ECONOMICS AND THE BUSINESS ENVIRONMENT

JOHN SLOMAN

SECOND EDITION

Prentice Hall
FINANCIAL TIMES

An imprint of **Pearson Education**

Harlow, England • London • New York • Boston • San Francisco • Toronto
Sydney • Tokyo • Singapore • Hong Kong • Seoul • Taipei • New Delhi
Cape Town • Madrid • Mexico City • Amsterdam • Munich • Paris • Milan

Pearson Education Limited
Edinburgh Gate
Harlow
Essex CM20 2JE
England

and Associated Companies throughout the world

Visit us on the World Wide Web at:
www.pearsoned.co.uk

First published 2005
Second edition 2008

ISBN 978-0-273-71037-0

British Library Cataloguing-in-Publication Data
A catalogue record for this book is available from the British Library

10 9 8 7 6 5 4 3 2 1
11 10 09 08 07

Typeset in 9/12 Stone Serif by 35
Printed and bound by Rotolito Lombarda, Italy

The publisher's policy is to use paper manufactured from sustainable forests.

Brief Contents

Contents

Supporting resources
Visit **www.pearsoned.co.uk/sloman** to find valuable online resources.

Companion Website with Grade Tracker for students
- Online workbook and study guide with interactive exercises, diagrams and videos
- Multiple choice questions with Grade Tracker function to test your learning and monitor your progress
- Business issues for each chapter
- Up-to-date case studies with questions for self study
- Topical economic issues relating directly to material in the book
- Economics news articles with features on topical stories, with analysis and links to the book
- Hotlinks to over 200 relevant sites on the web
- Answers to all in-chapter 'Pause for Thought' questions
- An online glossary to explain key terms

Also: The regularly maintained Companion Website with Grade Tracker provides the following features:

- Search tool to help locate specific items of content
- Online help and support to assist with website usage and troubleshooting

For lecturers
- By registering in our Companion Website with Grade Tracker as an instructor you can create a class and allow students to enrol to track individual and class progress
- TestGen testbank of customisable questions for formative or summative assessment
- Customisable lecture plans in PowerPoint with animated figures. One version contains multiple choice questions that can be used for lectures with an electronic audience response system
- Downloadable PowerPoint slides of all figures and most tables from the book
- A range of teaching and learning case studies
- Twelve workshops in Word for use in class or assessed work
- Answers to all box questions and end-of-chapter questions, and to questions in workshops, and Web Case Studies

These lecturer resources are also available on CD-ROM from your Pearson Education sales representative.

For more information please contact your local Pearson Education sales representative or visit **www.pearsoned.co.uk/sloman**

Guided tour

Navigation and setting the scene

The book is divided into four **parts**. Each part contains an introduction to the material covered.

Business issues and chapter maps, located at the start of each chapter, highlight and give an overview of the specific topics covered in each chapter.

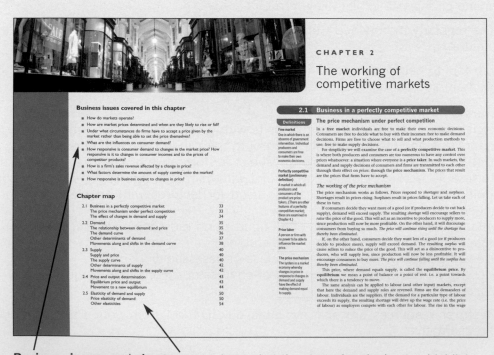

Business issues and **chapter maps**, located at the start of each chapter, highlight and give an overview of the specific topics covered in each chapter.

Aiding your understanding

Key terms are highlighted in the text where they first appear and are accompanied by paired **definitions** in the margin. This is very useful for revision and allows you to see the terms used in context. A full **glossary** also appears at the back of the book and online in the Companion Website (**www.pearsoned.co.uk/sloman**).

A total of 29 **key ideas** are highlighted and numbered in the text where they first appear. Key ideas are fundamental to being able 'think like an economist' and help you to see how the subject ties together. They also help you to develop a toolkit of concepts that can be used in a whole host of different contexts. Whenever key ideas re-occur later in the book, a numbered icon appears in the margin.

Pause for thought questions help you to reflect on what you have just read and show how the various ideas and theories relate to different issues. Answers to these questions are given on the book's Companion Website.

Throughout the text you will find **Recap boxes** at the end of each major section as well as consolidated at the end of chapters. Recap boxes allow you to check-up on your understanding of the material at frequent intervals and function as an important revision tool.

A **full-colour design** allows a consistent use of colour in the **figures**, letting you see at a glance how the figure or diagram is constructed and, additionally, the before and after positions when the diagram is used to illustrate the effects of a change in circumstance.

Practising and testing your learning

Multiple choice questions on the Companion Website provide a quick method for you to test and assess your progress.

Results graph for MCQs on the Companion Website gives you instant feedback.

The **Questions** section at the end of each chapter can be used for self testing, class exercises or class debate.

Applying economics to the real world

There are 53 boxed **Case Studies** and **Applications** for this edition. Applied material makes learning much more interesting and helps to bring the subject alive. This is particularly important to enable you to relate economic theory to your other subjects and to the world of business generally. All boxes include questions so as to relate the material back to the chapter in which the box is located.

Topical issues, news articles and **hotlinks** on the Companion Website (**www.pearsoned.co.uk/sloman**) provide further context for economic theory. Topical issues provide discussion of some of the key economic issues over the past sixth months related to passages in the book. Economics news articles are updated monthly and provide hotlinks to recent articles.

Web material at the end of each part lists additional case studies appearing on the book's Companion Website and references to various other useful websites.

Preface

To the student

Welcome to the second edition of this introduction to economics and the business environment. If you are a student on a business or management degree or diploma and taking a module which includes economics, then this book is written for you. Such modules may go under the title of Business Environment or Business Context, or they may simply be called Introduction to Economics or Introduction to Business Economics. Alternatively, you may be studying on an MBA and need a grounding in basic economic concepts and how they apply to the business environment.

The book covers the core economics that you will need as a business student, but it also covers various business-related topics not typically covered in an introductory economics textbook. These topics include elements of business organisation and business strategy.

As well as making considerable use of business examples throughout the text, I have included many case studies in boxes (53 in all). These illustrate how economics can be used to understand particular business problems or aspects of the business environment. Many of these case studies cover issues that you are likely to read about in the newspapers. Some cover general business issues; others look at specific companies. There are also many additional case studies appearing on the book's website (**www.pearsoned.co.uk/sloman**). These, along with references to various useful websites, are listed at the end of each of the four Parts of the book.

I hope that, in using this book, you will share my fascination for economics. It is a subject that is highly relevant to the world in which we live. And it is a world where many of our needs are served by business – whether as employers or as producers of the goods and services we buy. After graduating, you will probably take up employment in business. A grounding in economic principles and how they relate to the world of business should prove invaluable in the business decisions you may well have to make.

The aim throughout the book is to make this intriguing subject clear for you to understand and as relevant as possible to you as a student of business.

The written style is direct and straightforward, with short paragraphs to aid rapid comprehension. Definitions of all key terms are given in the margin, with defined terms appearing in bold. I have highlighted 29 Key Ideas, which are fundamental to 'thinking like an economist'. I refer back to these every time they recur throughout the book. This helps you to see how the subject ties together, and also helps you to develop a toolkit of concepts that can be used in a whole host of different contexts.

Summaries are given at the end of each section of each chapter. These should help you in reviewing the material you have just covered and in revising for exams. Each chapter finishes with a series of questions. These can be used to check your understanding of the chapter and help you to see how its material can be applied to various business problems.

There are also questions interspersed throughout the text in 'Pause for Thought' panels. These encourage you to reflect on what you are learning and to see how the various ideas and theories relate to different issues. Answers to these questions are given on the book's website.

I hope you enjoy the book and come to appreciate the crucial role that economics plays in all our lives, and in particular in the practice of business.

Good luck and enjoy. Perhaps this will be just the beginning of a life-long interest in economic issues and how they apply to the world of business – and in your own personal life too!

To the tutor

The aim of this book is to provide a short course in economic principles as they apply to the business environment. It is designed to be used by first-year undergraduates on business studies degrees and diplomas where economics is taught from the business perspective, either as a separate one-semester module or as part of a business environment module. It is also suitable for students studying economics on MBA, CMS, DMS and various professional courses.

In addition to covering core economic principles, various specialist business topics are also covered that do not appear in conventional introductory economics textbooks. The following are some examples of these additional topics:

- Business organisations
- Industrial structure
- STEEPLE analysis (as an extension of PEST analysis) (new to this edition)
- The structure–conduct–performance paradigm and its limitations
- The multinational corporation
- Globalisation and business
- Marketing the product
- Strategic analysis and choice
- Principal–agent analysis and the problem of asymmetric information as applied to various business situations
- The problems of adverse selection and moral hazard (expanded for this edition)
- Application of game theory to business situations (expanded for this edition to include extensive-form games)
- Porter's five forces model
- Growth strategy
- Transactions cost analysis (new to this edition)
- Alternative aims of firms
- Pricing in practice
- Price flexibility
- The product life cycle

- The small-firm sector
- Flexible labour markets and firms
- The economics of entrepreneurship (new to this edition)
- Business ethics and corporate social responsibility (extended for this edition)
- Government and the firm, including competition policy and regulation
- The macroeconomic environment of business, including the impact of macroeconomic policy on business
- The competitive advantage of nations (new to this edition)
- Trading blocs including the effect of the single European market on business
- Monetary union
- The implications of exchange rate movements and international capital flows for business.

The text is split into four Parts containing a total of 13 chapters. Each chapter could be covered in a week, giving enough material for a semester. Each chapter is divided into discrete sections, each with its own summary, providing an ideal coverage for a single study session for a student. Chapters finish with review questions, which can be used for seminars or discussion sessions.

The first nine chapters cover microeconomics and its relation to business. The final four cover the macroeconomic environment of business, both national and international. This higher weighting for microeconomics reflects the structure of many economics for business or business environment modules.

Special features

The book contains the following special features:

- *A direct and straightforward written style*, with short paragraphs to aid rapid comprehension. The aim all the time is to provide maximum clarity.
- *Attractive full-colour design*. The careful and consistent use of colour and shading makes the text more attractive to students and easier to use by giving clear signals as to the book's structure.
- *Figures with captions* (new to this edition). Most diagrams have captions to explain their properties and to highlight key features.
- *Key Ideas* highlighted and explained where they first appear. There are 29 of these ideas, which are fundamental to the study of economics on business courses. Students can see them recurring throughout the book, and an icon appears in the margin to refer back to the page where the idea first appears. Showing how ideas can be used in a variety of contexts helps students to 'think like an economist' and to relate the different parts of the subject together. All 29 Key Ideas are defined in a special section at the very end of the book.
- *'Pause for thought'* questions integrated throughout the text. These encourage students to reflect on what they have just read and make the learning process a more active one. Answers to these questions appear in the student section of the book's website. This new edition contains additional Pause for Thought questions.
- *Special Part opening sections* for each of the four Parts of the book, setting the scene and introducing the material to be covered.

■ *Chapter opening sections* that identify key business issues to be covered in that chapter.

■ *Chapter maps* (new to this edition). These occur at the beginning of each chapter and show the topics to be covered and on what pages.

■ *All technical terms are highlighted and clearly defined in the margin* on the page they appear. This feature is especially useful for students when revising.

■ *A comprehensive index*, including reference to all defined terms. This enables students to look up a definition as required and to see it used in context.

■ *Many boxes with additional applied material*. All boxes include questions so as to relate the material back to the chapter in which the box is located. The extensive use of applied material makes learning much more interesting for students and helps to bring the subject alive. This is particularly important for business students who need to relate economic theory to their other subjects and to the world of business generally. There are 21 more boxes in this edition to provide additional case-study material.

■ *Additional case studies appearing on the book's website* are referred to at the end of each Part.

■ *Detailed summaries appear at the end of each section*. These allow students not only to check their comprehension of a section's contents, but also to get a clear overview of the material they have been studying.

■ *Review questions at the end of each chapter*. These are designed to test students' understanding of the chapter's salient points. These questions can be used for seminars or as set work to be completed in the students' own time.

■ *A list of relevant websites given at the end of each Part*. Details of these websites can be found in the Web Appendix at the end of the book. You can easily access any of these sites from the book's own website (at **http://www.pearsoned.co.uk/ sloman**). When you enter the site, click on Hotlinks. You will find all the sites from the Web Appendix listed. Click on the one you want and the 'hotlink' will take you straight to it.

Supplements

WinEcon

The widely acclaimed, award-winning WinEcon software, produced and authored by the Economics Consortium of the Teaching and Learning Technology Programme (TLTP) and designed to support introductory economics, is now web-enabled and adapted by John Sloman in a special version designed for *Economics and the Business Environment*, Second Edition, for both institutions and students. There is a separate chapter in the Sloman version of WinEcon to correspond with the relevant chapter in the book. The software includes graphical interactive tutorials, relevant theory, self-assessment questions, economic databases and an economic glossary providing a comprehensive attractive and highly-interactive resource. For more information please go to **www.winecon.com/sloman**.

Website

Visit the book's Companion Website at **www.pearsoned.co.uk/sloman**. This has an extensive range of materials for students and tutors.

For students

- *Study material* designed to help you improve your results. This includes an online workbook and study guide, with interactive exercises, diagrams that you can manipulate, videos and links to articles and other material.

- *Economics news articles*, updated monthly: some 15 to 20 news items per month, with links to one or more newspaper articles per item. There are questions on each item and references to the relevant chapter(s) of the book.

- *Topical economic issues*, with analysis and links to key concepts and pages in the book.

- *Hotlinks* to over 200 useful websites listed in the book's Web Appendix and referenced at the end of each Part of the text.

- *Case studies* (85 in total) with questions for self study. These are the case studies referred to at the end of each Part of the text.

- *Answers to all Pause for Thought and odd-numbered end-of-chapter questions* to allow you to check your understanding as you progress.

- Self-test questions, organised chapter by chapter. You get a computer-generated answer to any test you take.

For tutors

- A range of *teaching and learning case studies*, with the focus on improving student learning outcomes.

- All *figures and tables* from the book in PowerPoint®, in two versions, each animated and in full colour.

- Customisable full-colour *lecture plans* in PowerPoint, with integrated animated diagrams and tables. Can also be used for handouts. There are five versions of these, including three with additional multiple-choice questions that can be used in lectures; two of these can be used with an electronic voting system.

- Full-colour OHTs of all *figures and tables* and all *lecture plans* with and without figures, tables and questions. These are all on a clear background and are suitable for both colour and black and white printing onto acetate. They can also be used for hand-outs.

- Thirteen workshops in Word: one per chapter. These are suitable for use in class or for homework. Answers are given to each workshop in separate Word files.

- *Answers* to all even-numbered end-of-chapter questions, boxes and Web case studies in a secure password protected area of the site.

These website materials are also available on a tutor's CD-ROM.

Acknowledgements

Many thanks to all the reviewers of the text, who have given me valuable advice for improvements. Thanks also to the team at Pearson, and especially Ellen Morgan, Julian Partridge, Joe Vella and Kevin Ancient.

Finally, thanks to all my family and especially, as always, to my wife Alison. Her continued patience, love and support make the task of writing considerably easier.

John Sloman

Custom publishing

Custom publishing allows academics to pick and choose content from one or more textbooks for their course and combine it into a definitive course text.

Here are some common examples of custom solutions which have helped over 500 courses across Europe:

- different chapters from across our publishing imprints combined into one book;
- lecturer's own material combined together with textbook chapters or published in a separate booklet;
- third-party cases and articles that you are keen for your students to read as part of the course;
- any combination of the above.

The Pearson Education custom text published for your course is professionally produced and bound – just as you would expect from a normal Pearson Education text. You can even choose your own cover design and add your university logo. Since many of our titles have online resources accompanying them we can even build a Custom website that matches your course text.

Whatever your choice, our dedicated Editorial and Production teams will work with you throughout the process, right up until you receive a copy of your Custom text.

Some adopters of Sloman's *Economics and the Business Environment* have found that the flexibility of custom publishing has allowed them to include additional material on certain aspects of the business environment subject area.

To give you an idea of which texts have proved popular, here is a list of titles covering particular subject areas that could provide extra chapters to match the emphasis of your course:

■ **Economics** – Sloman: *Economics*, Sixth Edition and Sloman: *Essentials of Economics*, Fourth Edition

■ **Legal environment** – Adams: *Law for Business Students*, Fourth Edition

■ **Ethics** – Lovell and Fisher: *Business Ethics and Values*, Second Edition

■ **Marketing** – Brassington: *Principles of Marketing*, Fourth Edition

■ **International marketing** – Hollensen: *Global Marketing*, Fourth Edition

■ **International business environment** – Brooks, Weatherston and Wilkinson: *The International Business Environment*, First Edition

■ **Business environment** – Worthington and Britton: *The Business Environment*, Fifth Edition

Examples of custom published texts containing material taken from the above list of textbooks:

For more details on any of these books or to browse other material from our entire portfolio, please visit: **www.pearsoned.co.uk**.

If, once you have had time to review this title, you feel Custom publishing might benefit you and your course, please do get in contact. However minor, or major the change – we can help you out.

You can contact us at: **www.pearsoncustom.co.uk** or via your local representative at: **www.pearsoned.co.uk/replocator**.

Publisher's acknowledgements

We are grateful to the following for permission to reproduce copyright material:

Figures and illustrations

Figure 1.5: Based on Scherer, F.M. and Ross, D. *Industrial Market Structure and Economic Performance*, Third Edition (New York: Houghton Mifflin, 1990). Copyright © 1990 by Houghton Mifflin. Reproduced with permission; Box 4.3, unnumbered figure: *Business clusters in the UK – A first assessment*, Figure 2, p. 7 (http://www.dti.gov.uk/ files/file17396.pdf) (Department of Trade and Industry). Reproduced under the terms of the click-use licence. Figure 6.1: Porter, M.E. *Competitive Strategy: Techniques for Analyzing Industries and Competitor* (New York: The Free Press, 1980). Copyright © 1980, 1998 by The Free Press. Reprinted with permission of The Free Press, a division of Simon & Schuster Adult Publishing Group. All rights reserved; Figure 6.5: Based on data in *Global Entrepreneurship Monitor 2006*. (Global Enterprise Research Association, 2007). Reproduced with permission; Figures 7.1 and 7.2: FDI database (www.unctad.org/fdistatistics) (UN Conference on Trade and Development [UNCTAD]). Reproduced with permission; Box 7.1, unnumbered figure: *World Investment Report 2006* (UN Conference on Trade and Development [UNCTAD], 2007), page 11. Reproduced with permission; Box 7.2, unnumbered figure: *Mergers & Acquisitions Note*, April 2007 (European Commission, DG ECFIN, 2007). Copyright © 2007 European Commission. Reproduced with permission; Box 9.2, unnumbered figure: *Stern Review on the Economics of Climate Change*, Executive Summary, Figure 1 (H.M. Treasury, 2006). (Prepared by Stern Review, from data drawn from World Resources Institute Climate Analysis Indicators Tool (CAIT) on-line database version 3.0.) Reproduced under terms of the click-use licence; Box 10.3, unnumbered figure (a): *European Economy, Statistical Annex* (European Commission, 2007) and unnumbered figure (b): *Business and Consumer Surveys* (European Commission, 2007). Reproduced with permission; Box 11.2, unnumbered figure (b): *Budget 2007*, Chart 2.3 (HM Treasury, 2007). Reproduced under terms of the click-use licence; Box 11.4, unnumbered figure: *Pre-Budget Report 2005*, Box 3.1, Chart (b) (HM Treasury, 2005). Reproduced under terms of the click-use licence; Figure 12.2: Based on data in *International Trade Statistics* (WTO, 2006). Reproduced by permission; Figure 12.3: Porter, M.E., *The Competitive Advantage of Nations*, p. 127 (New York: The Free Press, 1998). Copyright © 1980, 1998 by The Free Press. Reprinted with permission of The Free Press, a division of Simon & Schuster Adult Publishing Group. All rights reserved; Figure 13.1: Based on data from *OECD Economic Outlook* (Organisation for Economic Co-operation and Development, 2006). Copyright © 2006 OECD. Reproduce with permission.

Tables

Tables 1.1 and 1.2: Based on *Standard Industrial Classification 2003* (Office for National Statistics). Reproduced under the terms of the click-use licence; Table 1.3: Based on *UK Economic Accounts* and *Labour Market Statistics* (Office for National Statistics). Reproduced under the terms of the click-use licence; Box 4.4, Table (a): Pratten, C.F. 'A survey of the economies of scale', in *Research on the 'Costs of Non-Europe'*, Volume 2 (Luxembourg: Office for Official Publications of the European Communities, 1980) Copyright © 1988 European Communities. Reproduced with permission; Box 4.4 Table (b): European Commission / Economists Advisory Group Ltd 'Economies of scale', in *The Single Market Review*, Subseries V, Volume 4. (Luxembourg: Office for Official Publications of the European Communities, 1997). Copyright © 1997 European Communities. Reproduced with permission; Box 5.1, unnumbered table: Based on data in *United Kingdom Input-Output Analyses*, Table 8.31 (Office of National Statistics). Reproduced under terms of the click-use licence; Box 7.1, unnumbered table: *World Investment Report 2006* (UN Conference on Trade and Development [UNCTAD], 2007), extracts from Annex table A.I.11. Reproduced with permission; Box 7.4, unnumbered table: Based on data in FDI database (www.unctad.org/fdistatistics) (UN Conference on Trade and Development [UNCTAD]). Reproduced with permission; Table 11.2: Based on data in *European Economy Statistical Annex* (European Commission, 2007). Reproduced with permission; Table 13.1: *Financial Statistics* (Office for National Statistics). Reproduced under terms of the click-use licence; Table 13.2: Monetary and Financial Statistics Interactive Database (Bank of England). Reproduced with permission.

Text

Box 7.4: Text excerpt from Jane Macartney, 'New protectionism puts obstacles in the path of foreign investors', *The Times*, 12 February, 2007. © Jane Macartney, NI Syndication Limted. Reproduced with permission; Box 9.1: Text excerpt from Lee, Christine, 'Body Shop takeover – a bad day for animal welfare?', Environment Channel, 11 April 2006. (See http://www.999today.com/environment/news/story/3022.html). Reproduced with permission; Box 10.4: Text excerpt from 'Deflation turns into biggest economic risk' *The Times*, 11 May 2003. © NI Syndication Limited. Reproduced with permission.

In some instances we have been unable to trace the owners of copyright material, and we would appreciate any information that would enable us to do so.

PART A
Introduction

In this book we will be looking at the economic environment in which firms operate and at how economics can help in the process of business decision taking. In doing so, you will gain an insight into how economists think and the sorts of concepts they use to analyse business problems.

But what particular aspects of business does the economist study? Firms are essentially concerned with using inputs to make output. Inputs cost money and output earns money. The difference between the revenue earned and the costs incurred constitutes the firm's profit. Firms will normally want to make as much profit as possible, or at the very least to avoid a decline in profits.

In order to meet these and other objectives, managers will need to make choices: choices of what types of output to produce, how much to produce and at what price; choices of what techniques of production to use, what types of workers to employ and how many, what suppliers to use for raw materials, equipment, etc. In each case, when weighing up alternatives, managers will want to make the best choices. Business economists study these choices. They study economic decision making by firms.

Business issues covered in this chapter

- What things influence a firm's behaviour and performance?
- How are businesses organised and structured?
- What are the various legal categories of business and how do different legal forms suit different types of business?
- What are the aims of business?
- Will owners, managers and other employees necessarily have the same aims? How can those working in the firm be persuaded to achieve the objectives of their employers?
- How are businesses influenced by their national and global market environment?
- How are different types of industry classified in the official statistics?
- How do economists set about analysing business decision taking?
- What are the core economic concepts that are necessary to understand the economic choices that businesses have to make, such as what to produce, what inputs and what technology to use, where to locate their production and how best to compete with other firms?

Chapter map

CHAPTER I

Business and the economic environment

The world economy has undergone many changes in recent times, and these changes have had profound effects on business. For a start, most countries have increasingly embraced the 'market' as the means of boosting prosperity. You can see this in the abandonment of state planning in former communist countries, the privatisation of state industries around the world, the dismantling of barriers to international trade, the development of global financial markets, the use of government policies to promote competition and reductions in government regulation of business in order to attract inward investment. A consequence has been the growth of multinational businesses seeking the best market opportunities and the cheapest sources of supply.

Other important influences on businesses around the world have included the development of computers and IT, improvements in transport and communications and, more recently, a rapid growth in the use of the Internet. These technological advances have allowed businesses to take advantage of growing market opportunities.

Today, for many firms the world is their market. Their business environment is global. This is obviously the case with large multinational companies, such as McDonald's, Sony, VW, HSBC, Nestlé and Shell. But many small and medium-sized enterprises (SMEs) also have global reach, selling their products in various countries and buying their supplies from wherever in the world they get the best deal.

For other firms, however, their market is much more local. Take a restaurant or firm of heating engineers – in fact, look in the Yellow Pages and you will see a host of companies serving a market whose radius is no more than a few miles. But these firms also often face competition from global companies. A local shop is likely to face competition from a supermarket, such as Tesco or Wal-Mart, both of which have shops around the world and source their supplies from across the globe.

In this chapter, we take an overview of the types of environment in which firms operate and of the role of the economist in business decision taking.

We start by looking at the internal environment of the firm – the organisation and aims of the business. We then look at the external environment in which the firm operates – the nature of competition it faces, the type of industry in which it operates, the prices of its inputs, the general state of the economy (e.g. whether growing or in recession), the actions of the government and other authorities that might affect the firm (e.g. changes in taxes or interest rates or changes in competition legislation) and the global environment (e.g. the extent to which the company operates internationally and how it is influenced by global market opportunities and the state of the world economy).

Finally we look at the approach of the economist to analysing the business environment and business decision taking.

Box 1.1 introduces many of the topics that you will be covering in this book by taking the case of Gap and seeing how it is affected by its environment.

Box 1.1

Minding The Gap

Making the best of your business environment

Gap Inc. was founded in 1969 with the opening of a single shop in San Francisco. Today it has some 3200 stores, trading under The Gap, babyGap, Gap Kids, Banana Republic and Old Navy brands. With total sales of $16 billion and large markets in the USA, Canada, the UK, France, Ireland and Japan it is now America's largest clothing chain and one of the world's biggest fashion retailers. It employs 153 000 people worldwide.

What makes it a global company is not just its stores in several countries, but the fact that it produces its clothes in many locations, mainly in the developing world, where wages are much lower than in industrialised countries.

But has it continued to be successful? Has it made any mistakes? What lessons are there for other businesses? How has its performance been affected by its business environment – by consumer tastes, by the actions of its rivals, by the state of the national and world economies and by government policy?

In particular, how would an economist analyse Gap's performance so as to advise it on its best strategy for the future? This is the sort of thing that business economists do and the sort of thing we will be doing throughout this book. We will also look at the impact of the behaviour of businesses on their customers, on employees, on competitors and on society in general.

So let's have a look at some of the issues facing Gap and how they relate to business in general and to the topics covered in this book.

The market environment

To be a successful business, it is important for Gap to get its product right. This means that it must understand its market and how consumer demand responds to changes in price. We look at how markets work in general in Chapter 2 and then look specifically at consumer demand in Chapter 3.

To stay successful, Gap must both respond to changes in fashion and, to some extent, set fashion. To quote from the Gap website, 'We create emotional connections with customers around the world through inspiring product design, unique store experiences and compelling marketing.'[1]

But Gap hasn't always got things right. In 2000, it reported falling sales and profits and its share price plummeted. According to analyst Mike Goldman, from Verdict Research, 'There's a lack of innovation. Go into a store and the styles and ranges haven't

changed significantly. . . . The one-style-suits-all ethos of Gap may also have lost favour with consumers. Gap may have to embrace "glocalisation", where they have the reach of a global company but are able to take local tastes into account.'[2]

With an attempt to revitalise its brands, the Gap saw some turnaround in its fortunes between 2002 and 2004, with both sales and profits rising. But both fell again in 2005 and 2006. Part of the problem was a lack of responsiveness to fashion trends.

> The group's supply chain works with traditional lead times of around nine months, while competitors such as H&M, Charlotte Russe and Forever 21 have adopted "fast-fashion" lead times of less than three months, enabling them to respond far more quickly to fashion developments.'[3]

We look at strategies to estimate, respond to and influence demand in Chapter 3.

Success in selling is not just about the design of the product. It's also about getting the price right, and that depends a lot on what rival companies are doing. Gap's prices must be competitive with those of Next, H&M, Top Shop, Marks and Spencer, etc. Chapter 5 focuses on pricing decisions.

Over the longer term, Gap has to make decisions about which markets to target. In 1986 it launched GapKids and in 1994 GapScents. In 1997 it opened its online store. Should it expand to furnishing fabrics or to a greater range of fashion accessories? Should it expand to new countries, such as Australia, Mexico or Malaysia? Should it attempt to take over rivals?

> After repeatedly promising investors that a turnround was on the way, Gap has announced a brand strategy review at Old Navy and Gap, and has called in Goldman Sachs to advise it on possible next moves. This raises the possibility that some, or all, of the group might be sold to private investors or others.[4]

Strategic decisions such as these are examined in Chapters 6 and 7.

Production and employment

Being a profitable business depends not just on being able to sell a product. It also depends on how efficiently the product can be produced. This means choosing the most appropriate technology and deploying the labour force in the best way. We explore production and costs in Chapter 4 and the employment of labour in Chapter 8.

Gap is a vertically integrated company. This means that it is involved not only in retailing, but also in the production of the clothes it sells. To quote the Gap website again, 'Located around the globe, employees in Gap Inc.'s Sourcing and Logistics group, along with our buying agents, draw up production schedules and place orders with approved third-party factories in the more than 50 countries where our products are made.'

Gap, as with other companies, must decide on how many workers to employ, what wage rates to pay and what the conditions of employment should be. Such questions are explored in Chapter 8.

Most of Gap's garments are made in low-wage developing countries, where the garments can be made at a fraction of the cost in America or western Europe. One result is that Gap has come in for fierce criticism from the 'anti-globalisation' protestors about the employment conditions in its factories. According to the international human rights organisation, Global Exchange:

In Russia we were notified that Gap pays factory workers just 11 cents/hour and keeps them in slave-like conditions. Workers from Macao contacted the Asia Monitor Resource Centre in Hong Kong complaining of abusive treatment by factory managers, who forced them to work excessive overtime and cheated them out of their pay. A delegation from the National Labor Committee in June 1999 reported that Honduran Gap factory workers are subjected to forced pregnancy tests, forced overtime, exceedingly high production goals, locked bathrooms, and wages of $4/day, which only meet 1/3 of their basic needs.[5]

This raises questions of business ethics and what is known as 'corporate social responsibility'. We examine these broader social issues in Chapter 9, along with government policies to encourage, persuade or force firms to behave in the public interest.

Clearly Gap was worried about the adverse press it was receiving. It was particularly concerned by the campaign by the American labour union UNITE, which highlighted conditions in factories producing clothes for Gap and other US retailers. Gap was thus at pains to be seen to be addressing the problem. In April 2004, the *Corporate Social Responsibility Newswire Service* reported that:

UNITE and speciality apparel retailer Gap Inc. announced that they are supporting an effort by displaced garment workers in El Salvador to open that country's first independent and fully unionised apparel export factory. UNITE and Gap Inc. also said they plan to regularly discuss ways to co-operatively address garment factory issues that are of mutual concern to both organisations.

'My daughter asked me if it was OK to shop at Gap now, and when I said "yes," it instantly cost me $80,' said Bruce Raynor, president of UNITE.[6]

The economy

So do the fortunes of Gap and other companies depend solely on their policies and those of their competitors? The answer is no. One important element of a company's business environment is largely beyond its control. This is the state of the national economy and, for internationally trading companies, of the global economy. If the world economy is booming, then sales and profits are likely to grow without too much effort by the company. When the global economy slows down, however, as happened in the period 2001–03, trading conditions become much tougher.

We examine the national and international business environment in Part D. We also examine the impact on business of government policies to affect the economy – policies such as changes in taxation, interest rates, exchange rates and customs duties.

? **Question**

Choose a well-known company that trades globally and do a Web search to find out how well it has performed in recent years and how it has been influenced by various aspects of its business environment.

[1] www.gapinc.com

[2] http://news.bbc.co.uk/1/hi/uk/875926.stm

[3] 'Size matters in challenge to turn round Gap's fortunes', *Financial Times*, 10 January 2007

[4] ibid.

[5] http://www.globalexchange.org/campaigns/sweatshops/gap/background.html.pf

[6] http://www.csrwire.com/print.cgi?sfArticleId=2654

1.1 The business organisation

Three key things that affect the behaviour of firms are:

■ the legal status of the business;

■ the way in which the firm is organised – whether as a simple top-down organisation or as a more complex multi-department or multi-division organisation;

■ the aims of the firm – does the firm simply aim to maximise profits, or are there other aims?

The firm as a legal entity

In a small firm, the owner or owners are likely to play a major part in running the business. Such businesses will normally be one of two types.

The sole proprietor. This is where the business is owned by just one person. Owners of small shops, builders and farmers are typical examples. Such businesses are easy to set up and may require only a relatively small initial capital investment. They suffer two main disadvantages, however:

■ Limited scope for expansion. Finance is limited to what the owner can raise personally. Also there is a limit to the size of an organisation that one person can effectively control.

■ Unlimited liability. The owner is personally liable for any losses that the business might make. This could result in the owner's house, car and other assets being seized to pay off any outstanding debts.

The partnership. This is where two or more people own the business. In most partnerships there is a legal limit of 20 partners. Partnerships are common in the professions: solicitors, accountants, surveyors, etc. With more owners, there is more scope for expansion. More finance can be raised and the partners can each specialise in one aspect of the business.

Many partnerships, however, still have unlimited liability. This problem could be very serious. The mistakes of one partner could jeopardise the personal assets of all the other partners.

Where large amounts of capital are required and/or when the risks of business failure are relatively high, partnerships are not generally an appropriate form of organisation. In such cases it is best to form a company (or **joint-stock company**, to give it its full title).

Companies

A company is legally separate from its owners. This means that it can enter into contracts and own property. Any debts are its debts, not the owners'.

The owners are the shareholders. Each shareholder receives his or her share of the company's distributed profit. The payments to shareholders are called 'dividends'. The owners have only **limited liability**. This means that, if the company goes bankrupt, the owners will lose the amount of money they have invested in the company, but no more. This has the advantage of encouraging people to become shareholders, thereby providing more finance to businesses.

Definitions

Joint-stock company
A company where ownership is distributed between shareholders.

Limited liability
Where the liability of the owners for the debts of a company is limited to the amount they have invested in it.

Shareholders often take no part in the running of the firm. They may elect a board of directors which decides broad issues of company policy. The board of directors in turn appoints managers who make the day-to-day decisions.

There are two types of company: public and private.

Public limited companies. These are companies that can offer new shares publicly: by issuing a prospectus, they can invite the public to subscribe to a new share issue. In addition, many public limited companies are quoted on the Stock Exchange (see section 6.4), where existing shares can be bought and sold. A public limited company must hold an annual shareholders' meeting. Examples of well-known UK public limited companies are Marks & Spencer, BP, Barclays, BSkyB and Tesco.

Private limited companies. Private limited companies cannot offer their shares publicly. Shares have to be sold privately. This makes it more difficult for private limited companies to raise finance, and consequently they tend to be smaller than public companies. They are, however, easier to set up than public companies. One of the most famous examples of a private limited company is Manchester United football club, which, until it was bought out by the Glazer family in 2005, was a public limited company.

The internal organisation of the firm

The internal operating structures of firms are frequently governed by their size. Small firms tend to be centrally managed, with decision making operating through a clear managerial hierarchy. In large firms, however, the organisational structure tends to be more complex, although technological change is forcing many organisations to reassess the most suitable organisational structure for their business.

U form

In small to medium-sized firms, the managers of the various departments – marketing, finance, production, etc. – are normally directly responsible to a chief executive, whose function is to coordinate their activities: relaying the firm's overall strategy to them and being responsible for interdepartmental communication. We call this type of structure **U (unitary) form** (see Figure 1.1).

When firms expand beyond a certain size, however, a U-form structure is likely to become inefficient. This inefficiency arises from difficulties in communication,

Definition

U-form business organisation
One in which the central organisation of the firm (the chief executive or a managerial team) is responsible both for the firm's day-to-day administration and for formulating its business strategy.

Figure 1.1   U-form business organisation

Figure 1.2   M-form business organisation

coordination and control. It becomes too difficult to manage the whole organisation from the centre.

M form

To overcome these organisational problems, the firm can adopt an **M (multi-divisional) form** of managerial structure (see Figure 1.2).

This suits larger firms. The firm is divided into a number of 'divisions'. Each division could be responsible for a particular stage of production, a particular product or group of products, or a particular market (e.g. a specific country). The day-to-day running and even certain long-term decisions of each division would be the responsibility of the divisional manager(s). This leads to the following benefits:

- reduced length of information flows;
- the chief executive being able to concentrate on overall strategic planning;
- an enhanced level of control, with each division being run as a mini 'firm', competing with other divisions for the limited amount of company resources available.

The flat organisation

One of the major problems with M-form organisations is that they can become very bureaucratic with many layers of management. Recent technological innovations, however, especially in respect to computer systems such as e-mail and management information systems, have enabled senior managers to communicate easily and directly with those lower in the organisational structure. As a result, some companies in recent years have moved back towards simpler structures. These **flat organisations**, as they are called, dispense with various layers of middle management.

The holding company

As many businesses have expanded their operations, often on a global scale, so further more complex forms of business organisation have evolved. One such organisation is the **H-form** or **holding company**. A holding company (or parent company) is one that owns a controlling interest in other subsidiary companies. These subsidiaries, in turn, may also have controlling interests in other companies. There may thus be a complex web of interlocking holdings. While the parent company has ultimate control over its various subsidiaries, it is likely that both tactical and strategic decision making is left to the individual companies within the organisation.

> **Definition**
>
> **Holding company**
> A business organisation in which the present company holds interests in a number of other companies or subsidiaries.

The aims of the firm

Economists have traditionally assumed that firms want to maximise profits. The 'traditional theory of the firm', as it is called, shows how much output firms should produce and at what price, in order to make as much profit as possible. But do firms necessarily want to maximise profits?

It is reasonable to assume that the *owners* of firms will want to maximise profits. But even here, it is not always clear over what time period the owners want to maximise profits. For example, if a business adopts a strategy of rapid growth, this may result in the owners receiving smaller profits in the short run as more of the profits are invested in new plant and machinery, or more is spent on advertising or the firm engages in temporary price cutting in order to gain market share from its rivals. Such a strategy, however, could well lead to larger profits in the long run as the firm gets bigger. What is inconsistent with short-run profit maximisation, therefore, may be wholly consistent with long-run profit maximisation.

A more fundamental criticism of the assumption of profit maximisation, however, is that in large companies, it is not the owners that make the decisions about how much to produce and at what price. In such cases other objectives may be pursued.

The divorce of ownership from control

In public limited companies the shareholders elect directors. Directors in turn employ professional managers who are often given considerable discretion in making decisions. There is therefore a *separation between the ownership and control* of a firm.

But what are the objectives of managers? Will they want to maximise profits, or will they have some other aim? Managers may be assumed to want to maximise their *own* interests. This may well involve pursuits that conflict with profit maximisation. They may, for example, pursue higher salaries, greater power or prestige, greater sales, better working conditions or greater popularity with their subordinates. Different managers in the same firm may well pursue different aims.

> **Pause for thought**
>
> Make a list of four possible aims that a manager of a McDonald's restaurant might have. Which of these might conflict with the interests of McDonald's shareholders?

Managers will still have to ensure that *sufficient* profits are made to keep shareholders happy, but that may be very different from *maximising* profits. Alternative theories of the firm to those of profit maximisation, therefore, tend to assume that large firms are profit 'satisficers'. That is, managers strive hard for a minimum target level of profit, but are less interested in profits above this level.

The principal–agent relationship

Can the owners of a firm ever be sure that their managers will pursue the business strategy most appropriate to achieving the owners' goals (i.e. maximisation of profit)? This is an example of what is known as the **principal–agent problem**. One of the features of a complex modern economy is that people (principals) have to employ others (agents) to carry out their wishes. If you want to go on holiday, it is easier to go to a travel agent to sort out the arrangements than to do it all yourself. Likewise, if you want to sell a house, it is more convenient to go to an estate agent.

The crucial advantage that agents have over their principals is specialist knowledge and information. This is frequently the basis upon which agents are employed. For example, owners employ managers for their specialist knowledge of a market or their understanding of business practice. But this situation of **asymmetric information** – that one party (the agent) knows more than the other (the principal) – means that it will be very difficult for the principal to judge in whose interest the agent is operating. Are the manager's own goals rather than the goals of the owner being pursued? It is the same in other walks of life. The estate agent may try to convince you that it is necessary to accept a lower price, while the real reason may be to save the agent time, effort and expense.

The principal–agent problem.
Where people (principals), as a result of a lack of knowledge (asymmetric information), cannot ensure that their best interests are served by their agents. Agents may take advantage of this situation to the disadvantage of the principals.

Key Idea 1

Principals may attempt to reconcile the fact that they have imperfect information, and are thus in an inherently weak position, in the following ways.

■ *Monitoring* the performance of the agent. Shareholders could monitor the performance of their senior managers through attending annual general meetings. The managers could be questioned by shareholders and ultimately replaced if their performance is seen as unsatisfactory.

■ Establishing a series of *incentives* to ensure that agents act in the principals' best interest. For example, managerial pay could be closely linked to business performance.

Within any firm there will exist a complex chain of principal–agent relationships – between workers and managers, between junior managers and senior managers, between senior managers and directors, and between directors and shareholders. All groups will hold some specialist knowledge which might be used to further their own distinct goals. Predictably, the development of effective monitoring and evaluation programmes and the creation of performance-related pay schemes have been two central themes in the development of business practices in recent years – a sign that the principal is looking to fight back!

Staying in business

Aiming for profits, sales, salaries, power, etc. will be useless if the firm does not survive! Trying to *maximise* any of the various objectives may be risky. For example, if a firm tries to maximise its market share by aggressive advertising or price cutting, it might invoke a strong response from its rivals. The resulting war may drive it out of business. Concern with survival, therefore, may make firms cautious.

If a firm is too cautious, however, it may not after all survive. It may find that it loses markets to more aggressive competitors. Ultimately, therefore, if a firm is concerned to survive, it must be careful to balance caution against keeping up with competitors, ensuring that the customer is sufficiently satisfied and that costs are kept sufficiently low by efficient management and the introduction of new technology.

Recap

- There are four main types of legal organisation of firms: the sole proprietorship, the partnership, the private limited company and the public limited company. In the first two cases, the owners have unlimited liability. With companies, however, shareholders' liability is limited to the amount they have invested. This reduced risk encourages people to invest in companies.

- As firms grow, so they tend to move from a U-form to an M-form structure. In recent years, however, with the advance of information technology, many firms have adopted a flat organisation – a return to U-form. Multinational companies often adopt relatively complex forms of organisation. Many multinationals adopt a holding company (H-form) structure.

- Typically, owners of firms will seek to maximise profits. With large companies, however, there is a divorce of ownership from control. Control is by managers, who might pursue goals other than profit.

- The problem of managers not pursuing the same goals as the owners is an example of the *principal–agent problem*. Agents (in this case the managers) may not always carry out the wishes of their principals (in this case the owners). Because of asymmetric information, managers are able to pursue their own aims, just so long as they produce results that will satisfy the owners. The solution for owners is for there to be better means of monitoring the performance of managers, and incentives for the managers to behave in the owners' interests.

The external business environment   1.2

The decisions and performance of a firm are affected not just by its internal organisation and aims; they are also affected by the external environment in which the firm operates.

Dimensions of the external business environment

It is normal to identify various dimensions to the external business environment. These include political, economic, social/cultural and technological factors.

Political factors. Firms are directly affected by the actions of government and other political events. These might be major events affecting the whole of the business community, such as the collapse of communism, the Iraq War or a change of government. Alternatively, they may be actions affecting just one part of the economy. For example, the ban on smoking in pubs and restaurants affects the tobacco industry.

Economic factors. Businesses are affected by a whole range of economic factors, such as a rise in the cost of raw materials, or a price cut by a rival firm, or new taxes, or movements in interest rates or exchange rates. A firm must constantly take such factors into account when devising and implementing its business strategy.

It is normal to divide the economic environment in which the firm operates into two levels:

■ *The microeconomic environment.* This includes all the economic factors that are *specific* to a particular firm operating in its own particular market. Thus one firm may be operating in a highly competitive market, whereas another may not; one firm may be faced by rapidly changing consumer tastes (e.g. a designer clothing manufacturer), while another may be faced with a virtually constant consumer demand (e.g. a potato merchant); one firm may face rapidly rising costs, while another may find that costs are constant or falling.

■ *The macroeconomic environment.* This is the *national* and *international* economic situation in which business as a whole operates. Business in general will fare much better if the economy is growing than if it is in recession. In examining the macroeconomic environment, we will also be looking at the policies that governments adopt in their attempt to steer the economy, since these policies, by affecting things such as taxation, interest rates and exchange rates, will have a major impact on firms.

Social/cultural factors. This aspect of the business environment concerns social attitudes and values. These include attitudes towards working conditions and the length of the working day, equal opportunities for different groups of people (whether by ethnicity, gender, physical attributes, etc.), the nature and purity of products, the use and abuse of animals, and images portrayed in advertising. The social/cultural environment also includes social trends, such as an increase in the average age of the population, or changes in attitudes towards seeking paid employment while bringing up small children. In recent times, various ethical issues, especially concerning the protection of the environment, have had a big impact on the actions of business and the image that many firms seek to present.

Technological factors. Over the past 20 years the pace of technological change has quickened. This has had a huge impact not only on how firms produce products, but also on how their business is organised. The use of robots and other forms of computer-controlled production has changed the nature of work for many workers. It has also created a wide range of new opportunities for businesses, many of which have yet to be realised. The information-technology revolution is also enabling much more rapid communication and making it possible for many workers to do their job from home or while travelling, or from another country.

The division of the factors affecting a firm into political, economic, social and technological is commonly known as a **PEST analysis**. More recently, three more elements of the business environment have been added to give what is known as **STEEPLE analysis**. The extra elements are:

Environmental (ecological) factors. Increasingly firms are taking a greener approach to their activities and trying to find ways of minimising adverse effects on the environment, whether through cleaner technologies, or better waste management and recycling or through greener products. This might create extra costs for firms, but a greener image can also help to drive sales as consumers become more environmentally aware. Business attitudes towards the environment are examined in section 9.4.

PEST (or STEEPLE) analysis
Where the political, economic, social and technological factors shaping a business environment are assessed by a business so as to devise future business strategy. STEEPLE analysis would also take into account ethical, legal and environmental factors.

Legal factors. Businesses are affected by the legal framework in which they operate. Examples include industrial relations legislation, product safety standards, regulations governing pricing in the privatised industries and laws preventing collusion between firms to keep prices up. We examine some of these laws in sections 9.3–9.6.

Ethical factors. Firms are increasingly under pressure to adopt a more socially responsible attitude towards business. Corporate responsibility is a major concern of many firms, whether in terms of working conditions, the safety and quality of their products, truthful advertising, their attitudes towards the environment, concern for local residents and the general avoidance of what might be seen as 'suspect' business practices. Business ethics and corporate responsibility are examined in section 9.2.

The PEST or STEEPLE framework is widely used by organisations to audit their business environment and to help them establish a strategic approach to their business activities. It is nevertheless important to recognise that there is a great overlap and interaction among these sets of factors. Laws and government policies reflect social attitudes; technological factors determine economic ones, such as costs and productivity; technological progress often reflects the desire of researchers to meet social or environmental needs; and so on.

To be successful, a business needs to adapt to changes in its business environment and, wherever possible, take advantage of them. Ultimately, the better business managers understand the environment in which they operate, the more likely they are to be successful, either in exploiting ever-changing opportunities or in avoiding potential disasters.

The behaviour and performance of firms is affected by the business environment. The business environment includes social/cultural (S), technological (T), economic (E), ethical (E), political (P), legal (L) and environmental (E) factors. The mnemonic STEEPLE can be used to remember these.

Key Idea 2

Although we will be primarily concentrating on the economic environment, we will also look at the other dimensions in PEST and STEEPLE analysis at various points in the book, especially where they impact on the economic environment. Examples include competition legislation, the effect of social factors on consumer demand changing business attitudes towards pollution and social responsibility, and the effects of technology on costs.

> **Pause for thought**
>
> 1. Under which heading of a STEEPLE analysis would you locate training and education?
> 2. Identify at least one factor under each of the STEEPLE headings facing an electricity generating company.

Globalisation and the changing business environment

The external business environment of many firms is increasingly becoming a global one. International trade has grown much faster than countries' output, and so too has cross-border investment grown much faster than investment by companies within their home market. Many companies now see the world as their market and source their supplies from wherever in the world they can buy most cheaply. For some this simply means importing their inputs and exporting their products. Increasingly, however, companies set up their own factories or branches abroad.

Definition

Globalisation
The process whereby
the economies of the
world are becoming
increasingly integrated.

The world economy is becoming much more integrated. This process of **globalisation**, as it is called, has been hastened by various social/cultural, technological, economic, environmental, political and ethical factors (STEEPLE).

■ Social/cultural factors include the growing influence of Western consumerist culture as companies such as Nike, Levi, McDonald's and Disney sell their products around the world.

■ Technological factors include the communications revolution which, through the Internet, e-mails and computer linking, has allowed companies to communicate with their customers, suppliers and subsidiaries as easily halfway round the world as in the next town. Another key technological advance has been the reduction in size or weight of many products. The use of plastics rather than metals and the use of ever smaller and more powerful computer chips are just two examples of why it has become cheaper to transport goods long distance.

■ Economic factors include the globalisation of markets and production, as firms' activities spread across the globe. Markets around the world have tended to become more competitive as domestic firms increasingly face competition from abroad. Then at a macroeconomic level there is increasing convergence of economies, as interest rates, inflation rates and tax rates become more similar from one country to another.

■ Environmental and ethical factors include growing concerns worldwide over the burning of fossil fuels, the depletion of fish stocks, the pollution of land, sea and air, the cutting down of rainforests and the decline in bio-diversity. Increasingly these are seen as global rather than national problems. Another example is the growing worldwide concern for human rights and decent employment conditions.

■ Political and legal factors include the development of trading blocs such as the EU and the North America Free Trade Association (NAFTA) (consisting of the USA, Canada and Mexico), international agreements to dismantle barriers to trade and the international movement of finance, the growing influence of international bodies such as the World Trade Organisation, the political power of the USA to influence global events, and meetings of the Group of Eight (G8) major industrialised countries – Canada, France, Germany, Italy, Japan, Russia, the UK and the USA – to agree on means of harmonising their policies.

Pause for thought

Using the STEEPLE categories, in what ways has the USA influenced the business environment in countries outside the USA?

We explore the microeconomic effects of globalisation in detail in Chapter 7 and the macroeconomic effects in Chapters 12 and 13.

Classifying industries

One of the most important elements of the economic environment of a firm is the nature of the industry in which it operates and the amount of competition it faces. A knowledge of the structure of an industry is therefore crucial if we are to understand business behaviour and its likely outcomes.

In this section we will consider how the production of different types of goods and services are classified and how firms are located into different industrial groups.

Box 1.2
The biotechnology industry

Its business environment

There are few areas of business that cause such controversy as biotechnology. It has generated new medicines, created pest-resistant crops, developed eco-friendly industrial processes and, through genetic mapping, is providing incalculable advances in gene therapy. These developments, however, have raised profound ethical issues. Many areas of biotechnology are uncontentious, but genetic modification and cloning have met with considerable public hostility, colouring many people's views of biotechnology in general.

Biotechnology refers to the application of knowledge about living organisms and their components to make new products and develop new industrial processes. For many it is seen as the next wave in the development of the knowledge-based economy. According to EU estimates, by 2010 the biotechnology sector could well be worth some €2000 billion.

In global terms, the USA dominates this sector. In Europe, the UK is the region's leading biotechnology centre. It has some 460 specialist biotech companies, which is equivalent to 23 per cent of Europe's biotechnology sector, and is worth an estimated €5100 million in revenue. It employs some 22 000 staff, of which some 9600 are in research and development.

The industry is dominated by small and medium-sized businesses. In the EU some 51 per cent of these are in human healthcare, 35 per cent in service biotechnology (bioprocessing, chemicals, bioinformatics and genomics), and 14 per cent in agriculture, industrial and environmental products. As in the USA, biotech firms are geographically clustered, forming industry networks around key universities and research institutes. In the UK, clusters can be found in Cambridge, Oxford and London. The link with universities and research institutes taps into the UK's strong science base.

In addition to such clustering, the biotech industry is well supported by the UK government and other charitable organisations such as the Wellcome Trust. Such support helps to fund what is a highly research-intensive sector. The UK government not only provides finance, but encourages firms to form collaborative agreements, and through such collaboration hopes to encourage better management and use of the results that research generates. It also offers help for biotechnology business start-ups, and guidance on identifying and gaining financial support.

The EU too provides a range of resources to support business within the biotech sector. The EUREKA programme attempts to help create pan-EU partnerships, and the EU Seventh Framework Programme for research (2007–13) provides financing for such collaborative ventures. Such support by governments is seen as a crucial requirement for the creation of a successful biotechnology sector, as product development within the industry can take up to 12 years.

The majority of funding for the industry comes from 'venture capital' (investment by individuals and firms in new and possibly risky sectors). Even though the UK is Europe's largest venture capital market, such funding is highly volatile. Many of the biotech companies that are listed on the stock market, after significant share price rises in 1999 and 2000 then saw their share prices collapse, along with those of various hi-tech companies. With a depressed stock market, raising finance becomes much more difficult.

Since 2001 there has been a period of consolidation in the sector. Both public and private biotech companies in Europe have shown an increase in merger and acquisition activity, with 156 mergers between 2001 and 2004. Most of these mergers have been between European firms (49 per cent), though there has also been a significant number of purchases of European companies by US firms (29 per cent).

 Question

From the brief outline above, identify the political, economic, social and technological dimensions shaping the biotechnology industry's business environment.

Classifying production

When analysing production it is common to distinguish three broad categories.

■ **Primary production**. This refers to the production and extraction of natural resources such as minerals and sources of energy. It also includes output from agriculture.

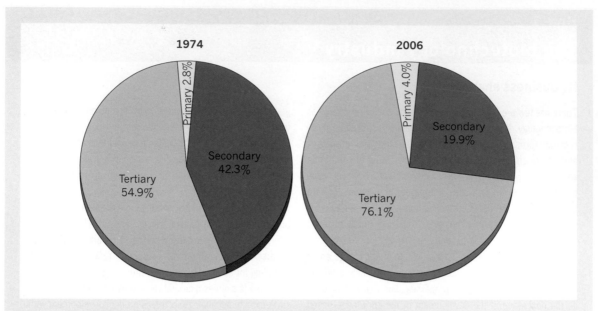

Figure 1.3   Output of industrial sectors (as % of GDP)

Source: Based on *UK National Accounts* (Blue Book) (Office for National Statistics)

Secondary production

The production from manufacturing and construction sectors of the economy.

Tertiary production

The production from the service sector of the economy.

Gross Domestic Product (GDP)

The value of output produced within the country over a 12-month period.

Deindustrialisation

The decline in the contribution to production of the manufacturing sector of the economy.

■ **Secondary production**. This refers to the output of the manufacturing and construction sectors of the economy.

■ **Tertiary production**. This refers to the production of services, and includes a wide range of sectors such as finance, the leisure industry, retailing and transport.

Figures 1.3 and 1.4 show the share of output (or **gross domestic product (GDP)**) and employment of these three sectors in 1974 and 2006. They illustrate how the tertiary sector has expanded rapidly. In 2006, it contributed 76.1 per cent to total output (up from 54.9 per cent in 1974) and employed 80.4 per cent of all workers (up from 54.7 per cent). By contrast, the share of output and employment of the secondary sector has declined. In 2006, it accounted for only 19.9 per cent of output (down from 42.3 per cent in 1974) and 17.6 per cent of employment (down from 41.9 per cent).

This trend is symptomatic of a process known as **deindustrialisation** – a decline in the share of the secondary sector in GDP. Many commentators argue that this process of deindustrialisation is inevitable and that the existence of a large and growing tertiary sector in the UK economy reflects its maturity. As people become richer, so a growing proportion of their consumption is of services such as leisure activities.

The classification of production into primary, secondary and tertiary allows us to consider broad changes in the economy. However, if we require a more

Pause for thought

Into which of the three sectors would you put (a) the fertiliser industry; (b) a marketing agency serving the electronics industry?

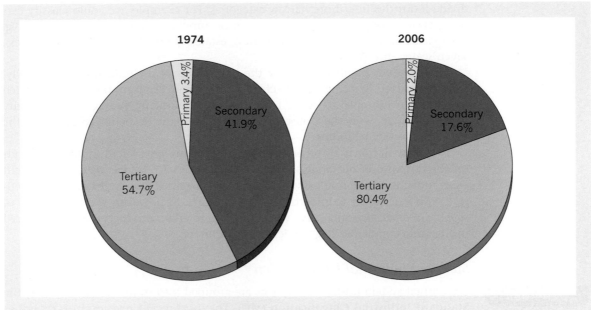

Figure 1.4   Employment by industrial sector (% of total employees)

Source: Based on data in various editions of *Labour Market Trends* and *Economic and Labour Market Review* (Office for National Statistics)

comprehensive analysis of the structure of industry and its changes over time, then such a general classification is of little value. What we need to do is to classify firms into particular industries.

Classifying firms into industries

An **industry** refers to a group of firms that produce a particular category of product. Thus we could refer to the electrical goods industry, the tourism industry, the aircraft industry or the insurance industry. Industries can then be grouped together into broad **industrial sectors**, such as manufacturing industry, or mining and quarrying, or construction, or transport.

Classifying firms into industrial groupings and subgroupings has a number of purposes. It helps us to analyse various trends in the economy and to identify areas of growth and areas of decline. It helps to identify parts of the economy with specific needs, such as training or transport infrastructure. Perhaps most importantly, it helps economists and business people to understand and predict the behaviour of firms that are in direct competition with each other. In such cases, however, it may be necessary to draw the boundaries of an industry quite narrowly.

To illustrate this, take the case of the vehicle industry. The vehicle industry produces cars, lorries, vans and coaches. The common characteristic of these vehicles is that they are self-propelled road transport vehicles. In other words, we could draw the boundaries of an industry in terms of the broad physical or technical characteristics of the products it produces. The problem with this type of categorisation, however, is that these products may not be substitutes in an *economic* sense. If I am thinking of buying a new vehicle to replace my car, I am hardly likely to consider buying a coach or a lorry! Lorries are not in competition with cars. If we are to group together products which are genuine competitors for each other, we will want to

Definitions

Industry
A group of firms producing a particular product or service.

Industrial sector
A grouping of industries producing similar products or services.

divide industries into more narrow categories. For example, we could classify cars into several groups according to size, price, function, engine capacity, etc.: e.g. luxury, saloon (of various size categories), estate (again of various size categories), seven seater and sports.

On the other hand, if we draw the boundaries of an industry too narrowly, we may end up ignoring the effects of competition from another closely related industry. For example, if we are to understand the pricing strategies of electricity supply companies in the household market, it might be better to focus on the whole domestic fuel industry.

Thus how narrowly or broadly we draw the boundaries of an industry depends on the purposes of our analysis. If the issue is one of *consumer demand* we might want to focus on the market and group goods together that are in direct competition with each other (e.g. particular types of car). If, however, the issue is one of *supply* – of *production* and *costs* – we might want to group products that are produced in the same companies (e.g. vehicle manufacturers).

Standard Industrial Classification

Definition
Standard Industrial Classification (SIC) The name given to the formal classification of firms into industries used by the government in order to collect data on business and industry trends.

The formal system under which firms are grouped into industries is known as the **Standard Industrial Classification (SIC)**. The most recent revision in 2003 brings the UK and EU systems of industry classification largely into alignment with each other. SIC (2003) is divided into 17 sections (A–Q), each representing a production classification (see Table 1.1). Two of the sections (C and D) are in turn divided into subsections. Sections or subsections are then divided into divisions; divisions are divided into groups; groups are divided into classes; and some classes are further

Table 1.1 Standard Industrial Classification

Section
A Agriculture, hunting and forestry
B Fishing
C Mining and quarrying
D Manufacturing
E Electricity, gas and water supply
F Construction
G Wholesale and retail trade, repair of motor vehicles and personal and household goods
H Hotels and restaurants
I Transport, storage and communication
J Financial intermediation
K Real estate, renting and business activities
L Public administration and defence; compulsory social security
M Education
N Health and social work
O Other community, social and personal service activities
P Private households with employed persons
Q Extra-territorial organisations and bodies

Source: Based on *Standard Industrial Classification 2003* (Office for National Statistics). Reproduced under terms of the click-use licence

Table 1.2   The classification of the manufacture of a milk carton

Section D	Manufacturing (comprising divisions 15 to 37)
Subsection DE	Manufacture of pulp, paper and paper products; publishing and printing (comprising divisions 21 and 22)
Division 21	Manufacture of pulp, paper and paper products (comprising groups 21.1 and 21.2)
Group 21.2	Manufacture of articles of paper and paperboard (comprising classes 21.21 to 21.25)
Class 21.21	Manufacture of corrugated paper and paperboard and of containers of paper and paperboard (comprising subclasses 21.21/1 to 21.21/9)
Subclass 21.21/5	Manufacture of cartons, boxes and similar containers of paper and paperboard specifically designed for carrying liquids, whether or not waxed

Source: Based on *Standard Industrial Classification 2003* (Office for National Statistics). Reproduced under terms of the click-use licence

divided into subclasses. Table 1.2 gives an example of how a manufacturer of a milk carton would be classified according to this system.

In total, SIC (2003) has 17 sections, 16 subsections, 62 divisions, 225 groups, 517 classes and 285 subclasses.

Changes in the structure of the UK economy

Given such a classification, how has UK industry changed over time? Table 1.3 shows the changes in output and employment of the various sectors identified by the SIC from 1980 to 2006.

Table 1.3   UK output and employment by industry in 2006 as a percentage of 1980

Industry	Output in 2006 as % of 1980	Employment in 2006 as % of 1980
A, B	129	69
C	90	25
E	173	
D	130	48
F	177	112
G, H	222	126
I	301	109
J, K	288	214
L–Q	158	146

Source: Based on *UK Economic Accounts* and *Labour Market Statistics* (Office for National Statistics). Reproduced under terms of the click-use licence

You can see from the table that the biggest increases in output have been in the service industries (sectors G to Q). Only in these industries has there been an increase in employment.

If we examine the subsections and divisions within the SIC, we can get a more detailed picture of how the structure of industry has changed. For example, we find that the process of deindustrialisation has not been experienced by all manufacturing industries. Certain divisions, such as instrument and electrical engineering, are in fact among the fastest growing in the whole UK economy. It is the more traditional manufacturing industries, such as metal manufacturing, that have experienced a substantial decline.

In respect to employment, there are again substantial variations between divisions. Thus whereas the financial services sector has seen a rapid growth in employment, there has been a decline in employment in parts of the retail banking sector (fewer counter staff are required in high street banks, given the growth in cash machines, direct debits, debit cards, etc.). And whereas there has been a decline in employment in primary industries (such as agriculture and mining) and in traditional manufacturing industries (such as shipbuilding and metal manufacturing), there has been a growth in employment in some of the more 'high-tech' industries.

Structure–conduct–performance

As we shall see throughout the book, business performance is strongly influenced by the market structure within which the firm operates. This is known as the *structure–conduct–performance paradigm* and is illustrated in Figure 1.5.

The structure of an industry depends on a number of basic conditions – some concerning production (supply) and some concerning consumer demand. For example, the availability of inputs and technology will influence whether it is more efficient to produce on a large scale or on a small scale. The nature of consumer tastes and whether there are close alternative products ('substitutes') available will influence the range of products produced and whether these should be highly differentiated from one producer to another or very similar across the industry. Such conditions will influence whether the market structure is highly competitive or

Figure 1.5 **The structure conduct performance paradigm**

Source: Based on Scherer, F.M. and Ross, D. *Industrial Market Structure and Economic Performance*, Third Edition (New York: Houghton Mifflin, 1990). Copyright © 1990 by Houghton Mifflin. Reproduced with permission dominated by just a few producers who are able to erect various barriers to the entry of competitors into the market.

A business operating in a highly competitive market structure will conduct its activities differently from a business in a market with relatively few competitors. For example, the more competitive the market, the more aggressive the business may have to be in order to sell its product and remain competitive. The less competitive the market structure, the greater the chance that collusion between producers might be the preferred strategy, as this reduces the excesses and uncertainties that outright competition might produce.

Such conduct will in turn influence how well businesses perform. Performance can be measured by several different indicators, such as efficiency in terms of cost per unit of output, current profitability or profitability over the longer term, market share or growth in market share, changes in share prices or share prices relative to those of other firms in the industry or to other firms in general, to name some of the most commonly used.

> ### Pause for thought
>
> *Why is a firm facing little competition from rivals likely to have higher profits, but also higher costs, than a firm facing intense competition?*

Throughout the book, we shall be seeing how market structure affects business conduct, and how business conduct affects business performance.

It would be wrong, however, to argue that business performance is totally shaped by external factors such as market structure. In fact, the internal aims, organisation and strategy of business may be very influential in determining success. We examine business strategy and the factors determining business competitiveness in Chapter 6.

Recap

- The external business environment is commonly divided into four dimensions: political, economic, social and technological (PEST analysis); or into seven dimensions, where the additional three are environmental, legal and ethical (STEEPLE analysis).

- The economic dimension of the business environment is divided into two: the microeconomic environment and the macroeconomic environment. The micro environment refers to the particular market in which the firm operates. The macro environment refers to the national and international economy in which all firms operate.

- The process of globalisation has meant that for many companies their external environment has an important international dimension.

- Production is divided into primary, secondary or tertiary. The contribution to output of these different sectors of production has changed over time. Over the years the tertiary sector has grown and the secondary sector contracted.

- Firms are classified into industries and industries into sectors. Such classification enables us to chart changes in industrial structure over time and to assess changing patterns of industrial concentration.

Box 1.3

The changing nature of business

Knowledge rules

In the knowledge-driven economy, innovation has become central to achievement in the business world. With this growth in importance, organisations large and small have begun to re-evaluate their products, their services, even their corporate culture in the attempt to maintain their competitiveness in the global markets of today. The more forward-thinking companies have recognised that only through such root and branch reform can they hope to survive in the face of increasing competition.

Innovation Management and the Knowledge-driven Economy European Commission, Directorate-general for Enterprise, (ECSC-EC-EAEC Brussels-Luxembourg, 2004)

Knowledge is fundamental to economic success in many industries and, for most firms, key knowledge resides in skilled members of the workforce. The result is a market in knowledge, with those having the knowledge being able to command high salaries and often being 'head hunted'. The 'knowledge economy' is fundamentally changing the nature, organisation and practice of business.

The traditional limited company was based around five fundamental principles:

■ Individual workers needed the business and the income it provided more than the business needed them. After all, employers could always find alternative workers. As such, the company was the dominant partner in the employment relationship.

■ Employees tended to be full time and depended upon this work as their sole source of income.

■ The company was integrated, with a single management structure overseeing all the various stages of production. This was seen as the most efficient way to organise productive activity.

■ Suppliers, and especially manufacturers, had considerable power over the customer by controlling information about their product or service.

■ Technology relevant to an industry was often developed within the industry.

In more recent times, with the advent of the knowledge economy, the principles above have all but been turned on their heads.

■ The key resource in a knowledge economy is knowledge itself, and the workers that hold such knowledge. Without such workers, the company is unlikely to succeed. As such, the balance of power between the business and the specialist worker in today's economy is far more equal.

■ Even though the vast majority of employees still work full time, the diversity in employment contracts, such as

1.3   The economist's approach to business

Tackling the problem of scarcity

We have looked at various aspects of the business environment and the influences on firms. We have also looked at some of the economic problems that businesses face. But what contribution can economists make to the analysis of these problems and to recommending solutions?

To answer this question we need to go one stage back and ask what it is that economists study in general. What is it that makes a problem an *economic* problem? The answer is that there is one central problem faced by all individuals and all societies. This is the problem of *scarcity*.

We define **scarcity** as 'the excess of human wants over what can actually be produced'.

Of course, we do not all face the problem of scarcity to the same degree. A poor person unable to afford enough to eat or a decent place to live will hardly see it as

Definition

Scarcity
The excess of human wants over what can actually be produced to fulfil these wants.

part-time and short-term contracts and consultancy, means that full-time work is not the only option. (We examine this in section 8.5.) The result is an increasing number of workers offering their services to business in non-conventional ways: e.g. as consultants.

■ As companies are increasingly supplying their products to a complex global marketplace, so many find they do not have the necessary expertise to do everything themselves – from production through all its stages, research and development, adapting their products to specific markets, to marketing and sales. With communication costs that have become insignificant, businesses are likely to be more efficient and flexible if they outsource and de-integrate. Not only are businesses outsourcing various stages of production, but many are employing specialist companies to provide key areas of management, such as HRM (human resource management) – hiring, firing, training, benefits, etc.

■ Whereas in the past businesses controlled information to their customers, today access to information via sources such as the Internet means that power is shifting towards the consumer.

■ Today, unlike in previous decades, technological developments are less specific to industries. Knowledge developments are diffuse and cut across industry boundaries. What this means for businesses, in a knowledge-driven economy, is that they must look beyond their own industry if they are to develop and grow. We frequently see partnerships and joint ventures between business that cut across industry types and technology.

What is clear from the above is that the dynamics of the knowledge economy require a quite fundamental change in the nature of business. Organisationally it needs to be more flexible, helping it to respond to the ever-changing market conditions it faces. Successful companies draw upon their core competencies to achieve market advantage, and thus ultimately specialise in what they do best. For other parts of their business, companies must learn to work with others, either through outsourcing specialist tasks, or through more formal strategic partnerships.

Within this new business model the key assets are the specialist people in the organisation – its 'knowledge workers'.

? Question

How is the development of the knowledge economy likely to affect the distribution of income in the economy? Will it become more equal or less equal? (Clue: think about the effects of specialist knowledge on the wage rates of specialists.)

---

a 'problem' that a rich person cannot afford a second Ferrari. But economists do not claim that we all face an *equal* problem of scarcity. The point is that people, both rich and poor, want more than they can have and this will cause them to behave in certain ways. Economics studies that behaviour.

Two of the key elements in satisfying wants are **consumption** and **production**. As far as consumption is concerned, economics studies how much the population spends; what the pattern of consumption is in the economy; and how much people buy of particular items. The business economist, in particular, studies consumer behaviour; how sensitive consumer demand is to changes in prices, advertising, fashion and other factors; and how the firm can seek to persuade the consumer to buy its products.

As far as production is concerned, economics studies how much the economy produces in total; what influences the rate of growth of production; and why the production of some goods increases and others falls. The business economist tends to focus on the role of the firm in this process: what determines the output

Definitions

Consumption
The act of using goods and services to satisfy wants. This will normally involve purchasing the goods and services.

Production
The transformation of inputs into outputs by firms in order to earn profit (or meet some other objective).

of individual businesses, the range of products they produce, the techniques they use and why, the amount they invest and how many workers they employ.

Demand and supply

We said that economics is concerned with consumption and production. Another way of looking at this is in terms of *demand* and *supply*. It is quite likely that you already knew that economics had something to do with demand and supply. In fact, demand and supply and the relationship between them lie at the very centre of economics. But what do we mean by the terms, and what is their relationship with the problem of scarcity?

Demand is related to wants. If goods and services were free, people would simply demand whatever they wanted. Such wants are virtually boundless: perhaps only limited by people's imagination. *Supply*, on the other hand, is limited. It is related to resources. The amount that firms can supply depends on the resources and technology available.

Given the problem of scarcity, given that human wants exceed what can actually be produced, *potential* demands will exceed *potential* supplies. Society therefore has to find some way of dealing with this problem. Somehow it has to try to match demand and supply. This applies at the level of the economy overall: *aggregate* demand will need to be balanced against *aggregate* supply. In other words, total spending in the economy must balance total production. It also applies at the level of individual goods and services. The demand and supply of cabbages must balance, and so must the demand and supply of DVD recorders, cars, houses and bus journeys.

But if potential demand exceeds potential supply, how are *actual* demand and supply to be made equal? Either demand has to be curtailed, or supply has to be increased, or a combination of the two. Economics studies this process. It studies how demand adjusts to available supplies, and how supply adjusts to consumer demands.

The business economist studies the role of firms in this process: how they respond to demand, or, indeed, try to create demand for their products; how they combine their inputs to achieve output in the most efficient way; how they decide the amount to produce and the price to charge their customers; and how they make their investment decisions. In this, firms are affected by the economic environment in which they operate. At a *microeconomic* level, they are affected by their competitors, by technology and by changing consumer tastes. At a *macroeconomic* level they are affected by the state of the economy and by government macroeconomic policies.

> **Pause for thought**
>
> *When you go into a supermarket, the shelves are normally well stocked. Does this mean that the problem of scarcity has been solved?*

Making choices

Because resources are scarce, choices have to be made. There are three main categories of choice that must be made in any society.

■ *What* goods and services are going to be produced and in what quantities, given that there are not enough resources to produce all the things that people desire?

How many cars, how much wheat, how much insurance, how many pop concerts, etc. will be produced?

■ *How* are things going to be produced, given that there is normally more than one way of producing things? What resources are going to be used and in what quantities? What techniques of production are going to be adopted? Will cars be produced by robots or by assembly-line workers? Will electricity be produced from coal, oil, gas, nuclear fission, renewable resources or a mixture of these?

■ *For whom* are things going to be produced? In other words, how is the nation's income going to be distributed? After all, the higher your income, the more you can consume of the nation's output. What will be the wages of farm workers, printers, cleaners and accountants? How much will pensioners receive? How much profit will owners of private companies receive or will state-owned industries make?

All societies have to make these choices, whether they be made by individuals, by business or by the government.

Choice and opportunity cost

Choice involves sacrifice. The more food you choose to buy, the less money you will have to spend on other goods. The more food a nation produces, the fewer resources there will be for producing other goods. In other words, the production or consumption of one thing involves the sacrifice of alternatives. This sacrifice of alternatives in the production (or consumption) of a good is known as its **opportunity cost**.

Opportunity cost.
The opportunity cost of something is what you give up to get it/do it. In other words, it is cost measured in terms of the best alternative forgone.

Key Idea 3

If the workers on a farm can produce either 1000 tonnes of wheat or 2000 tonnes of barley, then the opportunity cost of producing 1 tonne of wheat is the 2 tonnes of barley forgone. The opportunity cost of buying a textbook is the new pair of jeans you also wanted that you have had to go without. The opportunity cost of working overtime is the leisure you have sacrificed.

Rational choices

Economists often refer to **rational choices**. By this is simply meant the weighing-up of the *costs* and *benefits* of any activity, whether it be firms choosing what and how much to produce, workers choosing whether to take a particular job or to work extra hours, or consumers choosing what to buy.

Imagine you are doing your shopping in a supermarket and you want to buy some bread. Do you buy expensive 'speciality' bread or do you buy cheap basic bread, such as the supermarket's own 'value' bread? To make a rational (i.e. sensible) decision, you will need to weigh up the costs and benefits of each alternative. The expensive bread may give you a lot of enjoyment, but it has a high opportunity cost: because it is expensive, you will need to sacrifice quite a lot of consumption of other goods if you decide to buy it. If you buy the basic bread, however, although you will not enjoy it so much, you will have more money left over to buy other things: it has a lower opportunity cost.

Thus rational decision making, as far as consumers are concerned, involves choosing those items that give you the best value for money: i.e. the *greatest benefit relative to cost*.

The same principles apply to firms when deciding what to produce. For example, should a car firm open up another production line? A rational decision will again involve weighing up the benefits and costs. The benefits are the revenues that the firm will earn from selling the extra cars. The costs will include the extra labour costs, raw material costs, costs of component parts, etc. It will be profitable to open up the new production line only if the revenues earned exceed the costs entailed: in other words, if it earns a profit.

In the more complex situation of deciding which model of car to produce, or how many of each model, the firm must weigh up the relative benefits and costs of each: i.e. it will want to produce the most profitable product mix.

Marginal costs and benefits

Definitions

Marginal costs
The additional cost of doing a little bit more (or *1 unit* more if a unit can be measured) of an activity.

Marginal benefits
The additional benefits of doing a little bit more (or *1 unit* more if a unit can be measured) of an activity.

In economics we argue that rational choices involve weighing up **marginal costs** and **marginal benefits**. These are the costs and benefits of doing a little bit more or a little bit less of a given activity. They can be contrasted with the *total* costs and benefits of the activity. For example, the car manufacturer we were considering just now will weigh up the marginal costs and benefits of producing cars: in other words, it will compare the costs and revenue of producing *additional* cars. If additional cars add more to the firm's revenue than to its costs, it will be profitable to produce them.

> **Rational decision making involves weighing up the marginal benefit and marginal cost of any activity.**
>
> If the marginal benefit exceeds the marginal cost, it is rational to do the activity (or to do more of it). If the marginal cost exceeds the marginal benefit, it is rational not to do it (or to do less of it).
>
> **Key Idea 4**

Pause for thought

1. *Assume that you have an assignment to write. How would you make a rational choice about whether to work on it today or whether to do something else?*
2. *Assume that you are looking for a job and are offered two. One is more pleasant to do, but pays less. How would you make a rational choice between the two jobs?*

Choices and the firm

All economic decisions made by firms involve choices. The business economist studies these choices and their results.

We will look at the choices of how much to produce, what price to charge the customer, how many inputs to use and in what combination, whether to expand the scale of the firm's operations, whether to merge with or take over another company, whether to diversify into other markets, whether to export. The right choices (in terms of best meeting the firm's objectives) will vary according to the type of market in which the firm operates, its predictions about future demand, its degree of power in the market, the actions and reactions of competitors, the degree and type of government intervention, the current tax regime, the availability of finance, and so on. In short, we will be studying the whole range of economic choices made by firms and in a number of different scenarios.

In all these cases, the owners of firms will want the best possible choices to be made: i.e. those choices that best meet the objectives of the firm. Making the best choices, as we have seen, will involve weighing up the marginal benefits against the marginal opportunity costs of each decision.

Recap

- The central economic problem is that of scarcity. Given that there is a limited supply of resources, it is impossible to provide everybody with everything they want. Potential demands exceed potential supplies.

- Because resources are scarce, people have to make choices. Society has to choose by some means or other *what* goods and services to produce, *how* to produce them and *for whom* to produce them. Microeconomics studies these choices.

- Rational choices involve weighing up the marginal benefits of each activity against its marginal opportunity costs. If the marginal benefit exceeds the marginal cost, it is rational to choose to do more of that activity.

- Businesses are constantly faced with choices: how much to produce, what inputs to use, what price to charge, how much to invest, etc. We will study these choices.

QUESTIONS

1. Compare and contrast the relative strengths and weaknesses of unlimited liability partnerships with public limited companies.

2. Explain why the business objectives of owners and managers are likely to diverge. How might owners attempt to ensure that managers act in their interests and not in the managers' own interests?

3. Assume you are a UK car manufacturer and are seeking to devise an appropriate business strategy. Conduct a PEST analysis of the UK car industry and evaluate the various strategies that the business might pursue.

4. What is the Standard Industrial Classification (SIC)? In what ways might such a classification system be useful? Can you think of any limitations or problems such a system might have over time?

5. Outline the main determinants of the business performance. Distinguish whether these are micro- or macroeconomic.

6. Virtually every good is scarce in the sense we have defined it. There are, however, a few exceptions. Under *certain circumstances*, water and air are not scarce. When and where might this be true for (a) water and (b) air? Why is it important to define water and air very carefully before deciding whether they are scarce or abundant? Under circumstances where they are *not* scarce, would it be possible to charge for them?

7. Which of the following are macroeconomic issues, which are microeconomic ones and which could be either depending on the context?

   (a) Inflation.

   (b) Low wages in certain service industries.

   (c) The rate of exchange between the pound and the euro.

   (d) Why the price of cabbages fluctuates more than that of cars.

   (e) The rate of economic growth this year compared with last year.

   (f) The decline of traditional manufacturing industries.

8. Make a list of three things you did yesterday. What was the opportunity cost of each?

9. How would a firm use the principle of weighing up marginal costs and marginal benefits when deciding whether to (a) take on an additional worker; (b) offer overtime to existing workers?

Additional Part A case studies on the *Economics and the Business Environment* website (www.pearsoned.co.uk/sloman)

A.1 **The UK defence industry.** A PEST analysis of the changes in the defence industry in recent years.

A.2 **Downsizing and business reorganisation.** Many companies in recent years have 'downsized' their operations and focused on their core competences. This looks particularly at the case of IBM.

A.3 **Scarcity and abundance.** If scarcity is the central economic problem, is anything truly abundant?

A.4 **Global economics.** This examines how macroeconomics and microeconomics apply at the global level and identifies some key issues.

A.5 **The opportunity cost of studying at university.** An examination of the costs of being a student, using the concept of opportunity cost.

Websites relevant to Part A

Numbers and sections refer to websites listed in the Web Appendix and hotlinked from this book's website at www.pearsoned.co.uk/sloman/

■ For a tutorial on finding the best economics websites see site C8 (The Internet Economist).

■ For news articles relevant to Part A, see the Economics News Articles link from the book's website.

■ For general economics news sources see websites in section A of the Web Appendix at the end of the book, and particularly A1–9, 24, 35, 41. See also A38, 39 and 43 for links to newspapers worldwide; and A42 for links to economics news articles from newspapers worldwide.

■ For business news items, again see websites in section A of the Web Appendix at the end of the book, and particularly A1–3, 20–26, 35, 36.

■ For sources of economic and business data, see sites in section B and particularly B1–5, 27, 33, 34.

■ For general sites for students of economics for business, see sites in section C and particularly C1–7.

■ For sites giving links to relevant economics and business websites, organised by topic, see sites I4, 7, 8, 11, 12, 17, 18.

■ For details on companies, see sites B2 and A3.

PART B
Markets, demand and supply

One of the key determinants of a business's profitability is the price of its product. In most cases, firms have the option of changing their prices in order to increase their profits. Sometimes, a cut in price might be in order, if the firm anticipates that this will generate a lot more sales. At other times, a firm may prefer to raise its prices, believing there will be little effect on sales – perhaps it believes that its competitors will follow suit; or, perhaps, there are no close competitors, making it easy for the firm to get away with raising prices.

For some firms, however, the prices of the products they sell are determined not by them, but by the **market**. The 'market' is what we call the coming together of buyers and sellers: whether it be a street market, a shop, an auction, a mail-order system, the Internet or whatever. Thus we talk about the market for apples, the market for oil, for cars, for houses, for televisions and so on. As we shall see, market prices are determined by the interaction of demand (buyers) and supply (sellers).

When the price is determined by the market, the firm is called a *price taker*. It has to accept the market price as given. If the firm attempts to raise the price above the market price, it will simply be unable to sell its product: it will lose all its sales to its competitors. Take the case of farmers selling wheat. They have to accept the price as dictated by the market. If individually they try to sell above the market price, no one will buy.

So how does a competitive market work? How are prices determined in such markets? We examine this question in Chapter 2.

In Chapter 3 we look more closely at demand and at firms' attempt to understand demand and the behaviour of consumers. Then in Chapter 4 we look at supply and ask how much will a profit maximising firm produce at the market price.

Business issues covered in this chapter

- How do markets operate?
- How are market prices determined and when are they likely to rise or fall?
- Under what circumstances do firms have to accept a price given by the market rather than being able to set the price themselves?
- What are the influences on consumer demand?
- How responsive is consumer demand to changes in the market price? How responsive is it to changes in consumer incomes and to the prices of competitor products?
- How is a firm's sales revenue affected by a change in price?
- What factors determine the amount of supply coming onto the market?
- How responsive is business output to changes in price?

Chapter map

CHAPTER 2

The working of competitive markets

2.1 Business in a perfectly competitive market

The price mechanism under perfect competition

In a **free market** individuals are free to make their own economic decisions. Consumers are free to decide what to buy with their incomes: free to make demand decisions. Firms are free to choose what to sell and what production methods to use: free to make supply decisions.

For simplicity we will examine the case of a **perfectly competitive market**. This is where both producers and consumers are too numerous to have any control over prices whatsoever: a situation where everyone is a **price taker**. In such markets, the demand and supply decisions of consumers and firms are transmitted to each other through their effect on *prices*: through the **price mechanism**. The prices that result are the prices that firms have to accept.

The working of the price mechanism

The price mechanism works as follows. Prices respond to *shortages* and *surpluses*. Shortages result in prices rising. Surpluses result in prices falling. Let us take each of these in turn.

If consumers decide they want more of a good (or if producers decide to cut back supply), demand will exceed supply. The resulting *shortage* will encourage sellers to *raise* the price of the good. This will act as an incentive to producers to supply more, since production will now be more profitable. On the other hand, it will discourage consumers from buying so much. *The price will continue rising until the shortage has thereby been eliminated.*

If, on the other hand, consumers decide they want less of a good (or if producers decide to produce more), supply will exceed demand. The resulting *surplus* will cause sellers to *reduce* the price of the good. This will act as a disincentive to producers, who will supply less, since production will now be less profitable. It will encourage consumers to buy more. *The price will continue falling until the surplus has thereby been eliminated.*

This price, where demand equals supply, is called the **equilibrium price**. By **equilibrium** we mean a point of balance or a point of rest: i.e. a point towards which there is a tendency to move.

The same analysis can be applied to labour (and other input) markets, except that here the demand and supply roles are reversed. Firms are the demanders of labour. Individuals are the suppliers. If the demand for a particular type of labour exceeds its supply, the resulting shortage will drive up the wage rate (i.e. the price of labour) as employers compete with each other for labour. The rise in the wage

Definitions

Equilibrium price
The price where the quantity demanded equals the quantity supplied: the price where there is no shortage or surplus.

Equilibrium
A position of balance. A position from which there is no inherent tendency to move away.

rate will have the effect of curbing firms' demand for that type of labour and encouraging more workers to take up that type of job. Wages will continue rising until demand equals supply: until the shortage is eliminated.

Likewise, if there is a surplus of a particular type of labour, the wage will fall until demand equals supply.

As with price, the wage rate where the demand for labour equals the supply is known as the *equilibrium* wage rate.

The response of demand and supply to changes in price illustrates a very important feature of how economies work:

People respond to incentives, such as changes in prices or wages.
It is important, therefore, that incentives are appropriate and have the desired effect.

Key Idea 5

The effect of changes in demand and supply

How will the price mechanism respond to changes in consumer demand or producer supply? After all, the pattern of consumer demand changes over time. For example, people may decide they want more holidays abroad and fewer at home. Likewise the pattern of supply also changes. For example, changes in technology may allow the mass production of microchips at lower cost, while the production of hand-built furniture becomes relatively expensive.

A change in demand

A rise in demand causes a shortage and hence a rise in price. This then acts as an *incentive* for businesses to supply more: it is profitable for them to do so. They divert resources from products with lower prices relative to costs (and hence lower profits) to the product that has gone up in price and hence is now more profitable.

A fall in demand causes a surplus and hence a fall in price. This then acts as an incentive for businesses to supply less. These goods are now less profitable to produce.

A change in supply

A rise in supply (e.g. as a result of improved technology) causes a surplus and hence a fall in price. This then acts as an incentive for consumers to buy more. A fall in supply causes a rise in price. This then acts as an incentive for consumers to buy less.

Changes in demand or supply cause markets to adjust.
Whenever such changes occur, the resulting 'disequilibrium' will bring an automatic change in prices, thereby restoring 'equilibrium' (i.e. a balance of demand and supply).

Key Idea 6

Let us now turn to examine each side of the market – demand and supply – in more detail.

Pause for thought

If consumers want more of a product, how will the market create an incentive for more people to work in firms producing that product?

Recap

■ A firm is greatly affected by its market environment. The more competitive the market, the less discretion the firm has in determining its price. In the extreme case of a perfect market, the price is entirely outside the firm's control. The price is determined by demand and supply in the market, and the firm has to accept this price: the firm is a price taker.

■ In a perfect market, price changes act as the mechanism whereby demand and supply are balanced.

■ If there is a shortage, price will rise until the shortage is eliminated. If there is a surplus, price will fall until that is eliminated.

Demand   2.2

The relationship between demand and price

The headlines announce, 'Major crop failures in Brazil and East Africa: coffee prices soar.' Shortly afterwards you find that coffee prices have doubled in the shops. What do you do? Presumably you will cut back on the amount of coffee you drink. Perhaps you will reduce it from, say, six cups per day to two. Perhaps you will give up drinking coffee altogether.

This is simply an illustration of the general relationship between price and consumption: *when the price of a good rises, the quantity demanded will fall*. This relationship is known as the **law of demand**. There are two reasons for this law:

■ People will feel poorer. They will not be able to afford to buy so much of the good with their money. The purchasing power of their income (their *real income*) has fallen. This is called the **income effect** of a price rise.

■ The good will now be dearer relative to other goods. People will thus switch to alternative or 'substitute' goods. This is called the **substitution effect** of a price rise.

Similarly, when the price of a good falls, the quantity demanded will rise. People can afford to buy more (the income effect), and they will switch away from consuming alternative goods (the substitution effect).

Therefore, returning to our example of the increase in the price of coffee, we will not be able to afford to buy as much as before, and we will probably drink more tea, cocoa, fruit juices or even water instead.

A word of warning: be careful about the meaning of the words **quantity demanded**. They refer to the amount consumers are willing and able to purchase at a given price over a given time period (e.g. a week, or a month, or a year). They do *not* refer to what people would simply *like* to consume. You might like to own a luxury yacht, but your demand for luxury yachts will almost certainly be zero at current prices.

Definitions

The law of demand
The quantity of a good demanded per period of time will fall as the price rises and rise as the price falls, other things being equal (ceteris paribus).

Income effect
The effect of a change in price on quantity demanded arising from the consumer becoming better or worse off as a result of the price change.

Substitution effect
The effect of a change in price on quantity demanded arising from the consumer switching to or from alternative (substitute) products.

The demand curve

Consider the hypothetical data in Table 2.1. The table shows how many kilos of potatoes per month would be purchased at various prices.

Columns (2) and (3) show the **demand schedules** for two individuals, Tracey and Darren. Column (4), by contrast, shows the total **market demand schedule**. This is the total demand by all consumers. To obtain the market demand schedule for potatoes, we simply add up the quantities demanded at each price by *all* consumers: i.e. Tracey, Darren and everyone else who demands potatoes. Notice that we are talking about demand *over a period of time* (not at a *point* in time). Thus we would talk about daily demand or weekly demand or annual demand or whatever.

The demand schedule can be represented graphically as a **demand curve**. Figure 2.1 shows the market demand curve for potatoes corresponding to the schedule in

Table 2.1   The demand for potatoes (monthly)

	Price (pence per kg) (1)	Tracey's demand (kg) (2)	Darren's demand (kg) (3)	Total market demand (tonnes: 000s) (4)
A	20	28	16	700
B	40	15	11	500
C	60	5	9	350
D	80	1	7	200
E	100	0	6	100

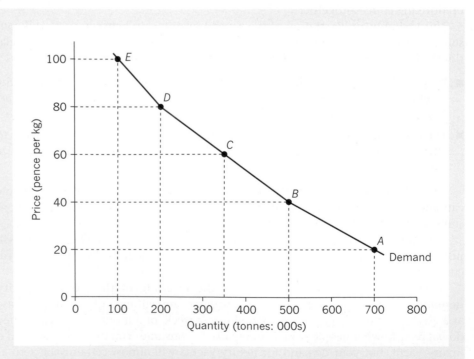

Figure 2.1   Market demand curve for potatoes (monthly)

Table 2.1. The price of potatoes is plotted on the vertical axis. The quantity demanded is plotted on the horizontal axis.

Point *E* shows that at a price of 100p per kilo, 100 000 tonnes of potatoes are demanded each month. When the price falls to 80p we move down the curve to point *D*. This shows that the quantity demanded has now risen to 200 000 tonnes per month. Similarly, if price falls to 60p, we move down the curve again to point *C*: 350 000 tonnes are now demanded. The five points on the graph (*A–E*) correspond to the figures in columns (1) and (4) of Table 2.1. The graph also enables us to read off the likely quantities demanded at prices other than those in the table.

> **Pause for thought**
>
> *Referring to Figure 2.1, what tonnage of potatoes would be purchased per month if the price were 70p per kg?*

A demand curve could also be drawn for an individual consumer. Like market demand curves, individuals' demand curves generally slope downward from left to right: the lower the price of the product, the more is a person likely to buy.

Two points should be noted at this stage:

■ In textbooks, demand curves (and other curves too) are only occasionally used to plot specific data. More frequently they are used to illustrate general theoretical arguments. In such cases the axes will simply be price and quantity, with the units unspecified.

■ The term 'curve' is used even when the graph is a straight line! In fact, when using demand curves to illustrate arguments we frequently draw them as straight lines – it's easier.

Other determinants of demand

Price is not the only factor that determines how much of a good people will buy. Demand is also affected by the following.

Tastes. The more desirable people find the good, the more they will demand. Tastes are affected by advertising, by fashion, by observing other consumers, by considerations of health and by the experiences from consuming the good on previous occasions.

The number and price of substitute goods (i.e. competitive goods). The higher the price of **substitute goods**, the higher will be the demand for this good as people switch from the substitutes. For example, the demand for coffee will depend on the price of tea. If tea goes up in price, the demand for coffee will rise.

The number and price of complementary goods. **Complementary goods** are those that are consumed together: coffee and milk, cars and petrol, shoes and polish. The higher the price of complementary goods, the fewer of them will be bought and hence the less the demand for this good. For example, the demand for electricity depends on the price of electrical goods. If the price of electrical goods goes up, so that fewer are bought, the demand for electricity will fall.

Income. As people's incomes rise, their demand for most goods will rise. Such goods are called **normal goods**. There are exceptions to this general rule, however. As people get richer, they spend less on **inferior goods**, such as cheap margarine, and switch to better quality goods.

Expectations of future price changes. If people think that prices are going to rise in the future, they are likely to buy more now before the price does go up.

Definitions

Substitute goods
A pair of goods which are considered by consumers to be alternatives to each other. As the price of one goes up, the demand for the other rises.

Complementary goods
A pair of goods consumed together. As the price of one goes up, the demand for both goods will fall.

Normal goods
Goods whose demand rises as people's incomes rise.

Inferior goods
Goods whose demand falls as people's incomes rise.

People's actions are influenced by their expectations.

People respond not just to what is happening now (such as a change in price), but to what they anticipate will happen in the future.

Key Idea 7

Movements along and shifts in the demand curve

A demand curve is constructed on the assumption that 'other things remain equal'. In other words, it is assumed that none of the determinants of demand, other than price, changes. The effect of a change in price is then simply illustrated by a movement along the demand curve: e.g. from point *B* to point *D* in Figure 2.1 when price rises from 40p to 80p per kilo.

Partial analysis: other things remaining equal (ceteris paribus).

In economics it is common to look at just one determinant of a variable such as demand or supply and see what happens when the determinant changes. For example, if price is taken as the determinant of demand, we can see what happens to quantity demanded as price changes. In the meantime we have to assume that other determinants remain unchanged. This is known as the 'other things being equal' assumption (or, using the Latin, the 'ceteris paribus' assumption). Once we have seen how our chosen determinant affects our variable, we can then see what happens when another determinant changes, and then another, and so on.

Key Idea 8

What happens, then, when one of these other determinants changes? The answer is that we have to construct a whole new demand curve: the curve shifts. If a change in one of the other determinants causes demand to rise – say, income rises – the whole curve will shift to the right. This shows that at each price more will be demanded than before. Thus in Figure 2.2 at a price of *P*, a quantity of Q_0 was originally demanded. But now, after the increase in demand, Q_1 is demanded. (Note that D_1 is not necessarily parallel to D_0.)

If a change in a determinant other than price causes demand to fall, the whole curve will shift to the left.

To distinguish between shifts in and movements along demand curves, it is usual to distinguish between a change in *demand* and a change in the *quantity demanded*. A shift in demand is referred to as a **change in demand**, whereas a movement along the demand curve as a result of a change in price is referred to as a **change in the quantity demanded**.

Pause for thought

The price of cinema tickets rises and yet it is observed that cinema attendance increases. Does this means that the demand for cinema tickets is upward sloping?

Definitions

Change in demand
The term used for a shift in the demand curve. It occurs when a determinant of demand other than price changes.

Change in the quantity demanded
The term used for a movement along the demand curve to a new point. It occurs when there is a change in price.

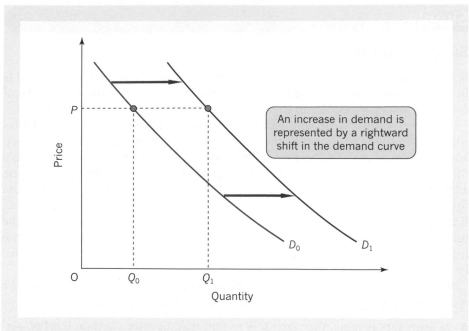

Figure 2.2   **An increase in demand**

Recap

■ When the price of a good rises, the quantity demanded per period of time will fall. This is known as the 'law of demand'. It applies both to individuals' demand and to the whole market demand.

■ The law of demand is explained by the income and substitution effects of a price change.

■ The relationship between price and quantity demanded per period of time can be shown in a table (or 'schedule') or as a graph. On the graph, price is plotted on the vertical axis and quantity demanded per period of time on the horizontal axis. The resulting demand curve is downward sloping (negatively sloped).

■ Other determinants of demand include tastes, the number and price of substitute goods, the number and price of complementary goods, income and expectations of future price changes.

■ If price changes, the effect is shown by a movement along the demand curve. We call this effect 'a change in the quantity demanded'.

■ If any other determinant of demand changes, the whole curve will shift. We call this effect 'a change in demand'. A rightward shift represents an increase in demand; a leftward shift represents a decrease in demand.

2.3 Supply

Supply and price

Imagine you are a farmer deciding what to do with your land. Part of your land is in a fertile valley. Part is on a hillside where the soil is poor. Perhaps, then, you will consider growing vegetables in the valley and keeping sheep on the hillside.

Your decision will depend to a large extent on the price that various vegetables will fetch in the market, and likewise the price you can expect to get from sheep and wool. As far as the valley is concerned, you will plant the vegetables that give the best return. If, for example, the price of potatoes is high, you will probably use a lot of the valley for growing potatoes. If the price gets higher, you may well use the whole of the valley, perhaps being prepared to run the risk of potato disease. If the price is very high indeed, you may even consider growing potatoes on the hillside, even though the yield per hectare is much lower there. In other words, the higher the price of a particular crop, the more you are likely to grow in preference to other crops.

This illustrates the general relationship between supply and price: *when the price of a good rises, the quantity supplied will also rise.* There are three reasons for this.

■ As firms supply more, they are likely to find that, beyond a certain level of output, costs rise more and more rapidly. Only if price rises will it be worth producing more and incurring these higher costs.

  In the case of the farm we have just considered, once potatoes have to be grown on the hillside, the costs of producing them will increase. Also if the land has to be used more intensively, say by the use of more and more fertilisers, again the cost of producing extra potatoes is likely to rise quite rapidly. It is the same for manufacturers. Beyond a certain level of output, costs are likely to rise rapidly as workers have to be paid overtime and as machines approach their full capacity. If higher output involves higher costs of production, producers will need to get a higher price if they are to be persuaded to produce extra output.

■ The higher the price of the good, the more profitable it becomes to produce. Firms will thus be encouraged to produce more of it by switching from producing less profitable goods.

■ Given time, if the price of a good remains high, new producers will be encouraged to set up in production. Total market supply thus rises.

The first two determinants affect supply in the short run. The third affects supply in the long run. We distinguish between short-run and long-run supply later (see pages 60–1).

The supply curve

The amount that producers would like to supply at various prices can be shown in a **supply schedule**. Table 2.2 shows a hypothetical monthly supply schedule for potatoes, both for an individual farmer (farmer X) and for all farmers together (the whole market).

The supply schedule can be represented graphically as a **supply curve**. A supply curve may be an individual firm's supply curve or a market supply curve (i.e. that of the whole industry).

Definitions

Supply schedule
A table showing the different quantities of a good that producers are willing and able to supply at various prices over a given time period. A supply schedule can be for an individual producer or group of producers, or for all producers (the market supply schedule).

Supply curve
A graph showing the relationship between the price of a good and the quantity of the good supplied over a given period of time.

Table 2.2   **The supply of potatoes (monthly)**

	Price of potatoes (pence per kg)	Farmer X's supply (tonnes)	Total market supply (tonnes: 000s)
a	20	50	100
b	40	70	200
c	60	100	350
d	80	120	530
e	100	130	700

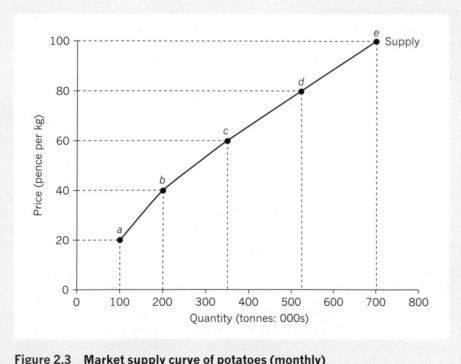

Figure 2.3   **Market supply curve of potatoes (monthly)**

Figure 2.3 shows the *market* supply curve of potatoes. As with demand curves, price is plotted on the vertical axis and quantity on the horizontal axis. Each of the points *a–e* corresponds to a figure in Table 2.2. Thus for example, a price rise from 60p per kilogram to 80p per kilogram causes a movement along the supply curve from point *c* to point *d*: total market supply rises from 350 000 tonnes per month to 530 000 tonnes per month.

Not all supply curves are upward sloping (positively sloped). Sometimes they are vertical, or horizontal, or even downward sloping. This depends largely on the time period over which the response of firms to price changes is considered. (This question is examined on pages 60–1.)

Pause for thought

1. How much would be supplied at a price of 70p per kilo?
2. Draw a supply curve for farmer X. Are the axes drawn to the same scale as in Figure 2.3?

Other determinants of supply

Like demand, supply is not determined simply by price. The other determinants of supply are as follows.

The costs of production. The higher the costs of production, the less profit will be made at any price. As costs rise, firms will cut back on production, probably switching to alternative products whose costs have not risen so much. Costs could change as a result of changing input prices, changes in technology, organisational changes within the firm, changes in taxation, etc.

The profitability of alternative products (substitutes in supply). If some alternative product (**a substitute in supply**) becomes more profitable to supply than before, producers are likely to switch from the first good to this alternative. Supply of the first good falls. Substitutes in supply are likely to become more profitable if their price rises or their cost of production falls. For example, if the price of carrots goes up, or the cost of producing carrots comes down, farmers may decide to cut down potato production in order to produce more carrots. The supply of potatoes is therefore likely to fall.

The profitability of goods in joint supply. Sometimes when one good is produced, another good is also produced at the same time. These are said to be **goods in joint supply**. An example is the refining of crude oil to produce petrol. Other grade fuels will be produced as well, such as diesel and paraffin. If more petrol is produced, due to a rise in demand, then the supply of these other fuels will rise too.

Nature, 'random shocks' and other unpredictable events. In this category we would include the weather and diseases affecting farm output, wars affecting the supply of imported raw materials, the breakdown of machinery, industrial disputes, earthquakes, floods and fire, and so on.

The aims of producers. A profit-maximising firm will supply a different quantity from a firm that has a different aim, such as maximising sales.

Expectations of future price changes. If price is expected to rise, producers may temporarily reduce the amount they sell. Instead they are likely to build up their stocks and only release them on to the market when the price does rise. At the same time they may plan to produce more, by installing new machines, or taking on more labour, so that they can be ready to supply more when the price has risen.

Movements along and shifts in the supply curve

The principle here is the same as with demand curves. The effect of a change in price is illustrated by a movement along the supply curve: e.g. from point *d* to point *e* in Figure 2.3 when price rises from 80p to 100p. Quantity supplied rises from 530 000 to 700 000 tonnes.

If any other determinant of supply changes, the whole supply curve will shift. A rightward shift illustrates an increase in supply. A leftward shift illustrates a decrease in supply. A movement along a supply curve is often referred to as a **change in the quantity supplied**, whereas a shift in the supply curve is simply referred to as a **change in supply**.

Definitions

Substitutes in supply
These are two goods where an increased production of one means diverting resources away from producing the other.

Goods in joint supply
These are two goods where the production of more of one leads to the production of more of the other.

Change in the quantity supplied
The term used for a movement along the supply curve to a new point. It occurs when there is a change in price.

Change in supply
The term used for a shift in the supply curve. It occurs when a determinant other than price changes.

Recap

■ When the price of a good rises, the quantity supplied per period of time will usually also rise. This applies both to individual producers' supply and to the whole market supply.

■ There are two reasons in the short run why a higher price encourages producers to supply more: (a) they are now willing to incur the higher costs per unit associated with producing more; (b) they will switch to producing this product and away from now less profitable ones. In the long run there is a third reason: new producers will be attracted into the market.

■ The relationship between price and quantity supplied per period of time can be shown in a table (or schedule) or as a graph. As with a demand curve, price is plotted on the vertical axis and quantity per period of time on the horizontal axis. The resulting supply curve is upward sloping (positively sloped).

■ Other determinants of supply include the costs of production, the profitability of alternative products, the profitability of goods in joint supply, random shocks and expectations of future price changes.

■ If price changes, the effect is shown by a movement along the supply curve. We call this effect 'a change in the quantity supplied'.

■ If any determinant *other* than price changes, the effect is shown by a shift in the whole supply curve. We call this effect 'a change in supply'. A rightward shift represents an increase in supply; a leftward shift represents a decrease in supply.

Price and output determination   2.4

Equilibrium price and output

We can now combine our analysis of demand and supply. This will show how the actual price of a product and the actual quantity bought and sold are determined in a free and competitive market.

Let us return to the example of the market demand and market supply of potatoes, and use the data from Tables 2.1 and 2.2. These figures are given again in Table 2.3.

What will be the price and output that actually prevail? If the price started at 20p per kilogram, demand would exceed supply by 600 000 tonnes (A – a). Consumers would be unable to obtain all they wanted and would thus be willing to pay a higher price. Producers, unable or unwilling to supply enough to meet the demand,

Table 2.3 **The market demand and supply of potatoes (monthly)**

Price of potatoes (pence per kg)	Total market demand (tonnes: 000s)	Total market supply (tonnes: 000s)
20	700 (A)	100 (a)
40	500 (B)	200 (b)
60	350 (C)	350 (c)
80	200 (D)	530 (d)
100	100 (E)	700 (e)

will be only too happy to accept a higher price. The effect of the shortage, then, will be to drive up the price. The same would happen at a price of 40p per kilogram. There would still be a shortage; price would still rise. But as the price rises, the quantity demanded falls and the quantity supplied rises. The shortage is progressively eliminated.

What would happen if the price started at a much higher level: say at 100p per kilogram? In this case supply would exceed demand by 600 000 tonnes ($e - E$). The effect of this surplus would be to drive the price down as farmers competed against each other to sell their excess supplies. The same would happen at a price of 80p per kilogram. There would still be a surplus; price would still fall.

In fact, only one price is sustainable. This is the price where demand equals supply: namely 60p per kilogram, where both demand and supply are 350 000 tonnes. When supply matches demand the market is said to **clear**. There is no shortage and no surplus.

As we have already seen, the price where demand equals supply is called the *equilibrium price*. In Table 2.3, if the price starts at other than 60p per kilogram, there will be a tendency for it to move towards 60p. The equilibrium price is the only price at which producers' and consumers' wishes are mutually reconciled: where the producers' plans to supply exactly match the consumers' plans to buy.

Equilibrium is the point where conflicting interests are balanced.
Only at this point is the amount that demanders are willing to purchase the same as the amount that suppliers are willing to supply. It is a point which will be automatically reached in a free market through the operation of the price mechanism.

Key Idea 9

Demand and supply curves

The determination of equilibrium price and output can be shown using demand and supply curves. Equilibrium is where the two curves intersect.

Figure 2.4 shows the demand and supply curves of potatoes corresponding to the data in Table 2.3. Equilibrium price is P_e (60p) and equilibrium quantity is Q_e (350 000 tonnes).

At any price above 60p, there would be a surplus. Thus at 80p there is a surplus of 330 000 tonnes ($d - D$). More is supplied than consumers are willing and able to purchase at that price. Thus a price of 80p fails to clear the market. Price will fall to the equilibrium price of 60p. As it does so, there will be a movement along the demand curve from point D to point C, and a movement along the supply curve from point d to point c.

At any price below 60p, there would be a shortage. Thus at 40p there is a shortage of 300 000 tonnes ($B - b$). Price will rise to 60p. This will cause a movement along the supply curve from point b to point c and along the demand curve from point B to point C.

Point Cc is the equilibrium: where demand equals supply.

Movement to a new equilibrium

The equilibrium price will remain unchanged only so long as the demand and supply curves remain unchanged. If either of the curves shifts, a new equilibrium will be formed.

Figure 2.4   The determination of market equilibrium (potatoes: monthly)

A change in demand

If one of the determinants of demand changes (other than price), the whole demand curve will shift. This will lead to a movement *along* the *supply* curve to the new intersection point.

For example, in Figure 2.5(a), if a rise in consumer incomes led to the demand curve shifting to D_2, there would be a shortage of $h - g$ at the original price P_{e_1}. This

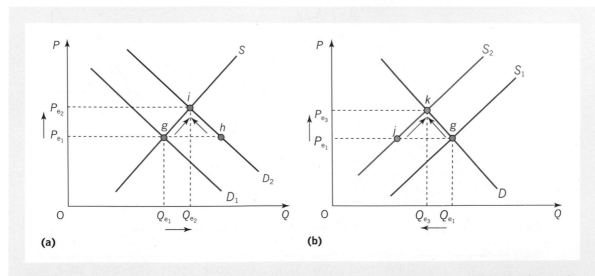

Figure 2.5   The effect of a shift in the demand or supply curve: (a) effect of a shift in the demand curve; (b) effect of a shift in the supply curve

Box 2.1

Stock market prices

Demand and supply in action

Firms that are quoted on the stock market (see page 183) can raise money by issuing shares. These are sold on the 'primary stock market'. People who own the shares receive a 'dividend' on them, normally paid six-monthly. The amount varies with the profitability of the company.

People or institutions that buy these shares, however, may not wish to hold on to them for ever. This is where the 'secondary stock market' comes in. It is where existing shares are bought and sold. There are stock markets, primary and secondary, in all the major countries of the world.

There are more than 3200 shares and other securities listed on the London Stock Exchange and trading in them takes place each Monday to Friday (excluding Bank Holidays). The prices of shares depend on demand and supply. For example, if the demand for Tesco shares at any one time exceeds the supply on offer, the price will rise until demand and supply are equal. Share prices fluctuate throughout the trading day and sometimes price changes can be substantial.

To give an overall impression of share price movements, stock exchanges publish share price indices. The best known one in the UK is the FTSE 100, which stands for the 'Financial Times

Stock Exchange' index of the 100 largest companies' shares. The index represents an average price of these 100 shares. The chart shows movements in the FTSE 100 from 1995 to 2007. The index was first calculated on 3 January 1984 with a base level of 1000 points. It reached a peak of 6930 points on 30 December 1999 and fell to 3287 on 12 March 2003.

But what causes share prices to change? Why were they so high in 1999, but only just over half that value just three years later? The answer lies in the determinants of the demand and supply of shares.

Demand

There are five main factors that affect the demand for shares.

The dividend yield. This is the dividend on a share as a percentage of its price. The higher the dividend yields on shares the more attractive they are as a form of saving. One of the main explanations of rising stock market prices since 2003 has been high profits and resulting high dividends.

The price of and/or return on substitutes. The main substitutes for shares in specific companies are other shares. Thus if, in

Financial Times Stock Exchange Index (FTSE) (3/1/84 = 1000)

comparison with other shares, Tesco shares are expected to pay high dividends relative to the share price, people will buy Tesco shares. As far as shares in general are concerned, the main substitutes are other forms of saving. Thus if the interest rate on savings accounts in banks and building societies fell, people with such accounts would be tempted to take their money out and buy shares instead.

Another major substitute is property. If house prices rise rapidly, as they did in 2002 and 2003, this will reduce the demand for shares as many people switch to buying property in anticipation of even higher prices. If house prices level off, as they did in 2005/06, this makes shares relatively more attractive as an investment and can boost the demand for them.

Incomes. If the economy is growing rapidly and people's incomes are thus rising rapidly, they are likely to buy more shares. Thus in the mid- to late 1990s, when UK incomes were rising at an average annual rate of over 3 per cent, share prices rose rapidly (see chart). As growth rates fell in the early 2000s, so share prices fell. But as growth rates then picked up, so share prices rose again.

Wealth. 'Wealth' is people's accumulated savings and property. Wealth rose in the 1990s and many people used their increased wealth to buy shares. It was a similar picture in the mid 2000s. Much of the wealth worldwide was in relatively 'liquid' form – i.e. in a form that can easily be turned into cash (and hence used to buy shares).

Expectations. In the mid- to late 1990s, people expected share prices to go on rising. They were optimistic about continued growth in the economy and that certain sectors, such as leisure and high-tech industries, would grow particularly strongly. But as people bought shares, this pushed their prices up even more, thereby fuelling further speculation that they would go on rising and encouraging further share buying.

In the early 2000s, by contrast, confidence was shaken. Most countries experienced a slowing down in economic growth, or even a recession (a fall in national output). This combined with other negative factors, such as the September 11 2001 attack on the World Trade Center and various corporate scandals, such as the accounting fraud concerning the giant US company Enron, caused share prices to plummet. As people anticipated further price falls, so they held back from buying, thereby pushing prices even lower. Conversely, as share prices began rising again from

2003 onwards, so this boosted the demand for shares, thereby fuelling the surge in share prices.

Worries in mid-2007, however, about the exposure of many companies to bad debts in the US mortgage market (the 'sub-prime market') and the effect this *could* have on dividends and share prices, led to bouts of selling and this saw shares prices fall.

Supply

The factors affecting supply are largely the same as those affecting demand, but in the opposite direction.

If the return on alternative forms of saving falls, people with shares are likely to hold on to them, as they represent a better form of saving. The supply of shares to the market will fall. If incomes or wealth rises, people again are likely to want to hold on to their shares.

As far as expectations are concerned, if people believe that share prices will rise, they will hold on to the shares they have. Supply to the market will fall, thereby pushing up prices. If, however, they believe that prices will fall, they will sell their shares now before prices do fall. Supply will increase, driving down the price.

Share prices and business

Companies are crucially affected by their share price. If a company's share price falls, this is taken as a sign that 'the market' is losing confidence in the company. This will make it more difficult to raise finance, not only by issuing additional shares in the primary market, but also from banks. It will also make the company more vulnerable to a takeover bid. This is where one company seeks to buy out another by offering to buy all its shares. A takeover will succeed if the owners of more than half of the company's shares vote to accept the offered price. Shareholders are more likely to agree to the takeover if the company's shares have not being doing very well recently.

Questions

1. If the rate of economic growth in the economy is 3 per cent in a particular year, why are share prices likely to rise by more than 3 per cent that year?
2. Find out what has happened to the FTSE 100 index over the past 12 months and explain why.

Box 2.2

UK house prices

The ups and downs of the housing market

If you are thinking of buying a house sometime in the future, then you may well follow the fortunes of the housing market with some trepidation. The chart shows what has happened to annual house price inflation since 1983. In the late 1980s there was a housing price explosion in the UK: in fact, between 1984 and 1989 house prices *doubled*. After several years of falling or gently rising house prices in the early and mid-1990s, there was another boom from 1996 to 2007, with house prices rising by 26 per cent per year at the peak (in the 12 months to January 2003). For many, owning a home of their own has become a mere dream.

House prices are determined by demand and supply. If demand rises (i.e. shifts to the right) or if supply falls (i.e. shifts to the left), the equilibrium price of houses will rise. Similarly, if demand falls or supply rises, the equilibrium price will fall.

So why did house prices rise so rapidly in the 1980s, only to fall in the early 1990s and then rise rapidly again in the late 1990s and 2000s? The answer lies primarily in changes in the *demand* for housing. Let us examine the various factors that affected the demand for houses.

Incomes (actual and anticipated). The second half of the 1980s and the mid-2000s were periods of rapidly rising incomes. The economy was experiencing an economic 'boom'. Many people wanted to spend their extra incomes on housing: either buying a house for the first time, or moving to a better one. What is more, many people thought that their incomes would continue to grow, and were thus prepared to stretch themselves financially in the short term by buying an expensive house, confident that their

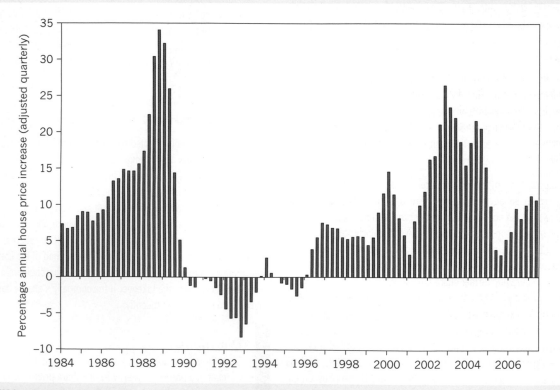

UK house price inflation

Source: Based on *Halifax House Price Index* (Halifax and Bank of Scotland [HBOS])

mortgage payments would become more and more affordable over time.

The early 1990s, by contrast, was a period of recession, with rising unemployment and much more slowly growing incomes. People had much less confidence about their ability to afford large mortgages.

The cost of mortgages. Most people have to borrow money to buy a house by taking out a mortgage. If mortgages become more affordable, people will tend to borrow more and this will fuel the demand for houses and hence drive up house prices. Mortgages will become more affordable if either the rate of interest falls or people are given longer to pay back the loan.

During the second half of the 1980s, mortgage interest rates were generally falling. Although they were still high compared with rates today, in *real* terms they were negative! In other words, house price inflation was greater than the rate of interest. Even if you paid back none of the mortgage and simply accumulated the interest owed, your house would be rising faster in price than you debt: your 'equity' in the house (i.e. the value of the house minus what you owe on it) would be rising.

In 1989, however, this trend was reversed. Mortgage interest rates were now rising. Many people found it difficult to maintain existing payments, let alone to take on a larger mortgage. From 1990 to 1995, house prices fell by 12.2 per cent. As a result of this, many people found themselves in a position of *negative equity*. This is the situation where the size of their mortgage is greater than the value of their house. In other words, if they sold their house, they would end up still owing money! For this reason many people found that they could not move house.

From 1996 to 2003 mortgage rates were generally reduced again, once more fuelling the demand for houses. Even given gently rising interest rates thereafter, mortgages were still relatively affordable

The availability of mortgages. In the late 1980s, mortgages were readily available. Banks and building societies were prepared to accept smaller deposits on houses, and to grant mortgages of $3\frac{1}{2}$ times a person's annual income, compared with $2\frac{1}{2}$ times in the early 1980s. In the early 1990s, however, banks and building societies were more cautious about granting mortgages. They were aware that, with falling house prices, rising unemployment and the growing problem of negative equity, there was a growing

danger that borrowers would default on payments. With the recovery of the economy in the mid-1990s, however, and with a growing number of mortgage lenders, mortgages became more readily available and for greater and greater amounts relative to people's income.

Speculation. In the 1980s, people generally believed that house prices would continue rising. This encouraged people to buy as soon as possible, and to take out the biggest mortgage possible, before prices went up any further. There was also an effect on supply. Those with houses to sell held back until the last possible moment in the hope of getting a higher price. The net effect was for a rightward shift in the demand curve for houses and a leftward shift in the supply curve. The effect of this speculation, therefore, was to help bring about the very effect that people were predicting (see Box 2.4).

In the early 1990s, the opposite occurred. People thinking of buying houses held back, hoping to buy at a lower price. People with houses to sell tried to sell as quickly as possible before prices fell any further. Again the effect of this speculation was to aggravate the change in prices – this time a fall in prices.

Then, in the late 1990s, the return of rapidly rising house prices encouraged people to buy more rapidly again, once more adding fuel to house price inflation. In the early 2000s, speculation was compounded by worries about falling stock market prices (see Box 2.1). Many investors turned to buying property instead of shares.

Demographics. The general rise in house prices over the whole period since 1983 has been compounded by demographics: population has grown more rapidly than the housing stock. This has caused demand to grow more rapidly than supply over the long term.

Questions

1. Draw supply and demand diagrams to illustrate what was happening to house prices (a) in the second half of the 1980s and since 1996; (b) in the early 1990s.
2. Are there any factors on the supply side that contribute to changes in house prices? If so, what are they?
3. Find out what has happened to house prices over the past two years. Attempt an explanation of what has happened.

Pause for thought

What would happen to price and quantity if the demand curve shifted to the left? Draw a diagram to illustrate your answer.

would cause price to rise to the new equilibrium P_{e_2}. As it did so there would be a movement along the supply curve from point g to point i, and along the new demand curve (D_2) from point h to point i. Equilibrium quantity would rise from Q_{e_1} to Q_{e_2}.

The effect of the shift in demand, therefore, has been a movement *along* the supply curve from the old equilibrium to the new: from point g to point i.

A change in supply

Likewise, if one of the determinants of supply changes (other than price), the whole supply curve will shift. This will lead to a movement *along* the *demand* curve to the new intersection point.

Pause for thought

Referring to Figure 2.4 and Table 2.3, what would happen to the equilibrium price of potatoes if there were a good harvest and the monthly supply of potatoes rose by 300 000 tonnes at all prices?

For example, in Figure 2.5(b) (on page 45), if costs of production rose, the supply curve would shift to the left: to S_2. There would be a shortage of $g - j$ at the old price of P_{e_1}. Price would rise from P_{e_1} to P_{e_3}. Quantity would fall from Q_{e_1} to Q_{e_3}. In other words, there would be a movement along the demand curve from point g to point k, and along the new supply curve (S_2) from point j to point k.

To summarise: a shift in one curve leads to a movement along the other curve to the new intersection point.

Sometimes a number of determinants might change. This may lead to a shift in *both* curves. When this happens, equilibrium simply moves from the point where the old curves intersected to the point where the new ones intersect.

Recap

- If the demand for a good exceeds the supply, there will be a shortage. This will result in a rise in the price of the good.

- If the supply of a good exceeds the demand, there will be a surplus. This will result in a fall in the price.

- Price will settle at the equilibrium. The equilibrium price is the one that clears the market: the price where demand equals supply. This is shown in a demand and supply diagram by the point where the two curves intersect.

- If the demand or supply curves shift, this will lead either to a shortage or to a surplus. Price will therefore either rise or fall until a new equilibrium is reached at the position where the supply and demand curves *now* intersect.

2.5 Elasticity of demand and supply

Price elasticity of demand

When the price of a good rises, the quantity demanded will fall. That much is fairly obvious. But in most cases we will want to know more than this. We will want to know just *how much* the quantity demanded will fall. In other words, we will want to know how *responsive* demand is to a rise in price.

Take the case of two products: oil and cauliflowers. In the case of oil, a rise in price is likely to result in only a slight fall in the quantity demanded. If people want to continue driving, they have to pay the higher prices for fuel. A few may turn to riding bicycles, and some people may try to make fewer journeys, but for most people, a rise in the price of petrol and diesel will make little difference to how much they use their cars.

In the case of cauliflowers, however, a rise in price may lead to a substantial fall in the quantity demanded. The reason is that there are alternative vegetables that people can buy. Many people, when buying vegetables, are very conscious of their prices and will buy whatever is reasonably priced.

We call the responsiveness of demand to a change in price the **price elasticity of demand**. If we know the price elasticity of demand for a product, we can predict the effect on price and quantity of a shift in the *supply* curve for that product.

Definition

Price elasticity of demand

A measure of the responsiveness of quantity demanded to a change in price.

Elasticity.

The responsiveness of one variable (e.g. demand) to a change in another (e.g. price). This concept is fundamental to understanding how markets work. The more elastic variables are, the more responsive is the market to changing circumstances.

Key Idea 10

Figure 2.6 shows the effect of a shift in supply with two quite different demand curves (D and D'). Curve D' is more elastic than curve D over any given price range. In other words, for any given change in price, there will be a larger change in quantity demanded along curve D' than along curve D.

Assume that initially the supply curve is S_1, and that it intersects with both demand curves at point a, at a price of P_1 and a quantity of Q_1. Now supply shifts to S_2. What will happen to price and quantity? In the case of the less elastic demand curve D, there is a relatively large rise in price (to P_2) and a relatively small fall in

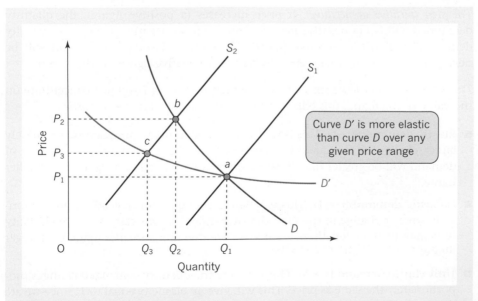

Figure 2.6   Market supply and demand

quantity (to Q_2): equilibrium is at point *b*. In the case of the more elastic demand curve *D′*, however, there is only a relatively small rise in price (to P_3) but a relatively large fall in quantity (to Q_3): equilibrium is at point *c*.

Defining price elasticity of demand

What we want to compare is the size of the change in quantity demanded of a given product with the size of the change in price. Price elasticity of demand does just this. It is defined as follows:

$$P\varepsilon_D = \frac{\text{Proportionate (or percentage) change in quantity demanded}}{\text{Proportionate (or percentage) change in price}}$$

If, for example, a 20 per cent rise in the price of a product causes a 10 per cent fall in the quantity demanded, the price elasticity of demand will be:

$$-10\%/20\% = -0.5$$

Three things should be noted about the figure that is calculated for elasticity.

The use of proportionate or percentage measures. Elasticity is measured in proportionate or percentage terms because this allows comparison of changes in two qualitatively different things, which are thus measured in two different types of unit: i.e. it allows comparison of quantity changes (quantity demanded) with monetary changes (price).

It is also the only sensible way of deciding *how big* a change in price or quantity is. Take a simple example. An item goes up in price by £1. Is this a big increase or a small increase? We can answer this only if we know what the original price was. If a can of beans goes up in price by £1, that is a huge price increase. If, however, the price of a house goes up by £1, that is a tiny price increase. In other words, it is the percentage or proportionate increase in price that we look at in deciding how big a price rise it is.

The sign (positive or negative). If price increases (a positive figure), the quantity demanded will fall (a negative figure). If price falls (a negative figure), the quantity demanded will rise (a positive figure). Thus price elasticity of demand will be negative: a positive figure is being divided by a negative figure (or vice versa).

The value (greater or less than 1). If we now ignore the sign and just concentrate on the value of the figure, this tells us whether demand is *elastic* or *inelastic*.

■ **Elastic demand** ($\varepsilon > 1$). This is where a change in price causes a proportionately larger change in the quantity demanded. In this case the price elasticity of demand will be greater than 1, since we are dividing a larger figure by a smaller figure.

■ **Inelastic demand** ($\varepsilon < 1$). This is where a change in price causes a proportionately smaller change in the quantity demanded. In this case the price elasticity of demand will be less than 1, since we are dividing a smaller figure by a larger figure.

■ **Unit elastic demand** ($\varepsilon = 1$). This is where the quantity demanded changes proportionately the same as price. This will give an elasticity equal to 1, since we are dividing a figure by itself.

Definitions

Elastic
If demand is (price) elastic, then any change in price will cause the quantity demanded to change proportionately more. (Ignoring the negative sign) it will have a value greater than 1.

Inelastic
If demand is (price) inelastic, then any change will cause the quantity demanded to change by a proportionately smaller amount. (Ignoring the negative sign) it will have a value less than 1.

Unit elasticity
When the price elasticity of demand is unity, this is where quantity demanded changes by the same proportion as the price. Price elasticity is equal to –1.

The determinants of price elasticity of demand

The price elasticity of demand varies enormously from one product to another. But why do some products have a highly elastic demand, whereas others have a highly *in*elastic demand? What determines price elasticity of demand?

The main determinant is the *number and closeness of substitute goods*. The more substitutes there are for a good, and the closer they are, the greater will be the price elasticity of demand. The reason is that people will be able to switch to the substitutes when the price of the good rises. The more numerous the substitutes and the closer they are, the more people will switch: in other words, the bigger will be the substitution effect of a price rise.

For example, the price elasticity of demand for a particular brand of a product will probably be fairly high, especially if there are many other, similar brands. If its price goes up, people can simply switch to another brand: there is a large substitution effect. By contrast the demand for a product in general will normally be pretty inelastic. If the price of food in general goes up, demand for food will fall only slightly. People will buy a little less, since they cannot now afford so much: this is the *income* effect of the price rise. But there is no alternative to food that can satisfy our hunger: there is therefore virtually no *substitution* effect.

Another important determinant is the *time period*. When price rises, people may take a time to adjust their consumption patterns and find alternatives. The longer the time period after a price change, then, the more elastic is the demand likely to be.

Pause for thought

Think of two products and estimate which is likely to have the higher price elasticity of demand. Explain your answer.

Price elasticity of demand and consumer expenditure

One of the most important applications of price elasticity of demand concerns its relationship with the total amount of money consumers spend on a product. **Total consumer expenditure (TE)** is simply price times quantity purchased:

$$TE = P \times Q$$

For example, if consumers buy 3 million units (Q) at a price of £2 per unit (P), they will spend a total of £6 million (TE).

Total consumer expenditure will be the same as the **total revenue (TR)** received by firms from the sale of the product (before any taxes or other deductions).

What will happen to consumer expenditure, and hence firms' revenue, if there is a change in price? The answer depends on the price elasticity of demand.

Elastic demand. As price rises, so quantity demanded falls, and vice versa. When demand is elastic, quantity changes proportionately more than price. Thus the change in quantity has a bigger effect on total consumer expenditure than does the change in price. This is summarised in Figure 2.7. In other words, total expenditure and total revenue change in the same direction as *quantity*.

This is illustrated in Figure 2.9(a). The areas of the rectangles in the diagram represent total expenditure. Why? The area of a rectangle is its height multiplied by its length. In this case, this is price multiplied by quantity purchased, which is total expenditure. Demand is elastic between points *a* and *b*. A rise in price from £4 to £5 causes a proportionately larger fall in quantity demanded: from 20m to 10m units. Total expenditure *falls* from £80m (the shaded area) to £50m (the striped area).

Definitions

Total consumer expenditure (TE) (per period)
The price of the product multiplied by the quantity purchased. $TE = P \times Q$.

Total revenue (TR) (per period)
The total amount received by firms from the sale of a product, before the deduction of taxes or any other costs. The price multiplied by the quantity sold. $TR = P \times Q$.

(a) Price *rises*; quantity *falls* proportionately more; therefore total expenditure ($P \times Q$) *falls*.

(b) Price *falls*; quantity *rises* proportionately more; therefore total expenditure ($P \times Q$) *rises*.

Figure 2.7   Effects of a change in price on total expenditure: price elastic demand

When demand is elastic, then, a rise in price will causes a fall in total expenditure and hence the total revenue earned by the firms selling the product. A reduction in price, however, will result in consumers spending more, and hence firms earning more.

So far we have been looking at the *market* demand curve. If we take the demand curve for a single firm, however, which is also a price taker, its demand curve will be perfectly elastic (i.e. horizontal). In other words, being a price taker, it can sell as much as it likes at the given market price. Any increase in its output and sales necessarily results in an increase in its total revenue, since it is selling a higher quantity at the *same* price. (When firms are not price takers, they face a downward-sloping demand curve. We consider such firms in Chapter 5.)

Inelastic demand. When demand is inelastic, price changes proportionately more than quantity. Thus the change in price has a bigger effect on total expenditure than does the change in quantity. This is summarised in Figure 2.8.

In other words, total expenditure changes in the same direction as *price*.

(a) Price *rises*; quantity *falls* proportionately *less*; therefore total expenditure ($P \times Q$) *rises*.

(b) Price *falls*; quantity *rises* proportionately *less*; therefore total expenditure ($P \times Q$) *falls*.

Figure 2.8   Effects of a change in price on total expenditure: price inelastic demand

This effect is illustrated in Figure 2.9(b). Demand is inelastic between points *a* and *c*. A rise in price from £4 to £8 causes a proportionately smaller fall in quantity demanded: from 20m to 15m units. Total revenue *rises* from £80m (the shaded area) to £120m (the striped area). In this case, firms' revenue will increase if there is an rise in price, and fall if there is a fall in price.

In the extreme case of a totally inelastic demand curve, this would be represented by a vertical straight line. No matter what happens to price, quantity demanded remains the same. It is obvious that the more the price rises, the bigger will be the level of consumer expenditure.

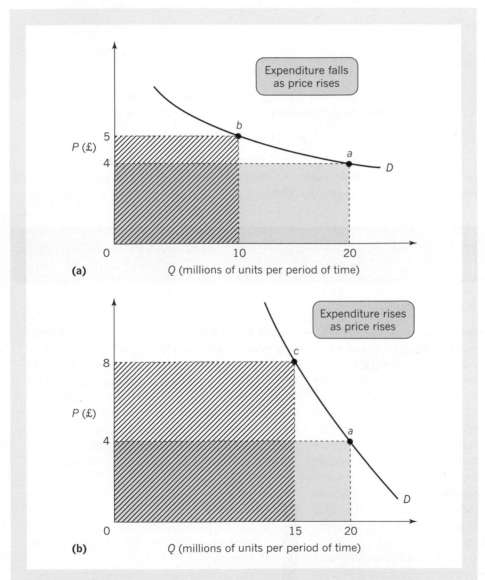

Figure 2.9   Price elasticity of demand and total expenditure: (a) elastic demand between two points; (b) inelastic demand between two points

Other elasticities

Firms are interested to know the responsiveness of demand not just to a change in price: they will also want to know the responsiveness of demand to changes in other determinants, such as consumers' incomes and the prices of substitute or complementary goods to theirs. They will want to know the **income elasticity of demand** – the responsiveness of demand to a change in consumers' incomes (Y); and the **cross-price elasticity of demand** – the responsiveness of demand for their good to a change in the price of another (whether a substitute or a complement).

Income elasticity of demand ($Y\varepsilon_D$)

We define the income elasticity of demand for a good as follows:

$$Y\varepsilon_D = \frac{\text{Proportionate (or percentage) change in quantity demanded}}{\text{Proportionate (or percentage) change in income}}$$

For example, if a 2 per cent rise in consumer incomes causes an 8 per cent rise in a product's demand, then its income elasticity of demand will be:

$$8\%/2\% = 4$$

Note that in the case of a normal good, the figure for income elasticity will be positive: a *rise* in income leads to a *rise* in demand (a positive figure divided by a positive figure gives a positive answer).

Box 2.3

Shall we put up our price?

Competition, price and revenue

When you buy a can of drink on a train, or an ice-cream in the cinema, or a bottle of wine in a restaurant, you may well be horrified by its price. How can they get away with it?

The answer is that these firms are *not* price takers. They can choose what price to charge. We will be examining the behaviour of such firms in Chapter 5, but here it is useful to see how price elasticity of demand can help to explain their behaviour.

Take the case of the can of drink on the train. If you are thirsty, and if you haven't brought a drink with you, then you will have to get one from the train's bar, or go without. There is no substitute. What we are saying here is that the demand for drink on the train is inelastic at the normal shop price. This means that the train operator can put up the price of its drinks, and food too, and earn *more* revenue.

Generally, the less the competition a firm faces, the lower will be the elasticity of demand for its products, since there will be fewer substitutes (competitors) to which consumers can turn. The lower the price elasticity of demand, the higher is likely to be the price that the firm charges.

When there is plenty of competition, it is quite a different story. Petrol stations in the same area may compete fiercely in terms of price. One station may hope that by reducing its price by 1p or even 0.1p per litre below that of its competitors, it can attract customers away from them. With a highly elastic demand, a small reduction in price may lead to a substantial increase in their revenue. The problem is, of course, that when they *all* reduce prices, no firm wins. No one attracts customers away from the others! In this case it is the customer who wins.

? *Questions*
1. Why might a restaurant charge very high prices for wine and bottled water and yet quite reasonable prices for food?
2. Why are clothes with designer labels so much more expensive than similar 'own brand' clothes from a chain store, even though they may cost a similar amount to produce?

The major determinant of income elasticity of demand is the degree of 'necessity' of the good. Typically, the demand for luxury goods expands rapidly as people's incomes rise, whereas the demand for more basic goods, such as bread, rises only a little. Thus items such as cars and foreign holidays have a high income elasticity of demand, whereas items such as potatoes and bus journeys have a low income elasticity of demand.

The demand for some goods actually decreases as income rises. These are inferior goods such as many of the 'value' products in supermarkets. As people earn more, so they switch to the supermarket's superior lines or to branded products. Unlike **normal goods**, which have a positive income elasticity of demand, **inferior goods** have a negative income elasticity of demand: a *rise* in income leads to a *fall* in demand (a negative figure divided by a positive figure gives a negative answer).

Income elasticity of demand is an important concept to firms considering the future size of the market for their product. If the product has a high income elasticity of demand, sales are likely to expand rapidly as national income rises, but may also fall significantly if the economy moves into recession.

Firms may also find that some parts of their market have a higher income elasticity of demand than others, and may thus choose to target their marketing campaigns on this group. For example, middle-income groups may have a higher income elasticity of demand for hi-tech products than lower-income groups (who are unlikely to be able to afford such products even if their incomes rise somewhat) or higher-income groups (who can probably afford them anyway, and thus would not buy much more if their incomes rose).

> **Definitions**
>
> **Normal goods**
> Goods whose demand increases as consumer incomes increase. They have a positive income elasticity of demand. Luxury goods will have a higher income elasticity of demand than more basic goods.
>
> **Inferior goods**
> Goods whose demand decreases as consumer incomes increase. Such goods have a negative income elasticity of demand.

Cross-price elasticity of demand ($C\varepsilon_{Dab}$)

This is often known by its less cumbersome title of *cross elasticity of demand*. It is a measure of the responsiveness of demand for one product to a change in the price of another (either a substitute or a complement). It enables us to predict how much the demand curve for the first product will shift when the price of the second product changes. For example, knowledge of the cross elasticity of demand for Coca-Cola with respect to the price of Pepsi would allow Coca-Cola to predict the effect on its own sales if the price of Pepsi were to change.

We define cross-price elasticity as follows:

$$C\varepsilon_D = \frac{\text{Proportionate (or percentage) change in quantity demand for good a}}{\text{Proportionate (or percentage) change in price of good b}}$$

If good b is a *substitute* for good a, a's demand will *rise* as b's price rises. For example, the demand for bicycles will rise as the price of public transport rises. In this case, cross elasticity will be a positive figure. If b is *complementary* to a, however, a's demand will *fall* as b's price rises and thus as the quantity of b demanded falls. For example, the demand for petrol falls as the price of cars rises. In this case, cross elasticity will be a negative figure.

The major determinant of cross elasticity of demand is the closeness of the substitute or complement. The closer it is, the bigger will be the effect on the first good of a change in the price of the substitute or complement, and hence the greater will be the cross elasticity – either positive or negative.

Firms will wish to know the cross elasticity of demand for their product when considering the effect on the

> **Pause for thought**
>
> If Good A had a cross-price elasticity of demand of zero with respect to Good B, would Good B be a substitute or a complement for Good A, or neither?

Box 2.4

Speculation

Taking a gamble on the future

In a world of shifting demand and supply curves, prices do not stay the same. Sometimes they go up; sometimes they come down.

If prices are likely to change in the foreseeable future, this will affect the behaviour of buyers and sellers *now*. If, for example, it is now December and you are thinking of buying a new winter coat, you might decide to wait until the January sales, and in the meantime make do with your old coat. If, on the other hand, when January comes you see a new summer jacket in the sales, you might well buy it now and not wait until the summer for fear that the price will have gone up by then. Thus a belief that prices will go up will cause people to buy now; a belief that prices will come down will cause them to wait.

The reverse applies to sellers. If you are thinking of selling your house and prices are falling, you will want to sell it as quickly as possible. If, on the other hand, prices are rising sharply, you will wait as long as possible so as to get the highest price. Thus a belief that prices will come down will cause people to sell now; a belief that prices will go up will cause them to wait.

This behaviour of looking into the future and making buying and selling decisions based on your predictions is called **speculation**. Speculation is often based on current trends in price behaviour. If prices are currently rising, people may try to decide whether they are about to peak and go back down again, or whether they are likely to go on rising. Having made their prediction, they will then act on it. This speculation will thus affect demand and supply, which in turn will affect price. Speculation is commonplace in many markets: the stock exchange (see Box 2.1), the foreign exchange market and the housing market (see Box 2.2) are three examples. Large firms often employ specialist buyers who choose the right time to buy inputs, depending on what they anticipate will happen to their price.

Speculation tends to be **self-fulfilling**. In other words, the actions of speculators tend to bring about the very effect on prices that speculators had anticipated. For example, if speculators believe that the price of BP shares is about to rise, they will buy more of them. The demand curve for BP shares shifts to the right. Those owning BP shares and thinking of selling will wait until the price has risen. In the meantime, the supply curve shifts to the left. The result of these two shifts is that the share price rises. In other words, the prophecy has become self-fulfilling.

Definitions

Speculation
This is where people make buying or selling decisions based on their anticipations of future prices.

Self-fulfilling speculation
The actions of speculators tend to cause the very effect that they had anticipated.

Speculation over commodity prices

The prices of two commodities, oil and copper, illustrate the process of speculation and how it can make price changes larger. Figure (a) shows changes in the prices of these two commodities from 2002 to 2007. As you can see, they rose dramatically from 2002 to 2006, only to fall back significantly. Why did this happen, and what part did speculation play in the process?

Oil prices. Take first the case of oil prices. After 2002 there was a significant increase in the demand for oil. This was partly the result of increased world economic growth after a slowdown in 2001/02 and partly the result of the massive growth in demand from China and India as their economies powered ahead. Their income elasticity of demand for oil is high, reflecting their high income elasticity of demand for manufacturing, transport and power.

There were also growing problems with supply. The war in Iraq and disruptions in supply in other parts of the world meant that supply could not match the growth in demand without substantial price increases. 'When Russia cut off gas supplies to Ukraine in January 2006, crude prices jumped 19 per cent within a few weeks.'[1]

Speculation compounded this process. As oil prices rose, so governments and oil companies increased demand so as to build

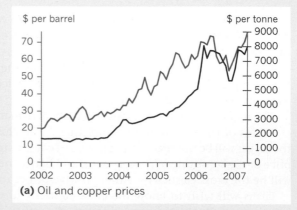

(a) Oil and copper prices

up stocks (or 'inventories') ahead of any further price increases. At the same time, holders of oil stocks released less onto the market, waiting for the price to rise further.

This is illustrated in Figure (b). A rise in demand from D_1 to D_2 caused by the underlying increase in demand for oil, plus a fall in supply from S_1 to S_2 caused by disruptions in supply, would have resulted in a price rise from P_1 to P_2. But speculation compounded this effect. A further rise in demand to D_3 caused by speculative building of stocks, plus a fall in supply to S_3 as a result of the speculative holding back of supplies, meant that price rose to P_3.

Then in 2006, things went into reverse. Price fell from $77 per barrel in early August 2006 to $50 in late January 2007. Oil stocks were near maximum and thus stock building slowed down. At the same time, investment in new oil wells, stimulated by earlier rises in prices, was beginning to increase supply. Later in the year a relatively mild winter in the northern hemisphere reduced the demand for oil. The resulting fall in prices put speculation into

reverse. Oil stocks were reduced as more was released onto the market before prices fell any further.

This is illustrated in Figure (c). A fall in demand from D_1 to D_2, plus a rise in supply from S_1 to S_2, would have caused price to fall from P_1 to P_2. But again, speculation compounded this effect, resulting in a further fall in demand to D_3 and a rise in supply to S_3. Price fell to P_3.

Speculation can be extremely volatile. A cold spell in the USA in late January 2007, plus a strike threat in Nigeria led to a 14 per cent increase in the price of oil in less than two weeks.

Copper prices. A similar picture of underlying changes in demand and supply, amplified by speculation, can be seen in the case of copper (see Figure (a)). Surging demand from China and India, with supply unable to keep pace, pushed up prices from 2004. This trend was exaggerated by speculation, as stocks were built in anticipation of further rises.

The trend was reversed in late 2006. Increased mining output, prompted by the earlier price increases, coupled with slowing worldwide demand and the perception that copper stocks were unnecessarily large, saw copper prices fall by some 35 per cent between June 2006 and February 2007.

These speculative trends in both oil and copper prices were exaggerated by another factor. Financial investors, such as investment banks and insurance companies, have increasingly held commodities in addition to shares, bonds and other assets.[2] They have done so as a means of 'diversifying their portfolios' (their asset holdings) and thereby spreading their risks. This has increased the amount of speculative buying or selling of copper, oil, gold, etc.

(b) Speculation compounding a price increase

> The rise in price to P_2 is compounded by speculation, resulting in a price rise to P_3

? Questions

1. Under what circumstances are people engaging in speculation likely to (a) gain, (b) lose from doing so?
2. Find out what has happened to the price of (a) oil and (b) copper over the past 12 months and give an explanation. To what extent have the price changes been influenced by speculation?

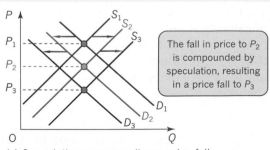

(c) Speculation compounding a price fall

> The fall in price to P_2 is compounded by speculation, resulting in a price fall to P_3

---

[1] 'Oil's not well', *The Economist*, 11 January 2007
[2] Note that if you buy copper, say, in this way, you don't physically take ownership of the copper, but acquire a paper or electronic asset denoting your ownership.

demand for their product of a change in the price of a rival's product (a substitute). If firm B cuts its price, will this make significant inroads into the sales of firm A? If so, firm A may feel forced to cut its prices too; if not, then firm A may keep its price unchanged. The cross-price elasticities of demand between a firm's product and those of each of its rivals are thus vital pieces of information for a firm when making its production, pricing and marketing plans.

Similarly, a firm will wish to know the cross-price elasticity of demand for its product with any complementary good. Car producers will wish to know the effect of petrol price increases on the sales of their cars.

Other elasticities of demand

We could look at the responsiveness of demand to any other determinant. For example, a business is likely to be very interested in how much demand will increase in response to expenditure on a particular advertising campaign or other forms of promotion. It will try to obtain evidence from advertising agencies on the success of their promotions elsewhere in order to estimate whether the likely increase in sales and revenue are worth the expenditure on the advertising. Of course, as with many aspects of business, the figures will only be an estimate, and may be a fairly rough one at that if the campaign is very different from any previous one.

Price elasticity of supply ($P\varepsilon_S$)

Just as we can measure the responsiveness of demand to a change in one of the determinants of demand, so too we can measure the responsiveness of supply to a change in one of the determinants of supply. The **price elasticity of supply** refers to the responsiveness of supply to a change in price. We define it as follows:

$$P\varepsilon_S = \frac{\text{Proportionate (or percentage) change in quantity supplied}}{\text{Proportionate (or percentage) change in price}}$$

Thus if a 15 per cent rise in the price of a product causes a 30 per cent rise in the quantity supplied, the price elasticity of supply will be:

$$30\%/15\% = 2$$

In Figure 2.10 curve S_2 is more elastic between any two prices than curve S_1. Thus, when price rises from P_0 to P_1 there is a larger increase in quantity supplied with S_2 (namely, Q_0 to Q_2) than there is with S_1 (namely, Q_0 to Q_1).

There are two main determinants of the price elasticity of supply.

The amount that costs rise as output rises. The less the additional costs of producing additional output, the more firms will be encouraged to produce for a given price rise: the more elastic will supply be.

Supply is thus likely to be elastic if firms have plenty of spare capacity, if they can readily get extra supplies of raw materials, if they can easily switch away from producing alternative products and if they can avoid having to introduce overtime working (at higher rates of pay). If all these conditions hold, costs will be little affected by a rise in output and supply will be relatively elastic. The less these conditions apply, the less elastic will supply be.

Time period

■ Immediate time period. Firms are unlikely to be able to increase supply by much immediately. Supply is virtually fixed, or can vary only according to available stocks. Supply is highly inelastic.

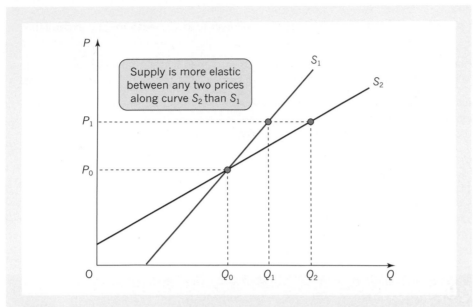

Figure 2.10   Supply curves with different price elasticity of supply

■ Short run. If a slightly longer time period is allowed to elapse, some inputs can be increased (e.g. raw materials), while others will remain fixed (e.g. heavy machinery). Supply can increase somewhat.

■ Long run. In the long run, there will be sufficient time for all inputs to be increased and for new firms to enter the industry. Supply, therefore, is likely to be highly elastic. In some circumstances the supply curve may even slope downward. (See the section on economies of scale in Chapter 4, pages 100–1.)

Recap

■ Price elasticity of demand measures the responsiveness of the quantity demanded to a change in price. It is defined as the proportionate (or percentage) change in quantity demanded divided by the proportionate (or percentage) change in price.

■ Given that demand curves are downward sloping, price elasticity of demand will have a negative value.

■ If quantity demanded changes proportionately more than price, the figure for elasticity will be greater than 1 (ignoring the sign): it is elastic. If the quantity demanded changes proportionately less than price, the figure for elasticity will be less than 1: it is inelastic. If they change by the same proportion, the elasticity has a value of 1: it is unit elastic.

■ Demand will be more elastic the greater the number and closeness of substitute goods and the longer the time period that elapses after the change in price.

■ When the demand for a firm's product is price elastic, a rise in price will lead to a reduction in consumer expenditure on the good and hence to a reduction in the total revenue of producers.

■ When demand is price inelastic, however, a rise in price will lead to an increase in total expenditure and revenue.

■ Income elasticity of demand measures the responsiveness of demand to a change in income. For normal goods it has a positive value. Demand will be more income elastic the more luxurious the good.

■ Cross-price elasticity of demand measures the responsiveness of demand for one good to a change in the price of another. For substitute goods the value will be positive; for complements it will be negative. The cross-price elasticity will be greater the closer the two goods are as substitutes or complements.

■ Price elasticity of supply measures the responsiveness of supply to a change in price. It has a positive value. Supply will be more elastic the less costs per unit rise as output rises and the longer the time period.

QUESTIONS

1. Referring to Table 2.1, assume that there are 200 consumers in the market. Of these, 100 have schedules like Tracey's and 100 have schedules like Darren's. What would be the total market demand schedule for potatoes now?

2. Refer to the list of determinants of demand (see page 37). For what reasons might the demand for butter fall?

3. Refer to the list of determinants of supply (see page 42). For what reasons might (a) the supply of potatoes fall; (b) the supply of leather rise?

4. This question is concerned with the supply of oil for central heating. In each case consider whether there is a movement along the supply curve (and in which direction) or a shift in it (and whether left or right): (a) new oil fields start up in production; (b) the demand for central heating rises; (c) the price of gas falls; (d) oil companies anticipate an upsurge in the demand for central-heating oil; (e) the demand for petrol rises; (f) new technology decreases the costs of oil refining; (g) all oil products become more expensive.

5. The price of cod is much higher today than it was 20 years ago. Using demand and supply diagrams, explain why this should be so.

6. What will happen to the equilibrium price and quantity of butter in each of the following cases? You should state whether demand or supply or both have shifted and in which direction: (a) a rise in the price of margarine; (b) a rise in the demand for yoghurt; (c) a rise in the price of bread; (d) a rise in the demand for bread; (e) an expected increase in the price of butter in the near future; (f) a tax on butter production; (g) the invention of a new, but expensive, process of removing all cholesterol from butter, plus the passing of a law which states that butter producers must use this process. In each case assume that other things remain the same.

7. Why does price elasticity of demand have a negative value, whereas price elasticity of supply has a positive value?

8. Rank the following in ascending order of elasticity: jeans, black Levi jeans, black jeans, black Levi 501 jeans, trousers, outer garments, clothes.

9. Will a general item of expenditure like food or clothing have a price elastic or inelastic demand? Explain.

10. Explain which of these two pairs are likely to have the highest cross-price elasticity of demand: two brands of coffee, or coffee and tea?

11. Why are both the price elasticity of demand and the price elasticity of supply likely to be greater in the long run?

Business issues covered in this chapter

- What determines the amount of a product that consumers wish to buy at each price?
- How are purchasing patterns dependent on human psychology?
- Why are purchasing decisions sometimes risky for consumers and how can insurance help to reduce or remove the level of risk?
- How do businesses set about gathering information on consumer attitudes and behaviour, and what methods can they use to forecast the demand for their products?
- In what ways can firms differentiate their products from those of their rivals?
- What strategies can firms adopt for gaining market share, developing their products and marketing them?
- What are the effects of advertising and what makes a successful advertising campaign?
- How has the growth of the Internet affected businesses' approach to advertising?

Chapter map

CHAPTER 3

Demand and the consumer

If a business is to be successful, it must be able to predict the strength of demand for its products and be able to respond to any changes in consumer tastes. It will also want to know how its customers are likely to react to changes in its price or its competitors' prices, or to changes in income. In other words, it will want to know the price, cross-price and income elasticities of demand for its product. The better the firm's knowledge of its market, the better will it be able to plan its output to meet demand, and the more able will it be to choose its optimum price, product design, marketing campaigns, etc.

3.1 Demand and the firm

In Chapter 2 we examined how prices are determined in perfectly competitive markets: by the interaction of market demand and market supply. In such markets, although the *market* demand curve is downward sloping, the demand curve faced by the individual firm will be horizontal. This is illustrated in Figure 3.1.

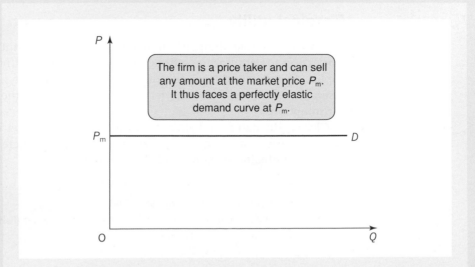

The firm is a price taker and can sell any amount at the market price P_m. It thus faces a perfectly elastic demand curve at P_m.

Figure 3.1   Market demand curve for an individual firm under conditions of perfect competition

The market price is P_m. The individual firm can sell as much as it likes at this market price: it is too small to have any influence on the market – it is a price taker. It will not force the price down by producing more because, in terms of the total market, this extra would be an infinitesimally small amount. If a farmer doubled the output of wheat sent to the market, it would be too small an increase to affect the world price of wheat!

In practice, however, most firms are not price takers; they have some discretion in choosing their price. Such firms face a downward-sloping demand curve. If they raise their price, they will sell less; if they lower their price, they will sell more. But firms will want to know more than this. They will want to know just *how much* the quantity demanded will change. In other words, they will want to know the price elasticity of demand for their product.

In general, the less price elastic the demand, the better it will be for firms, because this will give them more power over prices. In fact, where the price elasticity of demand for the firm's product is less than one, a rise in price will lead to an *increase* in the firm's revenue (see Figure 2.9(b) on page 55) despite the fall in sales.

It is clearly in firms' interests to try to make the demand for their product less elastic. Firms will generally try to do this by attempting to discriminate their product from those of their rivals. If they can produce a product that consumers feel does not have a close substitute, then demand will be relatively inelastic. Success here will depend partly on designing and producing a product that is clearly different, and partly on achieving an effective marketing and advertising programme.

3.2   Understanding consumer behaviour

In this section we examine the nature of consumer behaviour and in particular relate consumer demand to the amount of satisfaction that consumers get from products.

Marginal utility

When you buy something, it's normally because you want it. You want it because you expect to get pleasure, satisfaction or some other sort of benefit from it. This applies to everything from chocolate bars, to bus journeys, to CDs, to jeans, to insurance. Economists use the term 'utility' to refer to the benefit we get from consumption.

Clearly, the nature and amount of utility that people get varies from one product to another, and from one person to another. But there is a simple rule that applies to virtually all people and all products:

The principle of diminishing marginal utility.
As you consume more of a product, and thus become more satisfied, so your desire for additional units of it will decline.

Key
Idea
11

For example, the second cup of tea in the morning gives you less additional satisfaction than the first cup. The third cup gives less still.

We call the additional utility you get from consuming an extra unit of a product the **marginal utility** (*MU*). So what the rule is stating is that the marginal utility will fall as we consume more of a product over a given period of time.

There is a problem, however, with the concept of marginal utility. How can it be measured? After all, we cannot get inside each other's heads to find out just how much pleasure we are getting from consuming a product!

One way round the problem is to measure marginal utility in money terms: i.e. the amount that a person would be prepared to pay for one more unit of a product. Thus if you were prepared to pay 30p for an extra packet of crisps per week, then we would say that your marginal utility from consuming it is 30p. As long as you are prepared to pay more or the same as the actual price, you will buy an extra packet. If you are not prepared to pay that price, you will not.

> **Pause for thought**
>
> *Are there any goods or services where consumers do not experience diminishing marginal utility? If so, give some examples. If not, then explain why.*

> **Definition**
>
> **Marginal utility (*MU*)**
> The extra satisfaction gained from consuming one extra unit of a good within a given time period.

Marginal utility and the demand curve for a good

We can now see how marginal utility relates to a downward-sloping demand curve. As the price of a good falls, it will be worth buying extra units. You will buy more because the price will now be below the amount you are prepared to pay: i.e. price is less than your marginal utility. But as you buy more, your marginal utility from consuming each extra unit will get less and less. How many extra units do you buy? You will stop when the marginal utility has fallen to the new lower price of the good: when $MU = P$. Beyond that point, it's not worth buying any more.

An individual's demand curve

Individual people's demand curves for any good will be the same as their marginal utility curve for that good, measured in money.

This is demonstrated in Figure 3.2 (overleaf), which shows the marginal utility curve for a particular person and a particular good. The downward-sloping nature of the curve illustrates diminishing marginal utility.

If the price of the good were P_1, the person would consume Q_1: where $MU = P$. Thus point *a* would be one point on that person's demand curve. If the price fell to P_2, consumption would rise to Q_2, since this is where $MU = P_2$. Thus point *b* is a second point on the demand curve. Likewise if price fell to P_3, Q_3 would be consumed. Point *c* is a third point on the demand curve.

Thus as long as individuals consume where $P = MU$, their demand curve will be along the same line as their marginal utility curve.

The firm's demand curve

The firm's demand curve will simply be the (horizontal) sum of all individuals' demand curves for its product.

The shape of the demand curve. The price elasticity of demand will reflect the rate at which *MU* diminishes. If there are close substitutes for a good, it is likely to have an elastic demand, and its *MU* will diminish slowly as consumption increases. The reason is that increased consumption of this product will be accompanied by *decreased* consumption of the alternative product(s). Since total consumption of this

Figure 3.2 An individual person's demand curve

product *plus* the alternatives has increased only slightly (if at all), the marginal utility will fall only slowly.

For example, the demand for a given brand of petrol is likely to have a fairly high price elasticity, since other brands are substitutes. If there is a cut in the price of Esso petrol (assuming the prices of other brands stay constant), consumption of Esso will increase a lot. The *MU* of Esso petrol will fall slowly, since people consume less of other brands. Petrol consumption *in total* may be only slightly greater and hence the *MU* of petrol only slightly lower.

Shifts in the demand curve. How do *shifts* in demand relate to marginal utility? For example, how would the marginal utility of (and hence demand for) margarine be affected by a rise in the price of butter? The higher price of butter would cause less butter to be consumed. This would increase the marginal utility of margarine, since if people are using less butter, their desire for margarine is higher. The *MU* curve (and hence the demand curve) for margarine thus shifts to the right.

The problem of imperfect information

So far we have assumed that when people buy goods and services, they know exactly what price they will pay and how much utility they will gain. In many cases this is a reasonable assumption. When you buy a bar of chocolate, you clearly do know how much you are paying for it and have a very good idea how much you will like it. But what about a DVD recorder, or a car, or a washing machine, or any other **consumer durable**? In each of these cases you are buying something that will last you a long time, and the further into the future you look, the less certain you will be of its costs and benefits to you.

Take the case of a washing machine costing you £400. If you pay cash, your immediate outlay involves no uncertainty: it is £400. But washing machines can

Definition

Consumer durable
A consumer good that lasts a period of time, during which the consumer can continue gaining utility from it.

break down. In two years' time you could find yourself with a repair bill of £100. This cannot be predicted and yet it is a price you will have to pay, just like the original £400. In other words, when you buy the washing machine, you are uncertain as to the full 'price' it will entail over its lifetime.

If the costs of the washing machine are uncertain, so too are the benefits. You might have been attracted to buy it in the first place by the manufacturer's glossy brochure, or by the look of it, or by adverts on TV, in magazines, etc. When you have used it for a while, however, you will probably discover things you had not anticipated. The spin dryer does not get your clothes as dry as you had hoped; it is noisy; it leaks; the door sticks; and so on.

Buying consumer durables thus involves uncertainty. So too does the purchase of assets, whether a physical asset such as a house or financial assets such as shares. In the case of assets, the uncertainty is over their future *price*. If you buy shares in a currently profitable company, what will happen to their price in the future? Will they shoot up in price, thus enabling you to sell them at a large profit, or will they fall? You cannot know for certain. A lot depends on the company's future performance and what other people think that performance is likely to be.

At this point it is useful to distinguish between uncertainty and risk. **Risk** is where an outcome may or may not occur, but where the *probability* of its occurring is known. **Uncertainty** is where the probability is not known.

Insurance: a way of removing risks

Insurance is a means of eliminating, or at least reducing, uncertainty for people. If, for example, you could lose your job if you are injured, you can remove the risk of loss of income by taking out an appropriate insurance policy.

But why is it that the insurance companies are prepared to shoulder the risks that their customers were not? The answer is that the insurance company is able to **spread its risks**.

The spreading of risks

If there is a one in ten thousand chance of your house burning down each year, although it is only a small chance it would be so disastrous that you are simply not prepared to take the risk. You thus take out house insurance and are prepared to pay a premium of *more than* 0.01 per cent (one in ten thousand).

The insurance company, however, is not just insuring you. It is insuring many others at the same time. If your house burns down, there will be approximately 9999 others that do not. The premiums the insurance company has collected will be more than enough to cover its payments. The more houses it insures, the smaller will be the variation in the proportion that actually burn down each year.

This is an application of the **law of large numbers**. What is unpredictable for an individual becomes highly predictable in the mass. The more people the insurance company insures, the more predictable is the total outcome.

What is more, the insurance company will be in a position to estimate just what the risks are. It can thus work out what premiums it must charge in order to make a profit. With individuals, however, the precise risk is rarely known. Do you know your chances of living to 70? Almost certainly you do not. But a life assurance company will know precisely the chances of a person of your age, sex and occupation living to 70! It will have the statistical data to show this. In other words, an insurance company will be able to convert your *uncertainty* into their *risk*.

Box 3.1

Rogue traders

Buyer beware!

Markets are usually an efficient way of letting buyers and sellers exchange goods and services. However, this does not stop consumers making complaints about the quality of the goods or services they receive.

It is impossible to get a true measure of customer dissatisfaction because aggrieved consumers do not always complain and data are collected by a number of separate agencies. Particular sectors though seem to be more vulnerable to 'rogue traders' than others. For example, over the period 2000 to 2004, the largest proportion of consumer complaints received from the UK Trading Standards Offices relate to home maintenance, repairs and improvements, including the sale and installation of double glazing (15 per cent of all complaints), while the sale of second-hand motor vehicles and vehicle repairs comes a close second (13 per cent).

Consumer complaints are also of concern to cross-border sales as the growth of buying over the Internet has blossomed in recent times (see Box 4.6). The figure below reports data from 13 countries on complaints against e-commerce transactions. The largest proportion of complaints relate to internet shopping, online lotteries and internet auction sites such as eBay and Yahoo.

Adverse selection and moral hazard

But why does a market, which you would think would respond to consumer wishes, give rise to consumer complaints? Why is it that rogue traders can continue in business? The answer can be found in the concepts of adverse selection and moral hazard. In

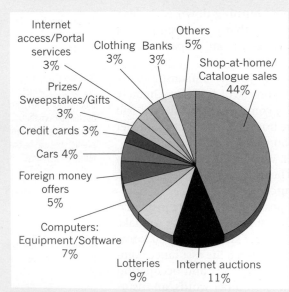

E-consumer complaints, 2006

Source: www.econsumer.gov

both cases, the problem is essentially one of 'information asymmetries' and is an example of the 'principal–agent problem' (see page 10). The buyer (the 'principal') has poorer information about the product than the agent (the 'seller').

Information asymmetries. Complaints by consumers are likely to be few if the product is fairly simple and information about the exchange process is publicly available. For example, if I buy apples from a market trader but subsequently return them because some are damaged, they are likely to exchange the apples, or offer a full refund, because failure to do so would lead to the trader's sales falling as information gets out that they sell poor-quality fruit. Here information asymmetries are minimal.

However, where the product is more complex, perhaps with consumers making large outlays, and information is more private, the situation can be very different. The greater the information 'gap' between sellers and consumers, the greater the scope for deception and fraud and the more likely are rogue traders to thrive. In these situations the number of consumer complaints increases.

Consider the sale of a conservatory, a large extension to a house usually comprising a number of various building products, including double-glazed windows and doors. A product such as this involves an expensive outlay for consumers, but they may have very limited information about the price of materials and labour, as well as the method of building a conservatory.

Assume that there is a standard-sized conservatory and that a high-quality seller would be prepared to supply this product at a price of £10 000. Such a price would reflect the quality of their work and would keep them in the business of selling high-quality products. On the other hand, assume that a poor-quality supplier, a 'rogue trader', could provide this conservatory at £5000.

Given information asymmetry, let us assume that consumers are not aware of who is a high-quality or low-quality seller. As a result, rogue traders offer to supply a standard conservatory for, say, £9000.

Adverse selection. This price of £9000, however, is not enough to cover the costs of high-quality sellers, and so they will not want to offer their services to build high-quality conservatories. On the other hand, 'rogue traders' will find this price very profitable and it will attract a higher than normal number of such sellers into the market. Of course, if consumers know that the only sellers in the market are likely to be 'rogue traders', they will not buy conservatories and the market will collapse.

The problem just described is an example of **adverse selection**. In this case a group of sellers ('rogue traders') have been attracted to the market by prices considerably greater than their costs even before any transactions have taken place.

Adverse selection.

Key Idea 12

Where information is imperfect, high-risk/poor-quality groups will be attracted to profitable market opportunities to the disadvantage of the average buyer (or seller).

Although information is imperfect, things aren't as bad as the above suggests. Consumers do try to find out about sellers before they buy and most consumers get a good product. However, 'rogue traders' also make sales. The poorer the information on the part of consumers, the more adverse will be their selection: the worse the likely quality of the products they buy.

Moral hazard. Once a contract has been signed, the problem of **moral hazard** occurs. In our example, the rogue trader might initially agree to supply and install the conservatory to meet particular high standards of quality for a particular price. However, unless the buyer has full information about the construction of conservatories or can keep a constant watch over the work, defective materials or poor-quality workmanship may be supplied. But the buyer will not know this until a later date when problems start to appear with the conservatory!

Idea 13

Moral hazard results because the seller has acted inappropriately (immorally) and to the detriment of the buyer. The 'hazard' arises because of imperfect information on the part of the consumer. Rogue traders are tempted to supply an inferior product, believing that they can get away with it.

Moral hazard.

Key Idea 13

Following a deal, if there are information asymmetries (see page 10), it is likely that one party will engage in problematic (immoral and/or hazardous) behaviour to the detriment of the other. In other words, lack of information by one party to the deal may result in the deal not being honoured by the other party.

Usually, the process of law would work in favour of the buyer because a contract had been established, but in many cases involving rogue traders the business has been declared bankrupt or the costs to buyers of pursuing a legal case are too great.

Solutions

So how can sellers signal to buyers that they offer high-quality products? And how can consumers trust this information? A number of methods exist.

Establishing a reputation. A single firm can establish a reputation for selling high-quality goods, usually over a number of years, or perhaps it has created a valued brand name through advertising. Alternatively, firms can offer guarantees and warranties on their products, although a ten-year guarantee on the building work associated with a conservatory is of no use if the firm has gone bankrupt!

Trade associations and other third parties. Firms can also band together collectively and establish a trade association. Examples include the Federation of Master Builders or the Association of British Travel Agents (ABTA). Firms that belong to a trade association have benefits that can extend beyond that of acting alone. For example, if one firm provides a poor-quality product, then consumers may get compensation via the association. ABTA, for example, guarantees to make sure customers will complete their holiday, or obtain a refund, if they have purchased it from a member that has gone bankrupt.

Trade associations are a means by which firms can demonstrate that they regulate themselves rather than have governments impose rules on them.

Sometimes third parties can help firms to signal high quality. The online auction site, eBay, for example, provides a feedback system for buyers and sellers so they can register their happiness or otherwise with sales. Likewise, the Office of Fair Trading, under the auspices of the Enterprise Act (2002), has created an Approved Codes of Practice scheme whereby trade associations and their members will guarantee that customers will receive high quality service. Successful associations can display an OFT Approved Codes logo.

Government intervention. On the whole, government does not like to intervene in particular industries, preferring a sector to regulate itself. However, in the case of the financial services industry, the government has directly intervened because the impact of the industry on consumers in recent times has been widespread and financially devastating. Following a number of financial scandals, including the mis-selling of pensions and mortgages, the government replaced ineffective self-regulation in 2000 with the Financial Services Authority, an independent industry regulator with statutory powers, whose Board is appointed by and accountable to the Treasury. In this instance the level of product complexity and information asymmetry between buyer and seller was viewed to be too great for the industry to control itself.

? Question

What are the disadvantages of trade associations?

Definitions

Adverse selection
Where information is imperfect, high-risk/poor-quality groups will be attracted to profitable market opportunities to the disadvantage of the average buyer (or seller).

Moral hazard
Following a deal, if there are information asymmetries, it is likely that one party will engage in problematic (immoral and/or hazardous) behaviour to the detriment of the other. In other words, lack of information by one party to the deal may result in the deal not being honoured by the other party.

Box 3.2

Problems for unwary insurance companies

'Adverse selection' and 'moral hazard'

In Box 3.1, we saw how consumers may suffer from adverse selection and from moral hazard on the part of suppliers. Adverse selection and moral hazard can also apply the other way round. Insurance companies may incur higher costs from adverse selection and moral hazard on the part of certain policyholders. These higher costs are then likely to be passed on to other policyholders.

Adverse selection

This occurs where the people taking out insurance are those who have the highest risk.

For example, suppose that a company offers medical insurance. It surveys the population and works out that the average person requires £200 of treatment per year. The company thus sets the premium at £250 (the extra £50 to cover its costs and provide a profit). But it is likely that the people most likely to take out the insurance are those most likely to fall sick: those who have been ill before, those whose families have a history of illness, those in jobs that are hazardous to health, etc. These people on average may require £500 of treatment per year. The insurance company would soon make a loss.

But cannot the company then simply raise premiums to £550 or £600? It can, but the problem is that it will thereby be depriving the person of *average* health of reasonably priced insurance.

The answer is for the company to discriminate more carefully between people. You may have to fill out a questionnaire so that the company can assess your own particular risk and set an appropriate premium. There may need to be legal penalties for people caught lying!

 Question
What details does an insurance company require to know before it will insure a person to drive a car?

Moral hazard

This occurs where having insurance makes you less careful and thus increases your risk to the insurance company. For example, if your bicycle is insured against theft, you may be less concerned to go through the hassle of chaining it up each time you leave it.

Again, if insurance companies work out risks by looking at the *total* number of bicycle thefts, these figures will understate the risks to the company because they will include thefts from *uninsured* people who are likely to be more careful.

 Question
How will the following reduce moral hazard?

(a) A no-claims bonus.
(b) Your having to pay the first so much of any claim.
(c) Offering lower premiums to those less likely to claim (e.g. lower house contents premiums for those with burglar alarms).

The problem of moral hazard occurs in many other walks of life. A good example is that of debt. If someone else is willing to pay your debts (e.g. your parents) it is likely to make you less careful in your spending! This argument has been used by some rich countries for not cancelling the debts of poor countries.

The spreading of risks does not just require that there should be a large number of policies. It also requires that the risks should be **independent**. If any insurance company insured 1000 houses *all in the same neighbourhood*, and then there was a major fire in the area, the claims would be enormous. The risks of fire were not independent. The company would, in fact, have been taking a gamble on a single event. If, however, it provides fire insurance for houses scattered all over the country, the risks *are* independent.

Another way in which insurance companies can spread their risks is by **diversification**. The more types of insurance a company offers (car, house, life, health, etc.), the greater is likely to be the independence of the risks.

Definitions

Independent risks
Where two risky events are unconnected. The occurrence of one will not affect the likelihood of the occurrence of the other.

Diversification
Where a firm expands into new types of business.

Recap

- Economists call consumer satisfaction 'utility'. Marginal utility diminishes as consumption increases.

- People will consume more of a good as long as its marginal utility to them (measured in terms of the price they are prepared to pay for it) exceeds its price. They will stop buying additional amounts once *MU* has fallen to equal the price.

- An individual's demand curve lies along the same line as the individual's marginal utility curve. The market demand curve is the sum of all individuals' marginal utility curves.

- When people buy consumer durables they may be uncertain of their benefits and any additional repair and maintenance costs. When they buy financial assets they may be uncertain of what will happen to their price in the future. Buying under these conditions of imperfect knowledge is therefore a form of gambling. When we take such gambles, if we know the odds we are said to be operating under conditions of *risk*. If we do not know the odds we are said to be operating under conditions of *uncertainty*.

- Insurance is a way of eliminating risks for policyholders. In order to avoid risks, people are prepared to pay premiums in order to obtain insurance. Insurance companies, on the other hand, are prepared to take on these risks because they can spread them over a large number of policies. According to the law of large numbers, what is unpredictable for a single policyholder becomes highly predictable for a large number of them provided that their risks are independent of each other.

Estimating and predicting demand   3.3

How might a business set about discovering the wants of consumers and hence the intensity of demand? The more effectively a business can identify such wants, the more likely it is to increase its sales and be successful. The clearer idea it can gain of the rate at which the typical consumer's utility will decline as consumption increases, the better estimate it can make of the product's price elasticity. Also the more it can assess the relative utility to the consumer of its product compared with those of its rivals, the more effectively will it be able to compete by differentiating its product from theirs.

In this section we first examine methods for gathering data on consumer behaviour and then see how firms set about forecasting changes in demand over time.

Methods of collecting data on consumer behaviour

There are three general approaches to gathering information about consumers. These are: **observations of market behaviour**, **market surveys** and **market experiments**.

Market observations

The firm can gather data on how demand for its product has changed over time. Virtually all firms will have detailed information on their sales broken down by week, and/or month, and/or year. They will probably also have information on how sales have varied from one part of the market to another.

In addition, the firm will need to obtain data on how the various determinants of demand (such as price, advertising and the price of competitors' products) have themselves changed over time. Firms are likely to have much of this information already: e.g. the amount spent on advertising and the prices of competitors' products. Other information might be relatively easy to obtain by paying an agency to do the research.

Having obtained this information, the firm can then use it to estimate how changes in the various determinants have affected demand in the past, and hence what effect they will be likely to have in the future.

Even the most sophisticated analysis based on market observations, however, will suffer from one major drawback. Relationships that held in the past will not necessarily hold in the future. Consumers are human, and humans change their minds. Their perceptions of products change (something that the advertising industry relies on!) and tastes change. It is for this reason that many firms turn to market surveys or market experiments to gain more information about the future.

Market surveys

It is not uncommon to be stopped in a city centre, or to have a knock at the door, and be asked whether you would kindly answer the questions of some market researcher. If the research interviewer misses you, then a postal questionnaire may well seek out the same type of information. A vast quantity of information can be collected in this way. It is a relatively quick and cheap method of data collection. Questions concerning all aspects of consumer behaviour might be asked, such as those relating to present and future patterns of expenditure, or how people might respond to changing product specifications or price, both of the firm in question and of its rivals.

A key feature of the market survey is that it can be targeted at distinct consumer groups, thereby reflecting the specific information requirements of a business. For example, businesses selling luxury goods will be interested only in consumers falling within higher income brackets. Other samples might be drawn from a particular age group or gender, or from those with a particular lifestyle, such as eating habits.

Definitions

Observations of market behaviour
Information gathered about consumers from the day-to-day activities of the business within the market.

Market surveys
Information gathered about consumers, usually via a questionnaire, that attempts to enhance the business's understanding of consumer behaviour.

Market experiments
Information gathered about consumers under artificial or simulated conditions: a method used widely in assessing the effects of advertising on consumers.

The major drawback with this technique concerns the accuracy of the information acquired. Accurate information requires various conditions to be met.

A random sample. If the sample is not randomly selected, it may fail to represent a cross-section of the population being surveyed.

Clarity of the questions. It is important for the questions to be phrased in an unambiguous way, so as not to mislead the respondent.

Avoidance of leading questions. It is very easy for the respondent to be led into giving the answer the firm wants to hear. For example, when asking whether the person would buy a new product that the firm is thinking of launching, the questionnaire might make the product sound really desirable. The respondents might, as a result, say that they would buy the product, but later, when they see the product in the shops, decide they do not want it.

Truthful response. It is very tempting for respondents who are 'keen to please' to give the answer that they think the questioner wants, or for other somewhat reluctant respondents to give 'mischievous' answers. In other words, people may lie!

Stability of demand. By the time the product is launched, or the changes to an existing product are made, time will have elapsed. The information may then be out of date. Consumer demand may have changed, as tastes and fashions have shifted, or as a result of the actions of competitors.

Market experiments

Rather than asking consumers questions and getting them to *imagine* how they *would* behave, the market experiment involves observing consumer *behaviour* under simulated conditions. It can be used to observe consumer reactions to a new product or to changes in an existing product.

A simple experiment might involve consumers being asked to conduct a blind taste test for a new brand of toothpaste. The experimenter will ensure that the same amount of paste is applied to the brush, and that the subjects swill their mouths prior to tasting a further brand. Once the experiment is over, the 'consumers' are quizzed about their perceptions of the product.

More sophisticated experiments could be conducted. For example, a *laboratory shop* might be set up to simulate a real shopping experience. People could be given a certain amount of money to spend in the 'shop' and their reactions to changes in prices, packaging, display, etc. could be monitored.

The major drawback with such 'laboratories' is that consumers might behave differently because they are being observed. For example, they might spend more time comparing prices than they would otherwise, simply because they think that this is what a *good*, rational consumer should do. With real shopping, however, it might simply be habit, or something 'irrational' such as the colour of the packaging, that determines which product they select (see Box 3.3).

> ### Pause for thought
>
> *Identify some other drawbacks in using market experiments to gather data on consumer behaviour.*

Another type of market experiment involves confining a marketing campaign to a particular town or region. The campaign could involve advertising, or giving out free samples, or discounting the price, or introducing an improved version of the product, but each confined to that particular locality. Sales in that area are then compared with sales in other areas in order to assess the effectiveness of the various campaigns.

Taking account of emotion

The shopping experience

Traditional 'neoclassical' economics assumes that consumers are rational: that they weigh up the marginal utility that they expect to gain from purchasing a product against the price they must pay. But is this how we behave when we go shopping. Are you a 'rational' shopper? Or do your emotions sometimes take over?

In many cases, the experience of the emotion of desire when contemplating buying something, such as a bar of chocolate, is merely an aid to rational behaviour. You imagine the pleasure you will receive: something that is borne out when you do actually eat the chocolate. Similarly, the emotion of displeasure at the thought of paying for the product helps you to be cautious and think of the opportunity cost of buying the product.

Sometimes, however, the emotion is misplaced. People may be lured by the packaging and the pleasure they imagine they will gain, rather than the pleasure they actually will gain. Advertisers know this well! To them, perceived pleasure at the time of purchase is more important than actual pleasure at the time of consumption.

In another departure from rationality, people may downplay the costs of a purchase. Research into the brain activity of consumers by George Loewenstein, an economist at Carnegie

Mellon University, in Pittsburgh suggests that 'rather than weighing the present good against future alternatives, as orthodox economics suggests happens, people actually balance the immediate pleasure of the prospective possession of a product with the immediate pain of paying for it.'[1]

This has profound implications for buying on credit. The abstract nature of credit cards and the fact that payment is deferred until some later date means that many people downplay the costs of the items they buy. No wonder many shops like to offer credit. Not only does it encourage people to buy things now rather than waiting: it may encourage them to buy things they would never otherwise have bought – neither now nor later!

Questions

1. Is it ever 'rational' to buy on credit? Explain.
2. In what other ways might consumer behaviour be regarded as irrational in the traditional sense? How might businesses take advantage of this 'irrationality'?

[1] 'The triumph of unreason?', *The Economist*, 11 January 2007

Forecasting demand

Businesses are interested not just in knowing the current strength of demand for their products and how demand is likely to be affected by changes in factors such as product specifications and the price of competitors' products. They are also interested in trying to predict *future* demand. After all, if demand is going to increase, they may well want to invest *now* so that they have the extra capacity to meet the extra demand. But it will be a costly mistake to invest in extra capacity if demand is not going to increase.

We now, therefore, turn to examine some of the forecasting techniques used by business.

Simple time-series analysis

Simple time-series analysis involves directly projecting from past sales data into the future. Thus if it is observed that sales of a firm's product have been growing steadily by 3 per cent per annum for the past few years, the firm can use this to predict that sales will continue to grow at approximately the same rate in the future. Similarly, if it is observed that there are clear seasonal fluctuations in demand, as in the case of the demand for holidays, ice cream or winter coats, then again it can be assumed that fluctuations of a similar magnitude will continue into the future.

Using simple time-series analysis assumes that demand in the future will continue to behave in the same way as in the past. The problem is that it may not. Just because demand has followed a clear pattern in the past, it does not inexorably follow that it will continue to exhibit the same pattern in the future. After all, the determinants of demand may well have changed. Successful forecasting, therefore, will usually involve a more sophisticated analysis of trends.

The decomposition of time paths

One way in which the analysis of past data can be made more sophisticated is to identify different elements in the time path of sales. Figure 3.3 illustrates one such time path: the (imaginary) sales of woollen jumpers by firm X. It is shown by the continuous green line, labelled 'Actual sales'. Four different sets of factors normally determine the shape of a time path like this.

Trends. These are increases or decreases in demand over a number of years. In our example, there is a long-term decrease in demand for this firm's woollen jumpers up to year 7 and then a recovery in demand thereafter.

Trends may reflect factors such as changes in population structure, or technological innovation or longer-term changes in fashion. Thus if wool were to become more expensive over time compared with other fibres, or if there were a gradual shift in tastes away from woollen jumpers and towards acrylic or cotton jumpers, or towards sweatshirts, this could explain the long-term decline in demand for the first few years. A gradual shift in tastes back towards natural fibres, and to wool

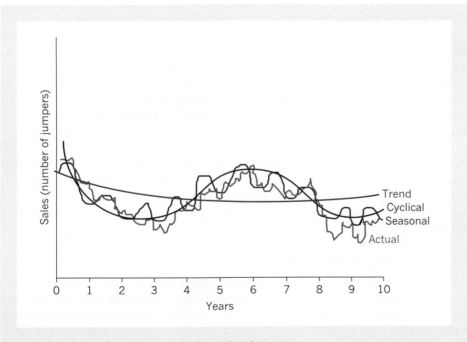

Figure 3.3   (Imaginary) sales of woollen jumpers

in particular, or a gradual reduction in the price of wool, could then explain the subsequent recovery in demand.

Alternatively, trends may reflect changes over time in the structure of an industry. For example, an industry might become more and more competitive, with new firms joining. This would tend to reduce sales for existing firms (unless the market were expanding very rapidly).

Cyclical fluctuations. In practice, the level of actual sales will not follow the trend line precisely. One reason for this is the cyclical upswings and downswings in business activity in the economy as a whole. In some years incomes are rising rapidly and thus demand is buoyant. In other years, the economy will be in recession, with incomes falling. In these years, demand may well also fall. In our example, in boom years people may spend much more on clothes (including woollen jumpers), whereas in a recession, people may make do with their old clothes. The cyclical variations line is thus above the trend line in boom years and below the trend line during a recession.

Seasonal fluctuations. The demand for many products also depends on the time of year. In the case of woollen jumpers, the peak demand is likely to be as winter approaches or just before Christmas. Thus the seasonal variations line is above the cyclical variations line in winter and below it in summer.

Short-term shifts in demand or supply. Finally, the actual sales line will also reflect various short-term shifts in demand or supply, causing it to diverge from the smooth seasonal variations line.

There are many reasons why the demand curve might shift. A competitor might increase its price, or there may be a sudden change in fashion, caused, say, by a pop group deciding to wear woollen jumpers for their new video: what was once seen as unfashionable by many people now suddenly becomes fashionable! Alternatively, there may be an unusually cold or hot, or wet or dry spell of weather.

Likewise there are various reasons for sudden shifts in supply conditions. For example, there may be a sheep disease which ruins the wool of infected sheep. As a result, the price of wool goes up, and sales of woollen jumpers fall.

These sudden shifts in demand or supply conditions are often referred to as 'random shocks' because they are usually unpredictable and temporarily move sales away from the trend. (Note that *long-term* shifts in demand and supply will be shown by a change in the trend line itself.)

Even with sophisticated time-series analysis, which breaks time paths into their constituent elements, there is still one major weakness: time-series analysis is merely a projection of the *past*. Most businesses will want to anticipate *changes* to sales trends – to forecast any deviations from the current time path. One method for doing this is *barometric forecasting*.

Barometric forecasting

Assume that you are a manager of a furniture business and are wondering whether to invest in new capital equipment. You would only want to do this if the demand for your product was likely to rise. You will probably, therefore, look for some indication of this. A good barometer of future demand for furniture would be the number of new houses being built. People will tend to buy new furniture some months after the building of their new house has commenced.

Barometric forecasting involves the use of **leading indicators**, such as housing starts, when attempting to predict the future. In fact some leading indicators, such as increased activity in the construction industry, rises in Stock Exchange prices, a rise in the rate of exchange and a rise in industrial confidence, are good indicators of a general upturn in the economy. In other words, firms use these indicators to predict what is likely to happen to their own demand.

Barometric forecasting suffers from two major weaknesses. The first is that it only allows forecasting a few months ahead – as far ahead as is the time lag between the change in the leading indicator and the variable being forecasted. The second is that it can give only a general indication of changes in demand. It is simply another form of time-series analysis. Just because a relationship existed in the past between a leading indicator and the variable being forecasted, it cannot be assumed that exactly the same relationship will exist in the future.

Normally, then, firms use barometric forecasting merely to give them a rough guide as to likely changes in demand for their product: i.e. whether it is likely to expand or contract, and by 'a lot' or by 'a little'. Nevertheless information on leading indicators is readily available in government or trade statistics.

> **Definitions**
>
> **Barometric forecasting**
> A technique used to predict future economic trends based upon analysing patterns of time-series data.
>
> **Leading indicators**
> Indicators that help predict future trends in the economy.

> **Pause for thought**
>
> *What might be a good leading indicator of the demand for a particular brand of printer ink?*

Recap

- Businesses seek information on consumer behaviour so as to predict market trends and improve strategic decision making.

- One source of data is the firm's own information on how its sales have varied in the past with changes in the various determinants of demand, such as consumer incomes and the prices of competitors' products.

- Another source of data is market surveys. These can generate a large quantity of cheap information. Care should be taken, however, to ensure that the sample of consumers investigated reflects the target consumer group.

- Market experiments involve investigating consumer behaviour within a controlled environment. This method is particularly useful when considering new products where information is scarce.

- It is not enough to know what will happen to demand if a determinant changes. Businesses will want to forecast what will actually happen to demand.

- Time-series analysis bases future trends on past events. Time-series data can be decomposed into different elements: trends, seasonal fluctuations, cyclical fluctuations and random shocks.

- Barometric forecasting involves making predictions based upon changes in key leading indicators.

Stimulating demand   3.4

For most firms, selling their product is not simply a question of estimating demand and then choosing an appropriate price and level of production. In other words, they do not simply take their market as given. Instead they will seek to *increase* demand. They will do this by developing their product and differentiating it from those of their rivals, and then marketing it by advertising and other forms of product promotion.

What firms are engaging in here is **non-price competition**. In such situations the job of the manager can be quite complex, involving strategic decisions about product design and quality, product promotion and the provision of various forms of after-sales service.

Product differentiation

Central to non-price competition is **product differentiation**. Most firms' products differ in various ways from those of their rivals. Take the case of washing machines. Although all washing machines wash clothes, and as such are close substitutes for each other, there are many differences between brands. They differ not only in price, but also in their capacity, their styling, their range of programmes, their economy in the use of electricity, hot water and detergent, their reliability, their noise, their after-sales service, etc. Firms will attempt to design their product so that they can stress its advantages (real or imaginary) over the competitor brands. Just think of the specific features of particular models of car, hi-fi equipment or brands of cosmetic, and then consider the ways in which these features are stressed by advertisements. In fact, think of virtually any advertisement and consider how it stresses the features of that particular brand.

Features of a product

A product has many dimensions, and a strategy to differentiate a product may focus on one or more of these. Dimensions include:

■ *Technical standards.* These relate to the product's level of technical sophistication: how advanced it is in relation to the current state of technology. This would be a very important product dimension if, for example, you were purchasing a PC.

■ *Quality standards.* These relate to aspects such as the quality of the materials used in the product's construction and the care taken in assembly. These will affect the product's durability and reliability. The purchase of consumer durables, such as televisions, furniture and toys, will be strongly influenced by quality standards.

■ *Design characteristics.* These relate to the product's direct appeal to the consumer in terms of appearance or operating features. Examples of design characteristics are colour, style and even packaging. The demand for fashion products such as clothing will be strongly influenced by design characteristics.

■ *Service characteristics.* This aspect is not directly concerned with the product itself, but with the support and back-up given to the customer after the product has been sold. Servicing, product maintenance and guarantees would be included under this heading. When purchasing a new car, the quality of after-sales service might strongly influence the choice you make.

Market segmentation

Different features of a product will appeal to different consumers. Where features are quite distinct, and where particular features or groups of features can be seen to appeal to a particular category of consumers, it might be useful for producers to divide the market into segments. Taking the example of cars again, the market could be divided into luxury cars, large, medium and small family cars, sports cars, multi-terrain vehicles, seven-seater people carriers, etc. Each type of car occupies a distinct market segment.

When consumer tastes change over time, or where existing models do not cater for every taste, a firm may be able to identify a new segment of the market – a **market niche**. Having identified the appropriate market niche for its product, the marketing division within the firm will then set about targeting the relevant consumer group(s) and developing an appropriate strategy for promoting the product.

Marketing the product

Marketing covers the following activities: establishing the strength of consumer demand in existing parts of the market, and potential demand in new niches; developing an attractive and distinct image for the product; informing potential consumers of various features of the product; fostering a desire by consumers for the product; and, in the light of all these, persuading consumers to buy the product.

Product/market strategy

Once the nature and strength of consumer demand (both current and potential) have been identified, the business will set about meeting and influencing this demand. In most cases it will be hoping to achieve a growth in sales. To do this, one of the first things the firm must decide is its *product/market strategy*. This will involve addressing two major questions:

■ Should it focus on promoting its existing product, or should it develop new products?

■ Should it focus on gaining a bigger share of its existing market, or should it seek to break into new markets?

These choices can be shown in a **growth vector matrix**. This is illustrated in Figure 3.4.

The four cells show the possible combinations of answers to the above questions: cell A – *market penetration* (current product, current market); cell B – *product*

Definitions

Market niche
A part of a market (or new market) that has not been filled by an existing brand or business.

Growth vector matrix
A means by which a business might assess its product/market strategy.

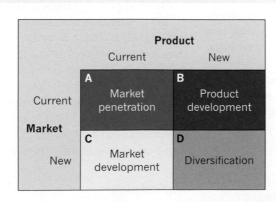

Figure 3.4   Growth vector components

Box 3.4

Brands and own-brands

What's in a name?

The rise of supermarket own-brands in the early 1990s was phe-nomenal. Their market penetration in the UK became so great that, by 1995, 54.5 per cent of all sales in the major supermarket chains were of own-branded products. In 1992, just three years earlier, the figure had been a mere 27 per cent. What makes this rise even more striking is that it followed a period when branded products dominated the market and seemed to be growing in strength. During the 1980s, the profits of companies such as Kellogg's and Heinz were increasing by as much as 15 per cent a year.

However, towards the end of the 1980s, things started to go horribly wrong for branded products:

■ The economic boom of the time came to an end, and the UK, along with many other countries, went into recession, with the result that consumers became more price conscious.

■ Supermarkets began to develop a more extensive range of own-label products.

As Alan Mitchell argued in *Marketing Week* (6 December 1996):

New technologies [were] allowing own-label manufacturers to produce smaller batch runs at lower costs: so the benefits of economies of scale [declined].

Own-label products also lay claim to cost advantages, both on marketing and distribution – a few dedicated trucks from factory to retailer regional distribution centre are noth-ing compared with the cost of a fleet serving every retailer, wholesaler, and convenience shop.

This means all the paraphernalia of advertising, distribu-tion, and new product development that made the brand manufacturing model so powerful decades ago is unravelling, and becoming an enormous cost burden instead – a burden that adds up to 50 per cent on to the final consumer price and allows retailers to undercut brands while creaming off higher margins. The virtuous cycle goes into reverse, and becomes a vicious circle.

Such were the cost advantages of the own-label alternative that, for many products, the price discrepancy between brands and own-brands had become staggering, forcing brand manu-facturers to make substantial price cuts. For example, the dairy producer Kraft was forced to slash prices on many of its cheese products, which in several cases were some 45 per cent more expensive than own-label alternatives.

The position of branded products was further undermined. Technology not only pushed down costs, but also raised the *qual-ity* of products, making it easier for own-label producers to copy established brands, and in many cases to innovate themselves. According to the *Grocer*[1], about two-thirds of shoppers believe the quality and innovation of own-label products are on a par with branded goods, while over two-thirds say that own-label is better value for money than branded goods.

The major supermarket chains such as Tesco, Asda, Sainsbury's and Morrisons have all developed their own premium brands, either to compete in particular segments, for example in healthy eating ranges such as 'Be Good to Yourself' or 'Taste the Difference' or, more generally, for example Tesco's 'Finest' range.

The brands fight back

What are brand manufacturers to do? One alternative is to extend a brand to new products and use the brand image to promote them. Not only will this help raise revenue but it will also reduce the producer's reliance on a single product. Take the case of Virgin. The brand no longer applies just to record stores. It now embraces airlines, trains, finance, soft drinks, mobile phones, holidays, bridal wear, cinemas, radio, virtual car showrooms, online books, an online wine store, an internet service provider, cosmetics, health clubs, balloon rides, gift 'experiences' and stem cell banks. With the launching of Virgin Galactic in 2004 and orders for five 'spaceliners', it now even includes space tourism! Other examples include Branston baked beans and Google Base (to rival eBay) and Google Checkout (to rival PayPal).

Another approach is to focus on the perceived high quality of branded products. Part of the reason for the decline in market share of own-brands since the mid-1990s has been a period of prolonged economic growth. The rise in disposable income leads to increased conspicuous consumption, and many branded goods are associated with affluence and increased quality of lifestyle. An example is the preference of many consumers for designer-label clothing rather than the supermarket's own clothing ranges, despite considerable differences in prices.

A mixed picture

Whilst the trend has been back towards brands, it is important to recognise that there is still substantial variability in own-label penetration across products. As the table illustrates, in some

Market Penetration of own-label brands in selected markets, 2005

Market Segment	Share (%)	Key Brand Competitors [a]
Cheese[b]	62.7	Kraft (6.6% – Dairylea), Dairy Crest (5% – Cathedral City)
Bottled water	46.7	Volvic (15.6%) Evian (13.5%)
Fresh ground coffee	40	Douwe Egberts (12%), Café Direct (8%)
Bread[b]	36	Kingsmill (18%), Hovis (17%), Warburtons (14%)
Take-home ice cream	35	Unilever (30% – includes Walls), Masterfoods (7% – includes Mars)
Carbonated drinks	25	Coca-Cola (15.2%), Diet Coke (10.2%), Pepsi (7%)
Butter	19	Lurpak (41%), Anchor (19%)
Breakfast cereals	14	Kelloggs (42% – includes Cornflakes, Rice Krispies, etc.), Cereal Partners (18% – includes all Nestlé products), Weetabix (14%)
Crisps[b]	12	Walkers Snack Foods (69% – includes Walkers Crisps, Walkers Sensations, Nobbys, Mr Potato Head), KP (9% – includes McCoys)
Instant coffee	11	Nescafé Original (33%), Nescafé Gold Blend (15%)
Snacks[b]	8	Walker Snack Foods (43% – Includes Wotsits, Doritos, Monster Munch, French Fries, Quavers) KP (20% – includes Hula hoops/Twiglets/Thai bites/Mini Cheddars)

[a] Market shares by value for key competitors in brackets where available (except Bottled water which is based on volume)
[b] Figures for 2004
Source: Based on various Mintel Reports (2005 and 2006)

product segments the penetration of supermarkets' own-brands is considerable, e.g. cheese, bottled water, fresh ground coffee, bread and take-home ice cream. In others, however, branded products dominate, e.g. breakfast cereals, crisps, snacks and instant coffee.

Where products are viewed as fairly homogenous, at least in the eyes of the consumer (e.g. cheese, water and freshly ground coffee), product differentiation by brand is difficult to achieve. There are no real cost advantages and prices are more competitive.

On the other hand, where products are more differentiated, consumers may identify their particular product by branding. Examples include products targeted at a particular group (defined by gender, age or socio-economic status), products that

reflect a certain style of living (e.g. healthy eating), products that embody high quality or innovative characteristics, or have a long history.

Questions

1. How has the improvement in the quality of own-brands affected the price elasticity of demand for branded products? What implications does this have for the pricing strategy of brand manufacturers?
2. Do the brand manufacturers have any actual or potential cost advantages over own-brand manufacturers?

[1] *The Grocer*, 1 April 2006

development (new product, current market); cell C – *market development* (current product, new market); cell D – *diversification* (new product, new market).

Market penetration. In the market penetration strategy, the business will seek not only to retain existing customers, but to expand its customer base with current products in current markets. Of the four strategies, this is generally the least risky: the business will be able to play to its product strengths and draw on its knowledge of the market. The business's marketing strategy will tend to focus upon aggressive product promotion and distribution. Such a strategy, however, is likely to lead to fierce competition from existing business rivals, especially if the overall market is not expanding and if the firm can therefore gain an increase in sales only by taking market share from its rivals.

Product development. Product development strategies will involve introducing new models and designs in current markets.

Market development. With a market development strategy the business will seek increased sales of current products by expanding into new markets. These may be in a different geographical location (e.g. overseas), or new market segments. Alternatively, the strategy may involve finding new uses and applications for the product.

Pause for thought

What unknown factors is the business likely to face following a diversification strategy?

Diversification. A diversification strategy will involve the business expanding into new markets with new products. Of all the strategies, this is the most risky given the unknown factors that the business is likely to face.

Once the product/market strategy has been decided upon, the business will then attempt to devise a suitable *marketing strategy*. This will involve looking at the marketing mix.

The marketing mix

In order to differentiate the firm's product from those of its rivals, there are four variables that can be adjusted. These are as follows:

- product;
- price;
- place (distribution);
- promotion.

Definition

Marketing mix
The mix of product, price, place (distribution) and promotion that will determine a business's marketing strategy.

The particular combination of these variables, known as 'the four Ps', represents the business's **marketing mix**, and it is around a manipulation of them that the business will devise its marketing strategy.

Product considerations. These involve issues such as quality and reliability, as well as branding, packaging and after-sales service.

Pricing considerations. These involve not only the product's basic price in relation to those of competitors' products, but also opportunities for practising price discrimination (the practice of charging different prices in different parts of the market: see section 5.6), offering discounts to particular customers, and adjusting the terms of payment for the product.

Place considerations. These focus on the product's distribution network, and involve issues such as where the business's retail outlets should be located, what warehouse facilities the business might require, and how the product should be transported to the market.

Promotion considerations. These focus primarily upon the amount and type of advertising the business should use. In addition, promotion issues might also include selling techniques, special offers, trial discounts and various other public relations 'gimmicks'.

Every product is likely to have a distinct marketing *mix* of these four variables. Thus we cannot talk about an ideal value for one (e.g. the best price), without considering the other three. What is more, the most appropriate mix will vary from product to product and from market to market.

What the firm must seek to do is to estimate how sensitive demand is to the various aspects of marketing. The greater the sensitivity (elasticity) in each case, the more the firms should focus on that particular aspect.

> **Pause for thought**
>
> *Give an example of how changing one of the four Ps might conflict with another of them.*

Advertising

One of the most important aspects of marketing is advertising. The major aim of advertising is to sell more products, and business spends a vast quantity of money on advertising to achieve this goal.

In fact, there is a bit more to it than this. Advertisers are trying to do two things:

■ Shift the product's demand curve to the right.

■ Make it less price elastic.

This is illustrated in Figure 3.5. D_1 shows the original demand curve with price at P_1 and sales at Q_1. D_2 shows the curve after an advertising campaign. The rightward

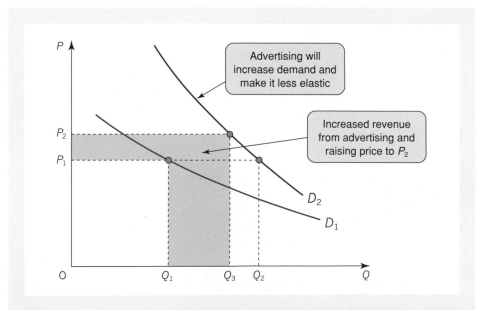

Figure 3.5   The effect of advertising on the demand curve

Box 3.5

Advertising and the long run

Promoting quality

It is relatively straightforward to measure the short-term impact of an advertising campaign; a simple before and after assessment of sales will normally give a good indication of the advertising's effectiveness. But what about the medium and longer-term effects of an advertising campaign? How will sales and profits be affected over, say, a five-year period?

The typical impact of advertising on a product's sales is shown in Figure (a). Assume that there is an advertising campaign for the product between time t_1 and t_2. There is a direct effect on sales while the advertising lasts and shortly afterwards. Sales rise from S_1 to S_2. After a while (beyond time t_3), the direct effect of the advertising begins to wear off, and wears off completely by time t_4. This is illustrated by the dashed line. But the higher level of sales declines much more slowly, given that many of the new customers continue to buy the product out of habit. Sales will eventually level off (at point t_5). It is likely, however, that sales will not return to the original level of S_1; there will be some new customers who will stick with the product over the long term. This long-term effect is shown by the increase in sales from S_1 to S_3.

But just what is this long-term effect? One way to explore the impact of advertising over the long run is to evaluate how advertising and profitability in general are linked. Figure (b) shows how advertising shapes the image of the product and its perceived

quality, which the customer then compares with price to determine the product's value. The more that advertising can enhance the perceived quality of a product, the more it will increase the product's profitability.

How this benefits the business over the longer term can be illustrated by the cases of VW Golf and the Famous Grouse whisky, winners of the 2006 Gold and Silver awards of the Institute of Practitioners in Advertising, the UK trade body and professional institute. To quote from the IPA site:

Thirty years ago, a small car called Golf was born. . . . Communications helped create, nourish and nurture the genuinely loved and financially valuable brand Golf is today. The story includes some of the UK's most famous ads – from 'Casino' and 'Changes' in the 1980s, to 'Singing in the Rain' in 2005 – but this is not just about them. It's about how Golf communications have become increasingly sophisticated, based on new thinking about the car buying process, and about the role of communications within it. Golf is now not just a much loved and enduring icon, it has also become the third biggest selling car in UK history.

The Famous Grouse was stuck in the middle of the whisky market in the UK; with its sector (Blended Scotch) declining

(a) Advertising and the long run

(b) Advertising, profit margins and company growth

while single malts and own-label brands experienced strong growth. It was a small Perthshire company with global ambitions, but without the scale of its global competitors. With the help of AMV.BBDO, they overcame this and built a brand-centric advertising platform – one that engaged the consumer, made them love the brand and helped The Famous Grouse stand out from the crowd. They invested in their brand equity in the UK while other brands retreated, and developed a campaign that more than returned their investment, producing a retail sales value in excess of over £513m in the UK.[1]

PG Tips, launched in 1930, is another brand that leads its respective market. The UK tea market has been dominated by PG Tips since 1958, when it became market leader. Today, with some 25 per cent of the market, it is neck and neck with Tetleys. The 'chimp' adverts, the Aardman T-Birds and more recently Monkey, have established a clear brand image, enabling PG Tips to hold its ground in a highly competitive market and charge a price premium. (Blind tests have revealed that consumers cannot distinguish between any of the leading tea brands!) Market analysis shows that PG Tips has a price elasticity of demand of

−0.4 compared with its nearest rival, Tetley, which has an elasticity of −1.4. It is estimated that between 1980 and 2000 advertising the PG Tips brand cost £100 million but generated in the region of £2 billion in extra sales.

The message is that advertising should seek to promote a product's quality. This is the key to long-term sales and profits. What is also apparent is that successful brands have advertising campaigns which have been consistent over time. A brand image of quality is not created overnight, but once it is established it can endure and yield profits over the longer term.

Questions

1. How are long-run profits and advertising linked?
2. Why does quality 'win out' in the end?
3. How would you advise the owner of the PG Tips brand (Unilever) on a pricing strategy?

[1] http://www.ipaeffectivenessawards.co.uk/text/2006/ shortlist06_text.html#link13

shift allows an increased quantity (Q_2) to be sold at the original price. If, at the same time, the demand is made less elastic, the firm can also raise its price and still experience an increase in sales. Thus in the diagram, price can be raised to P_2 and sales will be Q_3 – still substantially above Q_1. The total gain in revenue is shown by the shaded area.

How can advertising bring about this new demand curve?

Shifting the demand curve to the right. This will occur if the advertising brings the product to more people's attention and if it increases people's desire for the product.

Making the demand curve less elastic. This will occur if the advertising creates greater brand loyalty. People must be led to believe (rightly or wrongly) that competitors' brands are inferior. This will allow the firm to raise its price above that of its rivals with no significant fall in sales. There will be only a small substitution effect of this price rise because consumers have been led to believe that there are no close substitutes.

The more successful an advertising campaign is, the more it will shift the demand curve to the right and the more it will reduce the price elasticity of demand.

> **Pause for thought**
>
> *Assume that the government runs an advertising campaign to encourage people to stop smoking. How will this affect the position of the demand curve and the price elasticity of demand for cigarettes?*

Recap

- When firms seek to differentiate their product from those of their competitors, they can adjust one or more of four dimensions of the product: its technical standards, its quality, its design characteristics, and the level of customer service.

- Marketing involves developing a product image and then persuading consumers to purchase it.

- A business must choose an appropriate product/market strategy. Four such strategies can be identified: market penetration (focusing on existing product and market); product development (new product in existing market); market development (existing product in new markets); diversification (new products in new markets).

- The marketing strategy of a product involves the manipulation of four key variables: product, price, place and promotion. Every product has a distinct marketing mix.

- The aims of advertising are to increase demand and make the product less price elastic

QUESTIONS

1. How would marginal utility and market demand be affected by a rise in the price of (a) a substitute good, (b) a complementary good?

2. How can marginal utility by used to explain the price elasticity of demand for a particular brand of a product?

3. Why are insurance companies unwilling to provide insurance against losses arising from war or 'civil insurrection'? Name some other events where it would be impossible to obtain insurance.

4. What are the relative strengths and weaknesses of using (a) market observations, (b) market surveys and (c) market experiments as means of gathering evidence on consumer demand?

5. You are working for a record company which is thinking of signing up some new bands. What market observations, market surveys and market experiments could you conduct to help you decide which bands to sign?

6. You are about to launch a new range of cosmetics, but you are still to decide upon the content and structure of your advertising campaign. Consider how market surveys and market experiments might be used to help you assess consumer perceptions of the product. What limitations might each of the research methods have in helping you gather data?

7. Imagine that you are an airline attempting to forecast demand for seats over the next two or three years. What, do you think, could be used as leading indicators?

8. How might we account for the growth in non-price competition within the modern developed economy?

9. Consider how the selection of the product/market strategy (market penetration, market development, product development and diversification) will influence the business's marketing mix. Choose a particular and identify which elements in the marketing mix would be most significant in developing a successful marketing strategy for the product.

10. Think of some advertisements that deliberately seek to make demand less price elastic.

11. Imagine that 'Sunshine' sunflower margarine, a well-known brand, is advertised with the slogan, 'It helps you live longer' (the implication being that butter and margarines high in saturates shorten your life). What do you think would happen to the demand curve for a supermarket's *own* brand of sunflower margarine? Consider both the direction of shift and the effect on elasticity. Will the elasticity differ markedly at different prices? How will this affect the pricing policy and sales of the supermarket's own brand? Could the supermarket respond other than by adjusting the price of its margarine?

Business issues covered in this chapter

- What do profits consist of?
- What is the relationship between inputs and outputs in both the short and long run?
- How do costs vary with output and just what do we mean by 'costs'?
- What is meant by 'economies of scale' and what are the reasons for such economies?
- What are 'transactions costs' and how do these vary with the degree of vertical integration of the firm
- How does a business's sales revenue vary with output?
- How do we measure profits?
- At what output will a firm maximise its profits?
- Why does operating under conditions of perfect competition make being in business a constant battle for survival?

Chapter map

CHAPTER 4

Supply decisions in a perfectly competitive market

In this chapter we turn to supply. In other words, we focus on the amount that firms produce. In Part C we shall see how the supply decision is affected by the microeconomic environment in which a firm operates, and in particular by the amount of competition it faces. In this chapter, however, we assume that the firm is a price taker: that it has to accept the price as given by the market. We also assume that the firm seeks to maximise profits.

Profit is made by firms earning more from the sale of goods than the goods cost to produce. A firm's total profit ($T\Pi$) is thus the difference between its total sales revenue (TR) and its total costs of production (TC).

In order, then, to discover how a firm can maximise its profit, or even make a profit at all, we must first consider what determines costs and revenue. Sections 4.1 and 4.2 examine costs. Section 4.3 considers revenue, and then section 4.4 puts costs and revenue together to examine profit.

4.1 Production and costs: short run

Production in the short run

The cost of producing any level of output depends on the amount of inputs used and the price that the firm must pay for them. Let us first focus on the quantity of inputs used.

Short-run and long-run changes in production

If a firm wants to increase production, it will take time to acquire a greater quantity of certain inputs. For example, a manufacturer can use more electricity by turning on switches, but it might take a long time to obtain and install more machines, and longer still to build a second or third factory.

If, then, the firm wants to increase output in a hurry, it will only be able to increase the quantity of certain inputs. It can use more raw materials, more fuel, more tools and possibly more labour (by hiring extra workers or offering overtime to its existing workforce). But it will have to make do with its existing buildings and most of its machinery.

The distinction we are making here is between **fixed inputs** and **variable inputs**. A *fixed* input is an input that cannot be increased within a given time period (e.g. buildings). A *variable* input is one that can.

The distinction between fixed and variable inputs allows us to distinguish between the short run and the long run.

The short run. The **short run** is a time period during which at least one input is fixed. In the short run, then, output can be increased only by using more variable inputs. For example, if a shipping line wanted to carry more passengers in response to a rise in demand, it could accommodate more passengers on existing sailings if there was space. It could increase the number of sailings with its existing fleet, by hiring more crew and using more fuel. But in the short run it could not buy more ships: there would not be time for them to be built.

The long run. The **long run** is a time period long enough for all inputs to be varied. Given long enough, the shipping company can have a new ship built.

The actual length of the short run will differ from firm to firm. It is not a fixed period of time. Thus if it takes a farmer a year to obtain new land, buildings and equipment, the short run is any time period up to a year and the long run is any time period longer than a year. But if it takes a shipping company three years to obtain an extra ship, the short run is any period up to three years and the long run is any period longer than three years.

For this section we will concentrate on *short-run* production and costs. We will look at the long run in section 4.2.

Production in the short run: the law of diminishing returns

Production in the short run is subject to *diminishing returns*. You may well have heard of 'the law of diminishing returns': it is one of the most famous of all 'laws' of economics. To illustrate how this law underlies short-run production, let us take the simplest possible case where there are just two inputs: one fixed and one variable.

Take the case of a farm. Assume the fixed input is land and the variable input is labour. Since the land is fixed in supply, output per period of time can be increased only by increasing the number of workers employed. But imagine what would happen as more and more workers crowded on to a fixed area of land. The land cannot go on yielding more and more output indefinitely. After a point the additions to output from each extra worker will begin to diminish.

We can now state the **law of diminishing (marginal) returns**.

> **The law of diminishing marginal returns.**
> When increasing amounts of a variable input are used with a given amount of a fixed input, there will come a point when each extra unit of the variable input will produce less extra output than the previous unit.
>
> **Key Idea 14**

Opportunity cost

When measuring costs, economists always use the concept of **opportunity cost**. As we saw in section 1.3, opportunity cost is the cost of any activity measured in terms of the sacrifice made in doing it: i.e. the cost measured in terms of the opportunities forgone. If a car manufacturer can produce 10 small saloon cars with the same amount of inputs as it takes to produce 6 large saloon cars, then the opportunity

---

Definitions

Short run
The period of time over which at least one input is fixed.

Long run
The period of time long enough for *all* inputs to be varied.

Pause for thought

How will the length of the short run for the shipping company depend on the state of the shipbuilding industry?

Definitions

Law of diminishing (marginal) returns
When one or more inputs are held fixed, there will come a point beyond which the extra output from additional units of the variable input will diminish.

Opportunity cost
Cost measured in terms of the next best alternative forgone.

Box 4.1

Diminishing returns and business

What can managers do?

Everywhere you look in business you can see diminishing returns. It applies to both giant multinational corporations and the corner shop; to manufacturing, farming, mining and services. Let us take some examples.

A car manufacturer. In the short run, a company such as Toyota or Ford will have a particular number of factories. If it wants to increase output, there will not be enough time to build a new one. So what does it do? The answer is that it will have to use its existing plants more intensively. For example, it could increase the length of shifts. But as it does so, output per worker is likely to fall as workers become more tired or fed up. It could use its machines more intensively. But as it does so, breakdowns or maintenance problems are likely to increase.

Eventually, no matter how many extra people are employed, the factory will reach full capacity. At this point any additional workers would produce no extra output whatsoever. Returns from additional labour have diminished to zero.

The convenience store. Go into a shop and see what fixed inputs you can see. There will be the shelving, the tills, the warehouse space at the back and, of course, the floor space itself. At busy times the shop may take on more workers, but will each additional worker be able to serve the same number of customers? Probably not. Assume, for example, that there are two tills. Once they are fully in use, taking on more workers will not allow more customers to be served. True, additional workers can make sure the shelves are stocked, collect the trolleys, and so on; but diminishing returns to labour are obvious. Additional workers are permitting fewer and fewer extra customers to be served.

The problem applies similarly to supermarkets. At busy times, queues at the tills get longer and crowding in the shop slows down your progress around it.

The arable farm. In the short run, farmers have a fixed amount of land. They can increase crop yields by applying more fertiliser. However, beyond a certain quantity of fertiliser per hectare, diminishing returns to fertiliser will set in. Additional bags will yield less and less additional output. Case B.13 on the book's website looks at some evidence on diminishing returns to the application of nitrogen fertiliser on farmland.

The firm of solicitors. In the case of professional practices such as this, the number of partners will be fixed in the short run, along with the premises and much of the equipment. It might be possible to hire additional secretarial support or other office staff at short notice, but not another partner. But partners are only human. They get tired and less efficient as the work expands. Each additional hour they work beyond a certain level is likely to result in lower productivity.

The student. Which brings us to you! You have no doubt experienced diminishing returns to study time. Working that extra hour late at night may result in little if any extra learning!

? Questions

1. Give some other examples of diminishing returns to inputs other than labour (such as the fertiliser example above).
2. If all inputs were variable (as they are in the long run), would expanding output result in diminishing marginal returns? (We examine this question later when we consider the long run.)

cost of producing 1 small car is 0.6 of a large car. If a taxi and car hire firm uses its cars as taxis, then the opportunity cost includes not only the cost of employing taxi drivers and buying fuel, but also the sacrifice of rental income from hiring its vehicles out.

Measuring a firm's opportunity costs

Just how do we measure a firm's opportunity cost? First we must discover what inputs it has used. Then we must measure the sacrifice involved in using them. To do this it is necessary to put inputs into two categories.

Inputs not owned by the firm: explicit costs. The opportunity cost of those inputs not already owned by the firm is simply the price that the firm has to pay for them. Thus if the firm uses £100 worth of electricity, the opportunity cost is £100. The firm has sacrificed £100 which could have been spent on something else.

These costs are called **explicit costs** because they involve direct payment of money by firms.

Inputs already owned by the firm: implicit costs. When the firm already owns inputs (e.g. machinery) it does not as a rule have to pay out money to use them. Their opportunity costs are thus **implicit costs**. They are equal to what the inputs could earn for the firm in some alternative use, either within the firm or hired out to some other firm.

Here are some examples of implicit costs:

■ A firm owns some buildings. The opportunity cost of using them is the rent it could have received by letting them out to another firm.

■ A firm draws £100 000 from the bank out of its savings in order to invest in new plant and equipment. The opportunity cost of this investment is not just the £100 000 (an explicit cost), but also the interest it thereby forgoes (an implicit cost).

■ The owner of the firm could have earned £30 000 per annum by working for someone else. This £30 000 is the opportunity cost of the owner's time.

If there is no alternative use for an input, as in the case of a machine designed to produce a specific product, and if it has no scrap value, the opportunity cost of using it is *zero*. In such a case, if the output from the machine is worth more than the cost of all the *other* inputs involved, the firm might as well use the machine rather than let it stand idle.

What the firm paid for the machine – its **historic cost** – is irrelevant. Not using the machine will not bring that money back. It has been spent. These are sometimes referred to as 'sunk costs'.

Definitions

Explicit costs
The payments to outside suppliers of inputs.

Implicit costs
Costs which do not involve a direct payment of money to a third party, but which nevertheless involve a sacrifice of some alternative.

Historic costs
The original amount the firm paid for inputs it now owns.

Replacement costs
What the firm would have to pay to replace inputs it currently owns.

Sunk costs and the bygones principle.
The principle states that sunk (fixed) costs should be ignored when deciding whether to produce or sell more or less of a product. Only variable costs should be taken into account.

Key Idea 15

Pause for thought

Assume that a farmer decides to grow wheat on land that could be used for growing barley. Barley sells for £100 per tonne. Wheat sells for £150 per tonne. Seed, fertiliser, labour and other costs of growing crops are £80 per tonne for both wheat and barley. What are the farmer's costs and profit per tonne of growing wheat?

Likewise, the **replacement cost** is irrelevant. That should be taken into account only when the firm is considering replacing the machine.

Costs and inputs

A firm's costs of production will depend on the inputs it uses. The more inputs it uses, the greater will its costs be. More precisely, this relationship depends on two elements.

■ The productivity of the inputs. The greater their physical productivity, the smaller will be the quantity of them that is needed to produce a given level of output, and hence the lower will be the cost of that output.

■ The price of the inputs. The higher their price, the higher will be the costs of production.

In the short run, some inputs are fixed in supply. Their total costs (*TC*), therefore, are fixed, in the sense that they do not vary with output. Rent on land is a **fixed cost**. It is the same whether the firm produces a lot or a little.

The cost of variable inputs, however, does vary with output. The cost of raw materials is a **variable cost**. The more that is produced, the more raw materials are used and therefore the higher is their total cost.

Total cost is thus total fixed cost (*TFC*) plus total variable cost (*TVC*).

Average and marginal cost

In addition to the total cost of production (fixed and variable) there are two other measures of cost which are particularly important for our analysis of profits. These are average and marginal cost.

Average cost (*AC*) is cost per unit of production.

$$AC = TC/Q$$

Thus if it costs a firm £2000 to produce 100 units of a product, the average cost would be £20 for each unit (£2000/100).

Like total cost, average cost can be divided into the two components, fixed and variable. In other words, average cost equals **average fixed cost** (*AFC* = *TFC*/*Q*) plus **average variable cost** (*AVC* = *TVC*/*Q*).

$$AC = AFC + AVC$$

Marginal cost (*MC*) is the *extra* cost of producing *one more unit*: that is, the rise in total cost per one unit rise in output.

$$MC = \frac{\Delta TC}{\Delta Q}$$

where Δ means 'a change in'.

For example, assume that a firm is currently producing 1 000 000 boxes of matches a month. It now increases output by 1000 boxes (another batch): Δ*Q* = 1000. Assume that as a result its total costs rise by £30: Δ*TC* = £30. What is the cost of producing *one* more box of matches? It is:

$$MC = \frac{\Delta TC}{\Delta Q} = \frac{£30}{1000} = 3\text{p}$$

(Note that all marginal costs are variable, since, by definition, there can be no extra fixed costs as output rises.)

Table 4.1 shows costs for an imaginary firm, firm X, over a given period of time (e.g. a week). The table shows how average and marginal costs can be derived from total costs. It is assumed that total fixed costs are £12 000 (column 2) and that total variable costs are as shown in column 3.

The figures for *TVC* have been chosen to illustrate the law of diminishing returns. Initially, *before* diminishing returns set in, *TVC* rises less and less rapidly as more variable factors are added. For example, in the case of a factory with a fixed supply of machinery, initially as more workers are taken on the workers can do increasingly specialist tasks and make a fuller use of the capital equipment. Above a certain output (3 units in Table 4.1), diminishing returns set in. Given that extra workers (the extra variable factors) are producing less and less extra output, the extra units of output they do produce will be costing more and more in terms of wage costs. Thus *TVC* rises more and more rapidly. You can see this by examining column 3.

Definitions

Fixed costs
Total costs that do not vary with the amount of output produced.

Variable costs
Total costs that do vary with the amount of output produced.

Total cost (*TC*)
The sum of total fixed costs (*TFC*) and total variable costs (*TVC*): *TC* = *TFC* + *TVC*.

Average (total) cost (*AC*)
Total cost (fixed plus variable) per unit of output: *AC* = *TC*/*Q* = *AFC* + *AVC*.

Average fixed cost (*AFC*)
Total fixed cost per unit of output: *AFC* = *TFC*/*Q*.

Average variable cost (*AVC*)
Total variable cost per unit of output: *AVC* = *TVC*/*Q*.

Marginal cost (*MC*)
The cost of producing one more unit of output: *MC* = Δ*TC*/Δ*Q*.

Table 4.1   Costs for firm X

Output (Q) (1)	TFC (£000) (2)	TVC (£000) (3)	TC (TFC + TVC) (£000) (4)	AFC (TFC/Q) (£000) (5)	AVC (TVC/Q) (£000) (6)	AC (TC/Q) (£000) (7)	MC (ΔTC/ΔQ) (£000) (8)
0	12	0	12	–	–	–	
							10
1	12	10	22	12	10	22	
							6
2	12	16	28	6	8	14	
							5
3	12	21	33	4	7	11	
							7
4	12	28	40	3	7	10	
							12
5	12	40	52	2.4	8	10.4	
							20
6	12	60	72	2	10	12	
							31
7	12	91	103	1.7	13	14.7	

The figures in the remaining columns in Table 4.1 are derived from columns 1 to 3. Look at the figures in each of the columns and check how the figures are derived. Note the figures for marginal cost are plotted between the lines to illustrate that marginal cost represents the increase in costs as output increases from one unit to the next.

We can use the figures in Table 4.1 to draw MC, AFC, AVC and AC curves (see Figure 4.1 on p. 98).

Marginal cost (MC). The shape of the MC curve follows directly from the law of diminishing returns. Initially, in Figure 4.1, as more of the variable input is used, extra units of output cost less than previous units. MC falls.

Beyond a certain level of output, however, diminishing returns set in. This is shown as point x. Thereafter MC rises. Additional units of output cost more and more to produce, since they require ever-increasing amounts of the variable input.

Average fixed cost (AFC). This falls continuously as output rises, since total fixed costs are being spread over a greater and greater output.

Average (total) cost (AC). The shape of the AC curve depends on the shape of the MC curve. As long as new units of output cost less than the average, their production must pull the average cost down. That is, if MC is less than AC, AC must be falling.

Pause for thought

Use the figures in the first three columns of Table 4.1 to plot TFC, TVC and TC curves (where costs are plotted on the vertical axis and quantity on the horizontal axis). Mark the point on each of the TVC and TC curves where diminishing returns set in. What do you notice about the slope of the two curves at this output?

Pause for thought

Before you read can you explain why the marginal cost curve will always cut the average cost curve at its lowest point?

Box 4.2

Making use of your fixed inputs

Business practices to reduce average fixed costs

The distinction between fixed and variable costs has profound implications for the behaviour of any business. In the short run, if a firm increases its output, total variable costs will increase; total fixed costs will not. Put another way, average variable costs may well rise, but average fixed costs will fall (as Figure 4.1 illustrates).

So why is this so important for business? The answer is that no firm will want to have its fixed inputs under used, except for short periods of time. After all, using more of them incurs no extra fixed costs – by definition. The larger the proportion of fixed costs to variable costs, the more important this becomes. It becomes especially important when a business has more than one production plant and where the ratio of fixed and variable costs vary between them.

The case of electricity generation

Let's take the example of electricity generation and compare a gas-fired power station with a nuclear one. The average cost of generating electricity from these two types of power station is approximately the same: around 2.5 pence per kilowatt hour. However, the proportion of fixed and variable costs is very different.

A nuclear power station has very high fixed costs: average fixed cost at full capacity is around 82 per cent of average cost. The reason is that nuclear power stations are very expensive to build and maintain, and then to decommission at the end of their life. On the other hand, variable costs (mainly fuel) are very low compared with other forms of generation.

Gas-fired power stations, however, are relatively cheap to build. Average fixed cost at normal capacity account for only just over 30 per cent of average cost. Fuel costs, by contrast, are some four times as much per kilowatt as nuclear power.

So what are the implications of these differences? The answer is to keep nuclear power stations working to full capacity so as to spread their high total fixed costs over as much output as possible. In other words, because average fixed costs fall as more is produced, and because fixed costs account for such a large proportion of the total costs of nuclear generation, average costs fall substantially as output is increased. Put another way, the marginal cost of electricity generation from nuclear plants is low and so they should be used to full capacity.

With gas-fired power stations, the picture is very different. Because the demand for electricity fluctuates with the time of day and the weather, and because there must always be the capacity to meet demand (since electricity cannot be stored), there must always be some spare capacity to enable the system to respond to a surge in demand. Gas-fired power stations can fill this role, since they have low fixed costs. Cutting back production will not significantly increase average fixed cost.

Thus the output of nuclear power stations is virtually constant, while the output of gas-fired stations fluctuates with demand.

Lessons for business in general

Many businesses have more than one plant or more than one production line. For example, a firm could have a relatively new production line using the latest technology and an older one using a previous technology. It is quite likely that the new line will be more capital intensive, with high capital (fixed) costs, but using less labour, and possibly less raw material too, and thus with lower variable costs. The older technology is likely to be more labour intensive and thus have higher average variable costs and high marginal costs.

If demand for the firm's product fluctuates, it is likely to keep the automated production line working at full capacity (marginal cost is low) and vary output from the older line, since that has the higher marginal cost.

? *Question*
On a diagram similar to Figure 4.1, sketch the *AFC*, *AVC*, *AC* and *MC* curves for (a) a nuclear power station and (b) a gas-fired power station. For simplicity assume that both stations would produce the same amount of electricity at full capacity.

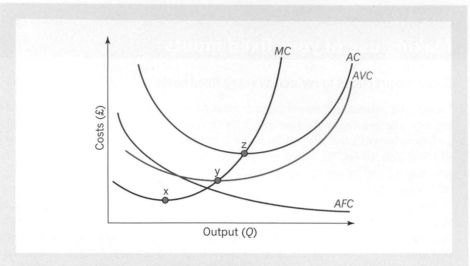

Figure 4.1   Average and marginal costs

Likewise, if new units cost more than the average, their production must drive the average up. That is, if *MC* is greater than *AC*, *AC* must be rising. Therefore, the *MC* curve crosses the *AC* curve at its minimum point (point *z* in Figure 4.1).

Average variable cost (AVC). Since *AVC* = *AC* − *AFC*, the *AVC* curve is simply the vertical difference between the *AC* and the *AFC* curves. Note that as *AFC* gets less, the gap between *AVC* and *AC* narrows. Since all marginal costs are variable (by definition, there are no marginal fixed costs), the same relationship holds between *MC* and *AVC* as it did between *MC* and *AC*. That is, if *MC* is less than *AVC*, *AVC* must be falling, and if *MC* is greater than *AVC*, *AVC* must be rising. Therefore, as with the *AC* curve, the *MC* curve crosses the *AVC* curve at its minimum point (point *y* in Figure 4.1).

Recap

■ Production in the short run is subject to diminishing returns. As greater quantities of the variable input(s) are used, so each additional unit of the variable input will add less to output than previous units: i.e. output will rise less and less rapidly.

■ When measuring costs of production, we should be careful to use the concept of opportunity cost. In the case of inputs not owned by the firm, the opportunity cost is simply the explicit cost of purchasing or hiring them. It is the price paid for them. In the case of inputs already owned by the firm, it is the implicit cost of what the factor could have earned for the firm in its best alternative use.

■ As some factors are fixed in supply in the short run, their total costs are fixed with respect to output. In the case of variable factors, their total cost increases as more output is produced and hence as more of them are used. Total cost can be divided into total fixed and total variable cost.

■ Marginal cost is the cost of producing one more unit of output. It will probably fall at first but will start to rise as soon as diminishing returns set in.

■ Average cost, like total cost, can be divided into fixed and variable costs. Average fixed cost will decline as more output is produced. The reason is that the total fixed cost is being spread over a greater and greater number of units of output. Average variable cost will tend to decline at first, but once the marginal cost has risen above it, it must then rise. The same applies to average cost.

Production and costs: long run   4.2

In the long run *all* inputs are variable. There is time for the firm to build a new factory (maybe in a different part of the country), to install new machines, to use different techniques of production, and in general to combine its inputs in whatever proportion and in whatever quantities it chooses.

In the long run, then, a firm will have to make a number of decisions: about the scale of its operations and the techniques of production it will use. These decisions will affect the costs of production. It is important, therefore, to get them right.

The scale of production

If a firm were to double all of its inputs – something it could do in the long run – would it double its output? Or would output more than double or less than double? We can distinguish three possible situations.

Constant returns to scale. This is where a given percentage increase in inputs will lead to the same percentage increase in output.

Increasing returns to scale. This is where a given percentage increase in inputs will lead to a larger percentage increase in output.

Decreasing returns to scale. This is where a given percentage increase in inputs will lead to a smaller percentage increase in output.

Notice the terminology here. The words 'to scale' mean that *all* inputs increase by the same proportion. Decreasing returns to *scale* are therefore quite different from *diminishing* marginal returns (where only the *variable* input increases). The differences between marginal returns to a variable input and returns to scale are illustrated in Table 4.2.

Table 4.2   Short-run and long-run increases in output

Short run			Long run		
Input 1	*Input 2*	*Output*	*Input 1*	*Input 2*	*Output*
3	1	25	1	1	15
3	2	45	2	2	35
3	3	60	3	3	60
3	4	70	4	4	90
3	5	75	5	5	125

In the short run, input 1 is assumed to be fixed in supply (at 3 units). Output can be increased only by using more of the variable input (input 2). In the long run, however, both input 1 and input 2 are variable.

In the short-run situation, diminishing returns can be seen from the fact that output increases at a decreasing rate (25 to 45 to 60 to 70 to 75) as input 2 is increased. In the long-run situation, the table illustrates increasing returns to scale. Output increases at an *increasing* rate (15 to 35 to 60 to 90 to 125) as both inputs are increased.

Economies of scale

The concept of increasing returns to scale is closely linked to that of **economies of scale**. A firm experiences economies of scale if costs per unit of output fall as the scale of production increases. Clearly, if a firm is getting increasing returns to scale from its inputs, then as it produces more, it will be using smaller and smaller amounts of inputs per unit of output. Other things being equal, this means that it will be producing at a lower unit cost.

There are a number of reasons why firms are likely to experience economies of scale. Some are due to increasing returns to scale; some are not.

Specialisation and division of labour. In large-scale plants, workers can do more simple repetitive jobs. With this **specialisation and division of labour**, less training is needed; workers can become highly efficient in their particular job, especially with long production runs; there is less time lost in workers switching from one operation to another; supervision is easier. Workers and managers who have specific skills in specific areas can be employed.

Indivisibilities. Some inputs are of a minimum size. They are indivisible. The most obvious example is machinery. Take the case of a combine harvester. A small-scale farmer could not make full use of one. They only become economical to use, therefore, on farms above a certain size. The problem of **indivisibilities** is made worse when different machines, each of which is part of the production process, are of a different size. For example, if there are two types of machine, one producing 6 units a day, the other packaging 4 units a day, a minimum of 12 units per day will have to be produced, involving two production machines and three packaging machines, if all machines are to be fully utilised.

The 'container principle'. Any capital equipment that contains things (blast furnaces, oil tankers, pipes, vats, etc.) will tend to cost less per unit of output, the larger its size. The reason has to do with the relationship between a container's volume and its surface area. A container's cost will depend largely on the materials used to build it and hence roughly on its *surface area*. Its output will depend largely on its *volume*. Large containers have a bigger volume relative to surface area than do small containers. For example, a container with a bottom, top and four sides, with each side measuring 1 metre, has a volume of 1 cubic metre and a surface area of 6 square metres (6 surfaces of 1 square metre each). If each side were now to be doubled in length to 2 metres, the volume would be 8 cubic metres and the surface area 24 square metres (6 surfaces of 4 square metres each). Thus an eightfold increase in capacity has been gained at only a fourfold increase in the container's surface area, and hence an approximate fourfold increase in cost.

Greater efficiency of large machines. Large machines may be more efficient, in the sense that more output can be gained for a given amount of inputs. For example, only one worker may be required to operate a machine whether it be large or small. Also, a large machine may make more efficient use of raw materials.

By-products. With production on a large scale, there may be sufficient waste products to enable them to make some by-product.

Multi-stage production. A large factory may be able to take a product through several stages in its manufacture. This saves time and cost moving the semi-finished product from one firm or factory to another. For example, a large cardboard-manufacturing firm may be able to convert trees or waste paper into cardboard and then into cardboard boxes in a continuous sequence.

All the above are examples of **plant economies of scale**. They are due to an individual factory or workplace or machine being large. There are other economies of scale that are associated with the business itself being large – perhaps with many factories.

Organisational. With a large business, individual plants can specialise in particular functions. There can also be centralised administration of the plants. Often, after a merger between two firms, savings can be made by **rationalising** their activities in this way.

Spreading overheads. Some expenditures are economic only when the *business* is large, such as research and development: only a large business can afford to set up a research laboratory. This is another example of indivisibilities, only this time at the level of the whole business rather than the plant. The greater the business's output, the more these **overhead costs** are spread.

Financial economies. Large businesses may be able to obtain finance at lower interest rates than small ones. They may be able to obtain certain inputs cheaper by buying in bulk.

Economies of scope. Often a business is large because it produces a range of products. This can result in each individual product being produced more cheaply than if it was produced in a single-product firm. The reason for these **economies of scope** is that various overhead costs and financial and organisational economies can be shared between the products. For example, a firm that produces a whole range of CD players, receivers, amplifiers and tuners can benefit from shared marketing and distribution costs and the bulk purchase of electronic components.

Diseconomies of scale

When businesses get beyond a certain size, costs per unit of output may start to increase. There are several reasons for such **diseconomies of scale**:

■ Management problems of coordination may increase as the business becomes larger and more complex, and as lines of communication get longer. There may be a lack of personal involvement by management.

■ Workers may feel 'alienated' if their jobs are boring and repetitive, and if they feel an insignificantly small part of a large organisation. Poor motivation may lead to shoddy work.

■ Industrial relations may deteriorate as a result of these factors and also as a result of the more complex inter-relationships between different categories of worker.

Definitions

Plant economies of scale
Economies of scale that arise because of the large size of the factory.

Rationalisation
The reorganising of production (often after a merger) so as to cut out waste and duplication and generally to reduce costs.

Overheads
Costs arising from the general running of an organisation, and only indirectly related to the level of output.

Economies of scope
When increasing the range of products produced by a firm reduces the cost of producing each one.

Diseconomies of scale
Where costs per unit of output increase as the scale of production increases.

Pause for thought

Which of the economies of scale we have considered are due to increasing returns to scale and which are due to other factors?

■ Production-line processes and the complex interdependencies of mass production can lead to great disruption if there are hold-ups in any one part of the business.

Whether businesses experience economies or diseconomies of scale will depend on the conditions applying in each individual one.

The size of the whole industry

As an *industry* grows in size, this can lead to **external economies of scale** for its member firms. This is where a firm, whatever its own individual size, benefits from the *whole industry* being large. For example, the firm may benefit from having access to specialist raw material or component suppliers, labour with specific skills, firms that specialise in marketing the finished product, and banks and other financial institutions with experience of the industry's requirements. What we are referring to here is the **industry's infrastructure**: the facilities, support services, skills and experience that can be shared by its members.

When industries form a cluster in an area, external economies are likely to be experienced. We examine such industrial clusters in Box 4.3.

The member firms of a particular industry might, however, experience **external diseconomies of scale**. For example, as an industry grows larger, this may create a growing shortage of specific raw materials or skilled labour. This will push up their prices, and hence the firms' costs.

Long-run average cost

We turn now to *long-run* cost curves. Since there are no fixed inputs in the long run, there are no long-run fixed costs. For example, a firm may rent more land in order to expand its operations. Its rent bill therefore goes up as it expands its output. All costs, then, in the long run are variable costs.

Although it is possible to draw long-run total, marginal and average cost curves, we will concentrate on **long-run average cost (*LRAC*) curves**. These can take various shapes, but a typical one is shown in Figure 4.2.

It is often assumed that, as a firm expands, it will initially experience economies of scale and thus face a downward-sloping *LRAC* curve. After a point, however, all such economies will have been achieved and thus the curve will flatten out. Then (possibly after a period of constant *LRAC*), the firm will get so large that it will start experiencing diseconomies of scale and thus a rising *LRAC*. At this stage, production and financial economies begin to be offset by the managerial problems of running a giant organisation.

Assumptions behind the long-run average cost curve

We make three key assumptions when constructing long-run average cost curves.

Input prices are given. At each output, a firm will be faced with a given set of input prices. If input prices *change*, therefore, both short- and long-run cost curves will shift. Thus an increase in wages would shift the curves upwards.

However, input prices might be different at *different* levels of output. For example, one of the economies of scale that many firms enjoy is the ability to obtain bulk discount on raw materials and other supplies. In such cases the curve does *not* shift.

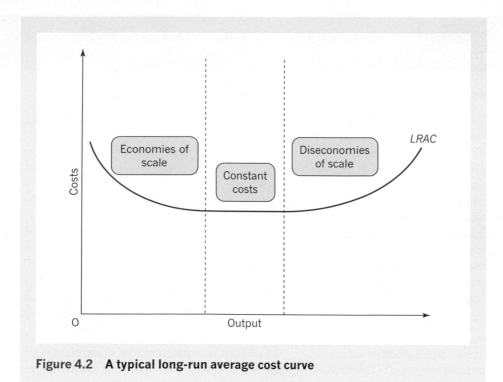

Figure 4.2   A typical long-run average cost curve

The different input prices are merely experienced at different points along the curve, and are reflected in the shape of the curve. Input prices are still given for any particular level of output.

The state of technology and input quality are given. These are assumed to change only in the *very* long run. If a firm gains economies of scale, it is because it is being able to exploit *existing* technologies and make better use of the existing availability of inputs.

Firms operate efficiently. The assumption here is that firms operate efficiently: that they choose the cheapest possible way of producing any level of output. If the firm did not operate efficiently, it would be producing at a point above the *LRAC* curve.

Transactions costs

So far we have concentrated largely on production costs: the cost of the inputs used in the production process. There is another category of costs, however, that businesses will need to take into account when considering the scale and scope of their organisation. These are **transactions costs**: costs associated with the process of buying or selling. There are four main categories of transactions costs.

Search costs. The firm will incur costs in searching out the best supplier in terms of price and/or quality. The problem here is that the firm starts with imperfect information and it takes time and money to obtain that information. It may employ a **logistics** company to seek out the best sources of supply, but obviously the logistics

Box 4.3

Industrial clusters and competitiveness

External economies of scale in practice

In May 2003, the Department of Trade and Industry published a report by Michael Porter and Christian Ketels of Harvard Business School on the UK's competitiveness and how it might be improved.[1] The authors declared that since 1980 the UK had done remarkably well in halting its economic decline on world markets, and had in fact matched and even bettered its main rivals in many industrial sectors. Other sectors, however, were faring less well.

According to Porter and Ketels, a key part in any country's success is the development of successful industrial clusters, such as IT in California's Silicon Valley and financial services in the City of London. Such clusters can bring substantial external economies of scale, with individual firms benefiting from being part of a cluster.

> Clusters are geographically proximate groups of interconnected companies, suppliers, service providers, and associated institutions in a particular field, linked by commonalties and complementarities.[2]

Porter suggests that clusters are vital for competitiveness in three crucial respects:

■ Clusters improve productivity. The close proximity of suppliers and other service providers enhances flexibility.

■ Clusters aid innovation. Interaction among business within a cluster stimulates new ideas and aids their dissemination.

■ Clusters contribute to new business formation. Clusters are self-reinforcing, in so far as specialist factors such as dedicated venture capital, and labour skills, help reduce costs and lower the risks of new business start-up.

The UK's industrial clusters were seen by Porter and Ketels as being relatively weak. In fact, many traditional clusters, such as steel and car manufacturing, had thinned to the point where they now lacked critical mass and failed to benefit from the clustering effect.

Where the UK had strengths were in the areas of services, such as financial services, media, defence, products for personal use, health care and telecommunications. Lesser clusters in entertainment, semiconductors and computers, transportation and office products could also be identified.

In 2001, the DTI produced a cluster map for the UK (see opposite). This showed that 'there were clusters throughout the UK: aerospace in the North West, textiles in the East Midlands, and IT around the M4 to name but three.'[3]

Porter and Katels conclude that, to improve its competitiveness, the UK must not only support what clusters it has but endeavour to up-grade and contribute to their development.

> The UK needs to mount a sustained programme of cluster development to create a more conducive environment for productivity growth and innovation through the collective action of companies and other institutions. . . . It will be essential to mobilise businesses and business institutions that are willing and able to engage in the upgrading of their clusters.[4]

Question

What policies or initiatives might a 'programme of cluster development' involve? Distinguish between policies that government and business might initiate.

---

[1] Michael E. Porter and Christian H. M. Ketels, 'UK competitiveness: moving to the next stage' (DTI and ESRC, May 2003)

[2] *Ibid*. page 27

[3] Ecotec Research & Consulting 'A practical guide to cluster development', (DTI, April 2004)

[4] Porter and Ketels, op. cit, page 46

UK cluster map

Source: *Business clusters in the UK – a first assessment*, Figure 2, p. 7 (http://www.dti.gov.uk/files/file17396.pdf) (Department of Trade and Industry). Reproduced under the terms of the click-use licence company will charge for its services. What is more, the firm may well run into the principal–agent problem unless it can monitor the behaviour of the logistics company – i.e. its agent (see page 10).

Contract costs. When a supplier is found, then time and effort may be incurred in bargaining over price and quality. If the supplier is to continue supplying over a period of time, then a contract will probably be negotiated. There will be costs in drawing up such contracts. These could include legal costs and the time of specialists to ensure that specifications are correct.

Monitoring and enforcement costs. When a contract has been drawn up, it is unlikely to cover every eventuality. To use the jargon, it is 'incomplete'. For example, if a logistics company is contracted to provide transportation of a manufacturing firm's products, the contract may specify maximum times for delivery. The manufacturing firm is then likely to incur costs in ensuring that the logistics firm sticks to the contract – and in taking action if it does not. What is more, there is a moral hazard involved (see page 71). If the logistics firm *could* deliver items more quickly than specified in the contract, it will have no incentive to do so, even though it would have been in the manufacturer's interests.

Transport and handling costs. The more firms rely on buying components from other firms, rather than making them in-house, the greater will be the costs of transporting and handling these materials.

Definitions

Vertically integrated firm
A firm that produces at more than one stage in the production and distribution of a product.

Supply chain
The flow of inputs into a finished product from the raw materials stage, though manufacturing and distribution right through to the sale to the final consumer.

Backward integration
Where a firm expands backwards down the supply chain to earlier stages of production.

Forward integration
Where a firm expands forward up the supply chain towards the sale of the finished product.

Transactions costs.

The costs associated with exchanging products. For buyers it is the costs over and above the price of the product. For sellers it is the costs over and above the costs of production. Transactions costs include search costs, contract costs, monitoring and enforcement costs, and transport and handling costs.

Key Idea 16

Transactions costs and the scale and scope of the firm

One way of reducing transactions costs is for the firm to produce more *within* the firm rather than buying inputs from other firms or supplying to other firms. What we are describing here is a **vertically integrated firm**. This is where a firm is involved in several stages of the production of a good, such as component production, assembly and wholesale and retail distribution.

Firms may expand their operations vertically by integrating backwards down the **supply chain** or forwards up it. **Backward integration** is where a firm itself produces the inputs it needs. Thus a car manufacturer may itself produce components such as body panels, engines and trimmings. **Forward integration** is where a firm itself moves into producing stages closer to the end consumer. Thus a manufacturer of building materials may move into construction or become a builder's merchant.

The costs of vertical integration. Even though vertical integration will save on transactions costs, it is likely to incur other costs. A large vertically integrated organisation could be more bureaucratic, with the increased complexity involving more complex management tasks. Although the firm is saving on the costs of monitoring contracts with other firms, managers are still having to monitor the behaviour of their own internal divisions and employees. Managers may set targets for the various divisions, but unless these are both carefully specified and comprehensive, the problem of moral hazard is likely to occur. Employees may meet the targets but may underperform in areas which are not specifically targeted. One response to this problem is to create more and more specific targets. This, however, is likely to remove flexibility and the opportunity for junior managers to take initiative.

Another problem is that, by producing components in-house, the firm will not then be able to source them from elsewhere if cheaper suppliers become available (see Box 4.5 on page 116). Similarly, if a manufacturer buys its components from outside, it could possibly change supplier if the first supplier lets it down. If it produces the components itself, however, switching to an outside supplier may prove more difficult if internal hold-ups occur. Thus in-house production can prove more risky.

Finally production costs may be higher. Despite the fact that a vertically integrated firm may be large, the *individual* parts of the company may be too small to gain full economies of scale. For example, if a car company produces its own carpets, this carpet production will be on a much smaller scale than if a specialist car carpet manufacturer were to supply *several* car companies.

In deciding its optimum degree of vertical integration, therefore, a firm must weigh up the transactions costs of not integrating against the internal costs of integrating.

Recap

■ In the long run, a firm is able to vary the quantity it uses of all inputs. There are no fixed inputs and hence there are no fixed costs.

■ If it increases all inputs by the same proportion, it may experience constant, increasing or decreasing returns to scale.

■ Economies of scale occur when costs per unit of output fall as the scale of production increases. This can be due to a number of factors, some of which are directly caused by increasing (physical) returns to scale. These include the benefits of specialisation and division of labour, the use of larger and more efficient machines, and the ability to have a more integrated system of production. Other economies of scale arise from the financial and administrative benefits of large-scale organisations.

■ Typically, *LRAC* curves are drawn as L-shaped or as saucer-shaped. As output expands, initially there are economies of scale. When these are exhausted, the curve will become flat. When the firm becomes very large, it may begin to experience diseconomies of scale. If this happens, the *LRAC* curve will begin to slope upward again.

■ Transactions costs are the costs associated with exchanging products. They include search costs, the costs of drawing up and monitoring contracts and transport and handling costs. The more firms rely on other firms as suppliers or buyers, the larger these costs are likely to be. Vertical integration can reduce transactions costs, but is likely to incur other costs instead.

Box 4.4

Minimum efficient scale

The extent of economies of scale in practice

Two of the most important studies of economies of scale have been those made by C. F. Pratten[1] in the late 1980s and by a group advising the European Commission[2] in 1997. Both studies found strong evidence that many firms, especially in manufacturing, experienced substantial economies of scale.

In a few cases long-run average costs fell continuously as output increased. For most firms, however, they fell up to a certain level of output and then remained constant.

The extent of economies of scale can be measured by looking at a firm's *minimum efficient scale* (*MES*). The *MES* is the size beyond which no significant additional economies of scale can be achieved: in other words, the point where the *LRAC* curve flattens off. In Pratten's studies he defined this level as the minimum scale above which any possible doubling in scale would reduce average costs by less than 5 per cent (i.e. virtually the bottom of the *LRAC* curve). In the diagram *MES* is shown at point *a*.

The *MES* can be expressed in terms either of an individual factory or of the whole firm. Where it refers to the minimum efficient scale of an individual factory, the *MES* is known as the *minimum efficient plant size* (*MEPS*).

The *MES* can then be expressed as a percentage of the total size of the market or of total domestic production. Table (a), based on the Pratten study, shows *MES* for plants and firms in various industries. The first column shows *MES* as a percentage of total UK production. The second column shows *MES* as a percentage of total EU production. Table (b), based on the 1997 study, shows *MES* for various plants as a percentage of total EU production.

Expressing *MES* as a percentage of total output gives an indication of how competitive the industry could be. In some industries (such as footwear and carpets), economies of scale were exhausted (i.e. *MES* was reached) with plants or firms that were still small relative to total UK production and even smaller relative to total EU production. In such industries there would be room for many firms and thus scope for considerable competition.

In other industries, however, even if a single plant or firm were large enough to produce the whole output of the industry in

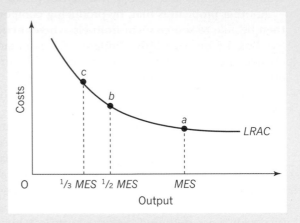

the UK, it would still not be large enough to experience the full potential economies of scale: the *MES* is greater than 100 per cent. Examples from Table (a) include factories producing cellulose fibres, and car manufacturers. In such industries there is no possibility of competition. In fact, as long as the *MES* exceeds 50 per cent there will not be room for more than one firm large enough to gain full economies of scale. In this case the industry is said to be a *natural monopoly*. As we shall see in the next few chapters, when competition is lacking consumers may suffer by firms charging prices considerably above costs.

A second way of measuring the extent of economies of scale is to see how much costs would increase if production were reduced to a certain fraction of *MES*. The normal fractions used are $\frac{1}{2}$ or $\frac{1}{3}$ *MES*. This is illustrated in the diagram. Point *b* corresponds to $\frac{1}{2}$ *MES*; point *c* to $\frac{1}{3}$ *MES*. The greater the percentage by which *LRAC* at point *b* or *c* is higher than at point *a*, the greater will be the economies of scale to be gained by producing at *MES* rather than at $\frac{1}{2}$ *MES* or $\frac{1}{3}$ *MES*. For example, in the table there are greater economies of scale to be gained from moving from $\frac{1}{2}$ *MES* to *MES* in the production of electric motors than in cigarettes.

Table (a)

Product	MES as % of production		% additional cost at ½ MES
	UK	EU	
Individual plants			
Cellulose fibres	125	16	3
Rolled aluminium semi-manufactures	114	15	15
Refrigerators	85	11	4
Steel	72	10	6
Electric motors	60	6	15
TV sets	40	9	9
Cigarettes	24	6	1.4
Ball-bearings	20	2	6
Beer	12	3	7
Nylon	4	1	12
Bricks	1	0.2	25
Tufted carpets	0.3	0.04	10
Shoes	0.3	0.03	1
Firms			
Cars	200	20	9
Lorries	104	21	7.5
Mainframe computers	>100	n.a.	5
Aircraft	100	n.a.	5
Tractors	98	19	6

Sources: see footnote 1 below

The main purpose of the studies was to determine whether a single EU market is big enough to allow both economies of scale and competition. The tables suggest that in all cases, other things being equal, the EU market is large enough for firms to gain the full economies of scale *and* for there to be enough firms for the market to be competitive.

Table (b)

Plants	MES as % of total EU production
Aerospace	12.19
Tractors and agricultural machinery	6.57
Electric lighting	3.76
Steel tubes	2.42
Shipbuilding	1.63
Rubber	1.06
Radio and TV	0.69
Footwear	0.08
Carpets	0.03

Source: see footnote 2 below

The second study also found that 47 of the 53 manufacturing sectors analysed had scope for further exploitation of economies of scale.

? Questions

1. Why might a firm operating with one plant achieve *MEPS* and yet not be large enough to achieve *MES*? (Clue: are all economies of scale achieved at plant level?)
2. Why might a firm producing bricks have an *MES* which is only 0.2 per cent of total EU production and yet face little effective competition from other EU countries?

[1] Pratten, C.F. 'A survey of the economies of scale', in *Research on the 'Costs of Non-Europe'*, Volume 2 (Luxembourg: Office for Official Publications of the European Communities, 1988). Copyright © 1988 European Communities

[2] European Commission/Economists Advisory Group Ltd, 'Economies of scale', in *The Single Market Review*, Subseries V, Volume 4 (Luxembourg: Office for Official Publications of the European Communities, 1997). Copyright © 1997 European Communities

4.3 Revenue

Remember that we defined a firm's total profit as its total revenue minus its total costs of production. In the last two sections we have examined costs. We now turn to revenue.

As with costs, we distinguish between three revenue concepts: total revenue (*TR*), average revenue (*AR*) and marginal revenue (*MR*).

Total, average and marginal revenue

Total revenue (TR)

Total revenue is the firm's total earnings per period of time from the sale of a particular amount of output (*Q*).

For example, if a firm sells 1000 units (*Q*) per month at a price of £5 each (*P*), then its monthly total revenue will be £5000: in other words, £5 × 1000 (*P* × *Q*). Thus:

$$TR = P \times Q$$

Average revenue (AR)

Average revenue is the amount the firm earns per unit sold. Thus:

$$AR = TR/Q$$

So if the firm earns £5000 (*TR*) from selling 1000 units (*Q*), it will earn £5 per unit. But this is simply the price! Thus:

$$AR = P$$

Marginal revenue (MR)

Marginal revenue is the extra total revenue gained by selling one more unit (per time period). So if a firm sells an extra 20 units this month compared with what it expected to sell, and in the process earns an extra £100, then it is getting an extra £5 for each extra unit sold: *MR* = £5. Thus:

$$MR = \Delta TR/\Delta Q$$

We now need to see how revenue varies with output. We concentrate on average and marginal revenue. We can show this relationship graphically in the same way as we did with costs.

The relationship will depend on the market conditions under which a firm operates. The revenue curves we look at in this section are for a price-taking firm: a firm that faces a horizontal demand curve (see section 3.1). When firms face a downward-sloping demand curve and are thus able to choose their price, they will face different revenue curves. We look at such curves in the next chapter.

Average and marginal revenue curves

Average revenue. We are assuming in this chapter that the firm is a price taker. That is, it has to accept the price given by the intersection of demand and supply in the whole market. But, being so small, it can sell as much as it is capable of producing at that price. This is illustrated in Figure 4.3.

Definitions

Total revenue (*TR*)
A firm's total earnings from a specified level of sales within a specified period: $TR = P \times Q$.

Average revenue (*AR*)
Total revenue per unit of output. When all output is sold at the same price, average revenue will be the same as price: $AR = TR/Q = P$.

Marginal revenue (*MR*)
The extra revenue gained by selling one or more unit per time period: $MR = \Delta TR/\Delta Q$.

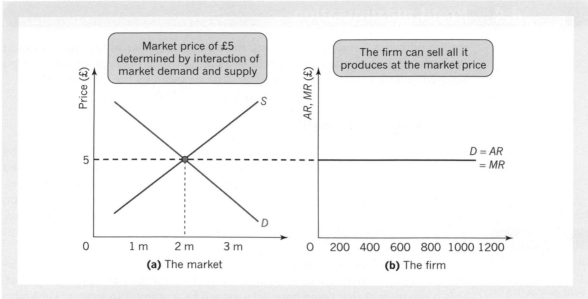

Figure 4.3   Deriving a firm's _AR_ and _MR_: price-taking firm

Figure 4.3(a) shows market demand and supply. Equilibrium price is £5. Figure 4.3(b) looks at the demand for an individual firm which is tiny relative to the whole market. (Look at the difference in the scale of the horizontal axes in the two diagrams.)

Being so small, any change in the firm's output will be too insignificant to affect the market price. The firm thus faces a horizontal demand 'curve' at this price. It can sell 200 units, 600 units, 1200 units or whatever without affecting this £5 price.

Average revenue is thus constant at £5. The firm's average revenue curve must therefore lie along exactly the same line as its demand curve.

Marginal revenue. In the case of a horizontal demand curve, the marginal revenue curve will be the same as the average revenue curve, since selling one more unit at a constant price (_AR_) merely adds that amount to total revenue. If an extra unit is sold at a constant price of £5, an extra £5 is earned.

Recap

- Total revenue (_TR_) is the total amount a firm earns from its sales in a given time period. It is simply price times quantity: $TR = P \times Q$.

- Average revenue (_AR_) is total revenue per unit: $AR = TR/Q$. In other words, $AR = P$.

- Marginal revenue is the extra revenue earned from the sale of one more unit per time period: $MR = \Delta TR/DQ$.

- The _AR_ curve will be the same as the demand curve for the firm's product. In the case of a price taker, the demand curve and hence the _AR_ curve will be a horizontal straight line and will also be the same as the _MR_ curve.

4.4   Profit maximisation

We are now in a position to put costs and revenue together to find the output at which profit is maximised, and also to find out how much that profit will be. First we need to look a little more precisely at what we mean by the term 'profit'.

The meaning of 'profit'

One element of cost is the opportunity cost to the owners of the firm incurred by being in business. This is the minimum return that the owners must make on their capital in order to prevent them from eventually deciding to close down and perhaps move into some alternative business. It is a *cost* since, just as with wages, rent, etc., it has to be covered if the firm is to continue producing. This opportunity cost to the owners is sometimes known as **normal profit**, and is included in the cost curves.

What determines this normal rate of profit? It has two components. First, someone setting up in business invests capital in it. There is thus an opportunity cost. This is the interest that could have been earned by lending it in some riskless form (e.g. by putting it in a savings account in a bank). Nobody would set up a business unless they expected to earn at least this rate of profit. Running a business is far from riskless, however, and hence a second element is a return to compensate for risk. Thus:

Normal profit (%) = rate of interest on a riskless loan + a risk premium

The risk premium varies according to the line of business. In those with fairly predictable patterns, such as food retailing, it is relatively low. Where outcomes are very uncertain, such as mineral exploration or the manufacture of fashion garments, it is relatively high.

Thus if owners of a business earn normal profit, they will (just) be content to remain in that industry.

Any excess of profit over normal profit is known as **supernormal profit**. If firms earn supernormal profit, they will clearly prefer to stay in this business. Such profit will also tend to attract new firms into the industry, since it will give them a better return on capital than elsewhere. If firms earn *less* than normal profit, however, then after a time they will consider leaving and using their capital for some other purpose.

Short-run profit maximising

In the **short run**, we assume that the number of firms in an industry cannot be increased: there is simply not time for new firms to enter the market.

Figure 4.4 shows a short-run equilibrium for an industry and the profit-maximising position for a firm under perfect competition. Both parts of the diagram have the same scale for the vertical axis. The horizontal axes have totally different scales, however. For example, if the horizontal axis for the firm were measured in, say, thousands of units, the horizontal axis for the whole industry might be measured in millions or tens of millions of units, depending on the number of firms in the industry.

Let us examine the determination of price, output and profit in turn.

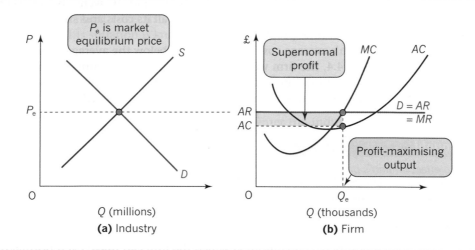

Figure 4.4   Short-run equilibrium of industry and firm under perfect competition

Price

The price is determined in the industry by the intersection of demand and supply. The firm faces a horizontal demand (or average revenue) 'curve' at this price. It can sell all it can produce at the market price (P_e), but nothing at a price above P_e.

Output

The firm will maximise profit where marginal cost equals marginal revenue ($MR = MC$), at an output of Q_e. In fact this **profit-maximising rule** will apply to firms in all types of market.

But why are profits maximised when $MR = MC$? The simplest way of answering this is to see what the position would be if MR did not equal MC.

Referring to Figure 4.4, at a level of output below Q_e, MR exceeds MC. This means that by producing more units there will be a bigger addition to revenue (MR) than to cost (MC). Total profit will *increase. As long as MR exceeds MC, profit can be increased by increasing production.*

At a level of output above Q_e, MC exceeds MR. All levels of output above Q_e thus add more to cost than to revenue and hence *reduce* profit. *As long as MC exceeds MR, profit can be increased by cutting back on production.*

Profits are thus maximised where $MC = MR$: at an output of Q_e.

Students worry sometimes about the argument that profits are maximised when $MR = MC$. Surely, they say, if the last unit is making no profit, how can profit be at a *maximum*? The answer is very simple. If you cannot add anything more to a total, the total must be at the maximum. Take the simple analogy of going up a hill. When you cannot go any higher, you must be at the top.

Profit

Once the profit-maximising output has been discovered, we now use the average curves to measure the *amount* of profit at the maximum. Remember that normal

> **Definition**
>
> **Profit-maximising rule**
> Profit is maximised where marginal revenue equals marginal cost.

Box 4.6

E-commerce

A modern form of perfect competition?

The relentless drive towards big business in recent decades has seen markets become more concentrated and increasingly dominated by large producers. And yet forces are at work that are undermining this dominance, and bringing more competition to markets. One of these forces is *e-commerce*.

In this case study, we shall first review the model of perfect competition and then consider how e-commerce is returning 'power to the people'.

A perfectly competitive market

As we have seen, under perfect competition firms are price takers: they have to accept the price as given by the market. Firms are faced with a constant battle for survival. The effect is to drive costs down. With firms freely entering the industry, only normal profits will be made in the long run. So only the fittest will survive, and the fittest will be in a constant struggle to produce at a lower cost.

So what conditions are necessary for the market for a particular good to be perfectly competitive and thus for firms to be price takers? In addition to freedom of entry to the market for new firms, consumers must have knowledge of the quality, availability and price of the good. There must be also be a large number of firms in the market. Only that way will competition be sufficient to ensure that no firm has any power over prices, and thus faces a perfectly elastic demand curve.

E-commerce and competition

How does e-commerce make markets more competitive and even, in some cases, become virtually perfectly competitive?

Consumer knowledge. There are various ways in which e-commerce is adding to the consumer's knowledge. There is greater price transparency, with consumers able to compare prices online. Online shopping agents such as Kelkoo, DealTime and Froogle can quickly locate a list of alternative suppliers. There is greater information on product availability and quality. Virtual shopping malls, full of e-retailers, place the high street retailer under intense competitive pressure.

The pressure is even greater in the market for intermediate products. Many firms are constantly searching for cheaper sources of supply, and the Internet provides a cheap and easy means of conducting such searches.

Large number of firms. The growth of e-commerce has led to many new firms starting up in business. It's not just large firms like Amazon that are providing increased competition for established firms, but the thousands of small online companies that are being established every day. Many of these firms are selling directly to us as consumers. This is known as 'B2C' e-commerce (business-to-consumers). But many more are selling to other firms ('B2B'). More and more companies, from the biggest to the smallest, are transferring their purchasing to the Web and are keen to get value for money.

The reach of the Web is global. This means that firms, whether conventional or web-based, are having to keep an eye on the prices and products of competitors in the rest of the world, not just in the local neighbourhood. Firms' demand curves are thus becoming very price elastic. This is especially so for goods that are cheap to transport, or for services such as travel agents, insurance and banking.

Freedom of entry. Internet companies often have lower start-up costs than their conventional rivals. Their premises are generally much smaller, with no 'shop-front' costs and lower levels of stock holding. Marketing costs can also be relatively low, especially given the ease with which companies can be located with search engines. Internet companies are often smaller and more specialist, relying on Internet 'outsourcing' (buying parts, equipment and other supplies through the Internet), rather than making everything themselves. They are also more likely to use delivery firms rather than having their own transport fleet.

All this makes it relatively cheap for new firms to set up and begin trading over the Internet.

In fact, the distinction between firms and consumers is becoming increasingly blurred. With the rise of eBay, more and more people are finding going into business incredibly easy. Suddenly people are finding a market for all the junk they've collected over the years! As the eBay TV advertisement says, 'someone wants everything'. There are some 200 million registered eBay users worldwide, and hundreds of thousands of people make a full-time living from buying and selling on eBay. Annual sales on eBay are worth over £30 billion.

The limits to e-commerce

In 20 years, will we be doing all our shopping on the net? Will the only shopping malls be virtual ones? Although e-commerce is revolutionising some markets, it is unlikely that things will go anything like that far.

The benefits of 'shop shopping' are that you get to see the good, touch it and use it. You can buy the good there and then, and take instant possession of it: you don't have to wait. Shopping is also an enjoyable experience. Many people like wandering round the shops, meeting friends, seeing what takes their fancy, trying on clothes, browsing through CDs and so on. 'Retail therapy' for many is an important means of 'de-stressing'.

Online shopping is limited by the screen; Internet access may be slow and frustrating; 'surfing' may instead become 'wading'; you have to wait for goods to be delivered; and what if deliveries are late or fail completely?

Also, costs might not be as low as expected. How efficient is it to have many small deliveries of goods? How significant are the lost cost savings from economies of scale that larger producers or retailers are likely to generate?

Nevertheless, e-commerce has made many markets, both retail and B2B, more competitive. This is especially so for services and for goods whose quality is easy to identify online. Many firms are being forced to face up to having their prices determined by the market.

? Questions

1. Why may the Internet work better for replacement buys than for new purchases?
2. Give three examples of products that are particularly suitable for selling over the Internet and three that are not. Explain your answer.

QUESTIONS

1. Are all explicit costs variable costs? Are all variable costs explicit costs?

2. Up to roughly how long is the short run in the following cases?

   (a) A mobile disco firm;

   (b) Electricity power generation;

   (c) A small grocery retailing business;

   (d) 'Superstore Hypermarkets plc'.

   In each case, specify your assumptions.

3. The following are some costs incurred by a shoe manufacturer. Decide whether each one is a fixed cost or a variable cost or has some element of both.

   (a) The cost of leather;

   (b) The fee paid to an advertising agency;

   (c) Wear and tear on machinery;

   (d) Business rates on the factory;

   (e) Electricity for heating and lighting;

   (f) Electricity for running the machines;

   (g) Basic minimum wages agreed with the union;

   (h) Overtime pay;

   (i) Depreciation of machines as a result purely of their age (irrespective of their condition).

4. Why does the marginal cost curve pass through the bottom of the average cost curve?

5. What economies of scale is a large department store likely to experience?

6. Why are many firms likely to experience economies of scale up to a certain size and then diseconomies of scale after some point beyond that?

7. Normal profits are regarded as a cost (and are included in the cost curves). Explain why.

8. What determines the size of normal profit? Will it vary with the general state of the economy?

9. A firm will continue producing in the short run even if it is making a loss, providing it can cover its variable costs. Explain why. Just how long will it be willing to continue making such a loss?

10. Would there ever be a point in a firm attempting to continue in production if it could not cover its *long-run* average (total) costs?

11. The price of pocket calculators and digital watches fell significantly in the years after they were first introduced and at the same time demand for them increased substantially. Use cost and revenue diagrams to illustrate these events. Explain the reasoning behind the diagram(s) you have drawn.

12. Illustrate on a diagram similar to Figure 4.6 what would happen in the long run if price were initially below P_L.

Additional Part B case studies on the *Economics and the Business Environment* website (www.pearsoned.co.uk/sloman)

B.1 **Coffee prices.** An examination of the coffee market and the implications of fluctuations in the coffee harvest for growers and coffee drinkers.

B.2 **The measurement of elasticity.** This examines how to work out the value for elasticity using the 'mid-point' method.

B.3 **Any more fares?** Pricing on the buses: an illustration of the relationship between price and total revenue.

B.4 **Elasticities of demand for various foodstuffs.** An examination of the evidence about price and income elasticities of demand for food in the UK.

B.5 **Adjusting to oil price shocks.** A case study showing how demand and supply analysis can be used to examine the price changes in the oil market since 1973.

B.6 **The role of the speculator.** This assesses whether the activities of speculators are beneficial or harmful to the rest of society.

B.7 **The demand for butter.** An examination of a real-world demand function.

B.8 **Markets where prices are controlled.** This examines what happens if price is set either above or below the equilibrium.

B.9 **Agriculture and minimum prices.** This shows how setting (high) minimum prices is likely to lead to surpluses.

B.10 **Diminishing returns in the bread shop.** An illustration of the law of diminishing returns.

B.11 **Dealing in futures markets.** How buying and selling in futures markets can reduce uncertainty.

B.12 **Short-run production.** An analysis of how output varies with increases in the quantity of variable inputs used.

B.13 **Diminishing returns to nitrogen fertiliser.** This case study provided a good illustration of diminishing returns in practice by showing the effects on grass yields of the application of increasing accounts of nitrogen fertiliser.

B.14 **The fallacy of using historic costs.** A demonstration of how it is important to use opportunity costs and not historic costs when working out prices and output.

B.15 **The relationship between averages and marginals.** An examination of the rules showing how an average curve relates to a marginal curve.

B.16 **Short-run cost curves in practice.** Why *AVC* and *MC* curves may have a flat bottom.

Websites relevant to Part B

Numbers and sections refer to websites listed in the Web Appendix and hotlinked from this book's website at www.pearsoned.co.uk/sloman/

■ For new articles relevant to Part B, see the *Economics News Articles* link from the book's website.

■ For general news on markets, demand and supply see websites in section A of the Web Appendix, and particularly A2, 3, 4, 5, 8, 9, 11, 12, 18, 20–26, 35, 36. See also sites A41, 43, 44 for links to economics news articles from newspapers worldwide.

■ For links to sites on markets, see the relevant sections of I4, 7, 11, 13, 17.

■ For data, information and sites on products and marketing, see sites B2, 10; I7, 11, 13, 17.

■ For data on advertising, see sites E37.

■ For links to sites on various aspects of advertising and marketing, see section *Industry and Commerce > Consumer Protection > Advertising* in site I7.

■ For links to sites on various aspects of production and costs, see section *Microeconomics > Production* in site I7.

■ For a case study examining costs, see site D2.

■ For student resources relevant to Part B, see sites C1–7, 9, 10, 14, 19, 20, 24; D3, 5, 14, 17, 19.

■ For sites favouring the free market, see C17 and E34.

PART C
The microeconomic environment of business

Whatever the aims of firms, if they are to be successful in pursuing them, they must take account of the environment in which they operate. In Part C we look at the microeconomic environment of firms: i.e. the market conditions that firms face in their particular industry.

Most firms are not price takers; they can choose the prices they charge. But in doing do they must take account of the reactions of their rivals. We look at pricing and output decisions in Chapter 5 and see how firms' aims affect these decisions.

And it is not just in terms of pricing and output decisions that firms must take account of rivals. They must also do so in planning out their longer-term strategy – in making decisions about developing and launching new products, how quickly and how much to expand, the methods of production to use, their supply chain, the balance of what should be produced in-house and what should be 'out-sourced' (i.e. bought in from other firms), their sources of finance, and whether to target international markets or to confine themselves to producing and selling domestically. These strategic decisions are the subject of Chapters 6 and 7.

In Chapter 8 we turn to the labour market environment of business. What power does the firm have in setting wages; what is the role of trade unions; how flexibly can the firm use labour? These issues all affect the profitability of business, its organisation and its choice of techniques.

Finally, in Chapter 9 we look at the impact of government policy towards business and how this in turn impacts on firms' decision making. How much does government legislation constrain business activity? How much can government force firms to behave in the society's interests and how much will firms choose to take a socially responsible attitude towards things such as ethical trading, the environment, product standards and conditions for their workforce?

Business issues covered in this chapter

- What determines the degree of market power of a firm?
- How do firms get to become monopolies and remain so?
- At what price and output will a monopolist maximise profits and how much profit will it make?
- How well or badly do monopolies serve the consumer?
- How are firms likely to behave when there are just a few of them competing ('oligopolies')? Will they engage in all-out competition or will they collude with each other?
- What strategic games are oligopolists likely to play in their attempt to out-do their rivals?
- Does oligopoly serve the consumer's interests?
- Why may managers pursue goals other than maximising profit? What other goals might they pursue and what will be the effect on price and output?
- How are prices determined in practice?
- Why do firms sometimes charge different prices to different customers for the same product (e.g. seats on a plane)?

Chapter map

CHAPTER 5

Pricing and output decisions in imperfectly competitive markets

In the previous chapter we looked at price-taking firms. In this chapter we examine firms that face a downward-sloping demand curve. Such firms are said to have 'market power'. In other words, they have the power to raise their price. Of course, if they do so, their sales will fall, and clearly they will have to trade off the benefit of higher prices against the cost of lower sales.

The degree of a firm's market power depends on the price elasticity of demand for its product. The less elastic the demand, the less will sales fall for any given rise in price, and the greater, therefore, is the firm's market power.

> **Market power benefits the powerful at the expense of others.**
> When firms have market power over prices, they can use this to raise prices and profits above the perfectly competitive level. Other things being equal, the firm will gain at the expense of the consumer. Similarly, if consumers or workers have market power they can use this to their own benefit.

Key Idea 17

The most extreme case of market power is **monopoly**. This is where there is just one firm in the industry, and hence no competition from *within* the industry. Normally the monopoly will have effective means of keeping other firms out of the industry. We look at monopoly in section 5.2.

Where firms face a downward-sloping curve but are not monopolies, we call this situation **imperfect competition**. The vast majority of firms in the real world operate under imperfect competition.

Imperfect competition is normally divided into two types. The more competitive of the two is **monopolistic competition**. This involves quite a lot of firms competing and there is freedom for new firms to enter the industry. As a result, if existing firms are making supernormal profits, new firms will enter the industry (given time). Thus, as under perfect competition, this will have the effect of driving profits down to the normal level.

Examples of monopolistic competition can be found by flicking through the *Yellow Pages*. Taxi companies, restaurants, small retailers, small builders, plumbers, electrical contractors, etc. all normally operate under monopolistic competition. As a result, their profits are kept down by the intense competition in the industry.

Definitions

Monopoly
A market structure where there is only one firm in the industry.

Imperfect competition
The collective name for monopolistic competition and oligopoly.

Monopolistic competition
A market structure where, like perfect competition, there are many firms and freedom of entry into the industry, but where each firm produces a differentiated product and thus has some control over its price.

Oligopoly
A market structure where there are few enough firms to enable barriers to be erected against the entry of new firms.

Box 5.2

Windows cleaning

Microsoft, the Internet and the US Justice Department

On 18 May 1998, the US government initiated its biggest competition case for 20 years: it sued Microsoft, the world's largest software company. It accused Microsoft of abusing its market power and seeking to crush its rivals. By controlling the *Windows* operating software, Microsoft could force its own Internet browser, *Internet Explorer*, on to consumers and computer manufacturers.

The case against Microsoft had been building for many years, but it was with the release of *Windows 98* that the US government decided to act. The US Justice Department alleged that Microsoft had committed the following anti-competitive actions:

■ Back in May 1995, Microsoft attempted to collude with Netscape Communications to divide the Internet browser market. Netscape Communications refused.

■ Microsoft had forced personal computer manufacturers to install Internet Explorer in order to obtain a *Windows 95 operating* licence.

■ Microsoft insisted that PC manufacturers conformed to a Microsoft front screen for Windows. This included specified icons, one of which was Microsoft's *Internet Explorer*.

■ It had set up reciprocal advertising arrangements with America's largest Internet service providers, such as America Online (AOL). Here Microsoft would promote AOL via Windows. In return, AOL would not promote Netscape's browsers.

Microsoft, in its defence, argued that the integration of its own browser into the Windows system was a natural part of the process of product innovation and development. If Microsoft were to do nothing with its Windows product, it would, over time, lose its dominant market position, and be replaced by a more innovative and superior product manufactured by a rival software producer.

In this respect, Microsoft could be seen to be operating in the consumer's interest. The argument is that, in an environment where technology is changing rapidly, Microsoft's control over standards gives the user a measure of stability, knowing that any new products and applications will be compatible with existing

ones. In other words, new software can be incorporated into existing systems.

Network effects

The key issue in respect to Microsoft, then, was not so much the browser war, but far more fundamentally to do with the operating system, and how Microsoft used its ownership of this system to extend its leverage into other related high-technology markets.

An operating system attracts software developed around that operating system, thereby discouraging new competition since any alternative faces not only the challenge of creating a better operating system but competing against a whole array of already existing software applications . . . These so-called 'network effects' give an incredible anti-competitive edge to companies like Microsoft that control so many different parts of the network.[1]

Network effects arise when consumers of a product benefit from it being used by other consumers. The more people that use it, the greater the benefit to each individual user. The problem for the consumer in such a scenario is that these network effects can lead to the establishment of a monopoly producer and hence to higher prices. There is also the problem of whether the best product is being produced by the monopolist. In such an instance, the consumer may be 'locked in' to using an inferior product or technology with limited opportunity (if any) to change.

Microsoft had been able to use consumer lock-in to drive competitors from the market. Where choice did exist, for example in Internet browsers, Microsoft was using its operating system dominance to promote its own product.

US Court findings

A verdict was reached on 7 June 2000, when Federal Judge Thomas Penfield Jackson ruled that Microsoft be split in two to prevent it operating as a monopoly. One company would produce and market the *Windows* operating system; the other would produce and market the applications software, such as *Microsoft Office* and the Web browser, *Internet Explorer*.

Microsoft appealed against the judgment to the US Federal Appeals Court, which in June 2001 overturned the ruling and referred the case to a different judge for reconsideration. Judge Colleen Kollar-Kotelly urged both sides (Microsoft and the US Justice Department) to try to reach a settlement and in November 2001 they did just that. They agreed that Microsoft would provide technical information about Windows to other companies to enable them to write software that would compete with Microsoft's own software. Also, Microsoft would not be allowed to retaliate against computer manufacturers that installed rival products or removed icons for Microsoft applications.

Nine states, however, refused to sign up to the agreement and a further year went past before Judge Kollar-Kotelly gave her final ruling. Whilst she agreed with many of Judge Jackson's original findings, she did not require that Microsoft be split into two companies. Instead, she upheld the November 2001 agreement.

European Commission findings

Legal action against Microsoft was not confined to the USA. In March 2004, the European Commission fined Microsoft a record €497 million for abusing its monopoly position.

In addition Microsoft was ordered to issue a version of *Windows XP* without *Windows Media Player* (*WMP*). The argument was similar to the earlier ones used in the USA over browsers. This time it was claimed that by bundling *WMP* with *XP*, Microsoft was gaining an unfair advantage over competitor media players, such as *RealPlayer* and Apple's *QuickTime*. Microsoft was also ordered to share programming code with rivals to allow them to develop servers compatible with *Windows*.

In December 2005, the Commission found that Microsoft was in breach of the 2004 ruling for failing to supply its rivals with 'the complete and accurate interoperability required'. It stated that it would impose daily fines on Microsoft of up to €2 million. In July 2006, the Commission decided that these fines had mounted to a total of €280 million. It would give Microsoft until November 23 to

supply satisfactory code, or face a further €2 million daily fine. Microsoft met this deadline – just!

Meanwhile, in April 2006, Microsoft launched an appeal against the judgment, claiming that, by forcing the company to share information with rivals, the Commission's ruling violated international law.

More battles

With the release of *Windows Vista* in Europe, along with *Office 2007* and *Exchange Server 2007*, the scene was set for another battle. The European Committee for Interoperable Systems (ECIS), an international association of IT hardware and software providers, including Nokia, Oracle and IBM, lodged a complaint with the EU. It claimed that these products ignore the principles established in the European Commission's 2004 ruling.

Specifically, the new software makes it difficult for non-Microsoft applications to run on *Windows*. Also, with its *Exchange server 2007* (for corporate e-mail systems based on *Outlook*) Microsoft is developing a new Web pages language to replace HTML for Web-based messaging. This, again, will make it difficult for users not using *Windows*. Finally, a new document file format in *Office 2007* operates seamlessly only in *Windows*.

You might want to follow subsequent events as the news unfolds (see section A of the Hotlinks section of this book's website for links to newspaper sites).

Questions

1. In what ways was Microsoft's behaviour (a) against the public interest; (b) in the public interest?
2. Being locked-in to a product or technology is only a problem if such a product can be clearly shown to be inferior to an alternative. What difficulties might there be in establishing such a case?

---

[1] N. Newman, from 'MS Word to MS world: how microsoft is building a global monopoly', www.netaction.org/msoft/world (1997)

- Since there are barriers to the entry of new firms, a monopolist's supernormal profits will not be competed away in the long run. There is no competition to drive the price down. The monopolist is not forced to operate at the bottom of the *LRAC* curve. Thus, other things being equal, long-run prices will tend to be higher, and hence output lower, under monopoly.

- The monopolist's cost curves may be higher. The sheer survival of a firm in the long run under perfect competition requires that it uses the most efficient known technique, and develops new techniques wherever possible. The monopolist, however, sheltered by barriers to entry, can still make large profits even if it is not using the most efficient technique. It has less incentive, therefore, to be efficient.

> ### Pause for thought
>
> *If the shares in a monopoly (such as a water company) were very widely distributed among the population, would the shareholders necessarily want the firm to use its monopoly power to make larger profits?*

It is possible, however, that a monopolist will operate with *lower* costs than an equivalent industry under perfect competition. The monopoly may be able to achieve substantial economies of scale due to larger plant, centralised administration and the avoidance of unnecessary duplication (e.g. a monopoly water company would eliminate the need for several sets of rival water mains under each street). If this results in an *MC* curve substantially below that of the same industry under perfect competition, the monopoly may even produce a *higher* output at a *lower* price.

Another reason why a monopolist may operate with lower costs is that it can use part of its supernormal profits for research and development and investment. It may not have the same *incentive* to become efficient as the perfectly competitive firm which is fighting for survival, but it may have a much greater *ability* to become efficient than has the small firm with limited funds.

Although a monopoly faces no competition in the goods market, it may face an alternative form of competition in financial markets. A monopoly, with potentially low costs, which is currently run inefficiently, is likely to be subject to a takeover bid from another company. This **competition for corporate control** may thus force the monopoly to be efficient in order to prevent it being taken over.

> ### Definition
>
> **Competition for corporate control**
> The competition for the control of companies through takeovers.

Finally, the promise of supernormal profits, protected perhaps by patents, may encourage the development of new (monopoly) industries producing new products. It is this chance of making monopoly profits that encourages many people to take the risks of going into business.

Recap

- There are four alternative market structures under which firms operate. In ascending order of firms' market power, they are: perfect competition, monopolistic competition, oligopoly and monopoly.

- A monopoly is where there is only one firm in an industry. In practice, it is difficult to determine where a monopoly exists because it depends on how narrowly an industry is defined.

- Barriers to the entry of new firms will normally be necessary to protect a monopoly from competition. Such barriers include economies of scale (making the firm a natural monopoly or at least giving it a cost advantage over new, smaller, competitors), control over supplies of inputs or over outlets, patents or copyright, and tactics to eliminate competition (such as takeovers or aggressive advertising).

- The demand curve (*AR* curve) for a monopolist is downward sloping. The *MR* curve is below it and steeper.

- Profits for the monopolist (as for other firms) are maximised where *MC* = *MR*.

- If demand and cost curves are the same in a monopoly and a perfectly competitive industry, the monopoly will produce a lower output and at a higher price than the perfectly competitive industry.

- On the other hand, any economies of scale will in part be passed on to consumers in lower prices, and the monopolist's high profits may be used for research and development and investment, which in turn may lead to better products at possibly lower prices.

Oligopoly   5.3

Oligopoly occurs when just a few firms between them share a large proportion of the industry. Most oligopolists produce differentiated products (e.g. cars, soap powder, soft drinks, electrical appliances). Much of the competition between such oligopolists is in terms of the marketing of their particular brand.

As with monopoly, there are barriers to the entry of new firms (see pages 128–9). The size of the barriers, however, varies from industry to industry. In some cases entry is relatively easy; in others it is virtually impossible.

Interdependence of the firms. Because there are only a few firms under oligopoly, each firm will have to take account of the others. This means that they are mutually dependent: they are **interdependent**. Each firm is affected by its rivals' actions. If a firm changes the price or specification of its product or the amount of its advertising, the sales of its rivals will be affected. The rivals may then respond by changing their price, specification or advertising. No firm can therefore afford to ignore the actions and reactions of other firms in the industry.

People often think and behave strategically.
How you think others will respond to your actions is likely to influence your own behaviour. Firms, for example, when considering a price or product change will often take into account the likely reactions of their rivals.

Key Idea 18

It is impossible, therefore, to predict the effect on a firm's sales of, say, a change in its price without first making some assumption about the reactions of other firms. Different assumptions will yield different predictions. For this reason there is no single generally accepted theory of oligopoly. Firms may react differently and unpredictably.

Competition and collusion

Oligopolists are pulled in two different directions:

- The interdependence of firms may make them wish to *collude* with each other. If they can club together and act as if they were a monopoly, they could jointly maximise industry profits.

■ On the other hand, they will be tempted to *compete* with their rivals to gain a bigger share of industry profits for themselves.

These two policies are incompatible. The more fiercely firms compete to gain a bigger share of industry profits, the smaller these industry profits will become! For example, price competition drives down the average industry price, while competition through advertising raises industry costs. Either way, industry profits fall.

Sometimes firms will collude. Sometimes they will not. The following sections examine first **collusive oligopoly** (both open and tacit), and then **non-collusive oligopoly**.

Collusive oligopoly

When firms under oligopoly engage in collusion, they may agree on prices, market share, advertising expenditure, etc. Such collusion reduces the uncertainty they face. It reduces the fear of engaging in competitive price cutting or retaliatory advertising, both of which could reduce total industry profits.

A cartel

A formal collusive agreement is called a **cartel**. The cartel will maximise profits if it acts like a monopoly: if the members behave as if they were a single firm. This is illustrated in Figure 5.3.

The total market demand curve is shown with the corresponding market *MR* curve. The cartel's *MC* curve is the *horizontal* sum of the *MC* curves of its members (since we are adding the *output* of each of the cartel members at each level of marginal cost). Profit for the whole industry is maximised at Q_1 where *MC* = *MR*. The cartel must therefore set a price of P_1 (at which Q_1 will be demanded).

Definitions

Collusive oligopoly

When oligopolists agree (formally or informally) to limit competition between themselves. They may set output quotas, fix prices, limit product promotion or development, or agree not to 'poach' each other's markets.

Non-collusive oligopoly

When oligopolists have no agreement between themselves – formal, informal or tacit.

Cartel

A formal collusive agreement.

Figure 5.3 Profit-maximising cartel

Having agreed on the cartel price, the members may then compete against each other using *non-price competition*, to gain as big a share of resulting sales (Q_1) as they can.

Alternatively, the cartel members may somehow agree to divide the market between them. Each member would be given a **quota**. The sum of all the quotas must add up to Q_1. If the quotas exceeded Q_1, either there would be output unsold if price remained fixed at P_1, or the price would fall.

In many countries cartels are illegal, being seen by the government as a means of driving up prices and profits and thereby as being against the public interest. Government policy towards cartels is examined in section 9.5.

Tacit collusion

Where open collusion is illegal, firms may simply break the law, or get round it. Alternatively, firms may stay within the law, but still *tacitly* collude by watching each other's prices and keeping theirs similar. Firms may tacitly 'agree' to avoid price wars or aggressive advertising campaigns.

One form of **tacit collusion** is where firms keep to the price that is set by an established leader. Such **price leadership** is more likely when there is a dominant firm in the industry, normally the largest.

Factors favouring collusion

Collusion between firms, whether formal or tacit, is more likely when firms can clearly identify with each other or some leader and when they trust each other not to break agreements. It will be easier for firms to collude if the following conditions apply:

■ There are only very few firms, all well known to each other.

■ They are open with each other about costs and production methods.

■ They have similar production methods and average costs, and are thus likely to want to change prices at the same time and by the same percentage.

■ They produce similar products and can thus more easily reach agreements on price.

■ There is a dominant firm.

■ There are significant barriers to entry and thus there is little fear of disruption by new firms.

■ The market is stable. If industry demand or production costs fluctuate wildly, it will be difficult to make agreements, partly due to difficulties in predicting and partly because agreements may frequently have to be amended. There is a particular problem in a declining market where firms may be tempted to undercut each other's price in order to maintain their sales.

■ There are no government measures to curb collusion.

Elements of competition under collusive oligopoly

Even when oligopolists collude over price, they may compete intensively though product development and marketing. As we saw in section 3.4, such 'non-price competition' can make the job of the manager quite complex, involving strategic decisions about product design and quality, product promotion and the provision of various forms of after-sales service.

Box 5.4

The prisoners' dilemma

When confession may be the best strategy

Game theory is relevant not just to business and economics. A famous non-economic example is the origin of the term 'prisoners' dilemma'. Take the case of Nigel and Amanda who have been arrested for a joint crime of serious fraud. Each is interviewed separately and given the following alternatives:

■ First, if they say nothing, the court has enough evidence to sentence both to a year's imprisonment.

■ Second, if either Nigel or Amanda *alone* confesses, he or she is likely to get only a three-month sentence but the partner could get up to ten years.

■ Third, if both confess, they are likely to get three years each.

Let us consider Nigel's dilemma. Should he confess in order to get the short sentence? This is better than the year he would get for not confessing. There is, however, an even better reason for confessing. Suppose Nigel doesn't confess but, unknown to him, Amanda does confess. Then Nigel ends up with the long sentence. Better than this is to confess and to get no more than three years: this is the safest strategy.

Amanda is in the same dilemma. The result is simple. When both prisoners act in their own self-interest by confessing, they both end up in position D with relatively long prison terms. Only when they collude will they end up in position A with relatively short prison terms, the best combined solution.

Of course the police know this and will do their best to prevent any collusion. They will keep Nigel and Amanda in separate cells and try to persuade each of them that the other is bound to confess.

Thus the choice of strategy depends on:

■ Nigel's and Amanda's risk attitudes: i.e. are they 'risk lovers' or 'risk averse'?

■ Nigel's and Amanda's estimates of how likely the other is to own up.

Questions

1. Why is this a dominant strategy game?
2. How would Nigel's choice of strategy be affected if he had instead been involved in a joint crime with Jeremy, Pauline, Diana and Dave, and they had all been caught?

Some other examples

Standing at concerts. When people go to some public event, such as a concert or a match, they often stand in order to get a better view. But once people start standing, everyone is likely to do so: after all, if they stayed sitting, they would not see at all. In this Nash equilibrium, most people are worse off, since, except for tall people, their view is likely to be worse and they lose the comfort of sitting down.

Too much advertising. Why do firms spend so much on advertising? If they are aggressive, they probably do so to get ahead of their rivals. If they are cautious, they probably do so for fear of their rivals increasing their advertising. Although in both cases it may be in the individual firm's best interests to increase advertising, the resulting Nash equilibrium is likely to be one of excessive advertising: the total spent on advertising (by all firms) is not recouped in additional sales.

Union membership. The more employees of a business there are who are members of a trade union, the more powerful will the union be and the bigger the pay rise it is likely to gain. But here is the prisoner's dilemma. Workers motivated by self-interest will be tempted *not* to join the union and thus save the membership subscription. But the more workers there are who do this, the smaller the union membership and the less the pay rise is likely to be.

Question

Give one or two other examples (economic or non-economic) of the prisoners' dilemma.

The importance of threats and promises

There are many situations where an oligopolist will make a threat or promise (either openly or implied) that it will act in a certain way. As long as the threat or promise is **credible** (i.e. its competitors believe it), the firm can gain and it will influence its rivals' behaviour.

Take the simple situation where a large oil company, such as Esso, states that it will match the price charged by any competitor within a given radius. Assume that competitors believe this 'price promise' but also that Esso will not try to *undercut* their price. In the simple situation where there is only one other filling station in the area, what price should it charge? Clearly it should charge the price which would maximise its profits, assuming that Esso will charge the *same* price. In the absence of other filling stations in the area, this is likely to be a relatively high price.

Now assume that there are several filling stations in the area. What should the company do now? Its best bet is probably to charge the same price as Esso and hope that no other company charges a lower price and forces Esso to cut its price. Assuming that Esso's threat is credible, other companies are likely to reason in a similar way.

The importance of timing: decision trees

Most decisions by oligopolists are made by one firm at a time rather than simultaneously by all firms. Sometimes a firm will take the initiative. At other times it will respond to decisions taken by other firms.

Take the case of a new generation of large passenger aircraft which can fly further without refuelling. Assume that there is a market for a 500-seater version of this type of aircraft and a 400-seater version, but that the market for each sized aircraft is not big enough for the two manufacturers, Boeing and Airbus, to share it profitably. Let us also assume that the 400-seater market would give an annual profit of £50 million to a single manufacturer and the 500-seater would give an annual profit of £30 million, but that if both manufacturers produced the same version, they would each make an annual loss of £10 million.

Assume that Boeing announces that it is building the 400-seater plane. What should Airbus do? The choice is illustrated in Figure 5.5 (overleaf). This diagram is called a **decision tree** and shows the sequence of events. The small square at the left of the diagram is Boeing's decision point (point A). If it had decided to build the 500-seater plane, we would move up the top branch. Airbus would now have to make a decision (point B_1). If it too built the 500-seater plane, we would move to outcome 1: a loss of £10m for both manufacturers. Clearly, with Boeing building a 500-seater plane, Airbus would choose the 400-seater plane: we would move to outcome 2, with Boeing making a profit of £30m and Airbus a profit £50m. Airbus would be very pleased!

Boeing's best strategy at point A, however, would be to build the 400-seater plane. We would then move to Airbus's decision point B_2. In this case, it is in Airbus's interests to build the 500-seater plane. Its profit would be only £30m (outcome 3), but this is better than a £10m loss if it too built the 400-seater plane (outcome 4). With Boeing deciding first, the Nash equilibrium will thus be outcome 3.

There is clearly a **first-mover advantage** here. Once Boeing has decided to build the more profitable version of the plane, Airbus is forced to build the less profitable

Pause for thought

Assume that there are two major oil companies operating filling stations in an area. The first promises to match the other's prices. The other promises to sell at 1p per litre cheaper than the first. Describe the likely sequence of events in this 'game' and the likely eventual outcome. Could the promise of the second company be seen as credible?

Definitions

Credible threat (or promise)
One that is believable to rivals because it is in the threatener's interests to carry it out.

Decision tree (or game tree)
A diagram showing the sequence of possible decisions by competitor firms and the outcome of each combination of decisions.

First-mover advantage
When a firm gains from being the first to take action.

Definition

Average cost or
mark-up pricing
Where firms set the
price by adding a profit
mark-up to average
costs.

Cost-based pricing

One approach is **average cost** or **mark-up pricing**. Here producers work out the price by simply adding a certain percentage (mark-up) for profit on top of average costs (average fixed costs plus average variable costs).

$$P = AFC + AVC + \text{Profit mark-up}$$

Choosing the mark-up

The level of profit mark-up on top of average cost will depend on the firm's aims: whether it is aiming for high or even maximum profits, or merely a target based on previous profit. It will also depend on the likely actions of rivals and their responses to changes in this firm's price and how these responses will affect demand.

If a firm could estimate its demand curve, it could then set its output and profit mark-up at levels to avoid a shortage or surplus. Thus in Figure 5.7 it could choose a lower output (Q_1) with a higher mark-up (fg), or a higher output (Q_2) with a lower mark-up (hj). If a firm could not estimate its demand curve, then it could adjust its mark-up and output over time by a process of trial and error, according to its success in meeting profit and sales aims.

Pause for thought

If a firm has a typical-shaped average cost curve and sets prices 10 per cent above average cost, what will its supply curve look like?

Variations in the mark-up

In most firms, the mark-up is not rigid. In expanding markets, or markets where firms have monopoly/oligopoly power, the size of the mark-up is likely to be greater. In contracting markets, or under conditions of rising costs and constant demand, a firm may well be forced to accept lower profits and thus reduce the mark-up.

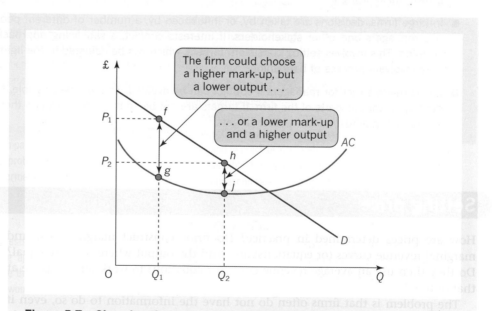

Figure 5.7 Choosing the output and profit mark-up

The firm is likely to take account of the actions and possible reactions of its competitors. It may well be unwilling to change prices when costs or demand change, for fear of the reactions of competitors (see the kinked demand curve theory on page 138). If prices are kept constant and yet costs change, either due to a movement along the *AC* curve in response to a change in demand, or due to a shift in the *AC* curve, the firm must necessarily change the size of the mark-up.

All this suggests that, whereas the mark-up may well be based on a target profit, firms are often prepared to change their target and hence their mark-up.

Pause for thought

If the firm adjusts the size of its mark-up according to changes in demand and the actions of competitors, could its actions approximate to setting price and output where MC = MR?

Price discrimination

Up to now we have assumed that a firm will sell its output at a single price. Sometimes, however, firms may practise **price discrimination**. This is where the firm charges different prices to different customers, where the price differences are *unrelated to costs*. Thus an airline may charge much higher ticket prices to late bookers than to early bookers for identical seats on the same flight (see Box 5.6).

Conditions necessary for price discrimination to operate

As we shall see, a firm will be able to increase its profits if it can engage in price discrimination. But under what circumstances will it be able to charge discriminatory prices? There are three conditions that must be met:

■ The firm must be able to set its price. Thus price discrimination will be impossible under perfect competition, where firms are price takers.

■ The markets must be separate. Consumers in the low-priced market must not be able to resell the product in the high-priced market. For example, children must not be able to resell a half-priced child's cinema ticket for use by an adult.

■ Demand elasticity must differ in each market. The firm will charge the higher price in the market where demand is less elastic, and thus less sensitive to a price rise.

Advantages to the firm

Price discrimination will allow the firm to earn a higher revenue from any given level of sales. Thus is illustrated in Figure 5.8, which shows a firm's overall demand curve. If it is to sell 200 units without price discrimination, it must charge a price of P_1. The total revenue it earns is shown by the grey area. If, however, it can practise price discrimination by selling 150 of those 200 units at the higher price of P_2, it will gain the mauve area in addition to the green area.

Another advantage to the firm of price discrimination is that it may be able to use it to drive competitors out of business. If a firm has a monopoly in one market (e.g. the home market), it may be able to charge a high price due to relatively inelastic demand, and thus make high profits. If it is under oligopoly in another market (e.g. the export market), it may use the high profits in the first market to subsidise a very low price in the oligopolistic market, thus forcing its competitors out of business.

Definition

Price discrimination Where a firm sells the same product at different prices in different markets for reasons unrelated to costs.

Pause for thought

To what extent do consumers gain or lose from price discrimination?

Box 5.6

Easy pricing

Getting the most revenue from a plane

A good example of price discrimination is the pricing strategy of easyJet. The first few seats on every flight are sold at a very low price (typically from £6.99 to £21.99 depending on the distance). Then as the plane fills up, so the prices rise (typically to around £170 to £200 for the last few seats). With carefully chosen prices, this strategy allows easyJet to maximise the revenue from its passengers. The last-minute business passengers will pay a high price, while those prepared to book a long time in advance for a cheap break, but willing to shop around to get a bargain, will be charged a low price – but probably close to the maximum they would be prepared to pay anyway.

This strategy can be illustrated with the demand curve shown in the diagram. Assume that the plane has 150 seats and that the pricing strategy manages to fill the plane. Assume also that the first 20 seats are sold at a price of £19.99. Seat prices then rise in bands with the final 20 seats being priced at £199.99.

What the demand curve shows is that there are 20 people who would be prepared to pay at least £199.99, but that to sell

all 150 seats, at least one must be offered at a price as low as £19.99. Of course, in practice, it's not quite as simple as this, as some of the people buying tickets at low prices might have been prepared to pay more.

The other part of easyJet's business model is to keep costs to a minimum. Practices include: no tickets; no seat allocations; direct web booking (including 18 language options); no agents; no free food; cabin crew collecting rubbish; avoiding congested airports; reduced turnaround times; maximum utilisation of planes; and a relatively modern fleet to reduce maintenance and operating costs.

? Questions

1. Would you advise easyJet to offer a business class option? Explain why or why not.
2. Referring to the above demand curve for an easyJet flight, how could additional revenue be earned from the same demand curve?

The revenue from a full 150-seater easyJet flight

Figure 5.8 Price discrimination

Pricing and the product life cycle

New products are launched and then become established. Later they may be replaced by more up-to-date products. Many products go through such a 'life cycle'. Four stages can be identified in a typical life cycle (see Figure 5.9):

1. Being launched.
2. A rapid growth in sales.
3. Maturity: a levelling off in sales.
4. Decline: sales begin to fall as the market becomes saturated, or as the product becomes out of date.

Analogue televisions, audio cassettes and gramophone records have all reached stage 4. Writable CDs, traditional mobile phones, DIY products and automatic washing machines have reached stage 3. Large LCD TVs, speed dating events, herbal teas, induction hobs, DVD recorders and city breaks using budget airlines are probably still in stage 2. Smart phones, HD multimedia entertainment devices and biodiesel are probably still in stage 1.

At each stage, the firm is likely to be faced with quite different market conditions: not only in terms of consumer demand, but also in terms of competition from rivals. What does this mean for pricing strategy?

The launch stage

In this stage the firm will probably have a monopoly (unless there is a simultaneous launch by rivals).

Given the lack of substitutes, the firm may be able to exploit its first-mover advantage (see page 145) and charge very high prices, thereby making large profits. This will be especially true if it is a radically new product – like the ballpoint pen,

How often individual prices move is an important question. Shifts in prices are like the traffic lights of an economy, signalling to people to buy more of this and less of that, to spend or to save, or to find new jobs. If the lights change readily, resources can be redirected smoothly; if they get stuck, so does the economy. In particular, if neither prices nor wages fall easily, the cost in output and jobs of reducing inflation can be high. Sticky prices also mean that an inflationary shock – an increase in oil prices, say – can take a long time to work its way through the system.[4]

As far as the magnitude of prices changes is concerned, in both the USA and Europe, price changes are typically much bigger than the rate of inflation. In Europe, average price increases are 8 per cent and average price reductions 10 per cent.

> **Pause for thought**
>
> *Why, do you think, are percentage price changes bigger, both up and down, than the rate of inflation?*

Recap

- Traditional economic theory assumes that businesses will set prices corresponding to the output where the marginal costs of production are equal to marginal revenue. They will do so in pursuit of maximum profits. The difficulties that a business faces in deriving its marginal cost and revenue curves suggest that this is unlikely to be a widely practised pricing strategy.

- Cost-based pricing involves the business adding a profit mark-up to its average costs of production. The profit mark-up set by the business is likely to alter depending upon market conditions.

- Many businesses practise price discrimination, in an attempt to maximise profits from the sale of a product. For a business to practise price discrimination it must be able to set prices, separate markets so as to prevent resale from the cheap to the expensive market, and identify distinct demand elasticities in each market.

- Products will be priced differently depending upon where they are in the product's life cycle. New products can be priced cheaply so as to gain market share, or priced expensively to recoup cost. Later on in the product's life cycle, prices will have to reflect the degree of competition, which may become intense as the market stabilises or even declines.

- Price flexibility varies from product to product. Generally the greater the proportion of raw materials in a product, the more frequently its price changes. In Europe, average price increases are 8 per cent and average price reductions 10 per cent.

[4] *Ibid.*

QUESTIONS

1. Think of four different products or services and estimate roughly how many firms there are in the market. You will need to decide whether 'the market' is a local one, a national one or an international one. In what ways do the firms compete in each of the cases you have identified?

2. As an illustration of the difficulty in identifying monopolies, try to decide which of the following are monopolies: a train operating company; your local evening newspaper; the village post office; the Royal Mail; Microsoft Office suite of programs; Interflora; the London Underground; ice creams in the cinema; Guinness; food on trains; the board game 'Monopoly'.

3. For what reasons would you expect a monopoly to charge (a) a higher price, and (b) a lower price than if the industry were operating under perfect competition?

4. Will competition between oligopolists always reduce total industry profits?

5. In which of the following industries is collusion likely to occur: bricks, beer, margarine, cement, crisps, washing powder, blank audio or video cassettes, carpets? Explain why.

6. Devise a box diagram like that in Table 5.3, only this time assume that there are three firms, each considering the two strategies of keeping price the same or reducing it by a set amount. Is the game still a 'dominant strategy game'?

7. What are the limitations of game theory in predicting oligopoly behaviour?

8. Make a list of six aims that a manager of a high street department store might have. Identify some conflicts that might arise between these aims.

9. When are increased profits in a manager's personal interest?

10. Since advertising increases a firm's costs, will prices necessarily be lower with sales revenue maximisation than with profit maximisation?

11. A frequent complaint of junior and some senior managers is that they are frequently faced with new targets from above, and that this makes their life difficult. If their complaint is true, does this conflict with the hypothesis that managers will try to build in slack?

12. Outline the main factors that might influence the size of the profit mark-up set by a business.

13. If a cinema could sell all its seats to adults in the evenings at the end of the week, but only a few on Mondays and Tuesdays, what price discrimination policy would you recommend to the cinema in order for it to maximise its weekly revenue?

14. How will a business's pricing strategy differ at each stage of its product's life cycle? First assume that the business has a monopoly position at the launch stage; then assume that it faces a high degree of competition right from the outset.

Business issues covered in this chapter

- What are the objectives of strategic management?
- What are the key competitive forces affecting a business?
- What choices of strategy towards competitors are open to a business?
- What internal strategic choices are open to a business and how can it make best use of its core competences when deciding on its internal organisation?
- By what means can a business grow and how can growth be financed?
- Should businesses seek to raise finance through the stock market?
- Under what circumstances might a business want to merge with another?
- What are the advantages and problems of remaining a small business?
- What issues arise in starting up a business?

Chapter map

CHAPTER 6

Business growth and strategy

6.1 Strategic analysis

For most of the time most managers are concerned with routine day-to-day activities of the business, such as dealing with personnel issues, checking budgets and looking for ways to enhance efficiency. In other words, they are involved in the detailed operational activities of the business.

Some managers, however, especially those high up in the business organisation, such as the managing director, will be busy in a different way, thinking about big, potentially complex issues, which affect the whole company. For example, they might be analysing the behaviour of competitors, or evaluating the company's share price or considering ways to expand the business. In other words, these managers are involved in the *strategic* long-term activities of the business. This is known as **strategic management**.

Strategic management involves *analysing* the alternative long-term courses of action for the firm and then *making choices* of what strategy to pursue.

The strategic choices that are made depend on the aims of the firm. Most firms have a 'mission statement' which sets out the broad aims, but as we saw in the last chapter, the aims in practice might be difficult to establish, given the number of different stakeholders in the business. It is thus in the *actual* decisions that are taken that the firm's aims can best be judged. In practice these aims are often complex, with economic objectives, such as profit, market share, product development and growth being mixed with broader social, ethical and environmental objectives.

We look at strategic analysis in this section and strategic choices in section 6.2.

Strategic analysis of the external business environment

In Chapter 1 we considered the various dimensions of the business environment and how they shape and influence business activity. We divided the business environment into four distinct sets of factors: political, economic, social and technological. Such factors comprise what we call a PEST analysis. In this section we will take our analysis of the business environment forward and consider more closely those factors that are likely to influence the **competitive advantage** of the organisation.

whether it lies in lower costs or product differentiation; (b) the nature of the target market – is it broad or a distinct market niche?

Cost leadership

As the title implies, a business that is a low-cost leader is able to manufacture and deliver its product more cheaply than its rivals, thereby gaining competitive advantage. The strategic emphasis here is on driving out inefficiency at every stage of the value chain. 'No-frills' budget airlines, such as easyJet and Ryanair, are classic examples of companies that pursue a cost-leadership strategy.

A strategy based upon cost leadership may require a fundamentally different use of resources or organisational structure if the firm is to stay ahead of its rivals. Wal-Mart's hub and spoke distribution system would be an example in point. Here the company distributes its products to shops from regional depots in order to minimise transport costs.

Box 6.1

Business strategy the Samsung way

Staying ahead of the game

Samsung is a major South Korean conglomerate involved in a number of industries, including machinery and heavy engineering, chemicals, financial services and consumer electronics. It has over 230 000 employees globally and is a major international investor and exporter.

This box outlines some of the strategic initiatives that have been taken in recent times by one of its most successful divisions, Samsung Electronics, which is the world's largest producer of colour monitors, LCD TVs, public display monitors, memory chips, flash memory, LCD panels for desktop and laptop computers, CDMA mobile phones and blue-ray players.

Samsung's success over the past few years is quite an achievement, given the massive financial problems it faced following the Asian financial crisis in the late 1990s. Since that time it has managed not only to shake off its debts and post significant improvements in profits, but to reposition itself in the upmarket segment of the consumer electronics industry.

How has Samsung achieved this? What have been the keys to its success?

Strong leadership. This has come from Mr Yun Jong Yong, vice-chairman and CEO of Samsung Electronics. He, in turn, is supported by a determined management team. Together they have a clear vision of the future of the sector. They want to become the leading electronics company in the world, measured by the quantity and quality of the goods that they produce. By 2006, they were already the third largest by sales, after Siemens and Hitachi.

Reorganisation. There has been a dramatic streamlining of the business and the decision-making structure following poor financial performance in the mid-1990s and an association with low-end brands in televisions and air-conditioning units. Mr Yun took aggressive measures to improve the division's finances by cutting jobs, closing unprofitable factories, reducing inventory levels and selling corporate assets. He then 'de-layered' the company, ensuring that managers had to go through fewer layers of bureaucracy, thereby speeding up the approval of new products, budgets and marketing plans.

New products. Samsung Electronics has been investing heavily in research and development (R&D) to increase its product portfolio and reduce the lead time from product conception to product launch. It has engaged in a number of strategic alliances with major players such as Sony, IBM and Hewlett Packard to share R&D costs. It aims to have 20 number-one products in terms of world market share by 2010 (currently the company has eight such products). This aggressive innovation strategy, coupled with low inventories and shortening product life cycles, allows Samsung to charge premium prices for state-of-the-art products.

This strategy is important in the rapidly changing world of consumer electronics, where a high-priced new product of today

In addition, firms that base their operations on low costs in order to achieve low prices (although that may not necessarily be the aim of low costs) are unlikely to have a high level of brand loyalty. In other words, if customer choice is going to be driven largely by price, demand is likely to be relatively price elastic. Other virtues of the product that might tie in buyers, such as quality or after-sales service, are largely absent from such firms' strategic goals.

Differentiation

A differentiation strategy aims to emphasise and promote the uniqueness of the firm's product: to make demand less elastic. As such, high rather than low prices are often attached to such products. Product characteristics such as quality, design and reliability are the basis of the firm's competitive advantage. Hence a strategy that adds to such differences and creates value for the customer needs to be identified.

can become a low-priced mass-produced product of tomorrow. Large panel LCD TVs, flash memory chips and mobile phones are all examples. In fact, Samsung saw its profits fall in late 2006 and early 2007 as prices of all these three products fell dramatically.

Driving down costs. Samsung invests heavily in modern factories that can cope with large production runs and gain maximum economies of scale. To this end Samsung also supplies components to its competitors as well as making them for its own product range. For example it sells flash memory chips for Apple's iPod, Nokia phones and digital cameras. Further, production systems are flexible enough to allow customisation for individual buyers, ensuring that selling prices are above the industry average. Alongside longer production runs, Samsung is concerned with ensuring that production costs are minimised by making its own business units compete with external rivals. For example, Samsung buys half of its colour filters from Sumitomo Chemical Company of Japan and the other half is sourced from its own factories.

Developing its brand image. Even though it makes most of its profits on semiconductors, investment in less profitable consumer products with a clear brand identity helps to raise the profile of all its products. It spends a great deal on sports sponsorship. For example, it sponsors Chelsea football club, it has invested heavily in successive Olympic games and it sponsors a range of

championships in golf, show jumping, running and Taekwondo. In both 2005 and 2006 Samsung Electronics was ranked number 1 consumer electronics brand by Businessweek's Interbrand, and 20th overall in the list of the top 100 global brands.

Consumers form especially strong bonds with cell phones and TVs. Most people carry their mobile phones with them everywhere, while their TV is the centre of the family room. 'We wanted the brand in users' presence 24/7,' says Peter Weedfald, head of Samsung's North American marketing and consumer electronics unit.

Now that strategy is paying off. Over the past five years, No. 20 Samsung has posted the biggest gain in value of any Global 100 brand, with a 186% surge. Even sweeter, last year Samsung surpassed No. 28 Sony, a far more entrenched rival that once owned the electronics category, in overall brand value.[1]

? Questions

1. What dangers do you see with Samsung's recent business strategy?
2. What makes Samsung's policies that we have examined in this box 'strategic' as opposed to merely 'operational'?

[1] *BusinessWeek Online*, 1 August 2005

Such a strategy might result in higher costs, especially in the short term, as the firm pursues constant product development through innovation, design and research. However, with the ability to charge premium prices, revenues may increase more than costs: i.e. the firm may achieve higher profits. Games console manufacturers, such as Sony with its PlayStation 3, Microsoft with its XBox 360 and Nintendo with Wii, are a good example. Even though they are in fierce competition with each other, each manufacturer focuses its strategy on trying to differentiate its product from the rivals'. This differentiation is in terms of features and performance, not price. Processor speed, online capabilities, player control, software support and product image are all characteristics used in the competitive battle.

Focus strategy

Rather than considering a whole market as a potential for sales, a focus strategy involves identifying market niches and designing and promoting products for them. In doing so a business may be able to exploit some advantage over its rivals, whether in terms of costs, or product difference. An example is Häagen-Dazs ice cream (a division of General Mills). The mass low-cost ice-cream market is served by a other large multinational food manufacturers and processors (such as Unilever, with its Wall's brand), and by supermarkets' own brands, but the existence of niche high-quality ice-cream markets offers opportunities for companies like Häagen-Dazs and Ben & Jerry's. By focusing on such consumers they are able to sell and market their product at premium prices.

Niche markets, however profitable, are by their nature small and as such limited in their growth potential. There is also the possibility that niches might shift over time or even disappear. This would require a business to be flexible in setting out its strategic position.

Internal resource-based strategic choices

Resource-based strategy focuses on exploiting a firm's internal organisation and production processes in order to develop its competitive advantage. It is important that the firm does certain things better or more cheaply than its rivals. What the firm will seek to exploit or to develop is one or more 'core competences'.

Core competences

Definition

Core competences
The key skills of a business that underpin its competitive advantage.

Core competences are those skills, knowledge, technologies and product specifications that underpin the organisation's competitive advantage over its rivals. These competences are likely to differ from one business to another, reflecting the uniqueness of each individual organisation, and ultimately determining its potential for success. The business should seek to exploit these competences, whether in the design of the product or in its methods of production.

Core competences.

The areas of specialised expertise within a business that underpin its competitive advantage over its rivals. These competences could be in production technologies or organisation, in relationships with suppliers, in the nature and specifications of the product, or in the firm's ability to innovate and develop its products and brand image.

Key
Idea
21

Thus Volvo has a core competence in building cars that are safe and reliable; Coca-Cola has a core competence in developing an image of a product; Tesco has a core competence in sourcing cheap but reliable supplies; Dell has a core competence in online selling of bespoke computers built to the consumer's specifications; Toys R Us, Mothercare and Saga have core competences in selling a wide variety of products to a very specific group of customers and in developing that customer base; Intel has a core competence in technological research and development that can yield significant continuing advances in the speed and efficiency of memory chips and processor cores; Ikea has a core competence in sourcing low-cost furniture and accessories and selling them at a highly competitive price in low-cost suburban sites where a wide choice is on view and instantly available.

In many cases, however, firms do not have any competences that give them a distinctive competitive advantage, even though they may still be profitable. In such instances, strategy often focuses either on *developing* such competences or simply on more effectively using the resources the firm already has.

Can a core competence be sustained?

A core competence (or core resource), if carefully exploited, will give the firm a competitive advantage over its rivals. If this advantage is to be sustained into the *long run*, however, the competence must satisfy the following four criteria. It must be:

■ *valuable*: a competence that helps the firm deal with threats or contributes to business opportunities;

■ *rare*: a competence or resource that is not possessed by competitors;

■ *costly to imitate*: a competence or resource that other firms find difficult to develop and copy;

■ *non-substitutable*: a competence or resource for which there is no alternative.

> **Pause for thought**
>
> *Referring back to Box 6.1, what core competences does Samsung have? Remember, you must justify a core competence in terms of all four listed criteria.*

Reactions of competitors

The success of a firm's strategic choices depends crucially on the reactions of rival firms. As we saw in the section on game theory (section 5.4), a firm has to be careful that strategic choices, such as developing new product lines or breaking into new markets, do not result in a 'war' with rivals that will end up with all 'players' worse off. The technology to produce a virtually everlasting light bulb has been available for many years, but it has not been in the interests of manufacturers to produce one, as it would force rivals to do the same with a resulting loss of future sales. To avoid this classic prisoners' dilemma (see pages 143–4) there has been tacit collusion between manufacturers not to launch such a product.

Sometimes, it is worth firms taking the risk of stimulating retaliatory action from rivals. If it estimates that its market position or core competences give it a competitive advantage, then it will take the risks of launching a new product, embarking on a marketing campaign, using a new technology or restructuring its organisation. If rivals do retaliate, its core competences may enable it to do well in any competitive battle.

Recap

■ Strategic choice often involves a consideration of both external and internal factors.

■ External environment- or market-based strategies are of three types: cost leadership strategy, where competitiveness is achieved by lower costs; differentiation strategy, where the business promotes the uniqueness of its product; focus strategy, where competitiveness is achieved by identifying market niches and tailoring products for different groups of consumers.

■ Internal strategy normally involves identifying core competences as the key to a business's competitive advantage. To give a business a sustained competitive advantage, core competences must be valuable, rare, costly to imitate and non-substitutable.

■ When making strategic choices, firms should take into account the likely reactions of competitors.

6.3 Growth strategy

Definitions

Internal expansion
Where a business adds to its productive capacity by adding to existing or by building new plant.

External expansion
Where business growth is achieved by merging with or taking over businesses within a market or industry.

Merger
The outcome of a mutual agreement made by two firms to combine their business activities.

Takeover (or acquisition)
Where one business acquires another. A takeover may not necessarily involve mutual agreement between the two parties. In such cases, the takeover might be viewed as 'hostile'.

Whether businesses wish to grow or not, many are forced to. The dynamic competitive process of the market drives producers on to expand in order to remain in the marketplace. If a business fails to grow, this may benefit its more aggressive rivals. They may secure a greater share of the market, leaving the first firm with reduced profits. Thus business growth is often vital if a firm is to survive.

In this section we consider the various growth strategies open to firms and assess their respective advantages and disadvantages. Growth may be achieved by one or both of the following:

Internal expansion. This is where a business looks to expand its productive capacity by adding to existing plant or by building new plant.

External expansion. This is where a business grows by engaging with another. It may do so in one of two ways.

■ The first is join with another firm to form a single legal identity, through merger or takeover. A **merger** is a situation in which, as a result of mutual agreement, two firms decide to bring together their business operations as one firm. A merger is distinct from a takeover in so far as a **takeover** involves one firm bidding for another's shares – often against the will of the directors of the target firm. One firm thereby acquires another. For simplicity, we will use the term 'merger' to refer to *both* mergers ('mutual agreements') and takeovers ('acquisitions').

■ The second is to form a **strategic alliance** with one or more firms. This is where firms agree to work together but retain their separate identities.

Whether the business embarks upon internal or external expansion, a number of alternative growth paths are open to it. Figure 6.3 shows these various routes, which are considered in the following pages.

Growth by internal expansion

Financing internal growth

Internal growth requires an increase in sales, which in turn requires an increase in the firm's productive capacity. In order to increase its *sales*, the firm is likely to

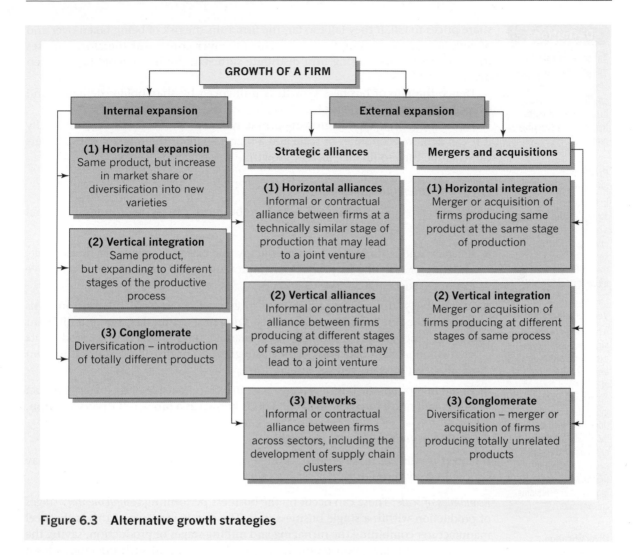

Figure 6.3   Alternative growth strategies

engage in extensive product promotion and to try to launch new products. In order to increase *productive capacity*, the firm will require new investment. Both product promotion and investment will require finance.

In the short run, the firm can finance growth by borrowing, by retaining profits or by a new issue of shares. What limits the amount of finance that a firm can acquire, and hence the rate at which it can grow?

If the firm *borrows* too much, the interest payments it incurs will make it difficult to maintain the level of dividends to shareholders. Similarly, if the firm *retains* too much *profit*, there will be less available to pay out in dividends. Also, if it attempts to raise capital by a *new issue of shares*, the distributed profits will have to be divided between a larger number of shares. Whichever way it finances investment, therefore, the more it invests, the more the dividends on shares in the short run will probably fall.

This could lead shareholders to sell their shares, unless they are confident that *long-run* profits and hence dividends will rise again, thus causing the share price to remain high in the long run. If shareholders do sell their shares, this will cause

Definition

Strategic alliance
Where two or more firms work together, formally or informally, to achieve a mutually desirable goal.

Definitions

Takeover constraint

The effect that the fear of being taken over has on a firm's willingness to undertake projects that reduce distributed profits.

Product differentiation

In the context of growth strategies, this is where a business upgrades existing products or services so as to make them different from those of rival firms.

Vertical integration

A business growth strategy that involves expanding within an existing market, but at a different stage of production. Vertical integration can be 'forward', such as moving into distribution or retail, or 'backward', such as expanding into extracting raw materials or producing components.

Diversification

A business growth strategy in which a business expands into new markets outside of its current interests.

share prices to fall. If they fall too far, the firm runs the risk of being taken over and of certain managers losing their jobs. This **takeover constraint** therefore requires that the growth-maximising firm distribute sufficient profits to avoid being taken over.

Hence the rate of business growth is influenced by shareholder demands and expectations and by the fear of takeover.

In the long run, a rapidly growing firm may find its profits increasing, especially if it can achieve economies of scale and a bigger share of the market. These profits can then be used to finance further growth.

Forms of internal expansion

There are three main ways in which a business can grow through internal expansion (see Figure 6.3):

■ It can expand or **differentiate its product** within existing markets, by, for example, updating or restyling its product, or improving its technical characteristics. We examined such strategies in Chapter 3.

■ Alternatively, the business might seek to expand via **vertical integration**. This involves the firm expanding within the same product market, but at a different stage of production. For example, a car manufacturer might wish to produce its own components ('backward vertical integration') or distribute and sell its own car models ('forward vertical integration').

■ As a third option, the business might seek to expand outside of its current product range, and move into new markets. This is known as a process of **diversification**.

Growth through vertical integration

If market conditions make growth through increased sales difficult, then a firm may choose to grow through vertical integration. This has a number of advantages:

Economies of scale. These can occur by the business performing *complementary* stages of production within a single business unit. The classic example of this is the steel manufacturer combining the furnacing and milling stages of production, saving the costs that would have been required to reheat the iron had such operations been undertaken by independent businesses. Clearly, for most firms, the performing of more than one stage on a single site is likely to reduce transport costs, as semi-finished products no longer have to be moved from one plant to another.

Reduced transactions costs. Vertical integration allows the firm to avoid the buying, selling and other costs associated with dealing with other firms, whether as suppliers or purchasers. We examined these costs on pages 103–7.

Consider two firms, one a motor vehicle manufacturer, the other a supplier of car exhausts. Both the car and the exhaust manufacturer will also be involved in frequent transactions between each other. The car manufacturer sells a lot of cars and so will need a lot of exhausts on a regular basis.

In addition, if the economic environment is uncertain and there is information asymmetry in the exchange, there is then the likelihood of a principal–agent problem, giving rise to a potential for moral hazard (see Boxes 3.1 and 3.2 on pages 70 and 72). One or both of the parties could exploit the situation to their own advantage because they have different sets of information about the markets in which they operate. The exhaust manufacturer could claim that rising steel prices forces it to put up prices. The car manufacturer could argue that poorer than expected sales forces it to reduce the price it can pay for the exhausts. Only if the contract between them is very tightly specified (is 'complete') can situations such as this be avoided.

If there is a binding contract, then this will prevent the car manufacturer from seeking alternative suppliers who could offer the exhausts more cheaply. Renegotiating the contract may be possible, but this too will incur costs. If a firm *is* free to seek alternative suppliers, then this may be risky (see below).

To avoid these transactions costs, then, firms may prefer to integrate vertically through internal expansion or merger.

Reduced uncertainty. A business that is not vertically integrated may find itself subject to various uncertainties in the marketplace. Examples include: uncertainty over future price movements, supply reliability or access to markets.

Backward vertical integration will enable the business to control its supply chain. Without such integration the firm may feel very vulnerable, especially if there are only a few suppliers within the market. In such cases the suppliers would be able to exert considerable control over price. Alternatively, suppliers may be unreliable.

Forward vertical integration creates greater certainty in so far as it gives the business guaranteed access to distribution and retailing on its own terms. As with supply, forward markets might be dominated by large buyers, which are able not only to dictate price, but also to threaten market foreclosure (being shut out from a market). Forward vertical integration can remove the possibility of such events occurring.

Barriers to entry. Vertical integration may give the firm greater power in the market by enabling it to erect entry barriers to potential competitors. For example, a firm that undertakes backward vertical integration and acquires a key input resource can effectively close the market to potential new entrants, either by simply refusing to supply a competitor, or by charging a very high price for the input such that new firms face an absolute cost disadvantage.

> ### Pause for thought
> See if you can identify two companies that are vertically integrated and what advantages they have from such integration.

The major problem with vertical integration is that it may reduce the firm's ability to respond to changing market demands. A business that integrates, either backward or forward, ties itself to particular supply sources or particular retail outlets. If, by contrast, it were free to choose between suppliers, inputs might be obtained at a lower price than the firm could achieve by supplying itself. In other words, outsourcing, rather than in-house production, can *save* costs by allowing the firm to buy from the cheapest and/or best suppliers. Such suppliers are likely to be in competition with each other and this helps to keep their prices down and quality up. Equally, the ability to shift between retail outlets would allow the firm's products to be sold in the best locations. This may not be possible if it is tied to its own retail network.

Many firms are finding that it is better *not* to be vertically integrated but to focus on their core competences and to outsource their supplies, their marketing and many other functions. That way they put alternative suppliers and distributors in competition with each other.

An alternative is to be *partially* vertically integrated, through a process known as **tapered vertical integration**.

Tapered vertical integration. This involves firms making part of a given input themselves and subcontracting the production of the remainder to one or more other

> ### Definition
> **Tapered vertical integration**
> Where a firm is partially integrated with an earlier stage of production: where it produces some of an input itself and buys some from another firm.

firms. For example, Coca-Cola and Pepsi are large vertically integrated enterprises. They have, as part of their operations, wholly-owned bottling subsidiaries. However, in certain markets they subcontract to independent bottlers both to produce and to market their product.

By making a certain amount of an input itself, the firm is less reliant on suppliers, but does not require as much capital equipment as if it produced all the input itself. A policy of tapered vertical integration suits many multinational companies. In certain countries, they produce the inputs themselves; in others, they rely on local suppliers, drawing on the supplier's competitive advantage in that local market.

Growth through diversification

An alternative internal growth strategy to vertical integration is that of diversification. A good example of a highly diversified company is Virgin. As we saw in Box 3.4 (page 82), Virgin's interests include planes, trains, cars, finance, music, mobile phones, holidays, wine, cinemas, radio, cosmetics, publishing, stem cells and even space travel.

If the current market is saturated, stagnant or in decline, diversification might be the only avenue open to the business if it wishes to maintain a high growth performance. In other words, it is not only the level of profits that may be limited in the current market, but also the growth of sales.

Diversification also has the advantage of spreading risks. So long as a business produces a single product in a single market, it is vulnerable to changes in that market's conditions. If a farmer produces nothing but potatoes, and the potato harvest fails, the farmer is ruined. If, however, the farmer produces a whole range of vegetable products, or even diversifies into livestock, then he or she is less subject to the forces of nature and the unpredictability of the market.

Growth through merger

Similar growth paths can be pursued via external expansion. However, in this case the business does not create the productive facilities itself, but purchases existing production. As Figure 6.3 identified, we can distinguish three types of merger: horizontal, vertical and conglomerate.

- A **horizontal merger** is where two firms at the same stage of production within an industry merge. An example of this is the merger in 2007 of travel companies Thomas Cook and MyTravel to form the Thomas Cook Group.

- A **vertical merger** is where businesses at different stages of production within the same industry merge. As such we might identify backward and forward vertical mergers for any given firm involved in the merger. In Europe there have been several vertical mergers in the electricity industry between generators and distributors, creating vertically integrated companies such as Electricité de France (EDF), and E.ON of Germany.

- A **conglomerate merger** is where firms in totally unrelated industries merge. Many of the big multinational corporations operate in a number of sectors and regularly buy other firms.

A further dimension of business growth that we should note at this point is that all of the above-mentioned growth paths can be achieved by the business looking beyond its national markets. In other words, the business might decide to become

Definitions

Horizontal merger
Where two firms in the same industry at the same stage of the production process merge.

Vertical merger
Where two firms in the same industry at different stages in the production process merge.

Conglomerate merger
Where two firms in different industries merge.

multinational and invest in expansion overseas. This raises a further set of issues, problems and advantages that a business might face. These will be discussed in Chapter 7 when we consider multinational business.

Why merge?

Why do firms want to merge with or take over others? Is it purely that they want to grow: are mergers simply evidence of the hypothesis that firms are growth max-imisers? Or are there other motives that influence the predatory drive?

Merger for growth. Mergers provide a much quicker means to growth than does internal expansion. Not only does the firm acquire new capacity, but also it acquires additional consumer demand. Building up this level of consumer demand by internal expansion might have taken a considerable length of time.

Merger for economies of scale. Once the merger has taken place, the constituent parts can be reorganised through a process of 'rationalisation'. The result can be a reduction in costs. For example, only one head office will now be needed. On the marketing side, the two parts of the newly merged company may now share distribution and retail channels, benefiting from each other's knowledge and operation in distinct market segments or geographical locations.

In fact, the evidence on costs suggests that most mergers result in few if any cost savings: either potential economies of scale are not exploited due to a lack of rationalisation, or diseconomies result from the disruptions of reorganisation. New managers installed by the parent company are often seen as unsympathetic, and morale may go down.

Merger for monopoly power. Here the motive is to reduce competition and thereby gain greater market power and larger profits. This applies mainly to horizontal mergers. With less competition, the firm will face a less elastic demand and be able to charge a higher percentage above marginal cost. What is more, the new more powerful company will be in a stronger position to regulate entry into the market by erecting effective entry barriers, thereby enhancing its monopoly position yet further.

> **Pause for thought**
>
> *Which of the three types of merger (horizontal, vertical and conglomerate) are most likely to lead to (a) reductions in average costs; (b) increased market power?*

Merger for increased market valuation. A merger can benefit shareholders of *both* firms if it leads to an increase in the stock market valuation of the merged firm. If both sets of shareholders believe that they will make a capital gain on their shares, then they are more likely to give the go-ahead for the merger.

What is the evidence? In the early stages of a merger boom, such as 2004–5 (see figure in Box 7.2 on page 204), when some good deals may be had, the share price of acquiring firms may rise. However, as the merger boom develops, more marginal firms are acquired. Take the merger boom of the late 1990s. In some 80 per cent of cases, there was a significant *fall* in the share value of the acquiring firm.

Merger to reduce uncertainty. Firms face uncertainty at two levels. The first is in their own markets. The behaviour of rivals may be highly unpredictable. Mergers, by reducing the number of rivals, can correspondingly reduce uncertainty. At the same time, they can reduce the *costs* of competition (e.g. reducing the need to advertise).

The second source of uncertainty is the economic environment. In a period of rapid change, such as often accompanies a boom, firms may seek to protect themselves by merging with others.

Box 6.2

Horizontal growth and vertical 'deintegration'

A dangerous recipe?

Look at most industries and they seem to be relatively competitive. With most oligopolies there are *several* firms competing for the consumer's custom. From cars, to supermarkets, to airlines, the competition seems intense.

But these companies are at the consumer end of the supply chain. Go further back down that chain and the degree of competition often declines: whether in industrial components, shipping, food processing, specialist services or even raw materials.

A 1999 earthquake in Taiwan shut down electronics factories around the world by interrupting supplies of semiconductors manufactured by just two companies in the same industrial park. One explosion at a chemical plant in Japan in 1993 cut off half the world's capacity for a resin used to make computer chips.[1]

One of the reasons for this worldwide pattern has been the relaxation of government policies towards oligopolistic collusion and the abuse of monopoly power. It began in the 1960s in the USA when Ronald Reagan was president. It has been continued by competition authorities in other many countries wanting to 'support' domestic industries in order to capture a larger share of world markets.

The general move to greater horizontal concentration in many parts of the supply chain is accompanied by another general move in the opposite direction: a reduction in vertical integration. This results in greater and greater outsourcing, often from overseas. Often this outsourcing is from specialist suppliers.

One result of giving big companies a licence to grow horizontally was that many producers, once they captured control over their markets, opted to sell off or shut down expensive and risky manufacturing and research and development operations and buy these 'services' from outside suppliers with few or no other pathways to the marketplace. Over time, many of these top-tier companies relied ever more on their power to dictate prices to their suppliers (including workers) to capture profits.

. . . In a production system marked by extreme outsourcing, oligopoly does not result in the end of competition so much as the redirection of competition downwards, as lead companies capture more power to set supplier against supplier, community against community and worker against worker.[2]

These trends are considered by Barry Lynn in his book *End of the Line: the Rise and Coming Fall of the Global Corporation*.

Using the examples of US multinationals such as Cisco Systems, Dell, FedEx, General Electric, General Motors, and Wal-Mart Stores, Lynn shows how cost-cutting and outsourcing by industry leaders have fed on themselves, leaving corporations dangerously open to even minor supply-chain interruptions. How has this happened? FedEx has encouraged US manufacturers to depend on daily delivery of global components to their assembly lines. Cisco has shown how a high-tech manufacturing behemoth can be created by assigning in advance most of the work to other companies, leaving little in-house.[3]

Dell was shocked to learn that key parts of its computers depended on a single supplier in Taiwan. Dell executives weren't aware of this, argues Lynn, because Dell doesn't actually make computers. Instead, it specializes in logistics, in managing the supply chain made up of the hundreds of companies that actually manufacture the thousands of parts that make up the modern computer. There are so many layers between Dell and the original supplier that no one really knows what's going on, from the top to the bottom of the supply chain.[4]

What we have then is a strange mix of large companies competing with each other in selling to consumers, but outsourcing their supplies from companies which, while being less powerful than the giant purchasing companies, nevertheless face little competition from other suppliers. The result is a growing vulnerability of the giant companies.

? Question

Would you advise large non-vertically integrated companies to move towards (a) tapered vertical integration; (b) buying any given type of supplies from at least two suppliers?

---

[1] 'Too lean a machine?' *BusinessWeek online*, 3 October 2005
[2] Barry Lynn, 'Wake up to the old-fashioned power of new oligopolies', *Financial Times*, 13 February 2006
[3] *BusinessWeek online, op. cit.*
[4] 'Our house of cards: a review by Andrew Leonard' (Powells.com)

Other motives. Other motives for mergers include:

■ Getting bigger so as to become less likely to be taken over oneself.

■ Merging with another firm so as to defend it from an unwanted predator (the 'White Knight' strategy).

■ Asset stripping. This is where a firm takes over another and then breaks it up, selling off the profitable bits and probably closing down the remainder.

■ Empire building. This is where owners or managers favour takeovers because of the power or prestige of owning or controlling several (preferably well-known) companies.

■ Geographical expansion. The motive here is to broaden the geographical base of the company by merging with a firm in a different part of the country or the world.

Mergers, especially horizontal ones, will generally have the effect of increasing the market power of those firms involved. This could lead to less choice and higher prices for the consumer. For this reason, mergers have become the target for government competition policy. Such policy is the subject of section 9.5.

Growth through strategic alliances

One means of achieving growth is through the formation of **strategic alliances** with other firms: either horizontally or vertically within an industry or as a network of firms across different industries. They are a means of expanding business operations relatively quickly and at relatively low cost, and are a common way in which firms can deepen their involvement in global markets.

A well-known example of strategic alliances is in the airline industry (see Figure 6.4 on page 180). Members co-operate over frequent flyer programmes, share business-class airport lounges and code share on various flights.

What forms can strategic alliances take?

Joint ventures. A **joint venture** is where two or more firms decide to create, and jointly own, a new independent organisation. An example is the Sony–NEC joint venture to produce hard disk drives. Another is the creation by BT and Securicor of Cellnet (now O2).

Consortia. A **consortium** is usually created for very specific projects, such as a large civil engineering work. As such, it has a very focused objective and once the project is completed the consortium is sometimes dissolved. TransManche Link, the Anglo-French company that built the Channel Tunnel, is an example of a defunct consortium. Camelot, by contrast, the company that runs the UK National Lottery, is still on-going. It is owned in equal shares by Cadbury Schweppes, De La Rue, Fujitsu Services, Royal Mail Enterprises and Thales Electronics, each of which had particular expertise to bring to the consortium.

Franchising and licensing. A less formal strategic alliance is where a business agrees to **franchise** its operations to third parties. McDonald's and Coca-Cola are good examples of businesses that use a franchise network. In such a relationship the franchisee is responsible for manufacturing and/or selling, and the franchiser retains responsibility for branding and marketing. A similar type of arrangement is that of **licensing**. Some lagers and beers sold in the UK, for example, are brewed under licence.

Definitions

Strategic alliance Where two firms work together, formally or informally, to achieve a mutually desirable goal.

Joint venture Where two or more firms set up and jointly own a new independent firm.

Consortium Where two or more firms work together on a specific project and create a separate company to run the project.

Franchise A formal agreement whereby a company uses another company to produce or sell some or all of its product.

Licensing Where the owner of a patented product allows another firm to produce it for a fee.

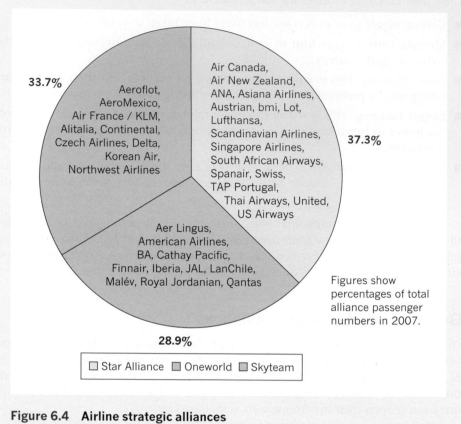

Figure 6.4   Airline strategic alliances

Subcontracting. Like franchising, **subcontracting** is a less formal source of strategic alliance, where companies maintain their independence. When a business subcontracts, it employs an independent business to manufacture or supply some service rather than conduct the activity itself. Car manufacturers are major subcontractors. Given the multitude and complexity of components that are required to manufacture a car, the use of subcontractors to supply specialist items, such as brakes and lights, seems a logical way to organise the business.

Networks. **Networks** are less formal than any of the above alliances. A network is where two or more businesses work collaboratively but without any formal relationship binding one to the other. Rather than a formal contract regulating the behaviour of the partners to the agreement, their relationship is based upon an understanding of trust and loyalty. Networks are common in the in the motor vehicle, electronics, pharmaceutical and other high-tech sectors.

Why form strategic alliances?

As a business expands, possibly internationally, it may well be advantageous to join with an existing player in the market. Such a business would have local knowledge and an established network of suppliers and distributors.

In addition, strategic alliances allow firms to share risk. The Channel Tunnel and the consortium of firms that built it is one such example. The construction of the Channel Tunnel was a massive undertaking and far too risky for any single firm to embark upon. With the creation of a consortium, risk was spread, and the various consortium members were able to specialise in their areas of expertise.

They also allow firms to pool capital. Projects that might have prohibitively high start-up costs, or running costs, may become feasible if firms cooperate and pool their capital. In addition, an alliance of firms, with their combined assets and credibility, may find it easier to generate finance, whether from investors in the stock market or from the banking sector.

The past 20 years have seen a flourishing of strategic alliances. They have become a key growth strategy for business both domestically and internationally. They are seen as a way of expanding business operations quickly without the difficulties associated with the more aggressive approach of acquisition or the more lengthy process of merger.

> **Pause for thought**
>
> *Give two reasons why a firm may prefer to form a strategic alliance with another firm rather than merging with it or taking it over.*

Recap

- A business can expand either internally, or externally by merging with other firms or by forming strategic alliances. In each case, there are three potential growth strategies open to business: product differentiation, vertical integration and diversification.

- Growth by internal expansion may be financed by ploughing back profits, by share issue or by borrowing. Whichever method a firm uses, it will require sufficient profits if it is to avoid becoming vulnerable to a takeover.

- Vertical integration involves remaining in the same market, but expanding into a different stage of production. Vertical integration can reduce a firm's costs through various economies of scale. It can eliminate the various transactions costs associated with dealing with other firms. It can also help to reduce uncertainty, as the vertically integrated business can hopefully secure supply routes and/or retail outlets. This strategy can also enhance the business's market power by enabling it to erect various barriers to entry.

- Diversification offers the business a growth strategy that not only frees it from the limitations of a particular market, but also enables it to spread its risks and seek profit in potentially fast-growing markets.

- There are three types of merger: horizontal, vertical and conglomerate. There are various possible advantages of mergers, including growth, economies of scale, market power, increased share values or reduction in uncertainty.

- One means of achieving growth is through the formation of strategic alliances with other firms. They have the advantage of allowing easier access to new markets, risk sharing and capital pooling.

6.4   Financing growth and investment

If businesses are to grow, they will need to invest. In this section we consider the sources of finance for investment, and the roles played by various financial institutions.

Sources of business finance

As mentioned in section 6.3 above, the firm can finance growth by borrowing, by retaining profits or by a new issue of shares.

The largest source of finance for investment in the UK is firms' own internal funds (i.e. ploughed-back profit). In a 2006 survey[1], 79 per cent of Chief Executive Officers stated that they planned to fund future activities in this way.

Given, however, that business profitability depends in large part on the general state of the economy, internal funds as a source of business finance are likely to show considerable cyclical variation. When profits are squeezed in a recession, this source of investment will decline (but so also will the *demand* for investment: after all, what is the point in investing if your market is declining?).

Other sources of finance, which include borrowing and the issue of shares and debentures, are known as 'external funds'. These are then categorised as short-term, medium-term or long-term sources of finance.

■ Short-term finance is usually in the form of a short-term bank loan or overdraft facility, and is used by firms as a form of working capital to aid them in their day-to-day business operations.

■ Medium-term finance, again provided largely by banks, is usually in the form of a loan with set repayment targets. It is common for such loans to be made at a fixed rate of interest, with repayments being designed to fit in with the business's expected cash flow. Bank lending tends to be the most volatile source of business finance, and has been particularly sensitive to the state of the economy. While part of the reason is the lower demand for loans during a recession, part of the reason is the caution of banks in granting loans if prospects for the economy are poor.

■ Long-term finance, especially in the UK, tends to be acquired through the stock and bond markets. The proportion of business financing from this source clearly depends on the state of the stock market. In the late 1990s, with a buoyant stock market, the proportion of funds obtained through share issue increased. Then with a decline in stock market prices from 2000 to early 2003, this proportion fell, only to rise again as the stock market surged ahead after 2004.

Definition

Short-termism
Where firms and investors take decisions based on the likely short-term performance of a company, rather than on its long-term prospects. Firms may thus sacrifice long-term profits and growth for the sake of quick return.

Despite the traditional reliance on the stock market for long-term sources of finance, there has been a growing involvement of banks in recent years. Banks have become more willing to provide finance for business start-ups and for diversification. Nevertheless, there is a concern that banks are still relatively cautious. This results in a problem of **short-termism**, with bankers often demanding a quick return on their money or charging high interest rates, and being less concerned to finance long-term investment.

Another source of finance is that from outside the country. Part of this is direct investment by externally based companies in the domestic economy. Part is finance from foreign financial institutions. In either case, a major determinant of the

[1] *Global CEO Survey 2006*, PricewaterhouseCoopers

amount of finance from this source is the current state of the economy and predictions of its future state. One of the major considerations here is anticipated changes in the exchange rate (see Chapter 13). If the exchange rate is expected to rise, this will increase the value of any given profit in terms of foreign currency. As would be expected, this source of finance is particularly volatile.

The stock market

In this section, we will look at the role of the stock market and consider the advantages and limitations of raising capital through it. We will also consider whether the stock market is efficient.

The role of the Stock Exchange

The London Stock Exchange operates as both a primary and secondary market in capital.

As a **primary market** it is where public limited companies (see page 7) can raise finance by issuing new shares, whether to new shareholders or to existing ones. To raise finance on the Stock Exchange a business must be 'listed'. The Listing Agreement involves directors agreeing to abide by a strict set of rules governing behaviour and levels of reporting to shareholders. A company must have at least three years' trading experience and make at least 25 per cent of its shares available to the public. In 2007, there were over 1200 UK and over 300 international companies on the Official List. In 2006, companies on this list raised £35.7 billion's worth of new capital by selling equity (ordinary shares) and fixed-interest securities on the London Stock Exchange.

As well as those on the Official List, there are some 1700 companies on what is known as the Alternative Investment Market (AIM). Companies listed here tend to be young but with growth potential, and do not have to meet the strict criteria or pay such high costs as companies on the Official List.

As a **secondary market**, the Stock Exchange operates as a market where investors can sell existing shares to one another. In 2006, on an average day's trading, £12.7 billion's worth of trading in UK equities and £13.7 billion's worth of trading in international equities took place.

The advantages and disadvantages of using the stock market to raise capital

As a market for raising capital the stock market has a number of advantages:

■ It brings together those that wish to invest and those that seek investment. It thus represents a way that savings can be mobilised to create output, and does so in a relatively low-cost way.

■ Firms that are listed on the Stock Exchange are subject to strict regulations. This is likely to stimulate investor confidence, making it easier for business to raise finance.

■ The process of merger and acquisition is facilitated by having a share system. It enables business more effectively to pursue this as a growth strategy.

The main weaknesses of the stock market for raising capital are:

■ The cost to a business of getting listed can be immense, not only in a financial sense, but also in being open to public scrutiny. Directors' and senior managers' decisions will often be driven by how the market is likely to react, rather by what they perceive to be in the business's best interests. They always have to think about the reactions of those large shareholders in the City that control a large proportion of their shares.

■ It is often claimed that the stock market suffers from *short-termism*. Investors on the Stock Exchange are more concerned with a company's short-term performance and its share value. In responding to this, the business might neglect its long-term performance and potential.

Is the stock market efficient?

One of the arguments made in favour of the stock market is that it acts as an arena within which share values can be accurately or efficiently priced. If new information comes on to the market concerning a business and its performance, this will be quickly and rationally transferred into the business's share value. This is known as the **efficient market hypothesis**. So for example, if an investment analyst found that, in terms of its actual and expected dividends, a particular share was underpriced and thus represented a 'bargain', the analyst would advise investors to buy. As people then bought the shares, their price would rise, pushing their value up to their full worth. So by attempting to gain from inefficiently priced securities, investors will encourage the market to become more efficient.

Definitions

Efficient (capital) market hypothesis
The hypothesis that new information about a company's current or future performance will be quickly and accurately reflected in its share price.

Random walk
Where fluctuations in the value of a share away from its 'correct' value are random. When charted over time, these share price movements would appear like a 'random walk' – like the path of someone staggering along drunk.

> **Efficient capital markets.**
> Capital markets are efficient when the prices of shares accurately reflect information about companies' current and expected future performance.
>
> **Key Idea 22**

If the market were perfectly efficient in this sense, then no gain could be made from studying a company's performance and prospects, as any such information would *already* be included in the current share price. In selecting shares, you would do just as well by pinning the financial pages of a newspaper on the wall, throwing darts at them, and buying the shares the darts hit!

If the stock market were perfectly efficient, it would only be unanticipated information that would cause share prices to deviate from that which reflected expected average yields. Such information must, by its nature, be random, and as such would cause share prices to deviate randomly from their expected price, or follow what we call a **random walk**. Evidence suggests that share prices do tend to follow random patterns.

> **Pause for thought**
>
> 1. For what reasons is the stock market not perfectly efficient?
> 2. How might some people gain from the lack of efficiency?

Recap

- Business finance can come from internal and external sources. Sources external to the firm include borrowing and the issue of shares.

- The stock market operates as both a primary and secondary market in capital. As a primary market it channels finance to companies as people purchase new shares. It is also a market for existing shares.

- It helps to stimulate growth and investment by bringing together companies and people who want to invest in them. By regulating firms and by keeping transaction costs of investment low, it helps to ensure that investment is efficient.

- It does impose costs on firms, however. It is expensive for firms to be listed and the public exposure may make them too keen to 'please' the market. It can also foster short-termism.

- The stock market is relatively efficient. It achieves efficiency by allowing share prices to respond quickly and fully to publicly available information.

Starting small   6.5

How often do you hear of small business making it big? Not very often, and yet many of the world's major corporations began life as small businesses. From acorns have grown oak trees! But small and large businesses are usually organised and run quite differently and face very different problems.

Unfortunately, there is no single agreed definition of a 'small' firm. In fact, a firm considered to be small in one sector of business, such as manufacturing, may be considerably different in size from one in, say, the road haulage business. Nevertheless, the most widely used definition is that adopted by the EU for its statistical data. Three categories of small and medium-sized enterprise (SME) are distinguished. These are shown in Table 6.1.

Of the whole UK economy in 2005, micro businesses (between 0 and 9 employees) accounted for 95.2 per cent of all firms, 21.0 per cent of turnover and provided 25.4 per cent of all employment. All SMEs together accounted for 99.9 per cent of all firms, 56.1 per cent of turnover and 52.1 per cent of employment.

Evidence suggests that a small business stands a significantly higher chance of failure than a large business, and yet many small businesses survive and some grow. What characteristics distinguish a successful small business from one that is likely to fail?

Pause for thought

Before you read on, try to identify what competitive advantages a small business might have over larger rivals.

Table 6.1   EU SME definitions

Criterion	Micro	Small	Medium
1. Maximum number of employees	9	49	249
2a. Maximum annual turnover	€2m	€10m	€50m
2b. Maximum annual balance sheet total	€2m	€10m	€43m
3. Maximum % owned by other firms which are large enterprise(s)	25%	25%	25%

Note: to qualify as an SME criteria 1 and 3 must be met and either 2a or 2b.

Competitive advantage and the small-firm sector

The following have been found to be the key competitive advantages that small firms might hold.

Flexibility. Small firms are more able to respond to changes in market conditions and to meet customer requirements effectively. For example, they may be able to develop or adapt products for specific needs. Small firms may also be able to make decisions quickly, avoiding the bureaucratic and formal decision-making processes that typify many larger companies.

Quality of service. Small firms are more able to deal with customers in a personal manner and offer a more effective after-sales service.

Production efficiency and low overhead costs. Small firms can avoid some of the dis-economies of scale that beset large companies. A small firm can benefit from: management that avoids waste; good labour relations; the employment of a skilled and motivated workforce; lower accommodation costs.

Product development. Many small businesses operate in niche markets, offering specialist goods or services. The distinctiveness of such products gives the small firm a crucial advantage over its larger rivals. A successful small business strategy, therefore, would be to produce products that are clearly differentiated from those of large firms in the market, thereby avoiding head-on competition – competition which the small firm would probably not be able to survive.

Innovation. Small businesses, especially those located in high-technology markets, are frequently product or process innovators. Such businesses, usually through entrepreneurial vision, manage successfully to match such innovations to changing market needs. Many small businesses are, in this respect, path breakers or market leaders.

Small businesses do, however, suffer from a number of significant limitations.

Problems facing small businesses

The following points have been found to hinder the success of small firms.

Selling and marketing. Small firms face many problems in selling and marketing their products, especially overseas. Small firms are perceived by their customers to be less stable and reliable than their larger rivals. This lack of credibility is likely to hinder their ability to trade. This is a particular problem for 'new' small firms which have not had long enough to establish a sound reputation.

Funding R&D. Given the specialist nature of many small firms, their long-run survival may depend upon developing new products and processes in order to keep pace with changing market needs. Such developments may require significant investment in research and development. However, the ability of small firms to attract finance is limited, as many of them have virtually no collateral and they are frequently perceived by banks as a highly risky investment.

Management skills. A crucial element in ensuring that small businesses not only survive but grow is the quality of management. If key management skills, such as being able to market a product effectively, are limited, then this will limit the success of the business.

Economies of scale. Small firms will have fewer opportunities and scope to gain economies of scale, and hence their costs may be somewhat higher than their larger rivals. This will obviously limit their ability to compete on price.

The role of the entrepreneur

Crucial to the success and growth of small businesses are the personality, skills and flair of the owner(s). Fostering their entrepreneurial talents has become a key element in government economic strategy around the world. Indeed, the creation of an entrepreneurial culture within society is often considered a pre-requisite for economic prosperity.

But what exactly is an entrepreneur? Entrepreneurs are sources of new ideas and new ways of doing things. That is, they are at the forefront of invention and innovation, providing new products and developing markets.

The *Global Entrepreneurship Monitor* (GEM) provides a framework for analysing entrepreneurship. It suggests that entrepreneurship is a complex phenomenon that can exist at various stages of the development of a business. So, someone who is just starting a venture and trying to make it in a highly competitive environment is entrepreneurial. And so too, but in a different way, are established business owners if they are innovative, competitive and growth-minded.

As far as new businesses are concerned, the GEM publishes a total entrepreneurial activity (TEA) index. This shows the proportion of the adult working age population to have established a firm within the past 42 months. Figure 6.5 shows the TEA

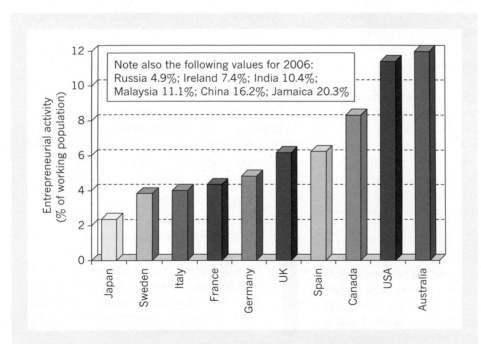

Figure 6.5   Entrepreneurial activity: TEA as % of adult population (average 2003–06)

Source: Based on data in *Global Entrepreneurship Monitor 2006* (Global Enterprise Research Association, 2007). Reproduced with permission

Box 6.3

The Dyson Dual Cyclone vacuum cleaner

A small business redefining the Hoover

In the 2007 New Years Honours, James Dyson, founder of Dyson Appliances, was knighted. Sir James said that he hoped that the honour would 'encourage other engineers and people who have ideas and inventions to go out and commercialise them and make them international successes'.

The tale of the Dyson Dual Cyclone vacuum cleaner records the successful and dramatic rise of James Dyson. As a budding entrepreneur, in the early 1980s he invented a revolutionary bagless vacuum cleaner, which worked, in effect, by creating a mini cyclone, whereby a high-speed air vortex pushed dust particles to the side of a collector. Without a bag, the suction power of the cleaner would not diminish over time, unlike conventional vacuums. When he initially developed this product (there were 5000 prototypes before a marketable product was finalised), neither Electrolux nor Hoover was interested – largely because of the profits they made from selling bags!

After an early and unsuccessful attempt to launch the project, Dyson managed to secure a deal with a Japanese company to produce and sell the vacuum in Japan. Launched in 1983, the pink-and-lavender 'G-Force' was a hit with Japanese consumers, who fell in love with its revolutionary design and looks. Nevertheless, at the staggering price of £1200, it was unlikely to yield the mass sales Dyson hoped for. Thus Dyson set out to manufacture it himself.

Finding it difficult to raise capital and find backers, Dyson reinvested his profits from the Japanese sales, and in 1993 managed to raise the £4.5 million required to design and patent his product, to establish a network of subcontractor suppliers, and to create an assembly plant near his home in the UK. With his DC01 vacuum cleaner priced at a relatively affordable £200, Dyson hoped to enter the mass market. By the end of the decade the Wiltshire plant was producing some 800 000 machines a year.

Today, Dyson's vacuum cleaner has nearly 50 per cent of the UK market, a fifth of the US and Western European markets and, with the launch of the compact DC12 vacuum, became the market leader in Japan, where homes are generally smaller.

The Dyson story is a classic example of how a small business with a revolutionary product can have a massive impact on a market, and within a short period of time become established as a market leader. The company now has an annual turnover of around £600 million, 80 per cent of it from exports. In 2005,

Dyson's salary was £31.5m – more than twice that of any FTSE 100 chief executive!

In recognition of his contribution to innovation, the Trade and Industry Secretary, Patricia Hewitt, in 2003 named James Dyson as her 'innovation tsar'.

The Dyson story has not, however, been all good news for the UK: in 2002, Dyson shifted production from the UK plant to Malaysia, with the loss of 560 UK jobs. Dyson countered criticisms of the move by arguing that fierce competition from competitors, who were selling bagless cleaners for half the price of Dysons, forced the company to relocate its manufacturing to a country where labour was much cheaper and which was close to suppliers of parts.

Yet things have turned out just as globalisation advocates would have hoped. Three factories in Malaysia now make 4m vacuum cleaners a year, with all the suppliers within a ten-mile radius, at one-third of the cost in Britain. The Wiltshire factory has become a research and design centre; Dyson employs more people than before, and in more highly skilled jobs. A new phase of R&D has produced a miniature digital motor with a power-to-weight ratio five times that of a Formula 1 racing car, which is being used in a tiny new vacuum cleaner and a super-hygienic, energy-efficient hand drier.

Innovative firms like Dyson can grow from small beginnings to world-beaters. Global competition is turning many products into commodities, so innovation is essential if companies – and countries – want to stay in business. [1]

? Questions

1. What conditions existed to enable James Dyson's small business to do so well in such a short period of time?
2. By 2007, a robotic Dyson vacuum cleaner (the DC06) had been over six years in development, involved several prototypes and cost a considerable amount of money. How would you assess whether the venture should have been scrapped?

---

[1] 'Suck it and see', *The Economist*, 1 February 2007

for various industrial countries. You can see that the UK is above its European counterparts but below the USA and Canada.

Attitudes towards entrepreneurship in the UK

Attitudes to entrepreneurship are generally positive in the UK with many creative and imaginative people starting businesses in niche markets, from organic and green products, to specialist computer services, to fashion products, to extreme sports, to painting and decorating, to financial services. A YouGov poll in 2006 found that a third of the population of working age wanted to run their own business. But, as Figure 6.5 shows, only 6.4 per cent had started a business within the previous 3½ years. According to the 2006 GEM, '7.8 per cent expect to start a business over the next three years, . . . 36.8 per cent see good business opportunities and 49.6% think that they have the skills to start a business.'[2]

However, the report also found that a significant proportion of the adult population of working age (36%) has a fear of business failure. Over 50 per cent perceive that getting finance for their business is the single most important obstacle to their entrepreneurial activity.

However, much of the fear of potential entrepreneurs is misplaced. Less than 20 per cent of loan applications are rejected; it is very easy to set up a business – you just have to inform HM Revenue and Customs; there is considerable support and advice available from various government agencies, such as *Business Link*; the amount of paperwork in running a small business is generally less than people expect; revenue from a new business's first year's trading on average turns out to be about double what the owners had expected.

Nevertheless, there are risks in setting up a business that should not be trivialised. The three-year survival rate is below 70 per cent. A dangerous period for a new business is between 12 and 18 months after start-up. It is then that a business often runs short of cash, and revenues are not coming in quickly enough. It is then, too, that initial interest from customers may wane.

> **Pause for thought**
>
> *Is business failure necessarily a 'bad thing' for a country?*

Recap

∎ Small firms survive because they provide or hold distinct advantages over their larger rivals. Such advantages include: greater flexibility, greater quality of service, production efficiency, low overhead costs and product innovation.

∎ Small businesses are prone to high rates of failure, however. This is due to problems of credibility, finance and limited management skills.

∎ Entrepreneurial activity varies from country to country, but most recognise that is an important ingredient in the health of the economy. Generally, the difficulties and risks of setting up a new business are less than people expect.

---

[2] *GEM Global Summary 2006: United Kingdom* (Babson and London Business School, 2007)

QUESTIONS

1. What do you understand by the term 'business strategy'? Explain why different types of business will see strategic management in different ways. Gives examples.

2. Outline the Five Forces Model of competition. Identify both the strengths and weaknesses of analysing industry in this manner.

3. Investigate a particular industry and assess its competitive environment using the Five Forces approach.

4. Distinguish between a business's primary and support activities in its value chain. Why might a business be inclined to outsource its support activities? Can you see any weaknesses in doing this?

5. What do you understand by the term 'core competence' when applied to a business? What are the arguments for and against a firm narrowly focusing on its core competences?

6. Explain the relationship between a business's rate of growth and its profitability.

7. Distinguish between internal and external growth strategy. Identify a range of factors which might determine whether an internal or external strategy is pursued.

8. What is meant by the term 'vertical integration'? Why might business wish to pursue such a growth strategy?

9. A firm can grow by merging with or taking over another firm. Such mergers or takeovers can be of three types: horizontal, vertical or conglomerate. Which of the following is an example of which type of merger (takeover)?

    (a) A soft drinks manufacturer merges with a pharmaceutical company.

    (b) A car manufacturer merges with a car distribution company.

    (c) A large supermarket chain takes over a number of independent grocers.

    To what extent will consumers gain or lose from the three different types of merger identified above?

10. Assume that an independent film company, which has up to now specialised in producing documentaries for a particular television broadcasting company, wishes to expand. Identify some possible horizontal, vertical and other closely related fields into which it may choose to expand.

11. What are the advantages and disadvantages for a company in using the stock market to raise finance for expansion?

12. In what sense can the stock market be said to be efficient? Why is it unlikely to be perfectly efficient?

13. Compare and contrast the competitive advantages held by both small and big business.

Business issues covered in this chapter

- What is the magnitude and pattern of global foreign direct investment?
- What forms do multinational corporations take?
- For what reasons do companies become multinational ones?
- In what ways do multinationals have a cost advantage over companies based in a single country?
- What competitive advantages do multinationals have over companies based in a single country?
- What disadvantages are companies likely to face from having their operations spread over a number of countries?
- What are the advantages and disadvantages of multinational investment for the host state and how can the multinational use its position to gain the best deal from the host state?

Chapter map

CHAPTER 7

Multinational corporations and business strategy in a global economy

In many respects a firm's global strategy is simply an extension of its strategy within its own domestic market. However, opening up to global markets can provide an obvious means for a business to expand its markets and spread its risks. It also is a means of reducing costs, whether through economies of scale or from accessing cheap sources of supply or low-wage production facilities.

A firm's global growth strategy may involve simply exporting or opening up factories or outlets abroad, or it may involve merging with businesses in other countries or forming strategic alliances. As barriers to trade and the international flow of capital have come down, so more and more businesses have sought to become multinational. The result is that the global business environment has tended to become more and more competitive.

For developing economies, such as India and China, the benefits of this new wave of globalisation are substantial. Foreign companies invest in high value-added, knowledge-rich production, most of which is subsequently exported. Economic growth is stimulated and wages rise. Increased consumption then spreads the benefits more widely throughout the economy. There are, however, costs. Many are left behind by the growth and inequalities deepen. There are also often significant environmental costs as rapid growth leads to increased pollution and environmental degradation.

7.1 Multinational corporations

There are some 80 000 **multinational corporations** (MNCs) worldwide. Between them they control a total of over 800 000 foreign subsidiaries, which employ some 65 million people. In 2006, the global stock of foreign direct investment (FDI) was over $11 trillion. Sales by foreign affiliates accounted for $22 trillion in 2005, or 49.6 per cent of world GDP. The largest MNCs have affiliates in an average of 40 foreign countries each.

But just what is an MNC? At the most basic level it is a business that either owns or controls subsidiaries in more than one country. It is this ownership or control of productive assets in other countries that makes the MNC distinct from an enterprise that does business overseas by simply exporting goods or services. However, merely to define an MNC as a company with overseas subsidiaries fails to reflect the immense diversity of multinationals.

Box 7.1

The transnationality index

A measure of global significance

As part of the UNCTAD annual World Investment Report, a 'transnationality' index is given for both host countries and multinational businesses. Transnationality refers to the significance of foreign activities in the country or for the business.

The transnationality index (TNI) for host countries

The transnationality index for a country is based on the average of four variables:

■ FDI inflows as a percentage of gross fixed capital formation (investment);

■ FDI inward stock as a percentage of GDP;

■ value added by foreign affiliates as a percentage of GDP;

■ employment by foreign affiliates as a percentage of total employment.

In 2003 the average transnationality index for the 74 countries for which it was calculated was just over 22 per cent. The world's most transnational host economy is Hong Kong (85.5%), followed

by Ireland (63.7%) Belgium (62.1%), Luxembourg (59.4%) and Singapore (59.3%) (see chart).

The transnationality index for business

The transnationality index for multinational business is composed of the average of three ratios:

■ foreign assets to total assets;

■ foreign sales to total sales;

■ foreign employment to total employment.

Between 1993 and 2004 the average transnationality index (TNI) for the world's 100 largest multinational companies rose from under 50 to 57 per cent, implying a growing level of transnationality. The top ten global companies ranked by transnationality are given in the table.

Another measure of the transnationality of business is the number of foreign affiliates relative to domestic ones. In 2004, 65 per cent of the affiliates of world's largest MNCs were located abroad.

The world's top ten MNCs in terms of transnationality (2004)

TNI[a] (ranking)	TNI (%)	Corporation	Home economy	Industry	Foreign assets (ranking)	Foreign assets ($m)
1	97.3	Thomson Corporation	Canada	Media	70	19 221
2	94.5	CRH plc	Ireland	Lumber and other building materials	88	15 192
3	93.5	Nestlé SA	Switzerland	Food & beverages	19	65 396
4	87.1	Vodaphone Group plc	UK	Telecommunications	2	247 850
5	85.6	Alcan Inc.	Canada	Metal and metal products	56	25 455
6	85.6	Koninklijke Ahold	USA/ Netherlands	Retail	57	24 659
7	84.0	Philips Electronics	Netherlands	Electrical and electronic equipment	47	30 330
8	83.2	Nortel Networks	Canada	Telecommunications	99	13 854
9	82.8	Unilever	UK/Netherlands	Diversified	38	38 415
10	81.5	BP	UK	Petroleum	5	154 513

[a] TNI = Transnationality index

Source: *World Investment Report 2006* (UN Conference on Trade and Development [UNCTAD], 2007), extracts from Annex table A.I.11. Reproduced with permission

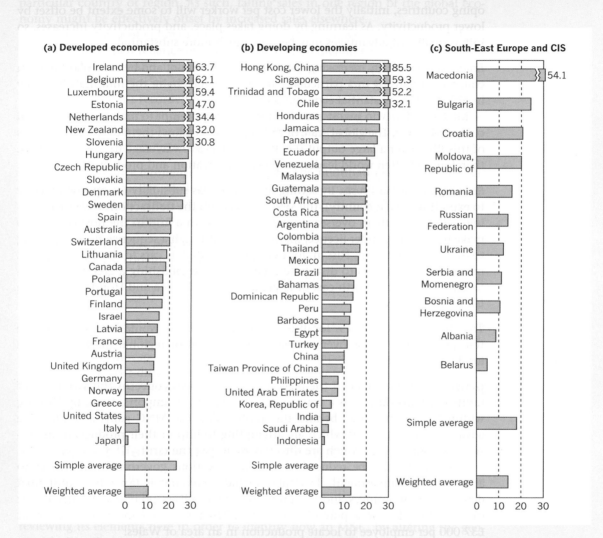

(a) Developed economies

Country	Value
Ireland	63.7
Belgium	62.1
Luxembourg	59.4
Estonia	47.0
Netherlands	34.4
New Zealand	32.0
Slovenia	30.8
Hungary	
Czech Republic	
Slovakia	
Denmark	
Sweden	
Spain	
Australia	
Switzerland	
Lithuania	
Canada	
Poland	
Portugal	
Finland	
Israel	
Latvia	
France	
Austria	
United Kingdom	
Germany	
Norway	
Greece	
United States	
Italy	
Japan	
Simple average	
Weighted average	

(b) Developing economies

Country	Value
Hong Kong, China	85.5
Singapore	59.3
Trinidad and Tobago	52.2
Chile	32.1
Honduras	
Jamaica	
Panama	
Ecuador	
Venezuela	
Malaysia	
Guatemala	
South Africa	
Costa Rica	
Argentina	
Colombia	
Thailand	
Mexico	
Brazil	
Bahamas	
Dominican Republic	
Peru	
Barbados	
Egypt	
Turkey	
China	
Taiwan Province of China	
Philippines	
United Arab Emirates	
Korea, Republic of	
India	
Saudi Arabia	
Indonesia	
Simple average	
Weighted average	

(c) South-East Europe and CIS

Country	Value
Macedonia	54.1
Bulgaria	
Croatia	
Moldova, Republic of	
Romania	
Russian Federation	
Ukraine	
Serbia and Momenegro	
Bosnia and Herzegovina	
Albania	
Belarus	
Simple average	
Weighted average	

Transnationality index of host economies, 2003 (percentage)

Source: *World Investment Report 2006* (UN Conference on Trade and Development [UNCTAD], 2007), page 11. Reproduced with permission

What are the most favoured economies for MNC investment? Excluding MNCs from the host economy itself, the most favoured location for affiliates is the USA, where 92.0 per cent of non-US companies from the largest 100 MNCs had affiliates. This was followed by the UK, where 91.0 per cent of non-UK companies in the top 100 had affiliates, followed by the Netherlands (89.6%), Germany (87.4%), France (83.5%), Italy (81.4%) and Brazil (81.0%). Percentages for other countries included: Singapore (73.7%), Japan (70.3%), China (66.0%), Russia (54%), Malaysia (53.5%) and S. Korea (49.5%).

Questions

1. Looking at the table, can you offer any explanation of why there is only one partly American owned and no Japanese owned company on this list?

2. How adequate do you feel such indices are in identifying how open or global an economy or business is? Should other indicators be considered as well? If so what?

3. The leading nations in the transnationality index are all small, whereas the most favoured economy for MNC investment is the USA. Explain this apparent paradox.

Box 7.2

Merger activity

An international perspective

What have been the trends, patterns and driving factors in mergers and acquisitions (M&A) around the world over the past ten years? An overview is given in the chart.

The 1990s saw a rapid growth in M&A as the world economy boomed. Then with a slowing down in economic growth after 2000, M&A activity declined, both in value and in the number of deals, only to pick up again after 2003 as the world economy surged ahead again. By 2006, the value of M&A had reached a record $4 trillion, surpassing the previous record in 2000.

The 1990s

The early years of the 1990s saw relatively low M&A activity as the world was in recession, but as world economic growth picked up, so worldwide M&A activity increased. Economic growth was

particularly rapid in the USA, which became the major target for acquisitions.

There was also an acceleration in the process of 'globalisation'. With the dismantling of trade barriers around the world and increasing financial deregulation, so international competition increased. Companies felt the need to become bigger in order to compete more effectively.

In Europe, M&A activity was boosted by the development of the Single Market, which came into being in January 1993. Companies took advantage of the abolition of trade barriers in the EU, which made it easier for them to operate on an EU-wide basis. As 1999 approached, and with it the arrival of the euro, so European merger activity reached fever pitch, stimulated also by the strong economic growth experienced throughout the EU.

By the end of the 1990s, annual worldwide M&A activity was three times the level of the beginning of the decade. At this time

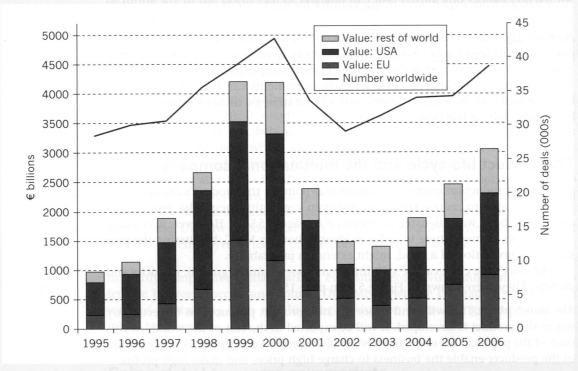

Mergers and acquisitions by target (deals valued at over $1 million)

Source: *Mergers & Acquisitions Note*, April 2007 (European Commission, DG ECFIN, 2007). Copyright © 2007 European Commission. Reproduced with permission there were some very large mergers indeed. These included a €29.4 billion marriage of pharmaceutical companies Zeneca of the UK and Astra of Sweden in 1998, a €205 billion takeover of telecomms giant Mannesmann of Germany by Vodafone of the UK in 1999 and a €50.8 billion takeover of Orange of the UK by France Telecom in 2000.

Other sectors in which merger activity was rife included financial services and the privatised utilities sector. In the UK, in particular, most of the privatised water and electricity companies were been taken over, with buyers attracted by the sector's monopoly profits. French and US buyers were prominent.

The 2000s

The 2000s have seen a change in the worldwide pattern of M&A activity. Whilst this predominantly involves a company in a neighbouring country, or a country that is a traditional trading partner, increasingly both European and US companies have looked to other parts of the world to expand their activities.

Two of the major target regions have been (a) the rest of Europe, especially the ten countries joining the EU in 2004 plus Russia, and (b) developing countries, especially China, Brazil and India. These new markets have the twin attractions of rapidly growing demand and low costs, including cheap skilled labour and low tax rates.

M&A activity has become more widespread across industrial sectors. In the 1997–2000 boom, the companies targeted were predominantly in the telecomms and media sectors. The boom of the mid-2000s, by contrast, saw companies involved in M&A from across the range of industries. According to a 2006 survey of Chief Executive Officers around the world[1], 47 per cent were actively engaged to some degree in M&A activity. The figure rises to 61 per cent for CEOs of large companies (those with revenue of more than $10 billion).

Overwhelmingly, gaining access to new markets and customers is the main purpose given for cross-border M&A, cited by nearly two-thirds of CEOs. However, CEOs do not underestimate the difficulties faced in cross-border acquisition and integration. Cultural issues and conflicts, differences in regulations and unexpected costs are the main obstacles to cross-border M&A activity cited by CEOs.

. . . The global winners of tomorrow are those that can change their outlook from local to global in the true sense, and learn to operate in a world now subject to far more influences from a wider array of sources than ever before.[2]

Types of M&A activity

Some 12 per cent of M&A deals are 'hostile' (up from 2 per cent in 2000). In other words, the company being taken over does not want to be. The deals are often concluded after prolonged boardroom battles, with bosses of the acquiring company seeking opportunities to build empires, and bosses of the target company attempting all sorts of manoeuvres to avoid being taken over. This may involve them seeking deals with alternative, more 'friendly' companies. Generally companies are increasingly using the services of investment banks to help them in the process of making or warding off deals.

Despite the growing number of horizontal mergers, there has also been a tendency for companies to become more focused, by selling off parts of their business which are not seen as 'core activities'. For example, not long after its takeover of Wellcome, Glaxo decided to concentrate on the production of prescription drugs, and as a consequence to sell its share of Warner Wellcome, which produced non-prescription drugs. Another example was Volvo. After unsuccessfully attempting to merge with Renault in 1993, it subsequently divested itself of several companies that it owned in a variety of industries, ranging from banking and finance to food, matches and pharmaceuticals.

This trend of horizontal mergers and conglomerate and vertical de-mergers has allowed companies to increase their market power in those specific sectors where they have expertise. Consumers may gain from lower costs, but the motives of the companies are largely to gain increased market power — something of dubious benefit to consumers.

 Question
Are the motives for merger likely to be different in a recession from in a period of rapid economic growth?

[1] *Global CEO Survey 2006*, PricewaterhouseCoopers
[2] 'Global CEOs' business confidence reaches record levels', PricewaterhouseCoopers Press Release, 24 January 2007

Business issues covered in this chapter

- How has the UK labour market changed over the years?
- How are wage rates determined in a perfect labour market?
- What are the determinants of the demand and supply of labour and their respective elasticities?
- What forms of market power exist in the labour market and what determines the power of employers and labour?
- What effects do powerful employers and trade unions have on wages and employment?
- How has the minimum wage affected business and employment?
- What is meant by a 'flexible' labour market and how has increased flexibility affected working practices, employment and wages?
- How will various incentives affect the motivation and productivity of workers?
- Should senior executives be given large bonuses and stock options?

Chapter map

CHAPTER 8

Labour and employment

In this chapter we consider how labour markets affect business. In particular, we will focus on the determination of wage rates in different types of market: ones where employers are wage takers, ones where they can choose the wage rate, and ones where wage rates are determined by a process of collective bargaining.

We start by examining some of the key trends in the structure of the labour market.

8.1 The UK labour market

The labour market has undergone great change in recent years. Advances in technology, changes in the pattern of output, a need to be competitive in international markets and various social changes have all contributed to changes in work practices and in the structure and composition of the workforce.

Major changes in the UK include the following:

- A shift from agricultural and manufacturing to service-sector employment. Figure 8.1 (overleaf) reveals that employment in agriculture has been falling over a long historical period. The fall in manufacturing employment, however, has been more recent, starting in the 1960s and gathering pace through the 1970s, 1980s and 1990s. By contrast, employment in the service industries has grown steadily since 1946. In fact since 1979, it has expanded by nearly 8 million jobs.

- A rise in part-time employment. In 1971 one in six workers was part time; by 2007 this had risen to one worker in four. In the EU as a whole, the figure is one in six. The growth in part-time work reflects the growth in the service sector, where many jobs are part time. Since 1979 part-time employment has risen by over 2.7 million.

- A rise in female participation rates. Women now constitute approximately half of the paid labour force. The rise in participation rates is strongly associated with the growth in the service sector and the creation of part-time positions. Some 43 per cent of female workers, about 5.7 million, are in part-time work.

- A rise in the proportion of workers employed on fixed-term contracts, or on a temporary or casual basis. Many firms nowadays prefer to employ only their core workers/managers on a permanent ('continuing') basis. They feel that it gives them more flexibility to respond to changing market conditions to have the remainder of their workers employed on a short-term basis and, perhaps, to make use of agency staff or to contract out work.

- **Downsizing**. It has become very fashionable in recent years for companies to try to 'trim' the numbers of their employees in order to reduce costs. There is now,

Definition

Downsizing
Where a business reorganises and reduces its size, especially in respect to levels of employment, in order to cut costs.

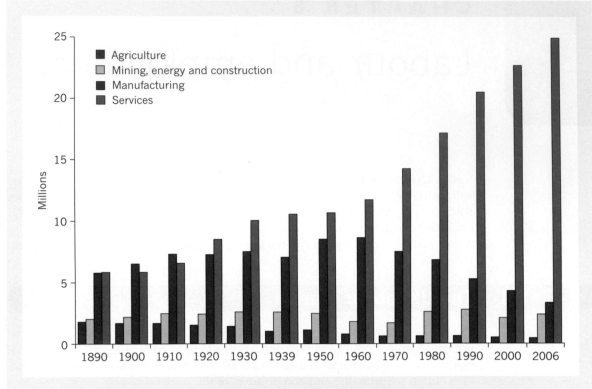

Figure 8.1   Jobs in different sectors of the UK economy (1890–2006)

Source: Based on data in Mitchell, B. R., *European Historical Statistics 1750–1970* (Macmillan Press, 1975); *Economic and Labour Market Review* time series data (Office for National Statistics)

however, a growing consensus that the process may have gone too far. The cost of reducing its workforce may be that a company loses revenue: if it cuts back on people employed to market its products, develop new products or ensure that quality is maintained, then it is likely to lose market share. It might reduce unit costs, but total profits could nevertheless fall, not rise.

8.2 Market-determined wage rates and employment

Perfect labour markets

When looking at the market for labour, it is useful to make a similar distinction to that made in the market for goods and services: the distinction between perfect and imperfect markets. Although in practice few labour markets are totally perfect, many do at least approximate to it.

The key assumption of a perfect labour market is that everyone is a **wage taker**. In other words, neither employers nor employees have any economic power to affect wage rates. This situation is not uncommon. Small employers are likely to have to pay the 'going wage rate' to their employees, especially where the employee

> **Definition**
>
> **Wage taker**
> The wage rate is determined by market forces.

Figure 8.2   A perfectly competitive labour market

is of a clear category, such as an electrician, a bar worker, a secretary or a porter. As far as employees are concerned, being a wage taker means not being a member of a union and therefore not being able to use collective bargaining to push up the wage rate.

Wage rates and employment under perfect competition are determined by the interaction of the market demand and supply of labour. This is illustrated in Figure 8.2. The curves show the total number of hours workers would supply and the number of hours of labour firms would demand for each wage rate in a particular labour market. The equilibrium market wage rate is W_e, where demand equals supply. Equilibrium employment in terms of the total number of hours people are employed in the market is Q_e.

Generally it would be expected that the supply and demand curves slope the same way as in goods markets. The higher the wage paid for a certain type of job, the more workers will want to do that job. This gives an upward-sloping supply curve of labour. On the other hand, the higher the wage that employers have to pay, the less labour they will want to employ. Either they will simply produce less output, or they will substitute other factors of production, like machinery, for labour. Thus the demand curve for labour slopes downwards.

We now turn to look at the supply and demand for labour in more detail.

The supply of labour

As we have seen, the supply of labour curve will typically be upward sloping. The *position* of the market supply curve of labour will depend on the number of people willing and able to do the job at each given wage rate. This depends on three things:

- the number of qualified people;
- the non-wage benefits or costs of the job, such as the pleasantness or otherwise of the working environment, job satisfaction or dissatisfaction, status, power, the degree of job security, holidays, perks and other fringe benefits;
- the wages and non-wage benefits in alternative jobs.

Pause for thought

Which way will the supply curve shift if the wage rates in alternative jobs rise?

A change in the wage rate will cause a movement along the supply curve. A change in any of these other three determinants will shift the whole curve.

The elasticity of the market supply of labour

How *responsive* will the supply of labour be to a change in the wage rate? If the market wage rate goes up, will a lot more labour become available or only a little? This responsiveness (elasticity) depends on (a) the difficulties and costs of changing jobs and (b) the time period.

Definition

Mobility of labour
The ease with which labour can either shift between jobs (occupational mobility) or move to other parts of the country in search of work (geographical mobility).

Another way of looking at the elasticity of supply of labour is in terms of the **mobility of labour**: the willingness and ability of labour to move to another job, whether in a different location (geographical mobility) or in a different industry (occupational mobility). The mobility of labour (and hence the elasticity of supply of labour) will be higher when there are alternative jobs in the same location, when alternative jobs require similar skills and when people have good information about these jobs.

It is also much higher in the long run, when people have the time to acquire new skills and when the education system has had time to adapt to the changing demands of industry.

Pause for thought

What effect has the entry of ten member states to the EU in 2004, including several from eastern Europe, had on the position and elasticity of the supply curve of various types of labour?

The demand for labour: the marginal productivity theory

The market demand curve for labour will typically be downward sloping. To see why, let us examine the behaviour of a profit-maximising firm.

The profit-maximising approach

How many workers will a profit-maximising firm want to employ? The firm will answer this question by weighing up the costs of employing extra labour against the benefits. It will use exactly the same principles as in deciding how much output to produce.

In the goods market, the firm will maximise profits where the marginal cost of an extra unit of *goods* produced equals the marginal revenue from selling it: $MC = MR$.

In the labour market, the firm will maximise profits where the marginal cost of employing an extra *worker* equals the marginal revenue that the worker's output earns for the firm: MC of labour = MR of labour. To understand this, consider what would happen if they were not equal. If an extra worker adds more to a firm's revenue than to its costs, the firm's profits will increase. It will be worth employing that worker. But as more workers are employed, diminishing returns to labour will set in (see page 92). Each extra worker will produce less than the previous one, and thus earn less revenue for the firm. Eventually the marginal revenue from extra workers will fall to the level of their marginal cost. At that point the firm will stop

Box 8.1

'Telecommuters'

The electronic cottage

The increasing sophistication of information technology, with direct computer linking, broadband access to the Internet, fax machines and mobile phones, has meant that many people can work at home. The number of these 'telecommuters' has grown steadily since the information technology revolution of the early 1980s. Some 16 per cent of US workers telecommute all or part of the time.

It has been found that where 'telecommuting networks' have been established, gains in productivity levels have been significant, when compared with comparable office workers. Most studies indicate rises in productivity of over 35 per cent. With fewer interruptions and less chatting with fellow workers, less working time is lost. Add to this the stress-free environment, free from the strain of commuting, and the individual worker's performance is enhanced.

With further savings in time, in the renting and maintenance of offices (often in high-cost inner city locations) and in heating and lighting costs, the economic arguments in favour of telecommuting seem very persuasive. What is more, concerns that managers lose control over their employees, and that the quality of work falls, appear unfounded. In fact the reverse seems to have occurred: the quality of work in many cases has improved.

These technological developments have been the equivalent of an increase in labour mobility. Work can be taken to the workers rather than the workers coming to the work. The effect is to reduce the premium that needs to be paid to workers in commercial centres, such as the City of London.

Then there are the broader gains to society. Telecommuting opens up the labour market to a wider group of workers who might find it difficult to leave the home – groups such as single parents and the disabled. Also there are environmental gains. Fewer journeys to work mean less traffic congestion and less pollution.

But do people working from home feel isolated? For many people, work is an important part of their social environment, providing them with an opportunity to meet others and to work as a team. For those who are unable to leave the home, however, telecommuting may be the *only* means of earning a living: the choice of travelling to work may simply not be open to them.

However, telecommuters can be exploited. The Low Pay Commission has found that many homeworkers are paid well below the minimum wage because employers pay by the amount of work done and underestimate the amount of time it takes to complete work.

International telecommuting

There is no reason, of course, why telecommuters cannot work in different countries. With the creation of trans-oceanic fibre optical cable networks, international data transmission has become both faster and cheaper. Increasingly, therefore, companies in developed countries are employing relatively low-wage workers in the developing world to do data processing, telesales and various 'back-office' work – work that is often highly skilled. More than 500 multinational companies employ IT workers in Bangalore alone.

Some of the international teleworkers work in call centres; others work from their own homes. Increasingly telecommuters in India are being provided with computers and broadband connection to enable them to do so.

Call-centres of tomorrow will not be the ones operating from under a single roof. Instead, it will be a network of customer service agents (CSAs) working from their own homes miles away from each other. . . . With all the push that the [Indian] government is giving to increase broadband penetration, this concept will trigger a revolution in the way call-centres of today operate.[1]

International telecommuting can be closer to home. Growing numbers of UK workers have moved to France or Spain, where property is much cheaper and, thanks to broadband, they can carry on their UK jobs from there. When they do have to come into the office, cheap travel by budget airline makes that possible.

Questions

1. What effect is telecommuting likely to have on (a) trade union membership; (b) trade union power?
2. How are the developments referred to in this box likely to affect relative house prices between capital cities and the regions?

---

[1] 'Telecommuting: the work-from-home option', DQChannels of India (http://www.dqchannels.com/content/mirror/105021801.asp)

employing extra workers. There are no additional profits to be gained. Profits are at a maximum.

Measuring the marginal cost and revenue of labour

Marginal cost of labour (MC_L). This is the extra cost of employing one more worker. Under perfect competition the firm is too small to affect the market wage. It faces a horizontal supply curve. In other words, it can employ as many workers as it chooses at the market wage rate. Thus the additional cost of employing one more person will simply be the wage rate: $MC_L = W$.

Marginal revenue of labour (MRP_L). The marginal revenue that the firm gains from employing one more worker is called the **marginal revenue product of labour** (MRP_L). The MRP_L is found by multiplying two elements – the *marginal physical product* of labour (MPP_L) and the marginal revenue gained by selling one more unit of output (MR).

$$MRP_L = MPP_L \times MR$$

The MPP_L is the extra output produced by the last worker. Thus if the last worker produces 100 tonnes of output per week (MPP_L), and if the firm earns an extra £2 for each additional tonne sold (MR), then the worker's MRP is £200. This extra worker is adding £200 to the firm's revenue.

The profit-maximising level of employment for a firm

The MRP_L curve is illustrated in Figure 8.3. As more workers are employed, there will come a point when diminishing returns set in (point *x*). Thereafter the MRP_L curve slopes downwards. The figure also shows the MC_L 'curve' at the current market wage W_e.

Profits are maximised at an employment level of Q_e, where MC_L (i.e. W) = MRP_L. Why? At levels of employment below Q_e, MRP_L exceeds MC_L. The firm will increase profits by employing more labour. At levels of employment above Q_e, MC_L exceeds MRP_L. In this case the firm will increase profits by reducing employment.

Derivation of the firm's demand curve for labour

No matter what the wage rate is, the quantity of labour demanded will be found from the intersection of W and MRP_L (see Figure 8.4). At a wage rate of W_1, Q_1 labour is demanded (point *a*); at W_2, Q_2 is demanded (point *b*); at W_3, Q_3 is demanded (point *c*).

Thus the MRP_L curve shows the quantity of labour employed at each wage rate. But this is just what the demand curve for labour shows. Thus the MRP_L curve is the demand curve for labour.

There are three determinants of the demand for labour:

■ The wage rate. This determines the position *on* the demand curve. (Strictly speaking, we would refer here to the wage determining the 'quantity demanded' rather than the 'demand'.)

■ The productivity of labour (MPP_L). This determines the position *of* the demand curve.

■ The demand for the good. The higher the market demand for the good, the higher will be its market price, and hence the higher will be the MR, and thus the MRP_L. This too determines the position of the demand curve. It shows

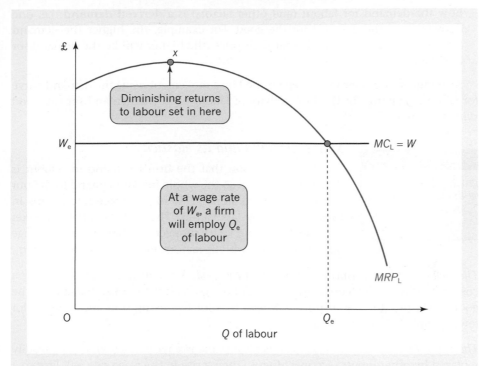

Figure 8.3   The profit-maximising level of employment

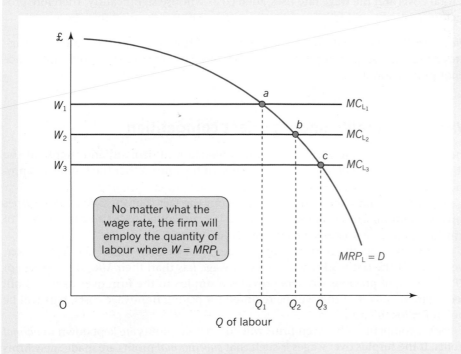

Figure 8.4   Deriving the firm's demand curve for labour

how the demand for labour (and other factors) is a **derived demand**: i.e. one derived from the demand for the good. For example, the higher the demand for houses, and hence the higher their price, the higher will be the demand for bricklayers.

A change in the wage rate is represented by a movement *along* the demand curve for labour. A change in the productivity of labour or in the demand for the good *shifts* the curve.

Market demand and its elasticity

For the same reason that the firm's demand for labour is downward sloping, so the whole market demand for labour will be downward sloping. At higher wage rates, firms in total will employ less labour. The *elasticity* of this market demand for labour (with respect to changes in the wage rate) depends on various factors. Elasticity will be greater:

The greater the price elasticity of demand for the good. A rise in the wage rate, being a cost of production, will drive up the price of the good. If the market demand for the good is elastic, this rise in price will lead to a lot less being sold and hence a lot fewer people being employed.

The easier it is to substitute labour for other inputs and vice versa. If labour can be readily replaced by other inputs (e.g. machinery), then a rise in the wage rate will lead to a large reduction in labour as workers are replaced by these other inputs.

The greater the wage cost as a proportion of total costs. If wages are a large proportion of total costs and the wage rate rises, total costs will rise significantly; therefore production and sales will fall significantly, and so will the demand for labour.

The longer the time period. Given sufficient time, firms can respond to a rise in wage rates by reorganising their production processes. For example they could introduce robot production lines.

Wages and profits under perfect competition

The wage rate (W) is determined by the interaction of demand and supply in the labour market. This will be equal to the value of the output that the last person produces (MRP_L).

Profits to the individual firm will arise from the fact that the MRP_L curve slopes downward (diminishing returns). Thus the last worker adds less to the revenue of firms than previous workers already employed.

If *all* workers in the firm receive a wage equal to the *MRP* of the *last* worker, everyone but the last worker will receive a wage *less* than their *MRP*. This excess of MRP_L over W of previous workers provides a surplus to the firm over its wages bill (see Figure 8.5). Part of this will be required for paying non-wage costs; part will be the profits for the firm.

Perfect competition between firms will ensure that profits are kept down to *normal* profits. If the surplus over wages is such that *supernormal* profits are made, new firms will enter the industry. The price of the good (and hence MRP_L) will fall, and the wage will be bid up, until only normal profits remain.

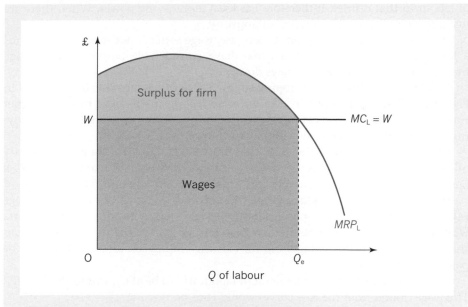

Figure 8.5   Wages and a firm's surplus over wages

Recap

- Wages in a competitive labour market are determined by the interaction of demand and supply. The market supply of labour in any labour market is likely to be upward sloping.

- The elasticity of labour supply will depend largely upon the geographical and occupational mobility of labour. The more readily labour can transfer between jobs and regions, the more elastic the supply.

- The demand for labour is traditionally assumed to be based upon labour's productivity. Marginal productivity theory assumes that the employer will demand labour up to the point where the cost of employing one additional worker (MC_L) is equal to the revenue earned from the output of that worker (MRP_L). The firm's demand curve for labour is its MRP_L curve.

- The elasticity of demand for labour is determined by: the price elasticity of demand for the good that labour produces; the substitutability of labour for other factors; the proportion of wages to total costs; and time.

Power in the labour market   8.3

Firms with power

In the real world, many firms have the power to influence wage rates: they are not wage takers. This is one of the major types of labour market 'imperfection'.

When a firm is the only employer of a particular type of labour, this situation is called a **monopsony**. The Post Office used to be a monopsony employer of postal workers. Another example is when a factory is the only employer of certain types

of labour in that district. It therefore has local monopsony power. When there are
just a few employers, this is called **oligopsony**.

Monopsonists (and oligopsonists too) are 'wage setters', not 'wage takers'. Thus
a large employer in a small town may have considerable power to resist wage
increases or even to force wage rates down.

Such firms face an upward-sloping supply curve of labour. This is illustrated in
Figure 8.6. If the firm wants to take on more labour, it will have to pay a higher
wage rate to attract workers away from other industries. But conversely, by employing less labour it can get away with paying a lower wage rate.

The supply curve shows the wage that must be paid to attract a given quantity
of labour. The wage it pays is the *average cost* to the firm of employing labour (AC_L):
i.e. the cost per worker. The supply curve is also therefore the AC_L curve.

The *marginal* cost of employing one more worker (MC_L) will be above the wage
(AC_L): see Figure 8.6. The reason is that the wage rate has to be raised to attract extra
workers. The MC_L will thus be the new higher wage paid to the new employee *plus*
the small rise in the total wages bill for existing employees: after all, they will be
paid the higher wage too.

The profit-maximising employment of labour would be at Q_1, where $MC_L = MRP_L$.
The wage (found from the AC_L curve) would thus be W_1.

If this had been a perfectly competitive labour market, employment would
have been at the higher level Q_2, with the wage rate at the higher level W_2, where
$W = MRP_L$. What in effect the monopsonist is doing, therefore, is forcing the wage
rate down by restricting the number of workers employed.

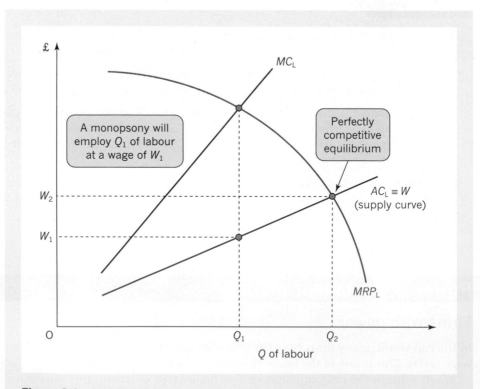

Figure 8.6 Monopsony

The role of trade unions

How can unions influence the determination of wages, and what might be the consequences of their actions?

The extent to which unions will succeed in pushing up wage rates depends on their power and militancy. It also depends on the power of firms to resist and on their ability to pay higher wages. In particular, the scope for unions to gain a better deal for their members depends on the sort of market in which the employers are producing.

Unions facing competitive employers

If the employers are producing in a highly competitive goods market, unions can raise wages only at the expense of employment. Firms are likely to be earning little more than normal profit. Thus if unions force up wages, the marginal firms will go bankrupt and leave the industry. Fewer workers will be employed. The fall in output will lead to higher prices. This will enable the remaining firms to pay a higher wage rate.

Figure 8.7 illustrates these effects. If unions force the wage rate up from W_1 to W_2, employment will fall from Q_1 to Q_2. There will be a surplus of people ($Q_3 - Q_2$) wishing to work in this industry for whom no jobs are available.

The union is in a doubly weak position. Not only will jobs be lost as a result of forcing up the wage rate, but also there is a danger that these unemployed people

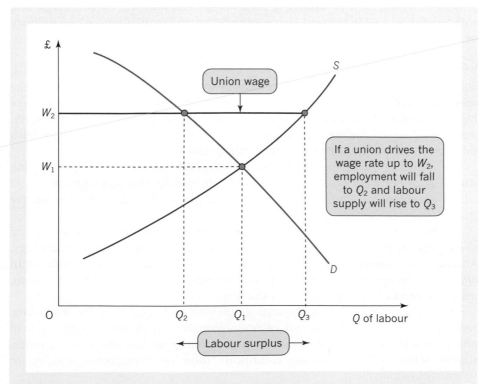

Figure 8.7   Monopoly union facing producers under perfect competition

could undercut the union wage, unless the union can prevent firms employing non-unionised labour.

In a competitive market, then, the union is faced with the choice between wages and jobs. Its actions will depend on its objectives.

Wages can be increased without a reduction in the level of employment only if, as part of the bargain, the productivity of labour is increased. This is called a **productivity deal**. The *MRP* curve, and hence the demand curve in Figure 8.7, shifts to the right.

Bilateral monopoly

What happens when a union monopoly faces a monopsony employer? What will the wage rate be? What will the level of employment be? Unfortunately, economic theory cannot give a precise answer to these questions. There is no 'equilibrium' level as such. Ultimately, the wage rate and level of employment will depend on the relative bargaining strengths and skills of unions and management.

Strange as it may seem, unions may be in a stronger position to make substantial gains for their members when they are facing a powerful employer. There is often considerable scope for them to increase wage rates *without* this leading to a reduction in employment, or even for them to increase both the wage rate *and* employment. The reason is that if firms have power in the *goods* market too, and are making supernormal profit, then there is scope for a powerful union to redistribute some of these profits to wages.

The actual wage rate under bilateral monopoly is usually determined through a process of negotiation or 'collective bargaining'. The outcome of this bargaining will depend on a wide range of factors, which vary substantially from one industry or firm to another.

Collective bargaining

Sometimes when unions and management negotiate, *both* sides can gain from the resulting agreement. For example, the introduction of new technology may allow higher wages, improved working conditions and higher profits. Usually, however, one side's gain is the other's loss. Higher wages mean lower profits. Either way, both sides will want to gain the maximum for themselves.

The outcome of the negotiations will depend on the relative bargaining strengths of both sides. In bargaining there are various threats or promises that either side can make. For these to be effective, of course, the other side must believe that they will be carried out.

Union *threats* might include strike action, **picketing**, **working to rule** or refusing to cooperate with management, for example in the introduction of new technology. Alternatively, in return for higher wages or better working conditions, unions might *offer* no strike agreements (or an informal promise not to take industrial action), increased productivity, reductions in the workforce or long-term deals over pay.

In turn, employers might threaten employees with plant closure, **lock-outs**, redundancies or the employment of non-union labour. Or they might offer, in return for lower wage increases, various 'perks' such as productivity bonuses, profit-sharing schemes, better working conditions, more overtime, better holidays or security of employment.

Strikes, lock-outs and other forms of industrial action impose costs on both unions and firms. Unions lose pay. Firms lose revenue. This is an example of a "prisoners' dilemma game" (see page 143). If played out, it will probably result in both sides losing. It is usually in both sides' interests, therefore, to settle by negotiation. Nevertheless, to gain the maximum advantage at the negotiations, each side must persuade the other that it will carry out its threats if pushed.

The approach described so far has essentially been one of confrontation. The alternative is for both sides to concentrate on increasing the total net income of the firm by cooperating on ways to increase efficiency or the quality of the product. This approach is more likely when unions and management have built up an atmosphere of trust over time.

Recap

■ In an imperfect labour market, where a business has monopoly power in employing labour, it is known as a monopsonist. Such a firm will employ workers to the point where $MRP_L = MC_L$. Since the wage is below the MC_L, the monopsonist, other things being equal, will employ fewer workers at a lower wage than would be employed in a perfectly competitive labour market.

■ If a union has monopoly power, its power to raise wages will be limited if the employer operates in a highly competitive goods market. A rise in wage rates will force the employer to cut back on employment, unless there is a corresponding rise in productivity.

■ In a situation of bilateral monopoly (where a monopoly union faces a monopsony employer), the union may have considerable scope to raise wages above the monopsony level, without the employer wishing to reduce the level of employment. There is no unique equilibrium wage. The wage will depend on the outcome of a process of collective bargaining between union and management.

Minimum wages   8.4

Many countries have a statutory minimum wage that businesses must pay, including the UK since 1999. In 2007/08 the UK minimum wage was £5.52 for those aged 22 and over, £4.60 for those between 18 and 21 and £3.40 for those aged 16 and 17. In the same year the minimum wage was 53.8 per cent of the median hourly wage. In 1999, the year that the minimum wage was introduced, it was 45.6 per cent of the median.

Many businesses argue that having to pay such wages erodes profit and leads to a reduction in employment. Supporters argue that not only does a minimum wage help to reduce poverty among the low paid, but also it has little or no adverse effects on unemployment. Some go further. They argue that it can actually *increase* employment. Let us analyse the effects.

Minimum wages in a competitive labour market

In a competitive labour market, workers will be hired up to the point where the marginal revenue product of labour (MRP_L), i.e. the demand for labour, is equal to the marginal cost of labour (MC_L), which gives the supply curve. Referring back to Figure 8.7 on page 227, the free-market equilibrium wage is W_1 in this particular industry and the level of employment is Q_1. A national minimum wage, set at W_2, will reduce the level of employment to Q_2 and increase the supply of labour to Q_3, thereby creating unemployment of the amount $Q_3 - Q_2$.

The level of unemployment created as a result of the national minimum wage will be determined not only by the level of the minimum wage, but also by the elasticity of labour demand and supply. The more elastic the demand and supply of labour, the bigger the unemployment effect will be. Evidence suggests that the demand for low-skilled workers by any given employer is likely to be relatively wage sensitive. The most likely reason for this is that many of the goods or services produced by low-paid workers are very price sensitive, the firms frequently operating in very competitive markets. If one firm alone raised its prices, it might well lose a considerable number of sales.

But with minimum wage legislation applying to *all* firms, if all the firms in an industry or sector put up their prices, demand for any one firm would fall much less. Here the problem of consumers switching away from a firm's products, and hence of that firm being forced to reduce its workforce, would mainly occur (a) if there were cheaper competitor products from abroad or (b) if other firms produced the products with more capital-intensive techniques, involving fewer workers to whom the minimum wage legislation applied.

Minimum wages and monopsony employers

In an imperfect labour market where the employer has some influence over rates of pay, the impact of the national minimum wage on levels of employment is even less clear cut.

The situation is illustrated in Figure 8.8 (which is similar to Figure 8.6 on page 226). With no minimum wage a monopsonistic employer will employ Q_1 workers: where the MC_L is equal to MRP_L. At this point the firm is maximising its return from the labour it employs. Remember that the MC_L curve lies above the supply of labour curve (AC_L), since the additional cost of employing one more unit of labour involves paying all existing employees the new wage. The wage rate paid by the monopsonist will be W_1.

If the minimum wage is set at W_2, the level of employment within the firm is likely to grow! Why should this be so? The reason is that the minimum wage cannot be bid down by the monopsonist cutting back on its workforce. The minimum wage rate is thus both the new AC_L and also the new MC_L: employers will thus choose to employ Q_1 workers, where $MRP_L =$ (the new) MC_L. Thus the imposition of a minimum wage rate has *increased* the level of employment.

Clearly, if the minimum wage rate were very high, then, other things being equal, the level of employment would fall. This would occur in Figure 8.8 if the minimum wage rate were above W_3. Employment would be below Q_1. But even this argument is not clear cut, given that (a) a higher wage rate may increase labour productivity by improving worker motivation and (b) other firms, with which the firm might compete in the product market, will also be faced with paying the higher minimum wage rate. The resulting rise in prices is likely to shift the MRP_L curve to the right.

On the other hand, to the extent that the imposition of a minimum wage rate reduces a firm's profits, this may lead it to cut down on investment, which may threaten long-term employment prospects.

Pause for thought

If a rise in the minimum wage causes employers to substitute machines for workers, will this necessarily lead to higher unemployment?

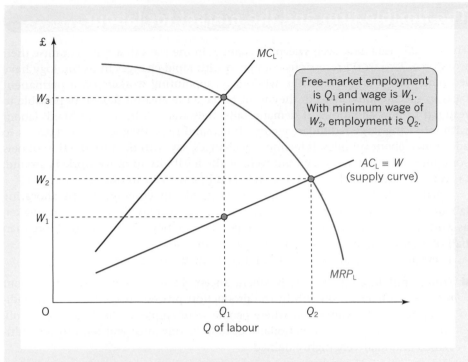

Figure 8.8   Minimum wage with a monopsony employer

Evidence on the effect of minimum wages

Which of the views concerning the effects of a national minimum wage are we to believe? Evidence from the USA and other countries suggests that modest increases in the minimum wage have had a neutral effect upon employment. Similarly in the UK, there is little evidence to suggest that employers have responded by employing fewer workers. In fact, unemployment rates have fallen. This, however, can be explained by a buoyant economy and increasing labour market flexibility (see section 8.5). Whether there would continue to be little effect if the minimum wage were to rise substantially is another matter! The issue, then, seems to be how *high* can the minimum wage be set before unemployment begins to rise.

Recap

- Statutory minimum wage rates have been adopted in many countries.

- In a perfect labour market, where employers are forced to accept the wage as determined by the market, any attempt to impose a minimum wage above this level will create unemployment. Amounts of additional unemployment are likely to be low, however, because the demand and supply of labour are relatively inelastic to changes in wage rates that apply to *all* firms.

- In an imperfect labour market, where an employer has some monopsonistic power, the impact of a minimum wage is uncertain. The impact will depend largely upon how much workers are currently paid below their *MRP* and whether a higher wage encourages them to work more productively.

8.5 The flexible firm and the market for labour

The past 25 years have seen sweeping changes in the ways that firms organise their workforce. Two world recessions combined with rapid changes in technology have led many firms to question the wisdom of appointing workers on a permanent basis to specific jobs. Instead, they want to have the greatest flexibility possible to respond to new situations. If demand falls, they want to be able to 'shed' labour without facing large redundancy costs. If demand rises, they want rapid access to additional labour supplies. If technology changes, say with the introduction of new computerised processes, they want to have the flexibility to move workers around, or to take on new workers in some areas and lose workers in others.

What many firms seek, therefore, is flexibility in employing and allocating labour. What countries are experiencing is an increasingly flexible labour market, as workers and employment agencies respond to the new 'flexible firm'. More than half of all firms today are using flexible forms of work.

There are three main types of flexibility in the use of labour:

■ **Functional flexibility.** This is where an employer is able to transfer labour between different tasks within the production process. It contrasts with traditional forms of organisation where people were employed to do a specific job, and then stuck to it. A functionally flexible labour force will tend to be multi-skilled and relatively highly trained.

■ **Numerical flexibility.** This is where the firm is able to adjust the size and composition of its workforce according to changing market conditions. To achieve this, the firm is likely to employ a large proportion of its labour on a part-time or casual basis, or even subcontract out specialist requirements, rather than employing such labour skills itself.

■ **Financial flexibility.** This is where the firm has flexibility in its wage costs. In large part it is a result of functional and numerical flexibility. Financial flexibility can be achieved by rewarding individual effort and productivity rather than paying a given rate for a particular job. Such rates of pay are increasingly negotiated at the local level rather than being nationally set. The result is not only a widening of pay differentials between skilled and unskilled workers, but also growing differentials in pay between workers within the same industry but in different parts of the country.

Figure 8.9 shows how these three forms of flexibility are reflected in the organisation of a **flexible firm**, an organisation quite different from that of the traditional firm. The most significant difference is that the labour force is segmented. The core group, drawn from the **primary labour market**, will be composed of *functionally* flexible workers, who have relatively secure employment and are generally on full-time permanent contracts. Such workers will be relatively well paid and receive wages reflecting their scarce skills.

The periphery, drawn from the **secondary labour market**, is more fragmented than the core, and can be subdivided into a first and a second peripheral group. The first peripheral group is composed of workers with a lower level of skill than those in the core, skills that tend to be general rather than firm specific. Thus workers in the first peripheral group can usually be drawn from the external labour market. Such workers may be employed on full-time contracts, but they will generally face less secure employment than those workers in the core.

Definitions

Functional flexibility
Where employers can switch workers from job to job as requirements change.

Numerical flexibility
Where employers can change the size of their workforce as their labour requirements change.

Financial flexibility
Where employers can vary their wage costs by changing the composition of their workforce or the terms on which workers are employed.

Flexible firm
A firm that has the flexibility to respond to changing market conditions by changing the composition of its workforce.

Primary labour market
The market for permanent full-time core workers.

Secondary labour market
The market for peripheral workers, usually employed on a temporary or part-time basis, or a less secure 'permanent' basis.

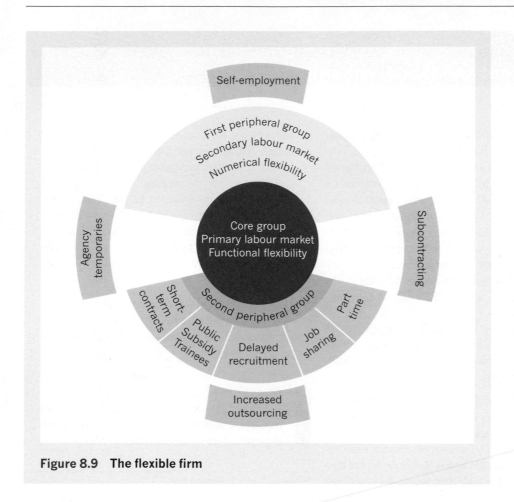

Figure 8.9   The flexible firm

The business gains a greater level of numerical flexibility by drawing labour from the second peripheral group. Here workers are employed on a variety of short-term, part-time contracts, often through a recruitment agency. Some of these workers may be working from home, or online from another country, such as India, where wage rates are much lower. Workers in the second peripheral group have little job security.

As well as supplementing the level of labour in the first peripheral group, the second periphery can also provide high-level specialist skills that supplement the core. In this instance the business can subcontract or hire self-employed labour, minimising its commitment to such workers. The business thereby gains both functional and numerical flexibility simultaneously.

> **Pause for thought**
>
> *How is the advent of flexible firms likely to alter the gender balance of employment and unemployment?*

The Japanese model

The application of new flexible working patterns is becoming more prevalent in businesses in the UK and elsewhere in Europe and North America. In Japan, flexibility has been part of the business way of life for many years and was crucial in shaping the country's economic success in the 1970s and 1980s. In fact we now talk of a Japanese model of business organisation, which many of its competitors seek to emulate.

Box 8.2

The Internet and labour mobility

Online flexibility

A firm may wish to be flexible, but is the labour market sufficiently flexible to meet the firm's needs?

It is all well and good a firm looking to expand employment in a prosperous period, but how will it find the individuals it needs, whether they be self-employed, subcontracted or added to the core labour group? This question becomes far more critical, the more highly skilled (and hence scarce) are the workers that the firm requires. Generally, it is the core/skilled workers that flexible firms find most difficulty in recruiting.

But the Internet is making the process much easier. The result is an increase in labour mobility and the speed with which jobs can be filled.

Employment agencies are increasingly using the Internet to match employers to job seekers. Agencies such as Reed, Manpower and Adecco have revolutionised the way in which people can search for jobs.

Paul Rapacioli is head of Reed Online, the Internet branch of the recruitment agency Reed. He says that '. . . People have been talking about labour market flexibility and mobility for years, but until recently the reality has been that a London-based worker prepared to work in Manchester has had to go up there and scout around.' Now, he says, the Internet can search the pool of jobs on offer across the country, identify suitable matches and automatically e-mail them to job-seekers, or send text messages to their mobile phones.

Economists say the behaviour of the whole labour market could be revolutionised by such developments. Professor Richard Layard, a leading labour market expert and government adviser at the London School of Economics, says the Internet could help bring a long-awaited improvement in the matching process between the unemployed and available jobs.[1]

The better the information on the jobs sites and the easier they are to use, the better the matching is likely to be and the more their use is likely to grow. Competition between these sites is aiding this process.

? Question

Explain how a firm's flexibility can be enhanced by online recruitment. What imperfection in information, for both employer and job seeker, still remains?

[1] *Financial Times*, 22 February 2000

The model is based around four principles:

- Total quality management (TQM). This involves all employees working towards continuously improving all aspects of quality, both of the finished product and of methods of production.

- Elimination of waste. According to the 'just-in-time' (JIT) principle, businesses should take delivery of just sufficient quantities of raw materials and parts, at the right time and place. Stocks are kept to a minimum and hence the whole system of production runs with little, if any, slack. For example, supermarkets today have smaller storerooms relative to the total shopping area than they did in the past, and take more frequent deliveries.

- A belief in the superiority of teamwork. Collective effort is a vital element in Japanese working practices. Teamwork is seen not only to enhance individual performance, but also to involve the individual in the running of the business and thus to create a sense of commitment.

- Functional and numerical flexibility. Both are seen as vital components in maintaining high levels of productivity.

The principles of this model are now widely accepted as being important in creating and maintaining a competitive business in a competitive marketplace.

Within the EU, the UK has been one of the most successful in cutting unemployment and creating jobs. Much of this has been attributed to increased labour market flexibility. As a result, other EU countries, such as Italy and Germany, are seeking to emulate many of the measures the UK has adopted.

Recap

- Changes in technology have had a massive impact upon the process of production and the experience of work. Labour markets and business organisations have become more flexible as a consequence.

- There are three major forms of flexibility: functional, numerical and financial. The flexible firm incorporates these different forms of flexibility into its business operations.

- It organises production around a core workforce, which it supplements with workers and skills drawn from a periphery. Peripheral workers tend to hold general skills rather than firm-specific skills, and are employed on part-time and temporary contracts.

- The application of the flexible firm model is closely mirrored in the practices of Japanese business. Commitments to improve quality, reduce waste, build teamwork and introduce flexible labour markets are seen as key components in the success of Japanese business organisation.

The labour market and incentives   8.6

Wages are a reward for labour. They are also, from a business perspective, a means of motivating the labour force. For example, the possibility of promotion to a post paying a higher wage can be a key incentive to employees to improve their performance. Another example is piece rates. This is where workers are paid according to the amount they produce. The more they produce, the higher their pay. Similarly a firm may pay commission to its sales force – as an incentive to sell more. Sometimes the firm will pay its senior executives bonuses related to company performance.

Because of the use of pay as a means of encouraging better performance by workers or management, firms will sometimes pay above the market rate. They pay what is known as an **efficiency wage rate**.

Efficiency wages

The **efficiency wage hypothesis** states that the productivity of workers rises as the wage rate rises. As a result, employers are frequently prepared to offer wage rates above the market-clearing level, attempting to balance increased wage costs against gains in productivity. But why may higher wage rates lead to higher productivity? There are three main explanations.

Less 'shirking'. In many jobs it is difficult to monitor the effort that individuals put into their work. In such cases piece rates or commission may be impracticable. Workers may thus get away with shirking or careless behaviour.

The business could attempt to reduce shirking by imposing a series of sanctions, the most serious of which would be dismissal. The greater the wage rate currently received, the greater will be the cost to the individual of dismissal, and the less likely it is that workers will shirk. The business will benefit not only from the additional output, but also from a reduction in the costs of having to monitor workers' performance. As a consequence, the efficiency wage rate for the business will lie above the market-determined wage rate.

Reduced labour turnover. If workers receive on-the-job training or retraining, then to lose a worker once the training has been completed is a significant cost to the business. Labour turnover, and hence its associated costs, can be reduced by paying a wage above the market-clearing rate. By paying such a wage, the business is seeking a degree of loyalty from its employees.

Morale. A simple reason for offering wage rates above the market-clearing level is to motivate the workforce – to create the feeling that the firm is a 'good' employer that cares about its employees. As a consequence, workers might be more industrious and more willing to accept the introduction of new technology (with the reorganisation that it involves).

> **Pause for thought**
>
> *Give some examples of things an employer could do to increase the morale of the workforce other than raising wages. How would you assess whether they were in the interests of the employer?*

The paying of efficiency wages above the market-clearing wage will depend upon the type of work involved. Workers who occupy skilled positions, especially where the business has invested time in their training (thus making them costly to replace), are likely to receive efficiency wages considerably above the market wage. By contrast, workers in unskilled positions, where shirking can be easily monitored, little training takes place and workers can be easily replaced, are unlikely to command an 'efficiency wage premium'. In such situations, rather than keeping wage rates high, the business will probably try to pay as little as possible.

Principal–agent relationships in the labour market

The need to pay efficiency wages above the market rate is an example of the principal–agent problem (see page 10). The worker, as an agent of the employer (the principal), is not necessarily going to act in the principal's interest.

At the time when people are interviewed for a job, they will clearly be keen to make a good impression on their potential employer and may promise all sorts of things. Once employed, however, a 'moral hazard' occurs (see pages 71–2) – workers will be tempted to take it easy. The principal (the firm) will therefore attempt to prevent this occurring. One solution, as we have seen, is to pay an efficiency wage. Another is to tighten up on job monitoring by managers. For example, regular performance appraisal could be instituted, with sanctions imposed on workers who underperform. Such sanctions could range from support in the form of additional training to penalties in the form of closer monitoring, lost pay, lost bonuses or even dismissal. Another solution is to offer rewards for good performance in the form of bonuses or promotion.

> **Pause for thought**
>
> *Does a moral hazard apply to employers as well as workers? If so, how might it affect employers' behaviour?*

In general, however, the poorer the information on the part of the principal (the greater the 'information asymmetry'), the more the employee will be able to get away with.

There is also an 'adverse selection' problem for the employer (see pages 71–2). The most able workers are those most likely to leave for a better job elsewhere. The workers who select to stay are likely to be the least able. To counter this problem, the employer might need to be willing to promote people to more senior posts to encourage them to stay.

Executive pay

There has been much resentment in recent years over the huge pay increases received by top managers. Up to the mid-1980s, the median pay of US executives was some 30 times higher than average wages. By 2000, the figure had soared to 120 times. Although it fell somewhat with the slowdown of the economy in 2001–03, it has risen back above that level since.

The picture is very similar in the UK. In 2007, the average remuneration for chief executives in the biggest companies was over £2.8 million, some 120 times the wage of the average worker. Pay rises for these top earners have been averaging around 25 per cent per annum. This compares with just 4 per cent for the average worker.

The nature of executive awards. For the top earners, salaries account for a relatively small percentage. Incentives and bonuses often considerably outstrip basic salaries. Incentives are normally related to company performance, such as profit or turnover (revenue). Bonuses, however, are given retrospectively and are often unrelated to performance. They are often given even when the company is underperforming.

Then there are shares and **share options**. These are normally given as a longer-term incentive. In the case of shares, these must be held for a period of time (say three years) before they can be cashed in. In the case of share options, the option is for the executive to buy shares at a price set when the option is granted, even though the current market price might be considerably higher. The argument is that both shares and share options give the executive an incentive to ensure that the company performs well and its share price rises as a result.

In addition to these rewards, top executives often receive generous pensions and large severance pay when they leave.

Incentive effects? So do these huge increases represent the necessary incentives and rewards for those leading industrial growth and taking risks? Or are they the result of market imperfections, where greedy executives can persuade complicit company boards of directors to give them what they want? Are they a sign of poor governance of industry?

> Extraordinary pay for great performance is fine, it is routinely said. But many executives have been paid a fortune for presiding over mediocrity. The Corporate Library, an American corporate-governance consultancy, last year [2006] identified 11 large and well known but poorly governed companies, including AT&T, Merck and Time Warner, where the chief executive had been paid at least $15m a year for two successive years even as the company's shares had underperformed. Robert Nardelli received a $210m pay-off when he lost his job earlier this month even though the shares of his company, Home Depot, fell slightly during his six years in charge. Carly Fiorina, ejected from Hewlett-Packard almost $180m better off – including a severance payment of $21.6m – after a

Definition
Share (or stock) options
The right to buy shares in the future at a fixed price set today. When granted to senior executives as a reward they do not involve any outlay by the company. They act as an incentive, however, since the better the company performs, the more the market value of its shares is likely to rise above the option price and the more the executive stands to gain by exercising the option to buy shares at the fixed price and then selling them at the market price.

Box 8.3

The market for talent

The price of brainpower

More and more companies are seeing talent as a key to their success.

Obsession with talent is no longer confined to blue-chip companies such as Goldman Sachs and General Electric. It can be found everywhere in the corporate world, from credit-card companies to hotel chains to the retail trade. Many firms reckon that they have pushed re-engineering and automation as hard as they can. Now they must raise productivity by managing talent better.

. . . When the Corporate Executive Board (CEB), a provider of business research and executive education based in Washington, DC, recently conducted an international poll of senior human-resources managers, three-quarters of them said that 'attracting and retaining' talent was their number one priority. Some 62% worried about company-wide talent shortages. The CEB also surveyed some 4000 hiring managers in more than 30 companies, and was told that the average quality of candidates had declined by 10% since 2004 and the average time to fill a vacancy had increased from 37 days to 51 days.[1]

But while hiring talented staff may be a necessary condition for success, it doesn't guarantee it. One problem is that talented staff may be very ambitious and are likely to be more concerned with their own careers than the long-term interests of their employers. There is a 'moral hazard' here (see pages 71–2). The firm may invest a lot of time and expense in training talented workers, only to see them leave for another job. In other words, employing a person does not guarantee a commitment on their part to stay. Such people are often sought out by other companies, which may use 'head hunting' agencies to find and recruit them.

Then there are the ethics of a number of these employees. There have been some spectacular cases of greed and malpractice in recent years, where accounting fraud has allowed some staff to get rich at the expense of customers and shareholders.

The most famous case was that of Enron. Not many companies come bigger than Enron, and none bigger has ever filed for bankruptcy, as Enron did on 1 December 2001. The company seemed to have everything going for it, being the largest energy trader in the USA with 25 per cent of the market. 'It recruited the best and the brightest, hiring up to 250 MBAs a year at the height of its fame.'[2] In 2000, Enron earned $100 billion in revenue and turned a profit of $1 billion. But by the time it filed for bankruptcy, the seventh largest company in the USA had seen its market value collapse from $80 billion to less than $400 million.

At the centre of this collapse was the greed and malpractices of some of its senior staff and its auditors, the accountancy firm

lacklustre tenure as chief executive, let it be known in her autobiography that money was not important to her. Not everyone believed her.[1]

As far as genuine incentive schemes are concerned, they may indeed encourage risk taking and good performance. High remuneration may be necessary in some cases to attract the right talent and persuade them to stay. Generous bonuses for executives of poorly performing companies, however, clearly have the opposite effect – as do generous severance packages for executives leaving early.

Then there are the incentives for workers. If they feel that their senior managers' pay is unjustified, this can breed resentment and harm industrial relations.

Ultimately, businesses function with the blessing of workers, shareholders, customers and voters. If business leaders are universally seen as immoral and grasping, cynicism and mistrust will flourish and choke enterprise.[2]

[1] 'In the money', *The Economist*, 18 January 2007
[2] *Ibid.*

Arthur Andersen. Through an accounting loophole Enron had been overstating its earnings since 1997 to the value of some $600 million. When they realised the end was in sight, many of the senior executives made massive gains by selling their shares before the company's problems became public knowledge and before the share price collapsed.

Clearly there is more to good management than hiring the best and the brightest. Among other things, it requires rewarding experience as well as talent, and applying strong ethical codes and internal controls. Indeed, talent-intensive businesses have a particular interest in maintaining high ethical standards. Whereas in manufacturing industries a decline in such standards is often slow, in talent-intensive ones it can be terrifyingly sudden, as Arthur Andersen and Enron found to their cost.[3]

Managing talent

Talent is a vital ingredient for many companies in the rapidly changing business environment in which they operate. It is something, however, that needs to be tamed and harnessed with the right incentives and careful monitoring. So what can be done to avoid the pitfalls?

One solution is to allow talented people to play to their strengths. This means carefully structuring jobs so that people feel challenged and valued and use their particular talents to the full. Another is to provide training schemes so that people's talents can be further developed. Another is for new recruits to work on projects that are seen as central to the success of the organisation. This helps make the recruits feel like insiders rather than as people merely hired for a particular skill.

Finally, companies should develop opportunities for promotions and transfers within the organisation. This can allow people to further their careers while at the same time developing a greater sense of loyalty to the company.

? Questions

1. How would you attempt to measure the marginal productivity of a person hired for a specific talent?
2. Why might companies be wise to pay talented people more than the value of their marginal product?

[1] 'The battle for brainpower', *The Economist*, 5 October 2006
[2] *Ibid.*
[3] *Ibid.*

Recap

- The efficiency wage hypothesis states that a business is likely to pay a wage above the market-clearing rate in order to: reduce shirking; reduce labour turnover; and stimulate worker morale.

- Employment is an example of a principal–agent relationship. Workers (the agents) may underperform as a result of lack of information on their performance by their employer (the principal). To combat this problem, employers may link pay more closely with output or monitor the performance of workers more closely.

- Executive pay has risen much more rapidly than average pay. In addition to high salaries, many senior managers receive considerable bonuses, shares, share options and other perks. High pay may be necessary to act as an incentive for risk taking and to attract high calibre people. It is also often, however, a reflection of poor governance at the top of industry and in many cases is unrelated to performance.

QUESTIONS

1. If a firm faces a shortage of workers with very specific skills, it may decide to undertake the necessary training itself. If on the other hand it faces a shortage of unskilled workers it may well offer a small wage increase in order to obtain the extra labour. In the first case it is responding to an increase in demand for labour by attempting to shift the supply curve. In the second case it is merely allowing a movement along the supply curve. Use a demand and supply diagram to illustrate each case. Given that elasticity of supply is different in each case, do you think that these are the best policies for the firm to follow?

2. The wage rate a firm has to pay and the output it can produce varies with the number of workers as follows (all figures are hourly):

Number of workers	1	2	3	4	5	6	7	8
Wage rate (AC_L) (£)	3	4	5	6	7	8	9	10
Total output (TPP_L)	10	22	32	40	46	50	52	52

Assume that output sells at £2 per unit.

(a) Copy the table and add additional rows for TC_L, MC_L, TRP_L and MRP_L. Put the figures for MC_L and MRP_L in the spaces between the columns.

(b) How many workers will the firm employ in order to maximise profits?

(c) What will be its hourly wage bill at this level of employment?

(d) How much hourly revenue will it earn at this level of employment?

(e) Assuming that the firm faces other (fixed) costs of £30 per hour, how much hourly profit will it make?

(f) Assume that the workers now form a union and that the firm agrees to pay the negotiated wage rate to all employees. What is the maximum to which the hourly wage rate could rise without causing the firm to try to reduce employment below that in (b) above? (See Figures 8.6 and 8.8.)

(g) What would be the firm's hourly profit now?

3. For what types of reason does the marginal revenue product differ between workers in different jobs?

4. If, unlike a perfectly competitive employer, a monopsonist has to pay a higher wage to attract more workers, why, other things being equal, will a monopsonist pay a lower wage than a perfectly competitive employer?

5. The following are figures for a monopsonist employer:

Number of workers (1)	Wage rate (£) (2)	Total cost of labour (£) (3)	Marginal cost of labour (£) (4)	Marginal revenue product (£) (5)
1	100	100		230
2	105	210	110	240
3	110	230	120	240
4	115			230
5	120			210
6	125			190
7	130			170
8	135			150
9	140			130
10	145			

Fill in the missing figures for columns (3) and (4). How many workers should the firm employ if it wishes to maximise profits?

6. To what extent could a trade union succeed in gaining a pay increase from an employer with no loss in employment?

7. Do any of the following contradict the theory that the demand for labour equals the marginal revenue product: wage scales related to length of service (incremental scales), nationally negotiated wage rates, discrimination, firms taking that lead from other firms in determining this year's pay increase?

8. What is the efficiency wage hypothesis? Explain what employers might gain from paying wages above the market-clearing level.

9. 'Statutory minimum wages will cause unemployment.' Is this so?

10. Identify the potential costs and benefits of the flexible firm to (a) employers and (b) employees.

Business issues covered in this chapter

- To what extent does business meet the interests of consumers and society in general?

- In what sense are perfect markets 'socially efficient' and why do most markets fail to achieve social efficiency?

- How do business ethics influence business behaviour?

- In what ways do governments intervene in markets and attempt to influence business behaviour?

- What forms do government environmental policies take, and how do they affect business?

- How does the government attempt to prevent both the abuse of monopoly power and collusion by oligopolists?

- How are privatised industries regulated and how has competition been increased in these industries?

Chapter map

CHAPTER 9

Government, the firm and the market

Despite the fact that most countries today can be classified as 'market economies', governments nevertheless intervene substantially in the activities of business in order to protect the interests of consumers, workers or the environment.

Firms might collude to fix prices, use misleading advertising, create pollution, produce unsafe products, or use unacceptable employment practices. In such cases, government is expected to intervene to correct for the failings of the market system: e.g. by outlawing collusion, by establishing advertising standards, by taxing or otherwise penalising polluting firms, by imposing safety standards on firms' behaviour and products, or by protecting employment rights.

In this chapter we examine the ways in which markets might fail to protect people's interests, whether as consumers or simply as members of society. We also look at the different types of policy the government can adopt to correct these 'market failures'.

9.1 Market failures

Markets and social objectives

One of the key arguments for government intervention in the behaviour of business is that, if left to its own devices, the private enterprise system will fail to achieve 'social efficiency'.

So what is meant by social efficiency? If the extra benefits to society – or **marginal social benefit** (*MSB*) – of producing more of any given good or service exceed the extra costs to society – or **marginal social cost** (*MSC*) – then it is said to be socially efficient to produce more. For example, if people's gains from having additional motorways exceed *all* the additional costs to society (both financial and non-financial) then it is socially efficient to construct more motorways.

If, however, the marginal social cost of producing more of any good or service exceeds the marginal social benefit, then it is socially efficient to produce less.

It follows that if the marginal social benefit of any activity is equal to the marginal social cost, then the current level is the optimum. To summarise: for **social efficiency** in the production of any good or service:

$$MSB > MSC \rightarrow \text{produce more}$$

$$MSC > MSB \rightarrow \text{produce less}$$

$$MSB = MSC \rightarrow \text{keep production at its current level}$$

Similar rules apply to consumption. For example, if the marginal social benefit of consuming more of any good or service exceeds the marginal social cost, then society would benefit from more of the good being consumed.

Social efficiency.
This is achieved where no further net social gain can be made by producing more or less of a good. This will occur where marginal social benefit equals marginal social cost.

Key Idea 23

In the real world, the market rarely leads to social efficiency: the marginal social benefits from the production of most goods and services do not equal the marginal social costs. In this section we examine why the free market fails to lead to social efficiency and what the government can do to rectify the situation.

Types of market failure

Externalities

The market will not lead to social efficiency if the actions of producers or consumers affect people *other than themselves*. These effects on other people are known as **externalities**: they are the side-effects, or 'third-party' effects, of production or consumption. Externalities can be either desirable or undesirable. Whenever other people are affected beneficially, there are said to be **external benefits**. Whenever other people are affected adversely, there are said to be **external costs**.

Externalities are spillover costs or benefits.
Where these exist, even an otherwise perfect market will fail to achieve social efficiency.

Key Idea 24

Thus the full cost to society (the **social cost**) of the production of any good or service is the private cost faced by firms plus any externalities of production (positive or negative). Likewise the full benefit to society (the **social benefit**) from the consumption of any good is the private benefit enjoyed by consumers plus any externalities of consumption (positive or negative).

External costs produced by business. Let us take the case of a chemical firm that dumps waste in a river or pollutes the air. In such a case, the community bears costs additional to those borne by the firm. The marginal social cost (*MSC*) of chemical production exceeds the marginal private cost (*MC*). Diagrammatically, the *MSC* curve is above the *MC* curve. This is shown in Figure 9.1, which assumes that the firm in other respects is operating in a perfect market, and is therefore a price taker (i.e. faces a horizontal demand curve).

The firm maximises profits at Q_1: the output where marginal cost equals price (see section 4.4 on page 112). The price is what people buying the good are prepared to pay for one more unit (if it wasn't they wouldn't buy it) and therefore reflects their marginal benefit. We assume no externalities from consumption, and therefore the marginal benefit to consumers is the same as the marginal *social* benefit (*MSB*).

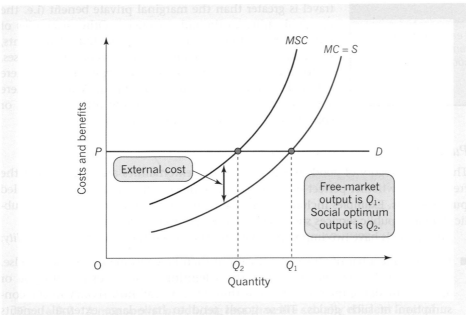

Figure 9.1   External costs of production

The socially optimum output would be Q_2, where P (i.e. MSB) = MSC. The firm, however, produces Q_1, which is more than the optimum. Thus external costs lead to *overproduction* from society's point of view.

The problem of external costs arises in a free-market economy because no one has legal ownership of the air or rivers and no one, therefore, can prevent or charge for their use as a dump for waste. Such a 'market' is missing. Control must, therefore, be left to the government or local authorities.

Other examples of firms producing external costs include extensive farming that destroys hedgerows and wildlife, acid rain caused by smoke from coal-fired power stations, nuclear waste from nuclear power stations and global warming from carbon emissions.

Other examples of externalities. Sometimes firms' actions *benefit* people other than consumers. An example is research and development. If other firms have access to the results of the research, then clearly the benefits extend beyond the firm that finances it. Since the firm only receives the private benefits, it will conduct a less than optimal amount of research. Similarly, a forestry company planting new woodlands will not take into account the beneficial effect on the atmosphere.

Externalities occur in consumption too. For example, when people use their cars, other people suffer from their exhaust, the added congestion, the noise, etc. These 'negative externalities' make the marginal social benefit of using cars less than the marginal private benefit (i.e. marginal utility to the car user). Other examples of negative externalities of consumption include noisy radios in public places, the smoke from cigarettes, and litter.

Consumption externalities could be positive. For example, when people travel by train rather than by car, other people benefit by there being less congestion and exhaust and fewer accidents on the roads. Thus the marginal social benefit of rail

Many economic decisions are based on expected future conditions. Since the future can never be known for certain, many decisions will be taken that later turn out to be wrong.

Protecting people's interests

Definition

Merit goods
Goods which the government feels that people will underconsume and which therefore ought to be subsidised or provided free.

The government may feel that people need protecting from poor economic decisions that they make on their own behalf. It may feel that in a free market people will consume too many harmful things. Thus if the government wants to discourage smoking and drinking, it can put taxes on tobacco and alcohol. In more extreme cases it could make various activities illegal: activities such as prostitution, certain types of gambling, and the sale and consumption of drugs.

On the other hand, the government may feel that people consume too little of things that are good for them: things such as education, health care and sports facilities. Such goods are known as **merit goods**. The government could either provide them free or subsidise their production.

Recap

- Social efficiency is achieved where $MSC = MSB$ for each good and service. In practice, however, markets will fail to achieve social efficiency. This provides a justification for government intervention in the market.

- Externalities are spillover costs or benefits. Whenever there are external costs, the market will (other things being equal) lead to a level of production and consumption above the socially efficient level. Whenever there are external benefits, the market will (other things being equal) lead to a level of production and consumption below the socially efficient level.

- Public goods will not be provided by the market. The problem is that they have large external benefits relative to private benefits, and without government intervention it would not be possible to prevent people having a 'free ride', thereby making it unprofitable to supply.

- Monopoly power will (other things being equal) lead to a level of output below the socially efficient level.

- Ignorance and uncertainty may prevent people and firms from consuming or producing at the levels they would otherwise choose.

- In a free market there may be inadequate provision for dependants and an inadequate output of merit goods.

9.2 Business ethics and corporate social responsibility

It is often assumed that firms are simply concerned to maximise profits: that they are not concerned with broader issues of **corporate social responsibility**. Indeed, many forms of market failure can be attributed directly to business practices that could not be classified as 'socially responsible': advertising campaigns that seek to misinform, or in some way deceive the consumer; monopoly producers exploiting their monopoly position through charging excessively high prices; the conscious decision to ignore water and air pollution limits, knowing that the chances of being caught are slim.

Changing business attitudes?

To some extent, however, the role of modern business has changed, and society expects business to adhere to certain moral and social principles. Indeed, social responsibility is a key component in many companies' **business ethics**.

Modern businesses often see themselves as more than economic institutions, as they are actively involved in society's social, political and legal environments. As such, all businesses are responsible not only to their shareholders but to all **stake-holders**. Stakeholders are all those affected by the business's operations: not only shareholders, but workers, customers, suppliers, creditors and people living in the neighbourhood. Given the far-reaching environmental effects of many businesses, stakeholding might extend to the whole of society.

In many top corporations, **environmental scanning** is now an integral part of the planning process. This involves the business surveying changing social and political trends in order to remain in tune with consumer concerns. For example, the general public's growing concern over 'green' issues has significantly influenced many businesses' product development programmes and R&D strategies. The more successful a business is in being able to associate the image of 'environmentally friendly' to a particular product or brand, the more likely it is to enhance its sales or establish a measure of brand loyalty, and thereby to strengthen its competitive position.

Several companies in recent years have made great play of their social respons-ibility. In 2007, Marks and Spencer launched its 'Plan A'. 'Plan A is our five-year, 100-point plan to tackle some of the biggest challenges facing our business and our world. It will see us working with our customers and our suppliers to combat cli-mate change, reduce waste, safeguard natural resources, trade ethically and build a healthier nation. We're doing this because it's what you want us to do. It's also the right thing to do. We're calling it Plan A because we believe it's now the only way to do business.'[1]

In the very same week that M&S launched Plan A, Tesco unveiled its plans to cut carbon emissions from existing stores worldwide by at least 50 per cent by 2020 and to make the reduction of its car-bon footprint 'a central business driver'. To help achieve this, it was commissioning independent research to map the total carbon footprint of its activities across the world. It would also encourage people to buy environmentally friendly products, with more special offers and more of such products in the value range. It was also introducing a carbon labelling system for all its products to help con-sumers make greener choices.

> ### Pause for thought
>
> *Green taxes (e.g. on carbon emission) are designed to 'internalise' environmental externalities and thereby force firms to take such externalities into account in their decision making. Should such taxes be reduced for firms that adopt a more environmentally responsible approach?*

Social responsibility and profitability

Clearly, M&S, Tesco and the many other companies that are openly committed to sustainability and ethical practices hope that such policies will also improve their

---

Definitions

Corporate social responsibility
Where a business takes into account the interests and concerns of a community rather than just its shareholders.

Business ethics
The values and principles that shape business behaviour.

Stakeholder
An individual affected by the operations of a business.

Environmental scanning
Where a business surveys social and political trends in order to take account of changes in its decision-making process.

---

[1] http://www2.marksandspencer.com/thecompany/plana/index.shtml

Box 9.1

The Body Shop

Is it 'worth it'?

The Body Shop shot to fame in the 1980s. It stood for environmental awareness and an ethical approach to business. But its success had as much to do with what it sold as what it stood for. It sold natural cosmetics, Raspberry Ripple Bathing Bubbles and Camomile Shampoo, products that were immensely popular with consumers.

Its profits increased from a little over £1 million in 1985 to nearly £40 million in 2005/06. Sales, meanwhile, grew even more dramatically, from £4.9 million to £772 million in 2005/06. By 2007, Body Shop International had over 2100 stores worldwide.

What makes this success so remarkable is that The Body Shop did virtually no advertising. Its promotion stemmed largely from the activities and environmental campaigning of its founder Anita Roddick, and the company's uncompromising claims that it sold only 'green' products and conducted its business operations with high ethical standards. It actively supported green causes such as saving whales and protecting rainforests, and it refused to allow its products to be tested on animals. Perhaps most surprising in the world of big business was its high-profile initiative 'trade not aid', whereby it claimed to pay 'fair' prices for its ingredients, especially those supplied from people in developing countries, who were open to exploitation by large companies.

The growth strategy of The Body Shop, since its founding in 1976, has focused on developing a distinctive and highly innovative product range, and at the same time identifying such products with major social issues of the day, such as the environment and animal rights.

Its initial expansion was based on a process of franchising.

... franchising. We didn't know what it was, but all these women came to us and said, if you can do this and you can't even read a balance sheet, then we can do it. I had a cabal of female friends all around Brighton, Hove and Chichester, and they started opening little units, all called The Body Shop. I just supplied them with gallons of products – we only had 19 different products, but we made it look like more as we sold them in five different sizes![1]

In 1984 the company went public. In the 1990s, however, sales growth was less rapid and in 1998 Anita Roddick stepped down as Chief Executive, but for a while she and her husband remained as co-chairmen. In 2003 she was awarded in knighthood and became Dame Anita Roddick. More recently The Body Shop has experienced rapid growth once more. In 2005 it opened 120 new stores.

A more dramatic event, however, occurred in 2006 when The Body Shop was sold to the French cosmetics giant L'Oréal, which was 26 per cent owned by Nestlé. The event resulted in the magazine, *Ethical Consumer*, downgrading The Body Shop's ethical

profitability. As consumers become more concerned with such issues, so they are likely to favour such companies.

As we saw in Box 1.1 (page 4), Gap received bad press coverage over the poor employment conditions in its factories in developing countries. The company, clearly worried about its image and the effect on sales, was at pains to be seen to be addressing this issue.

A reputation for social responsibility may also help the firm in raising finance and attracting trading partners. Investment in ethically screened investment funds has grown rapidly in recent years. This has been driven not only by the demands of shareholders for ethical funds, but also by a realisation from investors generally that socially responsible business has the potential to be hugely profitable.

Socially responsible companies also may find it easier to recruit and hold on to their employees. In a number of surveys of graduate employment intentions, students have claimed that they would be prepared to take a lower salary in order to work for a business with high ethical standards and a commitment to socially responsible business practices.

rating from 11 out of 20 to a mere 2.5 and calling for a boycott of the company.

But perhaps people are unaware that l'Oréal has been subject to accusations of testing on animals and of being part of a price-fixing cartel of French perfume houses, or indeed that l'Oréal is part-owned by the Nestlé corporation, which in turn is subject to boycott campaigns for using child labour on African cocoa farms, promoting formula milk for babies rather than breast milk, and various other issues.

Body Shop founder Anita Roddick (who in the past has been a harsh critic of both l'Oréal's animal testing policies and of its attitude towards women) claims that the acquisition will help the cosmetics giant to develop more ethical practices, while the l'Oréal chief executive Sir Lindsay Owen-Jones commented 'We are just as convinced that it is urgent and important to put an end to all animal testing in the cosmetics industry.' And even animal rights campaigning group PETA have stated they believe that l'Oréal will learn a lot from the Body Shop.

. . . In the meantime, PR Week magazine has revealed that the Body Shop has short listed a number of PR agencies specifically to address such campaigns. Evidently there is concern over retaining its ethical image. It will be interesting to see if l'Oréal does produce such a timeframe and 'walk its talk' to use one of Anita Roddick's phrases; it would be good to think that l'Oréal might opt for more openness about its policies (to use their own slogan) 'because it's worth it'.[2]

After the takeover in 2006, Body Shop International, as it is now called, was keen to be seen as separate from its new parent company. In a statement the company claimed that 'Body Shop has the highest ethical standards, particularly when it comes to animal testing, and that is not going to change at all.'

Questions

1. What assumptions has The Body Shop made about the 'rational consumer'?
2. How has The Body Shop's economic performance been affected by its attitudes towards ethical issues? (You could do an Internet search to find further evidence about its performance and the effects of its sale to L'Oréal.)

---

[1] Anita Roddick interview, Startups.co.uk
[2] From Lee, C., 'Body Shop takeover – a bad day for animal welfare?', *Environment Channel*, 11 April 2006 (www.999today.com/environment/news/story/3022.html). Reproduced with permission.

Social responsibility appears not only to bring a range of benefits to business and society, but also to be generally profitable. It is likely to enhance business performance, strengthen brand image, reduce employee turnover and increase access to stock market funds. Box 9.1 gives an example of a company that has built its reputation of being socially and environmentally responsible – The Body Shop.

It is nevertheless the case that there are still many firms that care little about the social or natural environment. There is thus a strong case for government intervention to correct market failures.

Recap

■ Sometimes firms are not aggressive profit maximisers but, instead, take a more socially responsible approach to business.

■ Evidence suggests that economic performance is often enhanced as the corporate responsibility of firms grows.

9.3 Government intervention in the market

What forms does government intervention take? There are several policy instruments that the government can use. At one extreme, it can totally replace the market by providing goods and services itself. At the other extreme, it can merely seek to persuade producers, consumers or workers to act differently. Between the two extremes the government has a number of instruments it can use to change the way markets operate. The major ones are taxes, subsidies, laws and regulatory bodies.

Taxes and subsidies

When there are imperfections in the market, social efficiency will not be achieved. Marginal social benefit (*MSB*) will not equal marginal social cost (*MSC*). A different level of output would be more desirable.

Taxes and subsidies can be used to correct these imperfections. Essentially the approach is to tax those goods or activities where the market produces too much, and subsidise those where the market produces too little.

In section 9.4 we examine how taxes and subsidies can be used to achieve various environmental and social goals.

Legislation and regulation

Laws are frequently used to correct market imperfections. Laws can be of three main types: those that prohibit or regulate behaviour that imposes external costs, those that prevent firms providing false or misleading information, and those that prevent or regulate monopolies and oligopolies.

Rather than using the blunt weapon of general legislation to ban or restrict various activities, a more 'subtle' approach can be adopted. This involves the use of various regulatory bodies. Having identified possible cases where action might be required (e.g. potential cases of pollution, misleading information or the abuse of monopoly power), the regulatory body would probably conduct an investigation and then prepare a report containing its findings and recommendations. It might also have the power to enforce its decisions.

In the UK there are regulatory bodies for each of the major privatised utilities (see section 9.6). Another example is the Office of Fair Trading (OFT), which investigates and reports on suspected cases of anti-competitive practices. The OFT can order such firms to cease or modify these practices. Alternatively it can refer them to the Competition Commission (CC), which then conducts an investigation, and makes a ruling (see section 9.5).

Recap

■ Governments intervene in markets in a number of ways. One is the use of taxes to curb production or subsidies to increase it.

■ Another is to use legislation or regulation to encourage or force businesses to behave in a more socially desirable way.

Environmental policy 9.4

Growing concerns over global warming, acid rain, the depletion of the ozone layer, industrial and domestic waste, traffic fumes and other forms of pollution have made the protection of the environment a major political and economic issue. So what policy instruments are open to government to tackle the problems?

Green taxes and subsidies

Increasingly countries are introducing 'green' taxes in order to discourage pollution as goods are produced, consumed or disposed of.

Table 9.1 shows the range of green taxes used around the world. Such green taxes are highest in Scandinavia, reflecting the strength of their environmental concerns. In 2004, green taxes revenues accounted for 5.1 per cent of GDP in Denmark. Of the major industrialised countries, they are lowest in the USA, accounting for just 0.88 per cent of GDP in 2004.

By far the largest green tax revenues come from fuel taxes. Fuel taxes are relatively high in the UK and so, therefore, are green tax revenues, accounting for 2.65 per cent in 2004.

Choosing the tax rate

The rule here is simple: to achieve the socially efficient output of a polluting activity, the government should impose a tax equal to the marginal external cost (or grant a subsidy equal to the marginal external benefit).

Assume, for example, that a chemical works emits smoke from a chimney and thus pollutes the atmosphere. This creates external costs for the people who breathe

Table 9.1 Types of environmental taxes and charges

Motor fuels	Other goods	Air transport
Leaded/unleaded	Batteries	Noise charges
Diesel (quality differential)	Plastic carrier bags	Aviation fuels
Carbon/energy taxation	Glass containers	**Water**
Sulphur tax	Drink cans	Water charges
Other energy products	Tyres	Sewage charges
Carbon/energy tax	CFCs/halons	Water effluent charges
Sulphur tax or charge	Disposable razors/cameras	Manure charges
NO_2 charge	Lubricant oil charge	**Direct tax provisions**
Methane charge	Oil pollutant charge	Tax relief on green investment
Agricultural inputs	Solvents	Taxation on free company cars
Fertilisers	**Waste disposal**	Employer-paid commuting expenses taxable
Pesticides	Municipal waste charges	Employer-paid parking expenses taxable
Manure	Waste-disposal charges	Employer-paid parking expenses taxable
Vehicle-related taxation	Hazardous waste charges	Commuter use of public transport tax deductible
Sales tax depends on car size	Landfill tax or charges	
Road tax depends on car size	Duties on waste water	

Box 9.2

A Stern warning

It's much cheaper to act now on global warming than to wait

The analysis of global warming is not just for climate scientists. Economists have a major part to play in examining its causes and consequences and the possible solutions. And these solutions are likely to have a major impact on business.

Perhaps the most influential study of climate change in recent times has been the Stern Review. This was an independent review, commissioned by the UK Chancellor of the Exchequer, and headed by Sir Nicholas Stern, head of the Government Economic Service and former chief economist of the World Bank. Here was an economist, using the methods of economics to analyse perhaps the most serious problem facing the world.

Climate change presents a unique challenge for economics: it is the greatest and widest-ranging market failure ever seen. The economic analysis must therefore be global, deal with long time horizons, have the economics of risk and

Total emissions in 2000: 42 GtCO$_2$e.
Energy emissions are mostly CO$_2$ (some non-CO$_2$ in industry and other energy related).
Non-energy emissions are CO$_2$ (land use) and non-CO$_2$ (agriculture and waste).

Greenhouse gas emissions in 2000, by source

Source: *Stern Review on the Economics of Climate Change*, Executive Summary, Figure 1 (H.M. Treasury, 2006). (Prepared by Stern Review, from data drawn from World Resources Institute Climate Analysis Indicators Tool (CAIT) on-line database version 3.0.) Reproduced under terms of the click-use licence

Pause for thought

Assume that production by a firm has beneficial spillover effects: i.e. that there are positive externalities which have the effect of positioning the MSC curve below the MC curve. Illustrate this on a diagram similar to Figure 9.3 and show (a) the profit-maximising level of output; (b) the socially efficient level of output; (c) the optimum level of subsidy.

in the smoke. The marginal social cost of producing the chemicals thus exceeds the marginal private cost to the firm: $MSC > MC$.

This is illustrated in Figure 9.3 (on page 256). For simplicity, it is assumed that the firm is a price taker. It produces Q_1 where $P = MC$ (its profit-maximising output), but in doing so takes no account of the external pollution costs it imposes on society. If the government imposes a tax on production equal to the marginal pollution cost, it will effectively 'internalise' the externality. The firm will have uncertainty at centre stage, and examine the possibility of major, non-marginal change. To meet these requirements, the Review draws on ideas and techniques from most of the important areas of economics, including many recent advances.[1]

First the bad news . . .

According to the Stern Report, if no action is taken, global temperatures will rise by some 2–3°C within the next 50 years. As a result the world economy will shrink by up to 20 per cent – and that would be just the average. The countries most seriously affected by floods, drought and crop failure could shrink by considerably more. These tend to be the poorest countries, least able to bear the costs of these changes.

Rising sea levels could displace some 200 million people; droughts could create tens or even hundreds of millions of 'climate refugees'. 'Ecosystems will be particularly vulnerable to climate change, with around 15–40% of species potentially facing extinction after only 2°C of warming.'

. . . Then the good

If action is taken now, these consequences could be averted – and at relatively low cost. According to the Stern Report, a sacrifice of just 1 per cent of global GDP (global income) could, if correctly targeted, be enough to stabilise greenhouse gases to an equivalent of 500–550 ppm of CO_2 – a level generally considered to be sustainable. To achieve this, action would need to be taken to cut emissions from their various sources (see the chart). This would involve a mixture of four things:

■ Reducing consumer demand for emissions-intensive goods and services.

■ Increased efficiency, which can save both money and emissions.

■ Action on non-energy emissions, such as avoiding deforestation.

■ Switching to lower-carbon technologies for power, heat and transport.

What policies did Sir Nicholas recommend to achieve these four objectives? Essentially the answer is to alter incentives. This could involve taxing polluting activities; subsidising green alternatives, including the development of green technology; establishing a price for carbon through trading carbon (see the section on tradable permits on page 257) and regulating its production; and encouraging behavioural change through education, better labelling of products, imposing minimum standards for building and encouraging public debate.

We consider some of these alternatives in this section of the chapter.

Questions

1. Would it be in the interests of a business to reduce its carbon emissions if this involved it in increased costs?
2. How is the concept of 'opportunity cost' relevant in analysing the impact of business decisions on the environment?

[1] Stern Review: Executive Summary (http://www.hm-treasury.gov.uk/media/8AC/F7/Executive_Summary)

to pay an amount equal to the external cost it creates. The firm's *MC* curve thus shifts upwards to become the same as the *MSC* curve. It will therefore now maximise profits at Q_2, which is the socially optimum output where $MSB = MSC$.

Advantages of taxes and subsidies

Many economists favour the tax/subsidy solution to market imperfections (especially the problem of externalities) because it still allows the market to operate. It forces firms to take on board the full social costs and benefits of their actions. It also has the flexibility of being adjustable according to the magnitude of the problem. For example, the bigger the external costs of a firm's actions, the bigger the tax can be.

Figure 9.3   Using taxes to reduce pollution

What is more, by taxing firms for polluting, they are encouraged to find cleaner ways of producing. The tax thus acts as an incentive over the longer run to reduce pollution: the more a firm can reduce its pollution, the more taxes it can save.

Likewise, when *good* practices are subsidised, firms are given the incentive to adopt more good practices.

Disadvantages of taxes and subsidies

Infeasible to use different tax and subsidy rates. Each firm produces different levels and types of externality and operates under different degrees of imperfect competition. It would be expensive and administratively very difficult, if not impossible, to charge every offending firm its own particular tax rate (or grant every relevant firm its own particular rate of subsidy).

Lack of knowledge. Even if a government did decide to charge a tax equal to each offending firm's marginal external costs, it would still have the problem of measuring that cost. The damage from pollution is often extremely difficult to assess. It is also difficult to apportion blame. For example, the damage to lakes and forests from acid rain has been a major concern since the beginning of the 1980s. But just how serious is that damage? What is its current monetary cost? How long lasting is the damage? What will be the position in 20 years? Just what and who are to blame? These are questions that cannot be answered precisely. It is thus impossible to fix the 'correct' pollution tax on, say, a particular coal-fired power station.

Despite these problems, it is nevertheless possible to charge firms by the amount of a particular emission. For example, firms could be charged for chimney smoke by so many parts per million of a given pollutant. Although it is difficult to 'fine-tune' such a system so that the charge reflects the precise number of people affected by the pollutant and by how much, it does go some way to internalising the externality.

> **Pause for thought**
>
> *Why is it easier to use taxes and subsidies to tackle the problem of car exhaust pollution than to tackle the problem of peak-time traffic congestion in cities?*

Laws and regulations

The traditional way of tackling pollution has been to set maximum permitted levels of emission or resource use, or minimum acceptable levels of environmental quality, and then to fine firms contravening these limits. Measures of this type are known as **command-and-control (CAC) systems**. Clearly, there have to be inspectors to monitor the amount of pollution, and the fines have to be large enough to deter firms from exceeding the limit.

Virtually all countries have environmental regulations of one sort or another. For example, the EU has over 200 items of legislation covering areas such as air and water pollution, noise, the marketing and use of dangerous chemicals, waste management, the environmental impacts of new projects (such as power stations, roads and quarries), recycling, depletion of the ozone layer and global warming.

Assessing CAC systems. Given the uncertainty over the environmental impacts of pollutants, especially over the longer term, it is often better to play safe and set tough emissions standards. These could always be relaxed at a later stage if the effects turn out not to be so damaging, but it might be too late to reverse damage if the effects turn out to be more serious. Taxes may be a more sophisticated means of reaching a socially efficient output, but CAC methods are usually more straightforward to devise, easier to understand by firms and easier to implement.

Where command-and-control systems are weak is that they fail to offer business any incentive to do better than the legally specified level. By contrast, with a pollution tax, the lower the pollution level, the less tax there will be to pay. There is thus a continuing incentive for businesses progressively to cut pollution levels and introduce cleaner technology.

Tradable permits

A policy measure that has grown in popularity in recent years is that of **tradable permits**. This is a combination of command-and-control and market-based systems. A maximum permitted level of emission is set for a given pollutant for a given factory, and the firm is given a permit to emit up to this amount. If it emits less than this amount, it is given a credit for the difference, which it can then use in another of its factories, or sell to another firm, to enable it to go that amount *over* its permitted level. Thus the overall level of emissions is set by CAC methods, whereas their distribution is determined by the market.

Take the example of firms A and B, which are currently producing 12 units of a pollutant each. Now assume that a standard is set permitting them to produce only 10 units each. If firm A managed to reduce the pollutant to 8 units, it would be given a credit for 2 units. It could then sell this to firm B, enabling B to continue emitting 12 units. The effect would still be a total reduction of 4 units between the two firms. However, by allowing them to trade in pollution permits, pollution reduction can be concentrated in the firms where it can be achieved at lowest cost. In our example, if it cost firm B more to reduce its pollution than firm A, then the permits could be sold from A to B at a price that was profitable to both (i.e. at a price above the cost of emission reduction to A, but below the cost of emission reduction to B).

> ### Definitions
>
> **Command-and-control (CAC) systems**
> The use of laws or regulations backed up by inspections and penalties (such as fines) for non-compliance.
>
> **Tradable permits**
> Each firm is given a permit to produce a given level of pollution. If less than the permitted amount is produced, the firm is given a credit. This can then be sold to another firm, allowing it to exceed its original limit.

> ### *Pause for thought*
>
> *To what extent will the introduction of tradable permits lead to a lower level of total pollution (as opposed to its redistribution)?*

Box 9.3

The problem of urban traffic congestion

Does London have the answer?

Traffic congestion is a classic example of the problem of exter-nalities. When people use their cars, not only do they incur private costs (petrol, wear and tear on the vehicle, tolls, the time taken to travel, etc.), but also they impose costs on other people. These external costs include the following:

Congestion costs: time. When a person uses a car on a congested road, it adds to the congestion. This therefore slows down the traffic even more and increases the journey time of other car users.

Congestion costs: monetary. Congestion increases fuel consump-tion, and the stopping and starting increases the costs of wear and tear. When a motorist adds to congestion, therefore, there are additional monetary costs imposed on other motorists.

Environmental costs. When motorists use a road they reduce the quality of the environment for others. Cars emit fumes and create noise. This is bad enough for pedestrians and other car users, but can be particularly distressing for people living along the road. Driving can cause accidents, a problem that increases as drivers become more impatient as a result of delays.

Exhaust gases cause long-term environmental damage and are one of the main causes of the greenhouse effect and of the increased acidity of lakes and rivers and the poisoning of forests. They can also cause long-term health problems (e.g. for asthma sufferers).

The socially efficient level of road usage

These externalities mean that road usage will be above the social optimum. This is illustrated in the diagram. Costs and benefits are shown on the vertical axis and are measured in money terms. Thus any non-monetary costs or benefits (such as time costs) must be given a monetary value. The horizontal axis measures road usage in terms of cars per minute passing a specified point on the road.

For simplicity it is assumed that there are no external benefits from car use and that therefore marginal private and marginal social benefits are the same. The *MSB* curve is shown as down-ward sloping. The reason for this is that different road users put

Actual and optimum road usage

a different value on any given journey. If the marginal (private) cost of making the journey were high, only those for whom the journey had a high marginal benefit would travel along the road. If the marginal cost of making the journey fell, more people would make the journey: people choosing to make the journey as long as the marginal cost of the journey was less than the marginal benefit. Thus the greater the number of cars, the lower the marginal benefit.

The marginal (private) cost curve (*MC*) is likely to be constant up to the level of traffic flow at which congestion begins to occur. This is shown as point *a* in the diagram. Beyond this point, marginal cost is likely to rise as time costs increase (i.e. journey times lengthen) and as fuel consumption rises.

The marginal *social* cost curve (*MSC*) is drawn above the marginal private cost curve. The vertical difference between the two represents the external costs. Up to point *b*, external costs are simply the environmental costs. Beyond point *b*, there are also external congestion costs, since additional road users slow down the journey of *other* road users. These external costs get pro-gressively greater as traffic grinds to a halt.

The actual level of traffic flow will be at Q_1, where marginal private costs and benefits are equal (point *e*). The socially efficient level of traffic flow, however, will be at the lower level of Q_2 where marginal social costs and benefits are equal (point d). In other words, there will be an excessive level of road usage.

So what can governments do to 'internalise' these externalities? To achieve a reduction in traffic to Q_2 the motorist should be charged an amount equal to $d-c$ in the diagram. How can this be achieved? In practice this is difficult, given that congestion and its costs vary with location and the time of day. Also the external cost is hard to measure. One, albeit imperfect, solution is to impose charges on cars entering a 'congestion zone'. This solution is the one adopted in London.

Congestion charging in London

In London, car drivers must pay £8 per day to enter the inner London area (or 'congestion zone') any time between 7.00 and 18.00, Monday to Friday. Payment can be made by various means, including post, Internet, telephone, mobile phone SMS text message and at various shops and petrol stations. Payment can be in advance or up to midnight on the day of travel, or up to midnight on the following charging day for an extra £2. Cars entering the congestion zone have their number plate recorded by camera and a computer check then leads to a fine of £100 being sent to those who have not paid (reduced to £50 for payment within 14 days).

The system was introduced in 2003 and the charging zone was extended in 2007. The initial effect was to reduce traffic in the zone by about 20 per cent and significantly increase the rate of traffic flow. Traffic in the zone has crept back somewhat since, but this is partly the result of a general increase in traffic.

The charge is not a marginal one, however, in the sense that it does not vary with the degree of congestion or the amount of time spent or distance travelled by a motorist within the zone. Nevertheless, its simplicity makes it easy to understand and relatively cheap to operate.

More sophisticated electronic road pricing

More sophisticated schemes attempt to relate directly the price charged to the motorist to the specific level of marginal external cost. In Singapore, for example, cars are fitted with a dashboard device into which you must insert a smart card which contains pre-paid units, much as a photocopying or telephone card. The cards can be recharged. On specified roads, overhead gantries read the device and deduct units from the card. Charges vary with the time of day. If a car does not have sufficient funds on its card, the car's details are relayed to a control centre and a fine is sent to the owner.

The most sophisticated scheme, still under development in parts of the world, would involve equipping all cars with a receiver. Their position is located by satellite tracking. Charges are then imposed according to location, distance travelled, time of day and type of vehicle. The charges can operate either through smart cards in a dashboard device or though central computerised billing.

Proposals to introduce a similar system in the UK have met with stiff opposition. People resent paying more to travel and many see such a scheme as merely a means of raising additional revenue. Many also worry that it would be unfair on people who are forced to travel long distances or through congested areas simply to get to work.

But such taxes can be revenue neutral if other taxes, such as the road fund licence, are cut. Also, they act as an incentive for people to reduce the amount they travel or to avoid peak times. They also put pressure on companies to use more flexible working times and to allow telecommuting (see Box 8.1 on page 221). Clearly congestion imposes large costs on society and tackling it is likely to involve increasing the costs of motoring one way or another. At least road pricing directly relates charging to congestion.

? Questions

1. Referring to a town or city with which you are familiar, consider what would be the most appropriate mix of policies to deal with its traffic congestion problems.
2. Explain how, by varying the charge to motorists according to the time of day or level of congestion, a socially optimal level of road use can be achieved.

A similar principle can be used for using natural resources. Thus fish quotas could be assigned to fishing boats or fleets or countries. Any parts of these quotas not used could then be sold.

The EU carbon trading system

In the EU, a carbon Emissions Trading Scheme (ETS) has been in place since January 2005 as part of the EU's approach to meeting its targets under the Kyoto Treaty (see Web Case C.17). Under the scheme, some 11 500 industrial plants have been allocated CO_2 emissions allowances, or credits, by their respective governments. Companies that exceed their limits must purchase credits to cover the difference, while those that reduce their emissions can sell their surplus credits for a profit. Companies can trade directly with each other or through brokers operating throughout Europe.

Assessing the system of tradable permits

The main advantage of tradable permits is that they combine the simplicity of CAC methods with the benefits of achieving pollution reduction in the most efficient way. There is also the advantage that firms have a financial incentive to cut pollution. This might then make it easier for governments to impose tougher standards (i.e. impose lower permitted levels of emission).

There are, however, various problems with tradable permits. One is the possibility that trade will lead to pollution being concentrated in certain geographical areas. Another is that it may reduce the pressure on dirtier factories (or countries) to cut their emissions. Finally, the system will lead to significant cuts in pollution only if the permitted levels are low. Once the system is in place, the government might then feel that the pressure is off to *reduce* the permitted levels.

A major criticism of the EU's initial ETS was that the carbon allowances were set far too high. Many firms found it easy to meet their target and had surplus allowances to sell. The result was that by 2007 carbon prices had plummeted from over €30 per tonne to under €10. According to the Stern Report (see Box 9.2), carbon prices of $30 to $50 are necessary to stabilise levels of CO_2. In response, the EU planned a reduction in permits of some 7 per cent in 2008 and a further reduction in 2012.

> **Pause for thought**
>
> *Should all emitters of carbon, including aircraft and agriculture, be included in carbon trading schemes?*

Recap

- There are three main types of environmental policy instrument: taxes and subsidies; command-and-control systems; tradable permits.

- Taxes and subsidies have the advantages of 'internalising' externalities and of providing incentives to reduce external costs. The problem with using taxes and subsidies is in identifying the appropriate rates, since these will vary according to the environmental impact.

- Command-and-control systems, such as making certain practices illegal or putting limits on discharges, are a less sophisticated alternative to taxes or subsidies. However, they may be preferable when the environmental costs of certain actions are unknown and it is wise to play safe.

- Tradable permits are where firms are given permits to emit a certain level of pollution and then these can be traded. A firm that can relatively cheaply reduce its pollution below its permitted level can sell this credit to another firm which finds it more costly to do so.

Competition policy and business behaviour   9.5

Competition, monopoly and the public interest

Most markets in the real world are imperfect, with firms having varying degrees of market power. But will this power be against the public interest? This question has been addressed by successive governments in framing legislation to deal with monopolies and oligopolies.

It might be thought that market power is always 'a bad thing', certainly as far as the consumer is concerned. After all, it enables firms to make supernormal profit, thereby 'exploiting' the consumer. The greater the firm's power, the higher will prices be relative to the costs of production. This is illustrated in Figure 9.4 (which is similar to Figure 5.2 on page 131).

The firm maximises profits at Q, where $MC = MR$. Profits are shown by the shaded area. The greater the firm's market power, the steeper will be the firm's AR curve and also the MR curve. The bigger will be the gap between price (point a) and marginal cost (point b). Remember that under perfect competition, price equals marginal cost (see Figure 4.4 on page 113). This is shown by point c, which is at a lower price and a higher output.

Not only does a lack of competition result in a higher price, it also removes the incentive to become more efficient.

But market power is not necessarily a bad thing. Firms may not fully exploit their position of power – perhaps for fear that very high profits would eventually lead to other firms overcoming entry barriers, or perhaps because they are not aggressive profit maximisers. Even if they do make large supernormal profits, they may still charge a lower price than more competitive sectors of the industry because of their economies of scale. Finally, they may use their profits for research and development

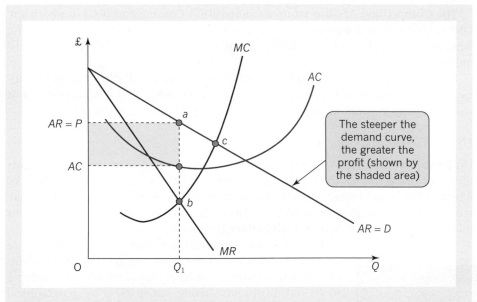

The steeper the demand curve, the greater the profit (shown by the shaded area)

Figure 9.4   Profit maximising under monopoly

and for capital investment. The consumer might then benefit from improved products at lower prices.

Competition policy could seek to ban various structures or activities. For example, it could ban mergers leading to market share of more than a certain amount, or it could ban price-fixing arrangements between oligopolists. However, most countries prefer to adopt a more flexible approach and examine each case on its merits. Such an approach does not presume that the mere possession of power is against the public interest, but rather that certain uses of that power may be.

UK competition policy

Current UK policy is based on the 1998 Competition Act and the 2002 Enterprise Act. These Acts bring UK policy in line with EU competition policy (which is largely confined to firms trading between EU members).

The Competition Act has two key sets (or 'chapters') of prohibitions. Chapter I prohibits various collusive practices of oligopolies ('restrictive practices') (see pages 136–8). Chapter II prohibits various abuses of monopoly power. The Enterprise Act strengthened the Competition Act and introduced new measures for the control of mergers.

Under the two Acts, the body charged with ensuring that the prohibitions are carried out is the Office of Fair Trading (OFT). The OFT can investigate any firms suspected of engaging in one or more of the prohibited practices. Its officers have the power to enter and search premises, and can require the production and explanation of documents.

Where the OFT decides that an infringement of one of the prohibitions has occurred, it can direct the offending firms to modify their behaviour or cease their practices altogether. Companies in breach of a prohibition are liable to fines of up to 10 per cent of their annual UK turnover. Third parties adversely affected by such breaches can seek compensation through the courts.

The Competition Act also set up a Competition Commission (CC) to which the OFT can refer cases for further investigation. The CC is charged with determining whether the structure of an industry or the practices of firms within it are detrimental to competition.

If a case is referred to the Competition Commission, it will carry out an investigation to establish whether competition is adversely affected. If it finds that it is, it will decide on the appropriate remedies, such as prohibiting various practices.

UK restrictive practices policy

Under the 2002 Enterprise Act it a *criminal* offence to engage in cartel agreements (i.e. horizontal, rather than vertical, agreements between firms), irrespective of whether there are appreciable effects on competition. Convicted offenders may receive a prison sentence of up to five years and/or an unlimited fine. Prosecutions may be brought by the Serious Fraud Office or the OFT.

But what practices constitute 'cartel agreements'? These involve one or more of the following agreements by firms: price fixing; limiting supply, perhaps by each firm agreeing to an output quota; sharing out markets by geographical area, type or size of customer or nature of outlet (e.g. bus companies agreeing not to run services in each other's

Pause for thought

Are all such agreements necessarily against the interests of consumers?

areas); **collusive tendering** for a contract, where two or more firms put in a tender at secretly agreed (high) prices; or agreements between purchasers (e.g. super-markets) to keep down prices paid to suppliers (e.g. farmers).

In the case of other types of agreement, the OFT has the discretion to decide, on a case-by-case basis, whether or not competition is appreciably restricted, and whether, therefore, they should be terminated or the firms should be exempted. Such cases include the following:

■ Vertical price-fixing agreements. These are price agreements between purchasing firms and their suppliers. An example of this is **resale price maintenance**. This is where a manufacturer or distributor sets the price for retailers to charge. It may well distribute a price list to retailers (e.g. a car manufacturer may distribute a price list to car showrooms). Resale price maintenance is a way of preventing competition between retailers driving down retail prices and ultimately the price they pay to the manufacturer. Both manufacturers and retailers, therefore, are likely to gain from resale price maintenance.

■ Agreements to exchange information that could have the effect of reducing competition. For example, if producers exchange information on their price intentions, it is a way of allowing price leadership (see page 137), a form of tacit collusion, to continue.

A problem with any policy to deal with collusion is the difficulty in rooting it out. When firms do all their deals 'behind closed doors' and are careful not to keep records or give clues, then collusion can be very hard to spot.

UK monopoly policy

Under the Chapter II prohibition of the 1998 Competition Act, it is illegal for a dominant firm to exercise its market power in such a way as to reduce competition. Any suspected case is investigated by the OFT, which uses a two-stage process in deciding whether an abuse has taken place.

The first stage is to establish whether a firm has a position of dominance. The firm does not literally have to be a monopoly. Rather 'dominance' normally involves the firm having at least a 40 per cent share of the market (national or local, whichever is appropriate), although this figure will vary from industry to industry. Also dominance depends on the barriers to entry to new competitors. The higher the barriers to the entry of new firms, the less 'contestable' will be the market, and the more dominant a firm is likely to be for any given current market share.

If the firm *is* deemed to be dominant, the second stage involves the OFT decid-ing whether the firm's practices constitute an abuse of its position. Examples of such practices include:

■ Charging excessively high prices. These are prices above those that the firm would charge if it faced effective competition. One sign of excessively high prices is abnormally high rates of profit.

■ Price discrimination. This is regarded as an abuse only to the extent that the higher prices are excessive or the lower prices are used to exclude competitors.

■ Predatory pricing. This is where the price of a product is set at loss-making levels, so as to undercut competitors and drive them out of business. The firm uses profitable parts of its business to subsidise this loss making.

Definitions

Collusive tendering
Where two or more firms secretly agree on the prices they will tender for a contract. These prices will be above those which would be put in under a genuinely competitive tendering process.

Resale price maintenance
Where the manufacturer of a product (legally) insists that the product should be sold at a specified retail price.

Box 9.4

A lift to profits?

Record EU fine for operating a lift and escalator cartel

EU competition policy applies to companies operating in two or more EU countries. The UK legislation described in this section of the chapter is very similar to EU legislation, which is largely contained in Articles 81 and 82 of the Treaty of Amsterdam. Article 81 is concerned with restrictive practices and Article 82 with the abuse of market power. The policy is implemented by the European Commission and it has the power to levy substantial fines on companies found to be in breach of the legislation.

In February 2007, the Commission imposed a record fine of €992 million on four lift and escalator manufacturers for operating a price-fixing cartel. According to the EU Commission, the companies – ThyssenKrupp of Germany, Otis of the USA, Kone of Finland and Schindler of Switzerland – sought to freeze market share and fix prices. 'Projects that were rigged included lifts and escalators for hospitals, railway stations, shopping centres and commercial buildings.'

The Commission last year passed new fining guidelines that will allow Brussels to further increase the financial pain on abusive companies in all new cases. Officials have argued that the new rules will mean that more companies will be hit with the maximum penalty – a fine equivalent to 10 per cent of their annual global turnover.

The lift cartel operated in Germany, the Netherlands, Belgium and Luxembourg between at least 1995 and 2004. According to the Commission, the groups co-ordinated their bids to ensure that a designated group would win specific contracts.

'[To agree on bids] they usually met in bars and restaurants, they travelled to the countryside or even abroad, and they used pre-paid mobile cards to avoid tracking,' the Commission said.[1]

According to Jonathan Todd of the EU, 'the result of this cartel is that taxpayers, public authorities and property developers have been ripped off big time. The companies ensured that, by rigging the bids [i.e. collusive tendering] and sharing the markets, the prices paid for the installation and the maintenance were way above what they would have been if there had been a competitive market.'

Neelie Kroes, the EU Competition Commissioner, said that 'the national management of these companies knew what they were doing was wrong, but they tried to conceal their action and went ahead anyway. The damage caused by this cartel will last for many years because it covered not only the initial supply but also the subsequent maintenance of lifts and escalators.'

Of the four companies, ThyssenKrupp was given the largest fine (€480 million), and the biggest ever for a single company, because it was a 'repeat offender'. It had received a previous fine of €3.2 million in 1998 for fixing stainless steel prices. Under guidelines issued in 2006, repeat offenders face an automatic 50 per cent increase in fines.

? Question

What factors determine the likelihood that firms will collude to fix prices – despite the prospect of facing fines of up to 10 per cent of their annual global turnover?

[1] 'Brussels imposes €992m fine on lift cartel', *Financial Times*, 22 February 2007

■ Vertical restraints. This is where a supplying firm imposes conditions on a purchasing firm (or *vice versa*). For example, a manufacturer may impose rules on retailers about displaying the product or the provision of after-sales service, or it may refuse to supply certain outlets (e.g. perfume manufacturers refusing to supply discount chains, such as Superdrug).

The simple *existence* of any of these practices may not constitute an abuse. The OFT has to decide whether their *effect* is to restrict competition. If the case is not straightforward, the OFT can refer it to the Competition Commission (CC). The CC will then carry out a detailed investigation to establish whether competition is restricted or distorted. If it is, the CC will rule what actions must be taken to remedy the situation.

Box 9.5

What price for peace of mind?

Exploiting monopoly power in the sale of extended warranties on electrical goods

If you go into Curry's, Comet, PC World or virtually any other High Street retailer to buy an electrical good, such as a DVD player, a fridge or PC, the sales assistant will probably be very keen to sell you an extended warranty (EW). These EWs are typically for three to five years and sometimes merely extend the product's guarantee against breakdown beyond its normal one- or two-year expiry date. Sometimes they go further and provide cover against other risks, such as accidental damage or theft.

These EWs are highly profitable for the retailer. In 2002 they accounted for approximately 40 per cent of Dixons' profits and 80 per cent of Comet's. It's hardly surprising that retailers are very keen to sell them to you!

In 2002 the Office of Fair Trading (OFT) published a report on EWs and concluded that 'there is insufficient competition and information to ensure that consumers get good value, and that many electrical retailers may make considerable profits on the sale of EWs'.

Research conducted by the OFT indicates that customers can feel pressurised to rush to a decision to buy an extended warranty when they buy their new appliance. A high percentage of consumers had not thought about buying an extended warranty before they arrive at the store.

Buyers should think whether extended warranties offer them value for money. OFT research found that the average washing machine repair costs between £45 to £65. So if a five year extended warranty costs £150 on a £300 washing machine, it would need to break down four times for a consumer to benefit.

A recent 'Which?' report highlights that modern domestic appliances are generally reliable. It found that 81 per cent of washing machines didn't break down at all in the first six years.

. . . Some sales staff are paid commission on each extended warranty they sell, so may be keen for a customer to sign on the dotted line.[1]

The OFT was concerned that retailers were using their market power at the point of sale and benefiting from consumers' ignorance. It decided, therefore, to refer the case to the Competition Commission (CC), which published its report in December 2003.

The CC report found that there was a 'complex monopoly'[2] in the market, worth £900 million per year, which was working against the public interest. It concluded that there had been an abuse of monopoly power, stating that:

> Were this market fully competitive such that the top five EW retailers' returns were no greater than their cost of capital,[3] we estimate that EW prices would have been, on average, up to one-third lower.
>
> . . . Many of the practices that we have identified during the course of our investigation operate or may be expected to operate against the public interest. They result in lack of choice, excessive prices, insufficient information, insufficient competition at point of sale, limited but not insignificant sales pressure, some terms which could be disadvantageous, and lack of information about the scope of protection under service-backed schemes.[4]

Despite these findings, the Competition Commission did not recommend banning shops from bundling warranties with electrical goods at the point of sale, despite many of the EWs being 'unfair and uncompetitive'. Instead, it recommended that retailers should display prices for EWs alongside the price of the goods, both in shops and in advertisements. It also recommended that the shops should provide information about customers' rights and that customers should get a full refund on the EW if they cancelled within 45 days.

The government minister, the Secretary of State for Trade and Industry, Patricia Hewitt, accepted these findings and ruled that they should be implemented – which they were in April 2005.

? Questions

1. What features of the market for EWs distort competition?
2. To what extent will the ruling by the government make the market for EWs competitive?

---

[1] OFT News Release, PN 68/02, October 2002

[2] A complex monopoly is where several companies separately (i.e. not collusively) are in a position to exploit a particular market advantage to the detriment of the consumer

[3] A measure of 'normal profit'

[4] Summary to 'Extended warranties on domestic electrical goods: a report on the supply of extended warranties on domestic electrical goods within the UK', Competition Commission, December 2003, (http://www.competition-commission.org.uk/reprpub/reports/2003/485xwars.htm#summary)

UK merger policy

Merger policy is covered by the 2002 Enterprise Act. It seeks to prevent mergers that are likely to result in a substantial lessening of competition.

A merger or takeover will be investigated by the OFT if the target company has a turnover of £70 million or more, or if the merger results in the new company having a market share of 25 per cent or more. The OFT conducts a preliminary investigation to see whether competition is likely to be threatened. If it is, and if there are unlikely to be any substantial compensating benefit to consumers, the OFT refers the case to the Competition Commission.

If reference is made to the CC, it conducts a detailed investigation to establish whether the merger is likely to lead to a significant reduction in competition. If so, it can prohibit the merger. Alternatively, it can require the merged firm to behave in certain ways in order to protect consumers' interests. In such cases, the OFT then monitors the firm to ensure that it is abiding by the CC's conditions. CC investigations must normally be completed within 24 weeks.

Recap

- Competition policy in most countries recognises that monopolies, mergers and restrictive practices can bring both costs and benefits to the consumer. Generally, though, restrictive practices tend to be more damaging to consumers' interests than simple monopoly power or mergers.

- UK legislation is covered by the 1998 Competition Act and 2002 Enterprise Act. The Office of Fair Trading (OFT) is charged with ensuring that firms abide by the legislation. Where there is doubt, it can refer cases to the Competition Commission for a ruling.

- Cartel agreements are a criminal offence and certain other types of collusive behaviour can be curtailed by the OFT if they are against the public interest.

- The abuse of monopoly power by a dominant firm can also be prevented by the OFT. Such abuses include charging excessively high prices.

- Mergers over a certain size are investigated by the OFT, with possible reference to the Competition Commission for a ruling as to whether they should be permitted.

9.6 The regulation of business

Regulation and the privatised industries

Definition

Nationalised industries
State-owned industries that produce goods or services that are sold in the market.

In the late 1940s and early 1950s the Labour government **nationalised** many of the key transport, communications and power industries, such as the railways, freight transport, airlines, coal, gas, electricity and steel. The Thatcher and Major governments in the 1980s and early 1990s sold these industries to the private sector in a programme of **privatisation**. However, many of these privatised industries had considerable market power and so it was felt necessary to regulate their behaviour.

Regulation in practice

To some extent the behaviour of privatised industries may be governed by general monopoly and restrictive practice legislation. For example, in the UK, privatised firms can be investigated by the Office of Fair Trading and if necessary referred to the Competition Commission.

In addition to this, there is a separate regulatory office to oversee the structure and behaviour of each of the privatised utilities. These regulators are as follows: the Office for Gas and Electricity Markets (Ofgem), the Office of Communications (Ofcom), the Office of the Rail Regulator (ORR) and the Office of Water Services (Ofwat). The regulators set terms under which the industries have to operate. For example, ORR sets the terms under which rail companies have access to the track and stations. The terms set by the regulator can be reviewed by negotiation between the regulator and the industry. If agreement cannot be reached, the Competition Commission acts as an appeal court and its decision is binding.

The regulator for each industry also sets limits to the prices that certain parts of the industry can charge. These parts are those where there is little or no competition: e.g. the charges made to electricity and gas retailers by National Grid Transco, the owner of the electricity grid and major gas pipelines.

The price-setting formulae are essentially of the '*RPI* minus *X*' variety. What this means is that the industries can raise their prices by the rate of increase in the retail price index (i.e. by the rate of inflation) *minus* a certain percentage (X) to take account of expected increases in efficiency. Thus if the rate of inflation were 6 per cent, and if the regulator considered that the industry (or firm) could be expected to reduce its costs by 2 per cent ($X = 2\%$), then price rises would be capped at 4 per cent. The $RPI - X$ system is thus an example of **price-cap regulation**. The idea of this system of regulation is that it forces the industry to pass cost savings on to the consumer.

Assessing the system of regulation in the UK

The system that has evolved in the UK has various advantages:

■ It is a *discretionary* system, with the regulator able to judge individual examples of the behaviour of the industry on their own merits. The regulator has a detailed knowledge of the industry which would not be available to government ministers or other bodies such as the Office of Fair Trading. The regulator could thus be argued to be the best person to decide on whether the industry is acting in the public interest.

■ The system is *flexible*, since it allows for the licence and price formula to be changed as circumstances change.

■ The '*RPI* minus *X*' formula provides an *incentive* for the privatised firms to be as efficient as possible. If they can lower their costs by more than X, they will, in theory, be able to make larger profits and keep them. If on the other hand, they do not succeed in reducing costs sufficiently, they will make a loss. There is thus a continuing pressure on them to cut costs.

There are, however, some inherent problems with the way in which regulation operates in the UK:

■ The '*RPI* minus X' formula was designed to provide an incentive for the firms to cut costs. But if X is too low, the firm might make excessive profits. Frequently,

Pause for thought

If an industry regulator adopts an RPI − X formula for price regulation, is it desirable that the value of X should be adjusted as soon as cost conditions change?

regulators have underestimated the scope for cost reductions resulting from new technology and reorganisation, and have thus initially set X too low. As a result, instead of X remaining constant for a number of years, as intended, new higher values for X have been set after only one or two years. Alternatively, one-off price cuts have been ordered, as happened when the water companies were required by Ofwat to cut prices by an average of 10 per cent in 2000. In either case, the incentive for the industry to cut costs is reduced. What is the point of being more efficient if the regulator is merely going to insist on a higher value for X and thus take away the extra profits?

■ Regulation is becoming increasingly complex. This makes it difficult for the industries to plan and may lead to a growth of 'short-termism'. One of the claimed advantages of privatisation was to give greater independence to the industries from short-term government interference, and allow them to plan for the longer term. In practice, one type of interference may have been replaced by another.

■ As regulation becomes more detailed and complex and as the regulator becomes more and more involved in the detailed running of the industry, so managers and regulators will become increasingly involved in a game of strategy: each trying to outwit the other. Information will become distorted and time and energy will be wasted in playing this game of cat and mouse. This is an example of the principal–agent problem (see page 10), where the agent (the company) is trying to avoid carrying out the wishes of the principal (the regulator).

One way in which the dangers of ineffective or over-intrusive regulation can be avoided is to replace regulation with competition wherever this is possible. Indeed, one of the major concerns of the regulators has been to do just this. (See Web Case C.24 for ways in which competition has been increased in the electricity industry.)

Regulation versus competition

Where natural monopoly exists (see page 128), competition is impossible in a free market. Of course, the industry *could* be broken up by the government, with firms prohibited from owning more than a certain percentage of the industry. But this would lead to higher costs of production. Firms would be operating further back up a downward-sloping long-run average cost curve.

But many parts of the privatised industries are not natural monopolies. Generally it is only the *grid* that is a natural monopoly. In the case of gas and water, it is the pipelines. It would be wasteful to duplicate these. In the case of electricity, it is the power lines: the national grid and the local power lines. In the case of the railways, it is the track.

Other parts of these industries, however, have generally been opened up to competition (with the exception of water). Thus there are now many producers and sellers of electricity and gas. This is possible because they are given access, by law, to the national and local electricity grids and gas pipelines. The telecommunications market too has become more competitive with the growth of mobile phones and lines supplied by cable operators.

As competition has been introduced into these industries, so price-cap regulation has been progressively abandoned. For example, in 2006 Ofcom abandoned price control of BT and other phone companies over line rentals and phone charges. This was in response to the growth in competition from cable operators, mobile phones and free Internet calls from companies such as Skype via VoIP (voice Internet protocol).

But despite attempts to introduce competition into the privatised industries, they are still dominated by giant companies. Even if they are no longer strictly monopolies, they still have considerable market power and the scope for price leadership or other forms of oligopolistic collusion is great. Thus although regulation through the price formula has been progressively abandoned as elements of competition have been introduced, the regulators have retained a role similar to that of the OFT: namely, to prevent cases of collusion and the abuse of monopoly power. The companies, however, do have the right of appeal to the Competition Commission.

Recap

- Regulation in the UK has involved setting up regulatory offices for the major privatised utilities. These generally operate informally, using negotiation and bargaining to persuade the industries to behave in the public interest.

- As far as prices are concerned, parts of the industries are required to abide by an '*RPI* minus *X*' formula. This forces them to pass potential cost reductions on to the consumer. At the same time they are allowed to retain any additional profits gained from cost reductions greater than *X*. This provides them with an incentive to achieve even greater increases in efficiency.

- Many parts of the privatised industries are not natural monopolies. In these parts, competition may be a more effective means of pursuing the public interest.

- Various attempts have been made to make the privatised industries more competitive, often at the instigation of the regulator. Nevertheless, considerable market power remains in the hands of many privatised firms, and thus the need for regulation will continue.

QUESTIONS

1. Assume that a firm discharges waste into a river. As a result, the marginal social costs (*MSC*) are greater than the firm's marginal (private) costs (*MC*). The following table shows how *MC*, *MSC*, *AR* and *MR* vary with output.

Output	1	2	3	4	5	6	7	8
MC (£)	23	21	23	25	27	30	35	42
MSC (£)	35	34	38	42	46	52	60	72
TR (£)	60	102	138	168	195	219	238	252
AR (£)	60	51	46	42	39	36.5	34	31.5
MR (£)	60	42	36	30	27	24	19	14

(a) How much will the firm produce if it seeks to maximise profits?

(b) What is the socially efficient level of output (assuming no externalities on the demand side)?

(c) How much is the marginal external cost at this level of output?

(d) What size tax would be necessary for the firm to reduce its output to the socially efficient level?

(e) Why is the tax less than the marginal externality?

(f) Why might it be equitable to impose a lump-sum tax on this firm?

(g) Why will a lump-sum tax not affect the firm's output (assuming that in the long run the firm can still make at least normal profit)?

2. Distinguish between publicly provided goods, public goods and merit goods.

3. Some roads could be regarded as a public good, but some could be provided by the market. Which types of road could be provided by the market? Why? Would it be a good idea?

4. Make a list of pieces of information a firm might want to know and consider whether it could buy the information and how reliable that information might be.

5. Why might it be better to ban certain activities that cause environmental damage rather than to tax them?

6. How suitable are legal restrictions in the following cases?

(a) Ensuring adequate vehicle safety (e.g. that tyres have sufficient tread or that the vehicle is roadworthy).

(b) Reducing traffic congestion.

(c) Preventing the use of monopoly power.

(d) Ensuring that mergers are in the public interest.

(e) Ensuring that firms charge a price equal to marginal cost.

7. In what ways might business be socially responsible?

8. What economic costs and benefits might a business experience if it decided to adopt a more socially responsible position? How might such costs and benefits change over the longer term?

9. What problems are likely to arise in identifying which firms' practices are anti-competitive? Should the OFT take firms' assurances into account when deciding whether to grant an exemption?

10. If anti-monopoly legislation is effective enough, is there ever any need to prevent mergers from going ahead?

11. If two or more firms were charging similar prices, what types of evidence would you look for to prove that this was collusion rather than mere coincidence?

12. Should governments or regulators always attempt to eliminate the supernormal profits of monopolists/oligopolists?

13. Should regulators of utilities that have been privatised into several separate companies permit (a) horizontal mergers (within the industry); (b) vertical mergers; (c) mergers with firms in other related industries (e.g. gas and electricity suppliers)?

Additional Part C case studies on the *Economics and the Business Environment* website (www.pearsoned.co.uk/sloman)

C.1   **B2B electronic marketplaces.** This case study examines the growth of firms trading with each other over the Internet (business to business or 'B2B') and considers the effects on competition.

C.2   **Measuring monopoly power.** This analyses how the degree of monopoly power possessed by a firm can be measured.

C.3   **Airline deregulation in the USA and Europe.** Whether the deregulation of various routes has led to more competition and lower prices.

C.4   **Bakeries: oligopoly or monopolistic competition.** A case study on the bread industry, showing that small-scale local bakeries can exist alongside giant national bakeries.

C.5   **Oligopoly in the brewing industry.** A case study showing how the UK brewing industry is becoming more concentrated.

C.6   **OPEC.** A case study examining OPEC's influence over oil prices from the early 1970s to the current day.

C.7   **Hybrid strategy.** Is it good for companies to use a mix of strategies?

C.8   **Stakeholder power.** An examination of the various stakeholders of a business and their influence on business behaviour.

C.9   **Logistics.** A case study of the use of the logistics industry by companies seeking to outsource their supply chain.

C.10   **Peak-load pricing.** An example of price discrimination: charging more when it costs more to produce.

C.11   **The rise and decline of the labour movement.** A brief history of trade unions in the UK.

C.12   **How useful is marginal productivity theory?** How accurately does the theory describe employment decisions by firms?

C.13   **Should health care provision be left to the market?** This identifies the market failures that would occur if health care provision were left to the free market.

C.14   **Corporate social responsibility.** An examination of social responsibility as a goal of firms and its effect on business performance.

C.15   **Technology and economic change.** How to get the benefits from technological advance.

C.16   **Green taxes.** Are they the perfect answer to the problem of pollution?

C.17   **Selling the environment.** The market-led solution of the Kyoto Protocol.

C.18 **Road pricing in Singapore.** A case study showing the methods Singapore has used to cut traffic congestion.

C.19 **Environmental auditing.** Are businesses becoming greener? A growing number of firms are subjecting themselves to an 'environmental audit' to judge just how 'green' they are.

C.20 **Cartels set in concrete, steel and cardboard.** This examines some of the best-known Europe-wide cartels of recent years.

C.21 **Taking your vitamins at a price.** A case study showing how vitamin-producing companies were fined for price fixing.

C.22 **The right track to reform.** Reorganising the railways in the UK.

C.23 **Competition in the pipeline.** An examination of attempts to introduce competition into the gas industry in the UK.

C.24 **Selling power to the people.** Attempts to introduce competition into the UK electricity industry.

Websites relevant to Part C

Numbers and sections refer to websites listed in the Web Appendix and hotlinked from this book's website at www.pearsoned.co.uk/sloman/

■ For news articles relevant to Part C, see the *Economics News Articles* link from the book's website.

■ For general news on the microeconomic environment of business see websites in section A of the Web Appendix, and particularly A1–5, 8, 9, 11, 12, 20–26, 35, 36. See also A38, 43 and 44 for links to newspapers worldwide; and A41 for links to economics news articles from newspapers worldwide.

■ For student resources relevant to Part C, see sites C1–7, 9, 10, 14, 19; D3.

■ For sites that looks at competition and market power, see B2; E4, 10, 18; G7, 8. See also links in I7, 11, 14 and 17. In particular see the following links in sites I7: *Microeconomics > Competition and Monopoly*.

■ For a site on game theory, see A40 including its home page. See also D4, 5, 13, 14, 18, 19; I17 and 4 (in the EconDirectory section).

■ For information on mergers, see sites E4, 10, 18, 20; G1, 8.

■ For information on stock markets, see sites F18 and A3, 22, 25, 26; B27.

■ Site I7 contains links to *Financial Economics*.

■ For data on SMEs, see the SME database in B3 or E10.

■ For information on pricing, see site E10 and the sites of the regulators of the privatised industries: E15, 16, 19, 22.

■ Site I7 in the Business section contains links to *Business > Management > Organisational Management.*

■ For data on labour markets, see links in B1, especially to *Labour Market Trends* on the National Statistics site. Also see B9 and links in B19. Also see the labour topic in B33 and the *resources > statistics* links in H3.

■ For information on international labour standards and employment rights, see site H3.

■ Site I7 contains links to Labour economics, Labour force and markets and Labour unions in the *Microeconomics* section and to Distribution of income and wealth in the *Macroeconomics* section. Site I4 has links in the Directory section to Labor and Labor Economics. Site I17 in the Labor Economics section has links to various topics, such as Labor Unions, Minimum Wage, Poverty and Work.

■ Links to the TUC and Confederation of British Industry sites can be found at E32 and 33.

■ Site I7 contains links to Competition and monopoly, Policy and regulation and Transport in the *Microeconomics* section; they also have an Industry and commerce section. Site I4 has links to Environmental and Environmental Economics in the EconDirectory section. Site I17 has several sections of links in the Issues in Society section.

■ Site I7 also contains links to sites related to corporate social responsibility: see *Industry and Commerce > Fair Trade > Corporate social Responsibility.*

■ For information on taxes and subsidies, see E30, 36; G13. For use of green taxes, see H5; G11; E2, 14, 30.

■ For information on health and the economics of health care (Web case C.13: see above), see E8; H9. See also links in I8 and 17.

■ For sites favouring the free market, see C17; D34. See also C18 for the development of ideas on the market and government intervention.

■ For the economics of the environment, see links in I4, 7, 11, 17. For policy on the environment and transport, see E2, 7, 11, 14, 29, 39; G10, 11. See also H11.

■ UK and EU departments relevant to competition policy can be found at sites E10; G7, 8.

■ UK regulatory bodies can be found at sites E4, 11, 15, 16, 18, 19, 22, 29.

PART D
The macroeconomic environment of business

The success of an individual business depends not only on its own particular market and its own particular decisions. It also depends on the whole *macroeconomic* environment in which it operates.

If the economy is booming, then individual businesses are likely to be more profitable than if the economy is in recession. It is thus important for businesses to understand the forces that affect the whole business climate.

One of these forces is the level of confidence, both of consumers and business. If business confidence is high, then firms are likely to invest. Similarly, if consumer confidence is high, spending in the shops is likely to be high and this will increase business profitability. The result will be economic growth. If, however, people are predicting a recession, firms will hold off investing and consumer spending may well decline. This could tip the economy into recession.

In Chapter 10 we look at the various national forces affecting the performance of the economy.

Another key ingredient of the macroeconomic environment is government policy and the actions of the central bank (the Bank of England in the UK). If the government raises taxes or the central bank raises interest rates this could impact directly on business profitability and on business confidence. We examine domestic macroeconomic policies in Chapter 11.

In the final two chapters we turn to the international macroeconomic environment. In Chapter 12 we look at the role of international trade. We see how countries and firms can gain from trade and why, despite this, governments sometimes choose to restrict trade.

Then in Chapter 13 we examine the flows of finance across international exchanges. We see how exchange rates are determined and how changes in exchange rates affect business. We study the euro and whether having a single currency for many EU countries benefits business. Finally, we look at attempts by governments worldwide to coordinate their macroeconomic policies.

Business issues covered in this chapter

- What determines the level of activity in the economy and hence the overall business climate?
- If a stimulus is given to the economy, what will be the effect on business output?
- Why do economies experience periods of boom followed by periods of recession? What determines the length and magnitude of these 'phases' of the business cycle?
- How are interest rates determined and what is the role of the money supply in the process?
- What determines the supply of money in the economy?
- What are the causes of unemployment and how does unemployment relate to the level of business activity?
- What are the causes of inflation and how does inflation relate to the level of business activity?

Chapter map

CHAPTER 10

The economy and business activity

10.1   Business activity and the circular flow of income

We start our examination of the macroeconomic environment by asking what determines the overall level of business activity. One of the most important determinants, at least in the short run, is the level of spending on firms' output. The more consumers spend, the more will firms want to produce in order to meet that consumer demand.

We use the term 'aggregate demand' (*AD*) to represent the total level of spending on the goods and services produced within the country over a given time period (normally a year). This spending consists of four elements: consumer spending on domestically produced goods and services (C_d), investment expenditure within the country by firms, whether on plant and equipment or on building up stocks (*I*), government spending on goods and services (such as health, education and transport) (*G*) and the expenditure by residents abroad on this country's exports (*X*). Thus:

$$AD = C_d + I + G + X$$

The total annual output of goods and services on which aggregate demand is spent is called GDP, or 'gross domestic product'. As long as there is spare capacity in the economy, a rise in aggregate demand will stimulate firms to produce more. GDP will rise.

A simple way of understanding this process is to use a 'circular flow of income diagram'. This is shown in Figure 10.1 overleaf.

In the diagram, the economy is divided into two major groups: *firms* and *households*. Each group has two roles. Firms are producers of goods and services; they are also the employers of labour. Households (which is the word we use for individuals) are the consumers of goods and services; they are also the suppliers of labour. In the diagram there is an inner flow and various outer flows of income between these two groups.

The inner flow, withdrawals and injections

The inner flow

Firms pay incomes to households in the form of wages and salaries. Some households also receive incomes from firms in the form of dividends on shares, or interest on loans or rent on property. Thus on the left-hand side of the diagram money flows directly from firms to households as household incomes.

Figure 10.6 Equilibrium in the money market

But the price of assets is inversely related to interest rates. The higher the price of an asset (such as a government bond), the less will any given interest payment be as a percentage of its price (e.g. £10 as a percentage of £100 is 10 per cent, but as a percentage of £200 is only 5 per cent). Thus a higher price of assets will correspond to lower interest rates.

As the rate of interest fell, so there would be a movement down along the M_s and M_d curves. The interest rate would go on falling until it reached r_e. Equilibrium would then be achieved.

Similarly, if the rate of interest were below r_e, people would have insufficient money balances. They would sell securities, thus lowering their prices and raising the rate of interest until it reached r_e.

Causes of changes in interest rates

We saw above what would cause an increase in the supply of money. If money supply does increase, the M_s line will shift to the right in Figure 10.6. This will cause a fall in the rate of interest to the point where the new M_s line intersects with the M_d curve.

A change in interest rates will also occur if the demand for money changes (i.e. the M_d curve shifts). For example, a rise in incomes would lead to people wanting to hold larger money balances. This would shift the M_d curve to the right and drive up the rate of interest.

In practice, the Bank of England seeks to *control* the rate of interest. We see how it achieves this in the next chapter.

Effects of changes in interest rates

A reduction in interest rates (e.g. from a rise in money supply) will lead to a rise in investment and consumer spending as firms and consumers borrow more. This rise in aggregate demand will then lead to a multiplied rise in GDP. How much aggregate demand increases depends on (a) the elasticity of the demand-for-money curve – the steeper the M_d curve, the more will interest rates fall for any given rise in money supply; (b) the responsiveness of businesses and consumers to a change in interest rates – the more responsive they are, the bigger will be the rise in aggregate demand and hence the bigger the multiplied rise in GDP.

> **Pause for thought**
>
> *Assume that interest rates fall. Under what circumstances will this lead to (a) a large rise in business investment; (b) little or no change in business investment?*

Recap

■ Interest rates are an important determinant of business activity. They are determined by the interaction of the demand and supply of money.

■ Money in its narrow sense includes just cash in circulation. Money is normally defined more broadly, however, to include all bank deposits, not just those in the form of cash. M4 is the name given in the UK to this broader measure of the money supply.

■ Bank deposits expand through a process of credit creation. If banks' liquid assets increase, they can be used as a base for increasing loans. When the loans are redeposited in banks, they form the base for yet more loans, and thus takes place a process of multiple credit expansion. The ratio of the increase of deposits to an expansion of banks' liquidity base is called the 'bank multiplier'. It is the inverse of the liquidity ratio.

■ Money supply will rise if (a) banks respond to an increased demand for money by increasing credit without an increase in liquidity; (b) there is an inflow of money from abroad; (c) the government has a PSNCR and finances it by borrowing from the banking sector.

■ The demand for money is determined mainly by people's incomes, the risk attached to alternatives to money and the rate of interest (the opportunity cost of holding money). The higher the rate of interest, the lower the demand for money.

■ The equilibrium rate of interest is where the supply of money is equal to the demand. A rise in the rate of interest can be caused by an increased demand for money or a reduced supply.

Unemployment   10.5

We saw in Chapter 8 how employment is determined in individual labour markets. In this section we look at the overall level of employment and unemployment in the economy. This, as we shall see, depends in part on the level of business activity. When the economy is booming, employment will be high and unemployment low as businesses take on more labour to meet the extra demand.

Measuring unemployment

Unemployment can be expressed either as a number (e.g. 1.5 million) or as a percentage (e.g. 5 per cent). If the figure is to be expressed as a percentage, then it is a

Definitions

Labour force

The number employed plus the number unemployed.

Unemployment rate

The number unemployed expressed as a percentage of the labour force.

Claimant unemployment

Those in receipt of unemployment-related benefits.

Standardised unemployment rate

The measure of the unemployment rate used by the ILO and OECD. The unemployed are defined as people of working age who are without work, available for work and actively seeking employment.

Aggregate supply of labour curve

A curve showing the total number of people willing and able to work at different average real wage rates.

Aggregate demand for labour curve

A curve showing the total demand for labour in the economy at different average real wage rates.

percentage of the total **labour force**. The labour force is defined as: *those in employment plus those unemployed*. Thus if 24 million people were employed and 1 million people were unemployed, the **unemployment rate** would be:

$$\frac{1}{24 + 1} \times 100 = 4 \text{ per cent}$$

Two common measures of unemployment are used in official statistics. The first is **claimant unemployment**. This is simply a measure of all those in receipt of unemployment-related benefits. In the UK, claimants receive the 'job-seeker's allowance'.

The second measure is the **standardised unemployment rate**. Since 1998, this has been the main measure used by the UK government. It is the measure used by the International Labour Organisation (ILO) and the Organisation for Economic Co-operation and Development (OECD), two international organisations that publish unemployment statistics for many countries.

In this measure, the unemployed are defined as people of working age who are without work, available to start work within two weeks and *actively seeking employment* or waiting to take up an appointment. The figures are compiled from the results of national labour force surveys. In the UK the labour force survey is conducted quarterly.

But is the standardised unemployment rate likely to be higher or lower than the claimant unemployment rate? The standardised rate is likely to be higher to the extent that it includes people seeking work who are nevertheless not entitled to claim benefits, but lower to the extent that it excludes those who are claiming benefits and yet who are not actively seeking work. Clearly, the tougher the benefit regulations, the lower the claimant rate will be relative to the standardised rate.

Unemployment and the labour market

We now turn to the causes of unemployment. These causes fall into two broad categories: *equilibrium* unemployment and *disequilibrium* unemployment. To make clear the distinction between the two, it is necessary to look at how the labour market works.

Figure 10.7 shows the aggregate demand for labour and the aggregate supply of labour: that is, the total demand and supply of labour in the whole economy. The *real* average wage rate is plotted on the vertical axis. This is the average wage rate expressed in terms of its purchasing power: in other words, after taking inflation into account.

The **aggregate supply of labour curve** (AS_L) shows the number of workers *willing to accept jobs* at each wage rate. This curve is relatively inelastic, since the size of the workforce at any one time cannot change significantly. Nevertheless, it is not totally inelastic because (a) a higher wage rate will encourage some people to enter the labour market (e.g. parents raising children) and (b) the unemployed will be more willing to accept job offers rather than continuing to search for a better-paid job.

The **aggregate demand for labour curve** (AD_L) slopes downward. The higher the wage rate, the more will firms attempt to economise on labour and to substitute other factors of production for labour.

The labour market is in equilibrium at a wage of W_e, where the demand for labour equals the supply. If the wage were above W_e, the labour market would be

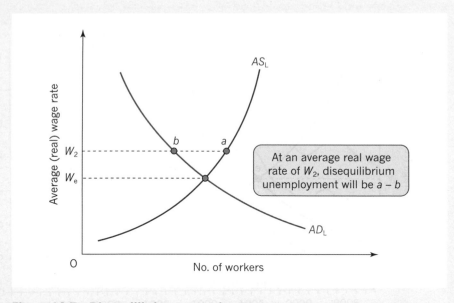

Figure 10.7 Disequilibrium unemployment

in a state of disequilibrium. At a wage rate of W_2, there is an excess supply of labour of $a - b$. This is called **disequilibrium unemployment**.

For disequilibrium unemployment to occur, two conditions must hold:

■ The aggregate supply of labour must exceed the aggregate demand.

■ There must be a 'stickiness' in wages. In other words, the wage rate must not immediately fall to W_e.

Even when the labour market *is* in equilibrium, however, not everyone looking for work will be employed. Some people will hold out, hoping to find a better job. The curve N in Figure 10.8 (overleaf) shows the total number in the labour force. The horizontal difference between it and the aggregate supply of labour curve (AS_L) represents the excess of people looking for work over those actually willing to accept jobs. Q_e represents the equilibrium level of employment and the distance $d - e$ represents the **equilibrium level of unemployment**. This is sometimes known as the *natural level of unemployment*.

Types of disequilibrium unemployment

There are two main causes of disequilibrium unemployment.

Real-wage unemployment

Real-wage unemployment is where wages are set above the market-clearing level, for example at W_2 in Figure 10.7. This could be the result of either minimum-wage legislation or the activities of trade unions. Excessive real wage rates were blamed by the Thatcher and Major governments for the high unemployment of the 1980s

Definitions

Disequilibrium unemployment
Unemployment resulting from real wages in the economy being above the equilibrium level.

Equilibrium ('natural') unemployment
The difference between those who would like employment at the current wage rate and those willing and able to take a job.

Real-wage unemployment
Disequilibrium unemployment caused by real wages being driven up above the market-clearing level.

Definitions

Structural unemployment

Unemployment that arises from changes in the pattern of demand or supply in the economy. People made redundant in one part of the economy cannot immediately take up jobs in other parts (even though there are vacancies).

Technological unemployment

Structural unemployment that occurs as a result of the introduction of labour-saving technology.

Regional unemployment

Structural unemployment occurring in specific regions of the country.

Seasonal unemployment

Unemployment associated with industries or regions where the demand for labour is lower at certain times of the year.

not to take the first job they are offered. Instead they may continue searching, hoping that a better one will turn up.

The problem is that information is imperfect. Employers are not fully informed about what labour is available; workers are not fully informed about what jobs are available and what they entail. Both employers and workers, therefore, have to search: employers search for the right labour and workers search for the right jobs.

Structural unemployment

Structural unemployment is where the structure of the economy changes. Employment in some industries may expand while in others it contracts. There are two main reasons for this.

A change in the pattern of demand. Some industries experience declining demand. This may be due to a change in consumer tastes. Certain goods may go out of fashion. Or it may be due to competition from other industries. For example, consumer demand may shift away from coal and to other fuels. This will lead to structural unemployment in mining areas.

A change in the methods of production (technological unemployment). New techniques of production often allow the same level of output to be produced with fewer workers. This is known as 'labour-saving technical progress'. Unless output expands sufficiently to absorb the surplus labour, people will be made redundant. This creates **technological unemployment**. An example is the job losses in the banking industry caused by the increase in the number of cash machines and by the development of telephone and Internet banking.

Structural unemployment often occurs in particular regions of the country. When it does, it is referred to as **regional unemployment**. This is most likely to occur when particular industries are concentrated in particular areas. For example, the decline in the South Wales coal mining industry led to high unemployment in the Welsh valleys.

Seasonal unemployment

Seasonal unemployment occurs when the demand for certain types of labour fluctuates with the seasons of the year. This problem is particularly severe in holiday areas such as Cornwall, where unemployment can reach very high levels in the winter months.

Recap

- The two most common measures of unemployment are claimant unemployment (those claiming unemployment-related benefits) and ILO/OECD standardised unemployment (those available for work and actively seeking work or waiting to take up an appointment).

- Unemployment can be divided into disequilibrium and equilibrium unemployment.

- Disequilibrium unemployment occurs when the average real wage rate is above the level that will equate the aggregate demand and supply of labour. It can be caused by unions or government pushing up wages (real-wage unemployment) or by a fall in aggregate demand but a downward 'stickiness' in real wages (demand-deficient or cyclical unemployment).

■ Equilibrium unemployment occurs when there are people unable or unwilling to fill job vacancies. This may be due to poor information in the labour market and hence a time lag before people find suitable jobs (frictional unemployment), to a changing pattern of demand or supply in the economy and hence a mismatching of labour with jobs (structural unemployment – specific types being technological and regional unemployment), or to seasonal fluctuations in the demand for labour.

Inflation   10.6

The rate of inflation measures the annual percentage increase in prices. The most usual measure is that of *consumer* prices. The government publishes a consumer prices index (CPI) each month, and the rate of inflation is the percentage increase in that index over the previous 12 months. Figure 10.10 shows the rates of inflation for various industrial economies from 1965 to 2008. As you can see, inflation was particularly severe between 1973 and 1983, and relatively low in the mid-1980s and in recent years.

It is also possible to give the rates of inflation for other prices. For example, indices are published for commodity prices, food prices, house prices, import prices, prices after taking taxes into account and so on. Their respective rates of inflation are simply their annual percentage increase. Likewise it is possible to give the rate of inflation of wage rates ('wage inflation').

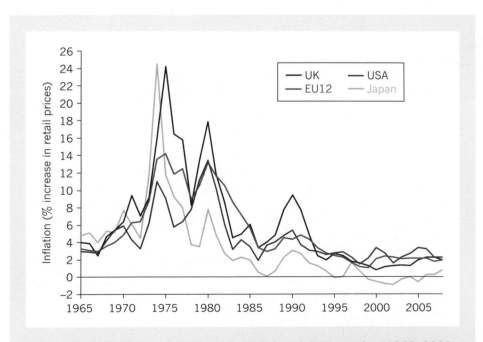

Figure 10.10   Inflation rates in selected industrial economies (1965–2008)

Definition

Real growth values
Values of the rate of growth in GDP or any other variable after taking inflation into account. The real value of the growth in a variable equals its growth in money (or 'nominal') value minus the rate of inflation.

When there is inflation, we have to be careful in assessing how much national output, consumption, wages, etc. are increasing. Take the case of GDP. GDP in year 2 may seem higher than in year 1, but this may be partly (or even wholly) the result of higher prices. Thus GDP in money terms may have risen by 5 per cent, but if inflation is 3 per cent, **real growth in GDP** will be only 2 per cent. In other words, the volume of output will be only 2 per cent higher.

The distinction between real and nominal values.
Nominal figures are those using current prices, interest rates, etc. Real figures are figures corrected for inflation.

Key Idea 27

Pause for thought

Why is inflation damaging to (a) business; (b) the economy in general?

Before we proceed, a word of caution: be careful not to confuse a rise or fall in *inflation* with a rise or fall in *prices*. A rise in inflation means a *faster* increase in prices. A fall in inflation means a *slower* increase in prices (but still an increase as long as inflation is positive).

Aggregate demand and supply and the level of prices

The level of prices in the economy is determined by the interaction of aggregate demand and aggregate supply. The analysis is similar to that of demand and supply in individual markets (see Chapter 2), but there are some crucial differences. Figure 10.11 shows aggregate demand and supply curves. Let us examine each in turn.

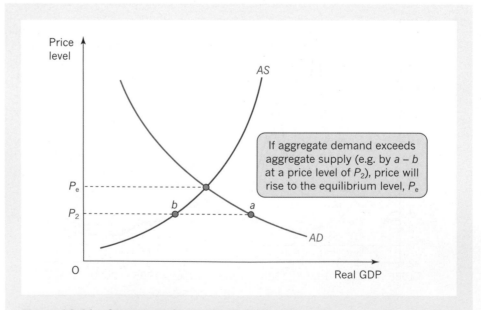

Figure 10.11   Aggregate demand and aggregate supply

Aggregate demand curve

Remember what we said about aggregate demand earlier in the chapter. It is the total level of spending on the country's products: that is, by consumers, by the government, by firms on investment, and by people residing abroad. The aggregate demand curve shows how much national output (real GDP) will be demanded at each level of prices. But why does the *AD* curve slope downwards: why do people demand fewer products as prices rise? There are three main reasons:

■ If prices rise, people will be encouraged to buy fewer of the country's products and more imports instead (which are now relatively cheaper); also the country will sell fewer exports. Thus aggregate demand will be lower.

■ As prices rise, people will need more money in their accounts to pay for their purchases. With a given supply of money in the economy, this will have the effect of driving up interest rates (the M_d curve shifts to the right in Figure 10.6 on page 296). The effect of higher interest rates will be to discourage borrowing and encourage saving. Both will have the effect of reducing spending and hence reducing aggregate demand.

■ If prices rise, the value of people's savings will be eroded. They may thus save more (and spend less) to compensate.

Aggregate supply curve

The aggregate supply curve slopes upwards – at least in the short run. In other words, the higher the level of prices, the more will be produced. The reason is simple: provided that input prices (and, in particular, wage rates) do not rise as rapidly as product prices, firms' profitability at each level of output will be higher than before. This will encourage them to produce more.

Equilibrium

The equilibrium price level will be where aggregate demand equals aggregate supply. To demonstrate this, consider what would happen if aggregate demand exceeded aggregate supply: e.g. at P_2 in Figure 10.11. The resulting shortages throughout the economy would drive up prices. This would cause a movement up along both the *AD* and *AS* curves until $AD = AS$ (at P_e).

Shifts in the AD or AS curves

If there is a change in the price level there will be a movement *along* the *AD* and *AS* curves. If any other determinant of *AD* or *AS* changes, the respective curve will shift. The analysis here is very similar to shifts and movements along demand and supply curves in individual markets (see pages 38 and 42).

The aggregate demand curve will shift if there is a change in any of its components – consumption of domestic products, investment, government expenditure or exports. Thus if the government decides to spend more, or if consumers spend more as a result of lower taxes, or if business confidence increases so that firms decide to invest more, the *AD* curve will shift to the right.

Similarly, the aggregate supply curve will shift to the right if there is a rise in labour productivity or in the stock of capital: i.e. if there is a rise in the capacity of the economy.

Figure 10.12 Demand-pull inflation

Causes of inflation

Demand-pull inflation

Demand-pull inflation
Inflation caused by
persistent rises in
aggregate demand.

Cost-push inflation
Inflation caused by
persistent rises in
costs of production
(independently of
demand).

Demand-pull inflation is caused by continuing rises in aggregate demand. In Figure 10.12, the AD curve shifts to the right, and continues doing so. Firms will respond to the rise in aggregate demand partly by raising prices and partly by increasing output (there is a move upwards along the AS curve). Just how much they raise prices depends on how much their costs rise as a result of increasing output. This in turn depends upon how close actual output is to output ceiling (see Figure 10.4 on page 286). The less slack there is in the economy, the more will firms respond to a rise in demand by raising their prices (the steeper will be the AS curve).

Demand-pull inflation is typically associated with a booming economy. Many economists therefore argue that it is the counterpart of demand-deficient unemployment. When the economy is in recession, demand-deficient unemployment will be high, but demand-pull inflation will be low. When, on the other hand, the economy is near the peak of the business cycle, demand-pull inflation will be high, but demand-deficient unemployment will be low.

Cost-push inflation

Cost-push inflation is associated with continuing rises in costs and hence continuing upward (leftward) shifts in the AS curve (see Figure 10.13). If firms face a rise in costs, they will respond partly by raising prices and passing the costs on to the consumer, and partly by cutting back on production (there is a movement back along the AD curve).

Just how much firms raise prices and cut back on production depends on the shape of the aggregate demand curve. The less elastic the AD curve – in other words,

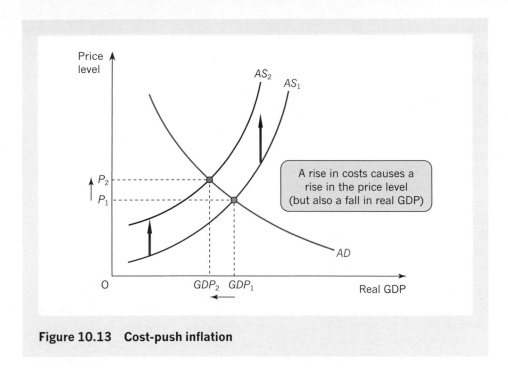

Figure 10.13   Cost-push inflation

the less consumers, firms and the government are prepared to cut back on real expenditure – the less sales will fall as a result of any price rise, and hence the more will firms be able to pass on the rise in their costs to consumers as higher prices.

The rise in costs may originate from a number of different sources, such as higher wages as a result of trade unions pushing up wages independently of the demand for labour, firms using their monopoly power to make bigger profits by pushing up prices independently of consumer demand, or import prices rising independently of the level of aggregate demand (e.g. OPEC putting up oil prices).

In all these cases, inflation occurs because one or more groups are exercising economic power. The problem is likely to get worse, therefore, if there is an increasing concentration of economic power over time (e.g. if firms or unions get bigger and bigger, and more monopolistic) or if groups become more militant. In practice, cost-push inflation has tended to get less around the world in recent years as the process of globalisation and freer trade has made international markets more competitive.

Demand-pull and cost-push inflation can occur together, since wage and price rises can be caused both by increases in aggregate demand and by independent causes pushing up costs. Even when an inflationary process *starts* as either demand-pull or cost-push, it is often difficult to separate the two. An initial cost-push inflation may encourage the government to expand aggregate demand to offset rises in unemployment. Alternatively, an initial demand-pull inflation may strengthen the power of certain groups, who then use this power to drive up costs. Either way, the result is likely to be continuing rightward shifts in the *AD* curve and upward shifts in the *AS* curve. Prices will carry on rising.

Box 10.4

Inflation or deflation

Where's the danger?

The spectre of deflation

In the first edition of this book, I wrote that 'Inflation no longer seems a serious worry in many developed economies. Instead, 'deflation' (i.e. falling prices) has become a source of concern. The Japanese economy has been in deflation for the past ten years, but more recently the US Federal Reserve – the 'Fed' (America's central bank) and the European Central Bank have sounded warnings that deflation is a real and present danger to us all, set to engulf the global economic system.'

That was back in 2003, and the box included a quote from *The Sunday Times* of 11 May of that year, which assessed the danger. The quote included the following:

Consumers have had a good run in America. Twenty years ago a Burger King Whopper cost $1.40. Today the same burger costs 99c. Ten years ago Delta Airlines charged $388 for a flight from New York to San Francisco; this weekend flights are available for $302. Five years ago the average new car cost $25 000; now it is $24 500.

The same is true for clothes, computers, holidays and television sets. As wages have risen, prices seem to have fallen across the board. But can you have too much of a good thing?

Last week, America's central bankers warned that falling prices could harm the US economy. The Federal Reserve even went as far as to raise the spectre of deflation – an economic malaise that has paralysed the Japanese economy for a decade and was last seen in America during the Great Depression of the 1930s.

Consumers normally welcome falling prices, but in a deflating economy such falls can create a damaging downward spiral. Profits fall as companies are unable to offset costs by raising prices. Companies then cut staff to save money. Job losses lead to falling sales.

Declining sales also make it harder for companies and people to meet their debts, leading to further declines in sales and a rise in bankruptcies. Falling prices also lead people to defer purchases in the belief that prices will come down further.[1]

One of the main causes of declining prices was the process of globalisation. Imports from low-cost countries, such as China and India, have driven prices down. What is more, outsourcing call-centre, back-office and IT work to developing countries has put downward pressure on wages. This downward effect on prices and wages in the USA and other developed economies has been dubbed the 'China price' effect.

A return of inflation?

The US and other OECD economies staged a rapid recovery after 2003. Between 2004 and 2006, US economic growth averaged 3.8 per cent and the OECD countries' averaged 3.1 per cent. These rates, however, were dwarfed by China and India, which experienced growth rates of 10.1 per cent and 8.4 per cent respectively over the same period.

The rapid growth in aggregate demand in many OECD countries put upward pressure on prices and wages but, unlike previously, the 'China price' effect was beginning to *reinforce* this upward pressure. As *The Economist* of 24 June 2006 stated:

China's excessive growth is not only of domestic concern. With much of the world increasingly worried about inflation, questions arise about what an overheating Chinese economy could do to global prices. . . . After being squeezed between rising input costs and falling factory-gate prices, China's manufacturers are starting to raise prices to rebuild margins – and getting away with it because both domestic demand and exports are still far stronger than they were two years ago. Add in higher domestic food and energy prices and surging labour costs, and the China price may soon be a good deal higher.

What is more, a rise in Chinese prices would be welcomed by industry in the developed world, which has suffered from consumers switching from their products to cheaper Chinese ones. To achieve this, the US and other governments have put China under pressure to allow the value of its currency, the yuan, to rise on foreign exchange markets. This would make its exports more expensive, and thus help competitor industries outside China. It would, however, boost inflation!

An alternative means of limiting Chinese imports is to put taxes (called 'tariffs') on them or to limit the quantity imported. European and other governments have been put under pressure to adopt such measures. Either way, this is again likely to raise the price of Chinese imports, putting upward pressure on inflation.

? Questions

1. What long-term economic benefits might deflation generate for business and the economy in general?
2. Would an inflationary China price effect be an example of demand-pull or cost-push inflation?

[1] From 'Deflation turns into biggest economic risk', *The Times*, 11 May 2003. © NI Syndication Limited. Reproduced with permission

Expectations and inflation

Workers and firms take account of the *expected* rate of inflation when making decisions.

Imagine that a union and an employer are negotiating a wage increase. Let us assume that both sides expect a rate of inflation of 5 per cent. The union will be happy to receive a wage rise somewhat above 5 per cent. That way the members would be getting a *real* rise in incomes. The employers will be happy to pay a wage rise somewhat below 5 per cent. After all, they can put their price up by 5 per cent, knowing that their rivals will do approximately the same. The actual wage rise that the two sides agree on will thus be somewhere around 5 per cent.

Now let us assume that the expected rate of inflation is 10 per cent. Both sides will now negotiate around this benchmark, with the outcome being somewhere round about 10 per cent.

Thus the higher the expected rate of inflation, the higher will be the level of pay settlements and price rises, and hence the higher will be the resulting actual rate of inflation.

In recent years the importance of expectations in explaining the actual rate of inflation has been increasingly recognised by economists, and it has prompted them to discover just what determines people's expectations.

Recap

- Inflation is the annual percentage increase in prices.

- Equilibrium in the economy occurs when aggregate demand equals aggregate supply. Prices will rise if there is a rightward shift in the aggregate demand curve or an upward (leftward) shift in the aggregate supply curve.

- Demand-pull inflation occurs as a result of increases in aggregate demand. It is typically associated with a booming economy.

- Cost-push inflation occurs when there are increases in the costs of production independent of rises in aggregate demand.

- Expectations play a crucial role in determining the level of inflation. The higher people expect inflation to be, the higher it will be.

QUESTIONS

1. The following table shows index numbers for real GDP (national output) for various countries (2000 = 100).

	2000	2001	2002	2003	2004	2005	2006
USA	100.0	100.8	102.7	105.8	110.5	114.1	117.8
Japan	100.0	100.4	100.1	102.6	106.7	108.9	111.3
Germany	100.0	101.0	101.1	101.0	102.2	103.6	104.8
France	100.0	102.1	103.2	103.7	105.9	108.0	109.9
UK	100.0	102.3	104.1	106.4	109.8	112.7	115.3

Sources: *Various*

Using the formula $G = (Y_t - Y_{t-1})/Y_{t-1} \times 100$ (where G is the rate of growth, Y is the index number of output, t is any given year and $t - 1$ is the previous year):

(a) Work out the growth rate for each country for each year from 2001–06.

(b) Plot the figures on a graph. Describe the pattern that emerges.

2. In terms of the UK circular flow of income, are the following net injections, net withdrawals or neither? If there is uncertainty, explain your assumptions.

(a) Firms are forced to take a cut in profits in order to give a pay rise.

(b) Firms spend money on research.

(c) The government increases personal tax allowances.

(d) The general public invests more money in building societies.

(e) UK investors earn higher dividends on overseas investments.

(f) The government purchases US military aircraft.

(g) People draw on their savings to finance holidays abroad.

(h) People draw on their savings to finance holidays in the UK.

(i) The government runs a budget deficit (spends more than it receives in tax revenues).

3. Assume that the multiplier has a value of 3. Now assume that the government decides to increase aggregate demand in an attempt to reduce unemployment. It raises government expenditure by £100 million with no increase in taxes. Firms, anticipating a rise in their sales, increase investment by £200 million, of which £50 million consists of purchases of foreign machinery. How much will GDP rise? (Assume that nothing else changes.)

4. What factors could explain why some countries have a higher multiplier than others?

5. At what point of the business cycle is the country now? What do you predict will happen to growth over the next two years? On what basis do you make your prediction?

6. Why does a booming economy not carry on booming indefinitely? Why does an economy in recession pull out of that recession?

7. For what possible reasons may one country experience a persistently faster rate of economic growth than another?

8. Imagine that the banking system receives additional deposits of £100 million and that all the individual banks wish to retain their current liquidity ratio of 20 per cent.

   (a) How much will banks choose to lend out initially?

   (b) What will happen to banks' deposits when the money that is lent out is spent and the recipients of it deposit it in their bank accounts?

   (c) How much of these latest deposits will be lent out by the banks?

   (d) By how much will total deposits (liabilities) eventually have risen, assuming that none of the additional liquidity is held outside the banking sector?

   (e) What is the size of the deposits multiplier?

9. What effects will the following have on the equilibrium rate of interest? (You should consider which way the demand and/or supply curves of money shift.)

   (a) Banks find that they have a higher liquidity ratio than they need.

   (b) A rise in incomes.

   (c) A growing belief that interest rates will rise from their current level.

10. Would it be desirable to have zero unemployment?

11. Consider the most appropriate policy for tackling each of the different types of unemployment.

12. Under what circumstances will a reduction in unemployment by accompanied by (a) an increase in inflation; (b) a decrease in inflation? Explain your answer.

13. Imagine that you had to determine whether a particular period of inflation was demand pull, or cost push, or a combination of the two. What information would you require in order to conduct your analysis?

Business issues covered in this chapter

- What sorts of government macroeconomic policy are likely to impact on business and in what way?
- What will be the impact on the economy and business of various fiscal policy measures?
- What determines the effectiveness of fiscal policy in smoothing out fluctuations in the economy?
- What fiscal rules are adopted by the government and is following them a good idea?
- How does monetary policy work in the UK and what is the role of the Bank of England?
- How does targeting inflation influence interest rates and hence business activity?
- Are there better rules for determining interest rates other than sticking to a simple inflation target?
- How can supply-side policy influence business and the economy?
- What types of supply-side policies can be pursued and what is their effectiveness?

Chapter map

CHAPTER 11

National macroeconomic policy

A key influence on the macroeconomic environment of business is the government. Governments like to achieve economic success, including sustained and stable economic growth, low unemployment and low inflation. To achieve these objectives, various types of policy are used. This chapter looks at the three main categories of macroeconomic policy.

The first is **fiscal policy**. This is where the government uses the balance of taxation (a withdrawal from the circular flow of income) and government expenditure (an injection) to influence the level of aggregate demand. If the economy is in recession, the government could increase government expenditure and/or cut taxes. The effect would be a higher level of aggregate demand and hence a multiplied rise in GDP and lower unemployment. If the economy was expanding too rapidly in a way that was unsustainable and hence with rising inflation, the government could do the reverse: it could cut government expenditure and/or raise taxes. This would help to slow the economy down and dampen inflation.

The second type of policy is **monetary policy**. Here the government sets the framework of policy, which in many countries, including the UK, means setting a target for the rate of inflation. In the UK the rate is 2 per cent, as it is also in the eurozone. The central bank is then charged with adjusting interest rates to keep inflation on target.

These first two types of policy are referred to as **demand-side** or **demand management policies** as they seek to control the level of aggregate demand. The third category of policy is **supply-side policy**. This seeks to control aggregate supply directly. For example, the government might seek ways of encouraging greater productivity through increased research and development or better training programmes. Or it might seek to improve the country's transport and communications infrastructure, for example by investing in the railways or building more roads.

The difference between demand-side and supply-side policies is illustrated in Figures 11.1(a) and (b) (overleaf). Both diagrams show an aggregate demand and an aggregate supply curve.

Demand-side policy seeks to shift the AD curve. This is illustrated in Figure 11.1(a). An expansionary fiscal or monetary policy would shift the AD curve to the right, say from AD_1 to AD_2. This will increase GDP (to GDP_2), thereby helping to reduce unemployment. On the other hand, it will result in higher prices: the price level will rise to P_2.

A contractionary fiscal or monetary policy would help to curb rightward shifts in the AD curve or even cause the curve to shift to the left. The policy could be used to tackle inflation, but would run the risk of a reduction in the rate of growth of GDP, or even a recession, and higher unemployment.

Definitions

Fiscal policy
Policy to affect aggregate demand by altering government expenditure and/or taxation.

Monetary policy
Policy to affect aggregate demand by central bank action to alter interest rates or money supply.

Demand-side or **demand management policy**
Policy to affect aggregate demand (i.e. fiscal or monetary policy).

Supply-side policy
Policy to affect aggregate supply directly.

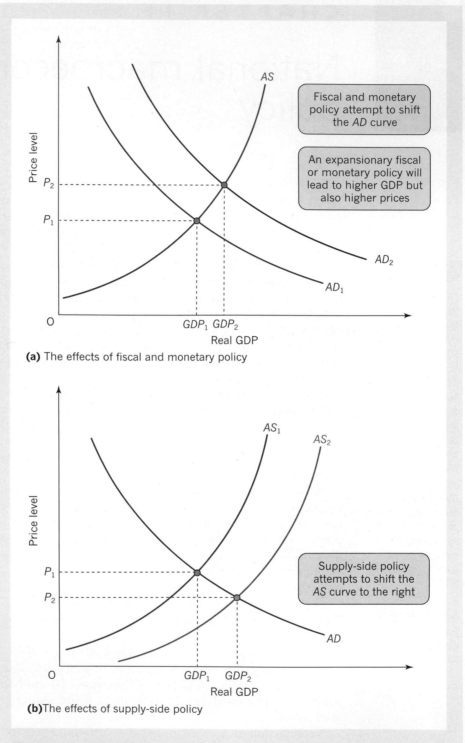

(a) The effects of fiscal and monetary policy

(b) The effects of supply-side policy

Figure 11.1   The effects of macroeconomic policies

Supply-side policy seeks to shift the *AS* curve to the right. If successful, it will lead to both higher GDP and employment and lower prices (or at least lower inflation). This is illustrated in Figure 11.1(b). A rightward shift in the aggregate supply curve from AS_1 to AS_2 results in a rise in GDP to GDP_2 and a fall in the price level to P_2.

Fiscal policy   **11.1**

Fiscal policy can be used to perform two main functions:

■ To prevent the occurrence of *fundamental* disequilibrium in the economy. In other words, expansionary fiscal policy could be used to prevent mass unemployment, such as that experienced in the Great Depression of the 1930s or in east and south-east Asia, Russia and Brazil in the late 1990s. Likewise deflationary fiscal policy could be used to prevent excessive inflation, such as that experienced in many countries in the early 1970s.

■ To smooth out the fluctuations in the economy associated with the business cycle. This would involve reducing government expenditure or raising taxes during the boom phase of the cycle. This would dampen down the expansion and prevent 'overheating' of the economy, with its attendant rising inflation. Conversely, during the recessionary phase, as unemployment grew and output declined, the government should cut taxes or raise government expenditure in order to boost the economy. If these stabilisation policies are successful, they will amount merely to **fine-tuning**. Problems of excess or deficient demand will never be allowed to get severe. Any movement of aggregate demand away from a steady growth path will be immediately 'nipped in the bud'.

Public finances

Central government deficits and surpluses

Since an expansionary fiscal policy involves raising government expenditure and/or lowering taxes, this has the effect of either increasing the **budget deficit** or reducing the **budget surplus**. A budget deficit in any one year is where central government's expenditure exceeds its revenue from taxation. A budget surplus is where tax revenues exceed central government expenditure. With the exception of short periods in 1969–70, 1987–90 and 1998–2001, governments in the UK, like most governments around the world, have run budget deficits.

Public-sector deficits and surpluses

To get a better view of the overall **stance of fiscal policy** – just how expansionary or contractionary it is – we would need to look at the deficit or surplus of the entire public sector: namely, central government, local government and public corporations.

If the public sector spends more than it earns (through taxes and the revenues of public corporations, etc.), the amount of this deficit is known as the **public-sector net cash requirement (PSNCR)**. The reason for the name 'public-sector net cash requirement' is simple. If the public sector

Pause for thought

If government is running a budget deficit, does this necessarily mean that GDP will increase?

Table 11.1   UK public-sector borrowing (public-sector net cash requirement, PSNCR)

	1986	1988	1990	1992	1994	1996	1998	2000	2001	2002	2003	2004	2005	2006
PSNCR (+ = deficit) (£bn)	+2.3	−12.1	−1.7	+28.4	+39.3	+24.7	−6.6	−37.4	−2.7	+18.3	+38.8	+41.4	+41.0	+33.3
PSNCR (% of GDP)	+0.6	−2.6	−0.3	+4.6	+5.8	+3.2	−0.8	−3.9	−0.3	+1.7	+3.5	+3.5	+3.3	+2.6

Definitions

General government debt

The accumulated central and local government deficits (less surpluses) over the years: i.e. the total amount owed by central and local government, both to domestic and overseas creditors.

Discretionary fiscal policy

Deliberate changes in tax rates or the level of government expenditure in order to influence the level of aggregate demand.

runs a deficit in the current year of, say, £1 billion, then it will have to borrow £1 billion this year (require 'cash') in order to finance it. Table 11.1 shows UK PSNCR from 1986 to 2006.

Deficits are shown as positive figures (the government must borrow). They add to the accumulated debts from the past. The accumulated debts of central and local government are known as the **general government debt**. If the public sector runs a surplus (a negative PSNCR), then this will be used to reduce the general government debt.

The use of fiscal policy

Automatic fiscal stabilisers

To some extent, government expenditure and taxation will have the effect of *automatically* stabilising the economy. For example, as GDP rises, the amount of tax people pay automatically rises. This rise in withdrawals from the circular flow of income will help to damp down the rise in GDP. This effect will be bigger if taxes are *progressive* (i.e. rise by a bigger percentage than GDP). Some government expenditure will have a similar effect. For example, total government expenditure on unemployment benefits will fall, if rises in GDP cause a fall in unemployment. This again will have the effect of dampening the rise in GDP.

Discretionary fiscal policy

Automatic stabilisers cannot *prevent* fluctuations; they merely reduce their magnitude. If there is a fundamental disequilibrium in the economy or substantial fluctuations in GDP, these automatic stabilisers will not be enough. The government may thus choose to *alter* the level of government expenditure or the rates of taxation. This is known as **discretionary fiscal policy**. Web Case D.12 looks at an example of discretionary fiscal policy in the USA.

If government expenditure on goods and services (roads, health care, education, etc.) is raised, this will create a full multiplied rise in GDP. The reason is that all the money gets spent and thus all of it goes to boosting aggregate demand.

Cutting taxes (or increasing benefits), however, will have a smaller effect on GDP than raising government expenditure on goods and services by the same amount. The reason

Pause for thought

Why will the multiplier effect of government transfer payments, such as child benefit, pensions and social security benefits be less than the full multiplier effect from government expenditure on goods and services?

Box 11.1

Fiscal policy and business

Indirect and direct effects

When the government adopts an expansionary fiscal policy there are indirect effects on virtually all firms from the expansion of the economy. Higher GDP means higher consumer demand. The greater the income elasticity of demand for a firm's products, the more it will benefit from increased sales as GDP expands.

Higher GDP, via the accelerator (see page 289), also means higher investment. This will benefit the construction industry as new factories and offices are built. It will also benefit businesses producing machinery and other capital equipment.

In addition to these indirect effects there are also *direct* effects on business from increased government expenditure. If new roads, hospitals or schools are built, the construction

industry will directly benefit. If the government spends money on refurbishing existing premises, then the building industry will directly benefit, as will the furnishing industry and businesses supplying computers and other equipment.

Similarly, there will be direct benefits from tax cuts. If corporation tax (the tax on business profits) is cut, after-tax profits will immediately increase. There will be a similar effect if employers' national insurance contributions are reduced.

Question
Apart from the industries mentioned above, what other industries are likely to benefit directly from an expansionary fiscal policy?

---

is that cutting taxes increases people's *disposable* incomes, of which only part will be spent. Part will be withdrawn into extra saving, imports and other taxes. In other words, not all the tax cuts will be passed on round the circular flow of income as extra expenditure. Thus if one-fifth of a cut in taxes is withdrawn and only four-fifths is spent, the tax multiplier will only be four-fifths as big as the government expenditure multiplier.

The effectiveness of fiscal policy

How successful will fiscal policy be? Will it be able to 'fine-tune' demand? Will it be able to achieve the level of GDP that the government would like it to achieve? Before changing government expenditure or taxation, the government will need to calculate the effect of any such change on GDP, employment and inflation. Predicting these effects, however, is often very unreliable.

Difficulty in predicting effects of changes in government expenditure. A rise in government expenditure of £x may lead to a rise in total injections (relative to withdrawals) that is smaller than £x. A major reason for this is a phenomenon known as **crowding out**. If the government relies on **pure fiscal policy** – that is, if it does not finance an increase in the budget deficit by increasing the money supply – it will have to borrow the money from individuals and firms. It will thus be competing with the private sector for finance and will have to offer higher interest rates. This will force the private sector also to offer higher interest rates, which may discourage firms from investing and individuals from buying on credit. Thus government borrowing *crowds out* private borrowing. In the extreme case, the fall in consumption and investment may completely offset the rise in government expenditure, with the result that aggregate demand does not rise at all.

Definitions

Crowding out
Where increased public expenditure diverts money or resources away from the private sector.

Pure fiscal policy
Fiscal policy which does not involve any change in money supply.

Difficulty in predicting effects of changes in taxes. A cut in taxes, by increasing people's disposable income, increases not only the amount they spend, but also the amount they save. The problem is that it is not easy to predict the relative size of these two increases. In part it will depend on whether people feel that the cut in tax is only temporary, in which case they may simply save the extra disposable income, or permanent, in which case they may adjust their consumption upwards.

Difficulty in predicting the resulting multiplied effect on GDP. The sizes of the multiplier and accelerator (see pages 283 and 289) are difficult to predict, mainly because the effects depend largely on people's confidence. For example, if the business community believes that a cut in taxes will be successful in pulling the economy out of recession, firms will invest. This will help to bring about the very recovery that firms predicted. There will be a big multiplier effect. If, however, businesses are pessimistic about the likely success of the policy, they are unlikely to invest. The economy may not recover.

Pause for thought

Give some other examples of 'random shocks' that could undermine the government's fiscal policy.

Random shocks. Forecasts cannot take into account the unpredictable. For that you would have to consult astrologers or fortune tellers! Unfortunately, unpredictable events, such as a war or a major industrial dispute, do occur and may seriously undermine the government's fiscal policy.

Problems of timing. Fiscal policy can involve considerable time lags. It may take time to recognise the nature of the problem before the government is willing to take action; tax or government expenditure changes take time to plan and implement – changes will have to wait until the next Budget to be announced and may come into effect some time later; the effects of such changes take time to work their way through the economy via the multiplier and accelerator.

If these time lags are long enough, fiscal policy could even be *de*stabilising. Expansionary policies taken to cure a recession may not take effect until the economy has *already* recovered and is experiencing a boom. Under these circumstances, expansionary policies are quite inappropriate: they simply worsen the problems of overheating. Similarly, deflationary (contractionary) policies taken to prevent excessive expansion may not take effect until the economy has already peaked and is plunging into recession. The deflationary policies only deepen the recession.

This problem is illustrated in Figure 11.2. Path (a) shows the course of the business cycle without government intervention. Ideally, with no time lags, the economy should be dampened in stage 2 and stimulated in stage 4. This would make the resulting course of the business cycle more like path (b), or even, if the policy were perfectly stabilising, a straight line. With the presence of time lags, however, deflationary policies taken in stage 2 may not come into effect until stage 4, and expansionary policies taken in stage 4 may not come into effect until stage 2. In this case the resulting course of the business cycle will be more like path (c). Quite obviously, in these circumstances 'stabilising' fiscal policy actually makes the economy *less* stable.

If the fluctuations in aggregate demand can be forecast, and if the lengths of the time lags are known, then all is not lost. At least the fiscal measures can be taken early and their delayed effects can be taken into account.

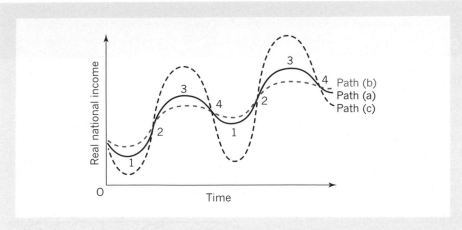

Figure 11.2   Fiscal policy: stabilising or destabilising?

Fiscal rules

Given the problems of pursuing active fiscal policy, many governments today take a much more passive approach. Instead of changing the policy as the economy changes, a rule is set for the level of public finances. This rule is then applied year after year, with taxes and government expenditure being planned to meet that rule. For example, a target could be set for the PSNCR, with government expenditure and taxes being adjusted to keep the PSNCR at or within its target level. Box 11.2 looks at some examples of fiscal targets.

The approach to fiscal policy in the UK

Since 1998, the government has set targets for government expenditure, not for just one year, but for a three-year period. Does this mean, therefore, that fiscal policy as a means of adjusting aggregate demand had been abandoned? In one sense, this is the case. The government is now committed to following its 'golden rule', whereby public-sector receipts should cover all current spending (e.g. spending on wages of public-sector employees, state pensions and other benefits, administration, repairs, heating and lighting) averaged over the course of the business cycle. This means that borrowing is allowed only for investment (e.g. on new roads and hospitals). See Box 11.2 for details.

But despite this apparent rejection of short-term discretionary fiscal adjustments, there is still a role for *automatic* fiscal stabilisers: with deficits rising in a recession and falling in a boom. There is also still the possibility, within the golden rule, of financing additional *investment* by borrowing, thereby providing a stimulus to a sluggish economy.

The golden rule also permits increased government expenditure (or tax cuts) if there is a budget surplus. Thus in the 2001 Budget the Chancellor announced spending increases of 3.7 per cent per year for three years. The effect was to provide a stimulus to the economy just at a time when the world economy was slowing down. This helped to make the slowdown in UK economic growth in the period 2001–03 much less severe than in many other countries.

Box 11.2

Following the golden rule

Fiscal policy in a strait-jacket?

If the government persistently runs a budget deficit, government debt will rise. If this debt rises faster than GDP, then it will account for a growing proportion of GDP. There is then likely to be an increasing problem of 'servicing' this debt: i.e. paying the interest on it. The government could find itself having to borrow more and more to meet the interest payments, and so government debt could rise faster still. As the government borrows more and more, so it has to pay higher interest rates to attract finances. If it is successful in this, borrowing and hence investment by the private sector could be crowded out (see page 317).

Recognising these problems, many governments in recent years have attempted to reduce their debts.

Preparing for the euro

In signing the Maastricht Treaty in 1992, the EU countries agreed that to be eligible to join the single currency (the euro), they should have sustainable deficits and debts. This was interpreted as follows: the general (i.e. central plus local) government deficit should be no more than 3 per cent of GDP and general government debt should be no more than 60 per cent of GDP, or should at least be falling towards that level at a satisfactory pace.

But in the mid-1990s, several of the countries which were subsequently to join the euro had deficits and debts substantially above these levels. Getting them down proved a painful business. Government expenditure had to be cut and taxes increased. Fiscal policy, unfortunately, proved to be powerful! Unemployment rose and growth remained low.

The EU Stability and Growth Pact

In June 1997, at the European Council in Amsterdam, the EU countries agreed on a Stability and Growth Pact. Under the Pact, which applied to countries adopting the euro, governments should seek to balance their budgets (or even aim for a surplus) averaged over the course of the business cycle. In addition, general government deficits should not exceed 3 per cent of GDP in any one year. A country's deficit is only permitted to exceed 3 per

(a) General government deficits in the eurozone

cent if its GDP has declined by at least 2 per cent (or 0.75 per cent with special permission from the Council of Ministers). Otherwise, countries with deficits exceeding 3 per cent are required to make deposits of money with the European Central Bank. These then become fines if the excessive budget deficit is not eliminated within two years.

There are two main aims of targeting a zero budget deficit over the business cycle. The first is to allow automatic stabilisers to work without 'bumping into' the 3 per cent deficit ceiling in years when economies are slowing. The second is to allow a reduction in government debts as a proportion of GDP (assuming that GDP grows on average at around 2–3 per cent per year).

The main criticism of aiming for a zero deficit over the cycle has been that this would mean a further reduction in deficits, which by the start of the euro in 1999 were typically only just meeting the 3 per cent ceiling. In other words, meeting the zero deficit target would mean further deflationary fiscal policies: something that most political leaders in Europe felt to be inappropriate at a time when there were fears of a world recession.

Later the criticisms turned on whether the Pact was flexible enough. From 2002, both Germany and France breached the 3 per cent ceiling (see diagram (a)). This was partly the result of slow growth and rising unemployment, and hence falling tax revenue and rising benefit payments. Not surprisingly, both countries were reluctant to cut government expenditure to bring the deficit in line for fear of dampening an already sluggish economy. Despite various promises by the two countries to rein in expenditure, they continued to have deficits in excess of 3 per cent.

Eventually, in March 2005 a deal was reached between European finance ministers. This allowed Germany to exclude reunification costs and France to exclude military and aid costs from the calculation of government expenditure. This compromise brought the deficits of the two countries below the 3 per cent ceiling and allowed them to escape having to adopt tighter fiscal policy.

It is interesting to note that the general government deficits in the USA and Japan in 2003 were 4.9 per cent and 8.0 per cent of GDP respectively, and both countries were adopting *expansionary* fiscal policy.

Labour's golden rule

The Labour government in the UK has adopted a similar approach to that of the Stability and Growth Pact. Under its 'golden rule', the government pledges that over the economic cycle, it will borrow only to invest (e.g. in roads, hospitals and schools) and not to fund current spending (e.g. on wages, administration and benefits). Investment is exempted from the zero borrowing rule, because it contributes towards the growth of GDP. Indeed, in its 1998 'Comprehensive Spending Review', the government announced that government investment expenditure would double as a percentage of GDP. The government has also set itself the target of maintaining a stable public-sector debt/GDP ratio below 40 per cent.

To allow the golden rule to operate, government departments are set three-year spending limits and each has separate current and capital (investment) budgets.

As with the Stability and Growth Pact, the argument is that by using an averaging rule over the cycle, automatic stabilisers will be allowed to work. Deficits of receipts over current spending

■ Average surplus on current budget since 1997–98
— Cyclically-adjusted surplus on current budget

(b) Meeting the Golden Rule?

Source: *Budget 2007*, Chart 2.3 (HM Treasury, 2007). Reproduced under the terms of the click-use licence

can occur when the economy is in recession or when growth is sluggish (as in 2001–03), helping to stimulate the economy. Surpluses can occur in boom periods (as in 1998–2000), helping to dampen the economy (see diagram (b)).

But as with the Stability and Growth Pact, a major concern is whether the policy provides too much of a strait-jacket. Does it prevent the government using substantial discretionary boosts to the economy at times of serious economic slowdown? Probably, yes, but the golden rule does permit some degree of discretionary fiscal policy and, unlike the Stability and Growth Pact, does not impose a ceiling to cyclical deficits.

? Questions

1. What effects will government investment expenditure have on general government deficits (a) in the short run; (b) in the long run?
2. If there is a danger of global recession, should governments loosen the strait-jacket of fiscal policy targets?

Recap

- The government's fiscal policy will determine the size of the budget deficit or surplus and the size of the PSNCR.

- Automatic fiscal stabilisers are tax revenues that rise and benefits that fall as GDP rises. They have the effect of reducing the size of the multiplier and thus reducing cyclical upswings and downswings.

- Discretionary fiscal policy is where the government deliberately changes taxes or government expenditure in order to alter the level of aggregate demand.

- There are problems in predicting the magnitude of the effects of discretionary fiscal policy. Expansionary fiscal policy can crowd out private expenditure, but the extent of crowding out is hard to predict and depends on business confidence. Also it is difficult to predict how people's spending will respond to changes in taxes. Various random shocks can knock fiscal policy off course.

- There are various time lags involved with fiscal policy. If these are very long, the policy could be destabilising rather than stabilising.

- Today many governments prefer a more passive approach towards fiscal policy. Targets are set for one or more measures of the public-sector finances, and then taxes and government expenditure are adjusted so as to keep to the target.

11.2 Monetary policy

Each month the Bank of England's Monetary Policy Committee meets to set interest rates. The event gets considerable media coverage. Pundits, for two or three days before the meeting, try to predict what the MPC will do and economists give their 'considered' opinions about what the MPC *ought* to do. Business leaders look at the potential impact on consumer spending, business confidence and investment.

The fact is that changes in interest rates have gained a central significance in macroeconomic policy. And it is not just in the UK. Whether it is the European Central Bank setting interest rates for the eurozone countries, or the Federal Reserve Bank setting US interest rates, or any other central bank around the world choosing what the level of interest rates should be, monetary policy is seen as having a major influence on a whole range of macroeconomic indicators.

But is monetary policy simply the setting of interest rates? In reality, it involves the central bank intervening in the money market to ensure that the interest rate that has been announced is also the *equilibrium* interest rate.

The policy setting

In framing its monetary policy, the government must decide on what the goals of the policy are. Is the aim simply to control inflation, or does the government wish also to affect output and employment, or does it want to control the exchange rate?

A decision also has to be made about who is to carry out the policy. There are three possible approaches here.

In the first, the government both sets the policy and decides the measures necessary to achieve it. Here the government would set the interest rate, with the central bank simply influencing money markets to achieve this rate. This first approach was used in the UK before 1997.

The second approach is for the government to set the policy *targets*, but for the central bank to be given independence in deciding interest rates. This is the approach adopted in the UK today. The government has set a target rate of inflation of 2 per cent, but then the MPC is free to choose the rate of interest.

The third approach is for the central bank to be given independence not only in carrying out policy, but in setting the policy targets themselves. The ECB, within the statutory objective of maintaining price stability over the medium term, decides on (a) the target rate of inflation – currently that inflation for the eurozone should be kept close to but below 2 per cent, and (b) the target rate of growth in money supply. It then sets interest rates to meet these targets.

Implementing monetary policy

Inflation may be off target. Alternatively, the government (or central bank) may wish to alter its monetary policy (e.g. choose a new target). What can it do? There are two main approaches. The first is to alter the money supply; the second is to alter interest rates. These are illustrated in Figure 11.3, which shows the demand for and supply of money (this is similar to Figure 10.6 on page 296). With an initial supply of money of M_S the equilibrium interest rate is r_1.

Assume that the central bank wants to tighten monetary policy in order to reduce inflation. It could (a) seek to shift the supply of money curve to the left, from M_S to M_S' (resulting in the equilibrium rate of interest rising from r_1 to r_2), (b) raise the interest rate directly from r_1 to r_2, and then manipulate the money supply to reduce it to M_S'.

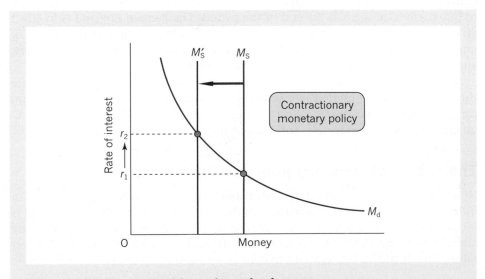

Figure 11.3   The demand for and supply of money

Techniques to control the money supply

The main way that the central bank seeks to control the money supply is through **open-market operations**. This involves the sale or purchase by the central bank of government securities (bonds or bills: see page 294) in the open market. These sales (or purchases) are *not* in response to changes in the PSNCR and are best understood, therefore, in the context of an unchanged PSNCR.

If the central bank wishes to *reduce* the money supply, it sells more securities. When people buy these securities, they pay for them with cheques drawn on banks. Thus banks' balances with the central bank are reduced. If this brings bank reserves below their prudent liquidity ratio, banks will reduce advances. There will be a multiple contraction of credit and hence of money supply.

Pause for thought

Explain how open-market operations could be used to increase the money supply.

Techniques to control interest rates

The approach to monetary control today in most countries is to focus directly on interest rates. Normally an interest rate change will be announced, and then open-market operations will be conducted by the central bank to ensure that the money supply is adjusted so as to make the announced interest rate the *equilibrium* one. Let us assume that the central bank decides to raise interest rates. What does it do?

In general, it will seek to keep banks short of liquidity. This will happen automatically on any day when tax payments by banks' customers exceed the money they receive from government expenditure. This excess is effectively withdrawn from banks and ends up in the government's account at the central bank. Even when this does not occur, sales of bills by the central bank will effectively keep the banking system short of liquidity.

How do banks acquire the necessary liquidity? The Bank of England (like other central banks) is willing to lend money to the banks on a short-term basis. It does this by entering into a **sale and repurchase ('repo') agreement** with the banks. This is an agreement whereby the banks sell some of their government bonds ('gilts') to the Bank of England on a temporary basis (normally two weeks), agreeing to buy them back again at the end of the period. The Bank of England is in effect giving a short-term loan to the banks and is thus tiding them over the period of liquidity shortage. In this role, the Bank of England is acting as **lender of last resort**, and ensures that the banks never run short of money.

Because banks frequently have to borrow from the Bank of England, it can use this to force through interest rate changes. The point is that the Bank of England can *choose the rate of interest to charge* (i.e. the repo rate). This will then have a knock-on effect on other interest rates throughout the banking system.

The impact of monetary policy on business

How much will a change in interest rates affect the level of business activity and/or inflation? This depends on the nature of the demand for loans. If this demand is (a) unresponsive to interest rate changes or (b) unstable because it is significantly affected by other determinants (such as anticipated income or foreign interest rates), then it will be very difficult to control by controlling the rate of interest.

Problem of an inelastic demand for loans. If the demand for loans is inelastic (i.e. a relatively steep M_d curve in Figure 11.3), any attempt to reduce demand will involve

Definitions

Open-market operations
The sale (or purchase) by the authorities of government securities in the open market in order to reduce (or increase) money supply.

Sale and repurchase agreement (repo)
An agreement between two financial institutions whereby one in effect borrows from another by selling some of its assets, agreeing to buy them back (repurchase them) at a fixed price and on a fixed date.

Lender of last resort
The role of the Bank of England as the guarantor of sufficient liquidity in the monetary system.

large rises in interest rates. The problem will be compounded if the demand curve shifts to the right, due, say, to a consumer spending boom. High interest rates lead to the following problems:

- They may discourage business investment and hence long-term economic growth.

- They add to the costs of production, to the costs of house purchase and generally to the cost of living. They are thus cost inflationary.

- They are politically unpopular, since the general public do not like paying higher interest rates on overdrafts, credit cards and mortgages.

- As we shall see in the next chapter, high interest rates encourage inflows of money from abroad. This drives up the exchange rate. A higher exchange rate makes domestically produced goods expensive relative to goods made abroad. This can be very damaging for export industries and industries competing with imports. Many firms in the UK have suffered badly in recent years from a high exchange rate, caused partly by higher interest rates in the UK than in both the eurozone and, until 2006, in the USA.

Evidence suggests that the demand for loans may indeed be quite inelastic. Especially in the short run, many firms and individuals simply cannot reduce their borrowing commitments. In fact, higher interest rates may force some people and firms to borrow *more* in order to finance the higher interest rate payments.

Problem of an unstable demand. Accurate monetary control requires the central bank to be able to predict the demand curve for money (in Figure 11.3). Only then can it set the appropriate level of interest rates. Unfortunately, the demand curve may shift unpredictably, making control very difficult. The major reason is *speculation.*

For example, if people think interest rates will rise and bond prices fall, in the meantime they will demand to hold their assets in liquid form. The demand for money will rise. Similarly, if people think exchange rates will rise, they will demand sterling while it is still relatively cheap. The demand for money will rise.

It is very difficult for the central bank to predict what people's expectations will be. Speculation depends so much on world political events, rumour and 'random shocks'.

If the demand curve shifts very much, and if it is inelastic, then monetary control will be very difficult. Furthermore, the central bank will have to make frequent and sizeable adjustments to interest rates. These fluctuations can be very damaging to business confidence and may discourage long-term investment.

> **Pause for thought**
>
> Assume that the central bank announces a rise in interest rates and backs this up with open-market operations. What determines the size of the resulting fall in aggregate demand?

The net result of an inelastic and unstable demand for money is that substantial interest rate changes may be necessary to bring about the required change in aggregate demand. An example occurred in 2001, when the US Federal Reserve, seeing the economy moving rapidly into recession, had to cut interest rates several times (see chart in Box 12.3). At the beginning of 2001, the US 'federal funds rate' was 6.5 per cent. By the end of the year it had been reduced to a mere 1.75 per cent.

Difficulties with choice of target

Assume that the government or central bank sets an inflation target. Should it then stick to that rate, come what may? Might not an extended period of relatively low

Goodhart's Law

Controlling a symptom or indicator of a problem is unlikely to cure the problem; it will simply mean that what is being controlled now becomes a poor indicator of the problem.

Taylor rule

A rule adopted by a central bank for setting the rate of interest. It will raise the interest rate if (a) inflation is above target or (b) economic growth is above the sustainable level (or unemployment below the equilibrium rate). The rule states how much interest rates will be changed in each case. In other words a relative weighting is attached to each of these two objectives.

inflation warrant a lower inflation target? The government must at least have the discretion to change the rules, even if only occasionally.

Then there is the question of whether success in achieving the target will bring success in achieving other macroeconomic objectives, such as low unemployment and stable economic growth. The problem is that something called **Goodhart's Law** is likely to apply. The law, named after Charles Goodhart, formerly of the Bank of England, states that attempts to control an indicator of a problem may, as a result, make it cease to be a good indicator of the problem.

Targeting inflation may make it become a poor indicator of the state of the economy. If people believe that the central bank will be successful in achieving its inflation target, then those expectations will feed into their inflationary expectations, and not surprisingly the target will be met. But that target rate of inflation may now be consistent with both a buoyant and a depressed economy. An example occurred in 2001/02 when the UK economy slowed down considerably and yet there was virtually no change in the rate of inflation. Thus achieving the inflation target may not tackle the much more serious problem of creating stable economic growth and an environment which will therefore encourage long-term investment.

Use of a Taylor rule. For this reason, many economists have advocated the use of a **Taylor rule**,[1] rather than a simple inflation target. A Taylor rule takes two objectives into account – (1) inflation and (2) either real GDP or unemployment – and seeks to get the optimum degree of stability of the two. The degree of importance attached to each of the two objectives can be decided by the government or central bank. The central bank adjusts interest rates when either the rate of inflation diverges from its target or the rate of economic growth (or unemployment) diverges from its sustainable (or equilibrium) level.

Take the case where inflation is above its target level. The central bank following a Taylor rule will raise the rate of interest. It knows, however, that this will reduce economic growth. This, therefore, limits the amount that the central bank is prepared to raise the rate of interest. The more weight it attaches to stabilising inflation, the more it will raise the rate of interest. The more weight it attaches to maintaining stable economic growth, the less it will raise the rate of interest.

Thus the central bank has to trade off inflation stability against stable economic growth.

The Bank of England's approach

The Bank of England uses a rule that is apparently more simple than the Taylor rule, but in reality is more sophisticated. The Bank of England targets inflation alone; in this sense the rule is more simple. But the inflation figure on which it bases its interest rate decisions is the *forecast* rate of inflation, not the current rate; in this sense it is more sophisticated.

The Bank of England publishes a quarterly *Inflation Report,* which contains projections for inflation for the next three years. These projections assume that interest

---

[1] Named after John Taylor, from Stanford University, who proposed that for every 1 per cent that GDP rises above sustainable GDP, real interest rates should be raised by 0.5 percentage points and for every 1 per cent that inflation rises above its target level, real interest rates should be raised by 0.5 percentage points (i.e. nominal rates should be raised by 1.5 percentage points).

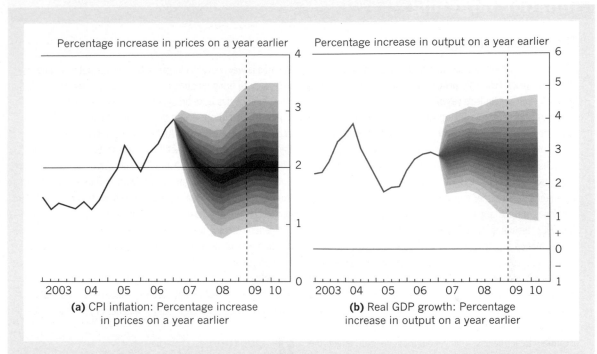

Figure 11.4 Fan chart of CPI inflation and GDP growth projections (made in 2007 Q2) based on market interest rate expectations

Source: *Inflation Report*, May (Bank of England, 2007)

rates follow market expectations. They form the basis for the Monetary Policy Committee's monthly deliberations. If the projected inflation in 24 months' time is off target, the MPC will change interest rates accordingly.

Two key projections of the MPC are shown in the Bank of England's *Inflation Report*, which is published each quarter. These are shown in Figure 11.4. They are known as 'fan charts'. The first plots the forecast range of inflation. The second plots the forecast range of real GDP growth. In each case, the darkest central band represents a 10 per cent likelihood, as does each of the eight subsequent pairs of lighter areas out from the central band. Thus inflation or GDP growth are considered to have a 90 per cent probability of being within the fan. The bands get wider as the time horizon is extended, indicating increasing uncertainty about the outcome. Also, the less reliable are considered to be the forecasts by the MPC, the wider will be the fan. The dashed line indicates the two-year target point. Thus in quarter 2 of 2007, the 2 per cent inflation target was for quarter 2 of 2009.

Although projections are made for GDP growth, these are to help inform the forecast for inflation. GDP growth is not itself an explicit target.

As it has turned out, inflation targeting has been successful in its prime purpose: keeping inflation at or near its target. For the whole period from 1997 to 2007, the chosen measure of inflation never diverged by more than 1 percentage point from the target. In the light of the history of macroeconomic management over the past 60 years, this would seem remarkable.

> **Pause for thought**
>
> *If people believe that the central bank will be successful in keeping inflation on target, does it matter whether a simple inflation rule or a Taylor rule is used? Explain.*

Box 11.3

Inflation targeting

The fashion of the age

More and more countries are turning to inflation targeting as their main macroeconomic policy. The table gives the targets for a selection of countries (as of 2007).

Part of the reason is the apparent failure of discretionary macroeconomic policies. Discretionary fiscal and monetary policies suffer from time lags, from being used for short-term political purposes and from failing to straighten out the business cycle. But if discretionary policies have seemed not to work, why choose an inflation target rather than a target for the money supply?

Money supply targets were adopted by many countries in the 1980s, including the UK, and this policy too was largely a failure. Money supply targets proved very difficult to achieve. As we have seen, money supply depends on the amount of credit banks create and this is not easy for the authorities to control. Then, even if money supply is controlled, this does not necessarily mean that aggregate demand will be controlled: people may simply adjust the amount they hold in their bank accounts. Nevertheless, many countries do still target the money supply, although in most cases it is not the main target.

Inflation targets, by contrast, have proved relatively easy to achieve. There may be problems at first, if the actual rate of inflation is way above the target level. The high rates of interest necessary to bring inflation down may cause a recession. But once inflation has been brought down and the objective is then simply to maintain it at the target level, most countries have been relatively successful. And the more successful they are, the more people will expect this success to be maintained, which in turn will help to ensure this success.

So, are there any problems with inflation targeting? Ironically, one of the main problems lies in its success. With worldwide inflation having fallen, and with global trade and competition helping to keep prices down, there is now less of a link between inflation and the business cycle. Booms no longer seem to generate the inflation they once did. Gearing interest-rate policy to maintaining low inflation could still see economies experiencing unsustainable booms, followed by recessions. Inflation may be controlled, but the business cycle may not be.

? Question

Why may there be a problem in targeting both inflation and the money supply (you might want to refer to Figure 11.3)?

Inflation targets

Country	Inflation target (%)	Details
Australia	2–3	Average over the business cycle
Brazil	4.5	Tolerance band of ±2 percentage points
Canada	1–3	6–8 quarter horizon
Chile	2–4	Over 12 to 24 months
Czech Republic	3	Tolerance band of ±1 percentage point
Eurozone	<2 but close to it	Average for eurozone as a whole; over medium term
Hungary	3.5	Tolerance band of ±1 percentage point
Iceland	2.5	Tolerance band of ±1.5 percentage points
Israel	1–3	
Mexico	3	Tolerance band of ±1 percentage point
New Zealand	1–3	On average over the medium term
Norway	2.5	Over 1–3 years
Peru	2.5	Tolerance band of ±1 percentage point
Poland	2.5	Tolerance band of ±1 percentage point
South Africa	3–6	
South Korea	2.5–3.5	
Sweden	2	1–2 year horizon; tolerance band of ±1 percentage point
Switzerland	<2 but close to it	
Thailand	0–3.5	
UK	2	2 year horizon; tolerance band of ±1 percentage point

Source: Reserve Bank of Australia (http://www.rba.gov.au/Education/monetary_policy.html)

Using monetary policy

It is impossible to use monetary policy as a precise means of controlling aggregate demand. It is especially weak when it is pulling against the expectations of firms and consumers and when it is implemented too late. However, if the authorities operate a tight monetary policy firmly enough and long enough, they should eventually be able to reduce lending and aggregate demand. But there will inevitably be time lags and imprecision in the process.

An expansionary monetary policy is even less reliable. If the economy is in recession, no matter how low interest rates are driven, people cannot be forced to borrow if they do not wish to. Firms will not borrow to invest if they predict a continuing recession.

A particular difficulty in using interest rate reductions to expand the economy arises if the repo rate is nearly zero but this is still not enough to stimulate the economy. The problem is that (nominal) interest rates cannot be negative, for clearly nobody would be willing to lend in these circumstances. Japan was in such a situation in the early 2000s. It was caught in what is known as the **liquidity trap**.

Despite these problems, changing interest rates can be quite effective. After all, they can be changed very rapidly. There are not the time lags of implementation that there are with fiscal policy. Indeed, since the early 1990s most governments or central banks in OECD countries have used interest rate changes as the major means of keeping aggregate demand and inflation under control.

Definition

Liquidity trap
When interest rates are at their floor and thus any further increases in money supply will not be spent but merely be held in bank accounts as people wait for the economy to recover and/or interest rates to rise.

Recap

- The government or central bank can use monetary policy to restrict the growth in aggregate demand by reducing money supply directly or by reducing the demand for money by raising interest rates.

- The money supply can be reduced directly by using open-market operations. This involves selling more government securities and thereby reducing banks' reserves when their customers pay for them from their bank accounts.

- The current method of control involves the Bank of England's Monetary Policy Committee announcing the interest rate and then the Bank of England bringing this rate about by its operations in the repo market. It keeps banks short of liquidity, and then supplies them with liquidity through gilt repos at the chosen interest rate (gilt repo rate). This then has a knock-on effect on interest rates throughout the economy.

- Higher interest rates, by reducing the demand for money, effectively also reduce the supply. However, with an inelastic demand for loans, interest rates may have to rise to very high levels in order to bring the required reduction in monetary growth.

- Controlling aggregate demand through interest rates is made even more difficult by *fluctuations* in the demand for money. These fluctuations are made more severe by speculation against changes in interest rates, exchange rates, the rate of inflation, etc.

- Nevertheless, controlling interest rates is a way of responding rapidly to changing forecasts, and can be an important signal to markets that inflation will be kept under control, especially when, as in the UK and the eurozone, there is a firm target for the rate of inflation.

■ Achieving inflation targets is becoming increasingly easy, but in the process inflation is becoming increasingly less related to other key objectives, such as economic growth or unemployment.

■ Some economists advocate using a Taylor rule, which involves targeting a weighted average of inflation and economic growth.

■ The Bank of England bases its decisions on the forecast inflation rate in two years' time. It adjusts interest rates if this forecast rate of inflation diverges from 2 per cent.

11.3 Supply-side policy

In considering economic policy up to this point we have focused our attention upon the demand side, where slow growth and unemployment are due to a lack of aggregate demand, and inflation is due to excessive aggregate demand. Many of the causes of these problems lie on the supply side, however, and as such require an alternative policy approach.

If successful, 'supply-side policies' will shift the aggregate supply curve to the right (see Figure 11.1(b) on page 314), thus increasing output for any given level of prices (or reducing the price level for any given level of output).

Supply-side policies can take various forms. They can be 'market orientated' and focus on ways of 'freeing up' the market, such as encouraging private enterprise, risk taking and competition; policies that provide incentives and reward initiative, hard work and productivity. Alternatively they can be *interventionist* in nature and focus on means of counteracting the deficiencies of the free market.

Either way, business leaders will be keen to have a supply-side policy that is favourable to them. This could be lower business taxes, improved education and training, a better transport and communications infrastructure or making regulation more 'light touch'. The Confederation of British Industry (and similar organisations in other countries), business pressure groups and also individual companies will seek to influence politicians in formulating supply-side policies. Frequently the argument is that 'business-friendly' policies will make the country more competitive.

Market-orientated supply-side policies

Radical market-orientated supply-side policies were first adopted in the early 1980s by the Thatcher government in the UK and the Reagan administration in the USA, but were subsequently copied by other right and centre-right governments around the world. The essence of this type of supply-side policy is to encourage and reward individual enterprise and initiative, and to reduce the role of government; to put more reliance on market forces and competition, and less on government intervention and regulation.

Reducing government expenditure

The desire of many governments to cut government expenditure is not just to reduce the size of the public-sector deficit and hence reduce the growth of money supply; it is also an essential ingredient of their supply-side strategy.

In most countries the size of the public sector, relative to GDP, grew substantially in the 1950s, 60s and 70s. A major aim of conservative governments throughout the world has been to reverse this trend. The public sector is portrayed as more bureaucratic and less efficient than the private sector. What is more, it is claimed that a growing proportion of public money has been spent on administration and other 'non-productive' activities, rather than on the direct provision of goods and services.

> **Pause for thought**
>
> *Why might a recovering economy (and hence a fall in government expenditure on social security benefits) make the government feel even more concerned to make discretionary cuts in government expenditure?*

Two things are needed, it is argued: (a) a more efficient use of resources within the public sector and (b) a reduction in the size of the public sector. This would allow private investment to increase with no overall rise in aggregate demand. Thus the supply-side benefits of higher investment could be achieved without the demand-side costs of higher inflation.

In practice, governments have found it very difficult to cut their expenditure without cutting services and the provision of infrastructure.

Tax cuts

Income tax cuts. Cutting the marginal rate of income tax was a major objective of the Thatcher and Major governments (1979–97). In 1979 the standard rate of income tax in the UK was 33 per cent and the top rate was 83 per cent. By 1997 the standard rate was only 23 per cent (with a starting rate of just 20 per cent), and the top rate was only 40 per cent. The Blair government continued with this policy. By 2008, the standard rate was 20 per cent (but the lower starting rate had been abolished). Cuts in the marginal rate of income tax are claimed to have many beneficial effects: e.g. people work longer hours; more people wish to work; people work more enthusiastically; unemployment falls; employment rises. The evidence regarding the truth of these claims, however, is less than certain.

For example, will people be prepared to work longer hours? On the one hand, each hour worked will be more valuable in terms of take-home pay, and thus people may be encouraged to work more and have less leisure time. This is a substitution effect (see page 35): people substitute work for leisure. On the other hand, a cut in income tax will make people better off, and therefore they may feel less need to do overtime than before. This is an income effect (see page 35): they can afford to work less. The evidence on these two effects suggests that they just about cancel each other out. Anyway, for many people there is no such choice in the short run. There is no chance of doing overtime or working a shorter week. In the long run, there may be some flexibility in that people can change jobs.

> **Pause for thought**
>
> *If the basic rate of income tax is cut, which will be the larger effect – the income effect or the substitution effect – for people (a) on low incomes just above the tax threshold and (b) on very high incomes? What will be the effect on hours worked in each case (assuming that the person has a choice)?*

Tax cuts for business and other investment incentives. A number of financial incentives can be given to encourage investment. Market-orientated policies seek to reduce the general level of taxation on profits, or to give greater tax relief to investment.

A cut in corporation tax (the tax on business profits) will increase after-tax profits. This will create more money for ploughing back into investment, and the higher after-tax return on investment will encourage more investment to take place. In 1983 the main rate of corporation tax in the UK stood at 52 per cent. A series of reductions have taken place since then – by 2009 the rate being 28 per cent for large companies and 22 per cent for small ones, with a zero per cent start-ing rate.

Reducing the power of labour

The argument here is that if labour costs to employers are reduced, their profits will probably rise. This could encourage and enable more investment and hence eco-nomic growth. If the monopoly power of labour is reduced, then cost-push inflation will also be reduced.

The Thatcher government took a number of measures to curtail the power of unions. These included the right of employees not to join unions, preventing workers taking action other than against their direct employers, and enforcing secret ballots on strike proposals. It set a lead in resisting strikes in the public sector.

As labour markets have become more flexible, with increased part-time working and short-term contracts, and as the process of globalisation has exposed more companies to international competition, so this has further eroded the power of labour in many sectors of the economy (see section 8.5).

Policies to encourage competition

If the government can encourage more competition, this should have the effect of increasing national output and reducing inflation. Four major types of policy have been pursued under this heading.

Privatisation. If privatisation simply involves the transfer of a natural monopoly to private hands (e.g. the water companies), the scope for increased competition is limited. However, where there is genuine scope for increased competition (e.g. in the supply of gas and electricity), privatisation can lead to increased efficiency, more consumer choice and lower prices.

Alternatively, privatisation can involve the introduction of private services into the public sector (e.g. private contractors providing cleaning services in hospitals, or refuse collection for local authorities). Private contractors may compete against each other for the franchise, thus driving down costs.

Introducing market relationships into the public sector. This is where the government tries to get different departments or elements within a particular part of the public sector to 'trade' with each other, so as to encourage competition and efficiency. The most well-known examples are within education and health.

The process often involves 'devolved budgeting'. For example, in the UK, under the local management of schools scheme (LMS), schools have become self-financing. Rather than the local authority meeting the bill for teachers' salaries, the schools have to manage their own budgets. The objective is to encourage them to cut costs, thereby reducing the burden on council tax payers. However, one result is that schools have tended to appoint inexperienced (and hence cheaper) teachers rather than those who can bring the benefits of their years of teaching.

Another example is in the National Health Service. In 2003, the government introduced a system of 'foundation trusts'. Hospitals can apply for foundation trust status. If successful, they are given much greater financial autonomy in terms of purchasing, employment and investment decisions. Applications are judged by Monitor, the independent health regulator. By 2007, there were 54 foundation trusts. Critics argue that funds have been diverted to foundation hospitals away from the less well-performing hospitals where greater funding could help that performance.

The Private Finance Initiative (PFI). This is where a private company, after a competitive tender, is contracted by a government department or local authority to finance and build a project, such as a new road or a prison. The government then pays the company to maintain and/or run it, or simply rents the assets from the company. The public sector thus becomes a purchaser of services rather than a direct provider itself.

The aim of these 'public–private partnerships' (PPPs) is to introduce competition (through the tendering process) and private-sector expertise into the provision of public services. It is hoped that the extra burden to the taxpayer of the private-sector profits will be more than offset by gains in efficiency. Critics, however, claim that PPPs have resulted in poorer quality of provision and that cost control has often been poor, resulting in a higher burden for the taxpayer in the long term.

Free trade and capital movements. The opening up of international trade and investment is central to a market-orientated supply-side policy. One of the first measures of the Thatcher government (in October 1979) was to remove all controls on the purchase and sale of foreign currencies, thereby permitting the free inflow and outflow of capital, both long term and short term. Most other industrialised countries also removed or relaxed exchange controls during the 1980s and early 1990s.

The Single European Act of 1987, which came into force in 1993, was another example of international liberalisation (we examine this in section 12.4). It was designed to create a 'single market' in the EU: a market without barriers to the movement of goods, services, capital and labour. This has been largely achieved, although some restrictions on trade between members do still apply.

Interventionist supply-side policy

For decades, the UK has had a lower level of investment relative to GDP than other industrialised countries. This is illustrated in Table 11.2. Only the USA has had similarly low rates of investment, but even here investment rates have been higher than in the UK over the past 10 years.

Private-sector research and development (R&D) is generally lower in the UK than in other major industrialised countries. This has meant that for many industries

Table 11.2 Gross fixed capital formation as a percentage of GDP: 1960–2008

Year (average)	UK	Germany[a]	Japan	EU (15)	USA
1960–70	18.7	25.5	32.4	23.5	18.1
1971–80	19.9	23.0	33.1	23.3	19.3
1981–90	18.7	20.9	29.5	21.0	18.8
1991–2000	16.7	22.0	28.1	20.1	17.9
2000–08	16.9	17.9	23.7	20.0	18.8

[a] West Germany prior to 1991
Note: 2007 and 2008 figures are forecasts
Source: Based on data in *European Economy Statistical Annex* (European Commission, 2007). Reproduced with permission

Box 11.4

Productivity and economic growth

The key to a better standard of living?

A country's potential output depends on the productivity of its factors of production. There are four common ways of measuring productivity. The first is output per worker. This is the most straightforward measure to calculate. All that is required is a measure of total output and employment.

The second measure is output per hour worked. This has the advantage that it is not influenced by the *number* of hours worked. So for an economy like the UK, with a very high percentage of part-time workers on the one hand, and long average hours worked by full-time employees on the other, such a measure would be more accurate in gauging worker efficiency.

The third measure is output per person of working age. This is influenced by the employment rate. The UK performs better on this measure than France and Germany because of much higher unemployment in those two countries.

The first three measures focus solely on the productivity of labour. In order to account directly for the productivity of capital we need to consider the growth in *total* factor productivity (TFP).

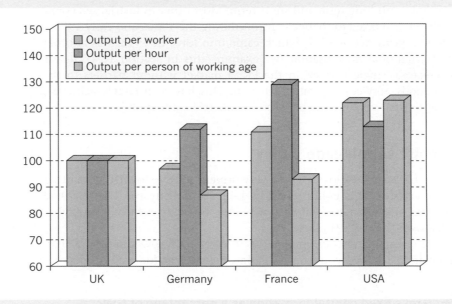

Productivity in selected countries, 2004 (UK = 100)

Source: *Pre-Budget Report 2005*, Box 3.1, Chart (b) (HM Treasury, 2005). Reproduced under terms of the click-use licence

there has emerged a widening technological gap between the UK and its major competitors such as Japan and Germany. Of the companies in the top 700 R&D spenders in the world in 2004, US companies' R&D as a percentage of sales was 4.9 per cent. For German companies the figure was 4.3 per cent, for Japanese companies it was 4.2 per cent, for French companies it was 3.1 per cent, while for UK companies it was only 2.3 per cent.

The poor performance of UK manufacturing firms has resulted in a growing import penetration of the UK market.

Pause for thought

How can the UK's low level of investment relative to GDP be explained?

This fourth measure gives output relative to the amount of factors used. Changes in total factor productivity over time provide a good indicator of technical progress.

The chart shows comparative productivity levels of four countries using the first three measures.

The importance of productivity

The faster the growth in productivity, the faster is likely to be the country's rate of economic growth. Any government seeking to raise the long-term growth rate, therefore, must find ways of stimulating productivity growth.

On what does the growth of productivity depend? There are seven main determinants:

■ Private investment in new physical capital (machinery and buildings) and in research and development (R&D).

■ Public investment in education, R&D and infrastructure.

■ Training and the development of labour skills.

■ Innovation and the application of new technology.

■ The organisation and management of factors of production.

■ The rate of entry of new firms into markets: generally such firms will have higher productivity than existing firms.

■ The business environment in which firms operate. Is there competition over the quality and design of products? Is there competitive pressure to reduce costs?

? Question

Identify some policies a government could pursue to stimulate productivity growth through each of the above means.

But what are the mechanisms whereby productivity growth feeds through into growth of the economy?

■ The capacity of the economy to grow will increase as productivity improvements extend potential output.

■ Productivity improvements will drive prices downwards, stimulating demand and actual growth.

■ With high returns from their investment, investors might be prepared to embark upon new projects and enterprises, stimulating yet further productivity growth and higher output.

■ As labour productivity rises, so wages are likely to rise. The higher wages will lead to higher consumption, and hence, via the multiplier and accelerator, to higher output and higher investment, thereby stimulating further advances in productivity.

■ In the longer term, businesses experiencing higher productivity growth would expect their lower costs, and hence enhanced competitiveness, to allow them to gain greater market share. This will encourage further investment and productivity growth.

It is clear that the prosperity of a nation rests upon its ability to improve its productivity. The more successful it is in doing this, the greater will be its rate of economic growth.

For decades the UK has invested a smaller proportion of its national income than most other industrialised nations. This has resulted in relatively low productivity growth and a comparatively low level of labour productivity. This is illustrated in the chart.

? Question

What could explain the differences in productivity between the four countries in the chart, and why do the differences vary according to which of the three measures is used?

Imports of manufactured products have grown more rapidly than UK manufactured exports, and since 1983 the UK has been a net importer of manufactured products.

These problems have led many economists to call for a much more active supply-side policy. Areas for intervention include the following:

Research and development. There are potentially large externalities (benefits) from research and development (see page 245). Firms investing in developing and improving products, and especially firms engaged in more general scientific research, may produce results that provide benefits to many other firms. Thus the *social* rate of return on investment may be much higher than the private rate of return. Investment that is privately unprofitable for a firm may therefore still be economically desirable for the nation.

The government may sponsor research and development in certain industries (e.g. aerospace) or in specific fields (e.g. microprocessors). The amount of government support in this field has been very small in the UK, however, compared with Japan, France and the USA. What is more, the amount of support declined between the mid-1980s and the late 1990s. In 1999, however, the Labour government introduced a system of tax credits for small firms which invest in research and development. In 2002, this was extended to offer tax relief of 20 per cent of R&D expenditure by large firms.

Direct provision. Improvements in infrastructure – such as a better motorway system – can be of direct benefit to industry. Alternatively, the government could provide factories or equipment to specific firms.

Training. The government may set up training schemes, or encourage educational institutions to make their courses more vocationally relevant, or introduce new vocational qualifications (such as the GNVQs, NVQs and foundation degrees in the UK). Alternatively, the government can provide grants or tax relief to firms which themselves provide training schemes.

Well-targeted training can lead to substantial improvements in labour productivity. The UK invests little in training programmes, however, compared with most of its industrial competitors.

Recap

- Supply-side policies, if successful, will shift the aggregate supply curve to the right, and help to achieve faster economic growth without higher inflation.

- Market-orientated supply-side policies aim to increase the rate of growth of aggregate supply and reduce the rate of unemployment by encouraging private enterprise and the freer play of market forces.

- Reducing government expenditure as a proportion of GDP is a major element of such policies.

- Tax cuts can be used to encourage more people to take up jobs, and people to work longer hours and more enthusiastically. The effects of tax cuts will depend on how people respond to incentives.

- Various policies can be introduced to increase competition. These include privatisation, introducing market relationships into the public sector, and freer international trade and capital movements.

- The UK has had a lower rate of investment than most other industrialised countries. This has contributed to a historically low rate of economic growth and imports of manufacture growing faster than exports. In response many argue for a more interventionist approach to supply-side policy.

- Intervention can take the form of grants, supporting research and development, advice and persuasion, investing in training and the direct provision of infrastructure.

QUESTIONS

1. 'The existence of a budget deficit or a budget surplus tells us very little about the stance of fiscal policy.' Explain and discuss.

2. Adam Smith, the founder of modern economics, remarked in *The Wealth of Nations* (1776) concerning the balancing of budgets, 'What is prudence in the conduct of every private family can scarce be folly in that of a great kingdom.' What problems might there be if the government decided to follow a balanced budget approach to its spending?

3. Imagine you were called in by the government to advise on whether it should attempt to prevent cyclical fluctuations by the use of fiscal policy. What advice would you give and how would you justify the advice?

4. Why is it difficult to use fiscal policy to 'fine-tune' the economy?

5. When the Bank of England announces that it is putting up interest rates, how will it achieve this, given that interest rates are determined by demand and supply?

6. How does the Bank of England attempt to achieve the target rate of inflation of 2 per cent? What determines its likelihood of success in meeting the target?

7. What is meant by a Taylor rule? In what way is it a better rule for central banks to follow than one of adhering to a simple inflation target?

8. Under what circumstances would adherence to an inflation target lead to (a) more stable interest rates, (b) less stable interest rates, than pursuing discretionary demand management policy?

9. Define demand-side and supply-side policies. Are there any ways in which such policies are incompatible?

10. What types of tax cuts are likely to create the greatest (a) incentives, (b) disincentives to effort?

11. Imagine that you are asked to advise the government on ways of increasing investment in the economy. What advice would you give and why?

12. In what ways can interventionist industrial policy work with the market, rather than against it? What are the arguments for and against such policy?

Business issues covered in this chapter

- What are the benefits to countries and firms of international trade?
- Which goods should a country export and which should it import?
- What determines the competitiveness of a particular country and any given industry within it?
- Why do countries sometimes try to restrict trade and protect their domestic industries?
- What is the role of the World Trade Organisation (WTO) in international trade?
- How has the 'single market' in the EU benefited its members?
- Has the business environment in the EU become more competitive?
- What benefits arise from the accession of new member states?

Chapter map

CHAPTER 12

The global trading environment

The macroeconomic environment of business extends beyond the domestic economy that we examined in the previous two chapters. As we saw in Chapter 7, many firms are global in their reach. They are clearly affected not only by the economic situation at home, but also by the various countries in which they are based. For many, this means the global economy.

But even firms that are based solely in one country are still affected by the global macroeconomic situation. They are likely to source some of their supplies from abroad; similarly, they are likely to export some of their output. In other words, they are locked into the global economy through the process of international trade.

Trading affects not only individual firms – it affects whole economies. Countries can become richer as a result of an open trading environment. We examine arguments for free trade in section 12.1.

Totally free trade, however, may bring problems to countries or to groups of people within those countries. Many people argue strongly for restrictions on trade. Textile workers see their jobs threatened by cheap imported cloth. Car manufacturers worry about falling sales as customers switch to Japanese models or other east Asian ones. But are people justified in fearing international competition, or are they merely trying to protect some vested interest at the expense of everyone else? Section 12.2 examines the arguments for restricting trade.

If there are conflicting views as to whether we should have more or less trade, what has been happening on the world stage? Section 12.3 looks at the various moves towards making trade freer and at the obstacles that have been met.

A step on the road to freer trade is for countries to enter free-trade agreements with just a limited number of other countries. In Section 12.4, we look at probably the world's most famous preferential trading system, the European Union and, in particular, at the development of a 'single European market'.

12.1 International trade

The growth of world trade

Since 1947, world trade has consistently grown faster than world GDP. This is illustrated in Figure 12.1 (overleaf). In 2007, world merchandise exports were worth nearly $13 trillion, some 31 per cent of world GDP.

The major industrial economies dominate world trade (see Figure 12.2, overleaf). Some 65 per cent of all merchandise trade is conducted by the developed economies and the top ten nations account for 53 per cent of all world trade. The country with

Table 12.1 Production possibilities for two countries

		Kilos of wheat		Metres of cloth
Developing country	Either	2	or	1
Advanced country	Either	4	or	8

Despite the advanced country having an absolute advantage in both wheat and cloth, the developing country has a *comparative* advantage in wheat, and the advanced country has a *comparative* advantage in cloth. This is because wheat is relatively cheaper in the developing country: only 1 metre of cloth has to be sacrificed to produce 2 kilos of wheat, whereas 8 metres of cloth would have to be sacrificed in the advanced country to produce 4 kilos of wheat. In other words, the opportunity cost of wheat is 4 times higher in the advanced country (8/4 compared with 1/2).

On the other hand, cloth is relatively cheaper in the advanced country. Here the opportunity cost of producing 8 metres of cloth is only 4 kilos of wheat, whereas in the developing country 1 metre of cloth costs 2 kilos of wheat. Thus the opportunity cost of cloth is 4 times higher in the developing country (2/1 compared with 4/8).

To summarise: countries have a comparative advantage in those goods that can be produced at a lower opportunity cost than in other countries.

If countries are to gain from trade, they should export those goods in which they have a comparative advantage and import those goods in which they have a comparative disadvantage. Given this, we can state a **law of comparative advantage**.

> **Pause for thought**
>
> *Draw up a similar table to Table 12.1, only this time assume that the figures are:*
> *Developing country 6 wheat or 2 cloth;*
> *Advanced country: 8 wheat or 20 cloth.*
> *What are the opportunity cost ratios now?*

> **Definitions**
>
> **Comparative advantage**
> A country has a comparative advantage over another in the production of a good if it can produce it at a lower opportunity cost: i.e. if it has to forgo less of other goods in order to produce it.
>
> **The law of comparative advantage**
> Trade can benefit all countries if they specialise in the goods in which they have a comparative advantage.

> **The law of comparative advantage.**
> Provided opportunity costs of various goods differ in two countries, both of them can gain from mutual trade if they specialise in producing (and exporting) those goods that have relatively low opportunity costs compared with the other country.
>
>
> Key Idea 28

But why do they gain if they specialise according to this law? And just what will that gain be? We will consider these questions next.

The gains from trade based on comparative advantage

Before trade, unless markets are very imperfect, the prices of the two goods are likely to reflect their opportunity costs. For example, in Table 12.1, since the developing country can produce 2 kilos of wheat for 1 metre of cloth, the *price* of 2 kilos of wheat will roughly equal 1 metre of cloth.

Assume, then, that the pre-trade exchange ratios of wheat for cloth are as follows:

Developing country : 2 wheat for 1 cloth

Advanced country : 1 wheat for 2 cloth (i.e. 4 for 8)

Both countries will now gain from trade, provided the exchange ratio is somewhere between 2:1 and 1:2. Assume, for the sake of argument, that it is 1:1. In other words, 1 wheat trades internationally for 1 cloth. How will each country gain?

The developing country gains by exporting wheat and importing cloth. At an exchange ratio of 1:1, it now only has to give up 1 kilo of wheat to obtain a metre of cloth, whereas before trade it had to give up 2 kilos of wheat.

The advanced country gains by exporting cloth and importing wheat. Again at an exchange ratio of 1:1, it now only has to give up 1 metre of cloth to obtain a kilo of wheat, whereas before it had to give up 2 metres of cloth.

Thus both countries have gained from trade.

The actual exchange ratios will depend on the relative prices of wheat and cloth after trade takes place. These prices will depend on total demand for and supply of the two goods. It may be that the trade exchange ratio is nearer to the pre-trade exchange ratio of one country than the other. Thus the gains to the two countries need not be equal.

Pause for thought

Show how each country could gain from trade if the developing country could produce (before trade) 3 wheat for 1 cloth and the advanced country could produce (before trade) 2 wheat for 5 cloth, and if the exchange ratio (with trade) was 1 wheat for 2 cloth. Would they both still gain if the exchange ratio was (a) 1 wheat for 1 cloth; (b) 1 wheat for 3 cloth?

Increased competition from trade

The other major advantage from trade is the extra competition it brings. Competition from imports may stimulate greater efficiency at home and may prevent domestic monopolies/oligopolies from charging high prices. It may stimulate greater research and development and the more rapid adoption of new technology. It may lead to a greater variety of products being made available to consumers. Finally, the extra price competition will help to keep inflation low.

The competitive advantage of nations

The theory of comparative advantage shows how countries can gain from trade, but why do countries have a comparative advantage in some goods rather than others?

One explanation is that it depends on the resources that countries have. If a country has plenty of land, then it makes sense to specialise in products that make use of this abundant resource. Thus Canada produces and exports wheat. If a country has a highly skilled workforce and an established research base, then it makes sense to specialise in high-tech products and export these. Thus Germany exports many highly sophisticated manufactured products. Many developing countries, by contrast, with plentiful but relatively low-skilled workers specialise in primary products or simple manufactured products.

In other words, countries should specialise in goods which make intensive use of their abundant resources. But this still does not give enough detail as to why countries specialise in the precise range of products that they do. Also, why do countries both export and import the *same* products. Why do many countries produce and export cars, but also import many cars too?

According to Porter[1], there are four key determinants of why nations are highly competitive in certain products but less so in others. These are illustrated in a diagram which has become known as the 'Porter diamond' (see Figure 12.3).

[1] Michael E. Porter, *The Competitive Advantage of Nations* (New York: The Free Press, 1998)

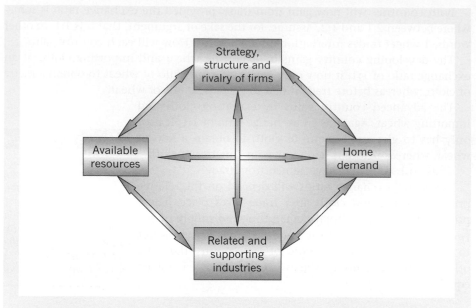

Figure 12.3   The competitive advantage of nations: Porter's diamond model

Source: Porter, M.E., *The Competitive Advantage of Nations*, p. 127 (New York: The Free Press, 1998). Copyright © 1980, 1998 by The Free Press. Reprinted with permission of The Free Press, a division of Simon & Schuster Adult Publishing Group. All rights reserved

Available resources. These include 'given' resources, such as raw materials, population and climate, but also specialised resources that have been developed by humans, such as the skills of the labour force, the amount and type of capital, the transport and communications infrastructure, and the science and technology base. These specialised resources vary in detail from one country to another and give them a competitive advantage in very specific products. Once an industry has started to develop, this may attract further research and development, capital investment and training, all of which are very specific to that industry. This then further builds the country's competitive advantage in that industry. Thus the highly developed engineering skills and equipment in Germany gives it a competitive advantage in producing well-engineered cars.

Demand conditions in the home market. The more discerning customers are within the country, the more this will drive the development of each firm's products and the more competitive the firm will then become in international markets. The demand for IT solutions within the USA drove the development of the software industry and gave companies such as Microsoft, Intel and Google an international advantage.

Strategy, structure and rivalry of firms. Competition between firms is not just in terms of price. Competitive rivalry extends to all aspects of business strategy, from product design, to marketing, to internal organisation, to production efficiency, to logistics. The very particular competitive conditions within each industry can have a profound effect on the development of firms within that industry and determine whether of not they gain an international competitive advantage. Strategic investments and rivalry gave Japanese electronic companies an international competitive advantage.

Related and supporting industries. Firms are more likely to be successful internationally if there are well-developed supporting industries within the home economy. These may be industries providing specialist equipment or specialist consultancy, or they may simply be other parts of the main value chain, from suppliers of inputs to distributors of the firms' output. The more efficient this value chain, the greater the competitive advantage of firms within the industry.

The competitive advantage of nations.

The ability of countries to compete in the market for exports and with potential importers to their country. The competitiveness of any one industry depends on the availability and quality of resources, demand conditions at home in that industry, the strategies and rivalry of firms within the industry and the quality of supporting industries and infrastructure. It also depends on government policies, and there is also an element of chance.

Key Idea 29

As the arrows in Figure 12.3 show, the four determinants of competitive advantage are interlinked and influence each other. For example, the nature of related and supporting industries can influence a firm's strategic decision about whether to embark on a process of vertical integration or de-integration. Similarly, the nature of related and supporting industries depends on demand conditions in these industries and the availability of resources.

With each of the four determinants in Figure 12.3, competitive advantage can be stimulated by appropriate government supply-side policies, such as a supportive tax regime, investment in transport and communications infrastructure, investment in education and training, competition policy and sound macroeconomic management of the economy. Also chance often has a large part to play. Which pharmaceutical company in which part of the world discovers a cure for AIDS or for various types of cancer will then have a significant competitive advantage.

> **Pause for thought**
>
> *Give two other examples of ways in which the determinants of competitive advantage are interlinked.*

The terms of trade

What price will our exports fetch abroad? What will we have to pay for imports? The answer to these questions is given by the **terms of trade**. The terms of trade are defined as:

$$\frac{\text{The average price of exports}}{\text{The average price of imports}}$$

expressed as an index, where prices are measured against a base year in which the terms of trade are assumed to be 100. Thus if the average price of exports relative to the average price of imports has risen by 20 per cent since the base year, the terms of trade will now be 120. If the terms of trade rise (export prices rising relative to import prices), they are said to have 'improved', since fewer exports now have to be sold to purchase any given quantity of imports. Changes in the terms of trade are caused by changes in the demand and supply of imports and exports and by changes in the exchange rate.

> **Definition**
>
> **Terms of trade**
> The price index of exports divided by the price index of imports and then expressed as a percentage. This means that the terms of trade will be 100 in the base year.

> **Pause for thought**
>
> *Assume that a developing country exports primary products whose demand on world markets is inelastic with respect to income. Assume also that it imports manufactured products whose demand in the country is elastic with respect to income. What is likely to happen to its terms of trade over the years as this country and other countries around the world experience economic growth?*

Recap

- World trade has grown, for many years, significantly faster than the growth in world output. World trade is highly concentrated in the developed world and in particular between the top few trading nations.

- Countries can gain from trade if they specialise in producing those goods in which they have a comparative advantage: i.e. those goods that can be produced at relatively low opportunity costs.

- If two countries trade, then, provided that the trade price ratio of exports and imports is between the pre-trade price ratios of these goods in the two countries, both countries can gain.

- Gains from trade also arise from increased competition.

- The terms of trade give the price of exports relative to the price of imports expressed as an index, where the base year is 100.

12.2   Trade restrictions

We have seen how trade can bring benefits to all countries. But when we look around the world, we often see countries erecting barriers to trade. Their politicians know that trade involves costs as well as benefits.

In this section, we examine the arguments for restricting trade. Are people justified in fearing international competition, or are they merely trying to protect some vested interest at the expense of everyone else?

Types of restriction

Countries may impose customs duties (or **tariffs**) on imports; they may put restrictions on the amount of certain goods that can be imported ('quotas'); they may subsidise domestic products to give them a price advantage over imports; they may impose administrative regulations designed to exclude imports, such as customs delays or excessive paperwork; or governments may favour domestic producers when purchasing equipment (e.g. defence equipment). Alternatively, governments may favour domestic producers by subsidising their exports in a process known as **dumping**. The goods are 'dumped' at artificially low prices in the foreign market.

In looking at the costs and benefits of trade, the choice is not the stark one of whether to have free trade or no trade at all. Although countries may sometimes contemplate having completely free trade, typically they limit their trade. However, they certainly do not ban it altogether.

Definitions

Tariffs
Taxes (customs duties) on imports. These could be a percentage of the value of the good (an 'ad valorem' tariff), or a fixed amount per unit (a 'specific' tariff).

Dumping
Where exports are sold at prices below marginal cost – often as a result of government subsidy.

Arguments for restricting trade

The following are the main arguments that have been used to restrict trade.

The infant industry argument. Some industries in a country may be in their infancy but have a potential comparative advantage. This is particularly likely in developing countries. Such industries are too small yet to have gained economies of scale; their workers are inexperienced; there is a lack of back-up facilities – communications networks, specialist research and development, specialist suppliers, etc. – and they may have only limited access to finance for expansion. Without protection, these **infant industries** will not survive competition from abroad.

Protection from foreign competition, however, will allow them to expand and become more efficient. Once they have achieved a comparative advantage, the protection can then be removed to enable them to compete internationally.

To prevent 'dumping' and other unfair trade practices. A country may engage in dumping by subsidising its exports. The result is that prices may no longer reflect comparative costs. Thus the world would benefit from tariffs being imposed by importers to counteract the subsidy.

It can also be argued that there is a case for retaliating against countries which impose restrictions on your exports. In the short run, both countries are likely to be made worse off by a contraction in trade. But if the retaliation persuades the other country to remove its restrictions, it may have a longer-term benefit. In some cases, the mere threat of retaliation may be enough to get another country to remove its protection.

To prevent the establishment of a foreign-based monopoly. Competition from abroad could drive domestic producers out of business. The foreign company, now having a monopoly of the market, could charge high prices with a resulting misallocation of resources. The problem could be tackled either by restricting imports or by subsidising the domestic producer(s).

All the above arguments suggest that governments should adopt a 'strategic' approach to trade. **Strategic trade theory** argues that protecting certain industries allows a net gain in the *long* run from increased competition in the market (see Box 12.1).

To spread the risks of fluctuating markets. A highly specialised economy – Zambia with copper, Cuba with sugar – will be highly susceptible to world market fluctuations. Greater diversity and greater self-sufficiency, although maybe leading to less efficiency, can reduce these risks.

To reduce the influence of trade on consumer tastes. The assumption of fixed consumer tastes dictating the pattern of production through trade is false. Multinational companies through their advertising and other forms of sales promotion may influence consumer tastes. Many developing countries object to the insidious influence of western consumerist values expounded by companies such as Coca-Cola and McDonald's.

To take account of externalities. Free trade will tend to reflect private costs. Both imports and exports, however, can involve externalities. The mining of many

---

Definition

Infant industry
An industry which has a potential comparative advantage, but which is as yet too underdeveloped to be able to realise this potential.

Pause for thought

How would you set about judging whether an industry had a genuine case for infant industry protection?

Pause for thought

Does the consumer in the importing country gain or lose from dumping?

Definition

Strategic trade theory
The theory that protecting/supporting certain industries can enable them to compete more effectively with large monopolistic rivals abroad. The effect of the protection is to increase long-run competition and may enable the protected firms to exploit a comparative advantage that they could not have done otherwise.

Box 12.1

Strategic trade theory

The case of Airbus

Supporters of *strategic trade theory* hold that comparative advantage need not be the result of luck or circumstance, but may in fact be created by government. By diverting resources into selective industries, usually high tech and high skilled, a comparative advantage can be created through intervention.

An example of such intervention was the European aircraft industry, and in particular the creation of the European Airbus Consortium.

The Consortium was established in the late 1960s, its four members being Aérospatiale (France), British Aerospace (now BAE Systems) (UK), CASA (Spain) and DASA (Germany). The setting up of this consortium was seen as essential for the future of the European aircraft industry for three reasons:

■ To share high R&D costs.

■ To generate economies of scale.

■ To compete successfully with the market's major players in the USA – Boeing and McDonnell Douglas (which have since merged).

Airbus, although privately owned, was sponsored by government and received state aid, especially in its early years when the company failed to make a profit. Then, in 2000, the French, Geman and Spanish partners of the consortium merged to form the European Aeronautic Defence and Space Company (EADS), which had an 80 per cent share of Airbus (BAE Systems having the remaining 20 per cent share). Shortly afterwards, it was announced that enough orders had been secured for the planned new 550-seater A380 for production to go ahead. This new jumbo would be a serious competitor to the long-established Boeing 747.

By 2006 Airbus had become very successful, capturing a larger and larger share of the world commercial aircraft market. In that year Airbus delivered 434 commercial aircraft – 36 more than its rival.

So does the experience of Airbus support the arguments of the strategic trade theorists? Essentially two key benefits are claimed to flow from Airbus and its presence in the aircraft market: lower prices and economic spillovers.

■ Without Airbus the civil aircraft market would have been dominated by one giant American firm, Boeing (or possibly two, if the 1997 merger of Boeing and McDonnell Douglas had not taken place). Therefore the presence of Airbus would be expected to promote competition and thereby keep prices down. Studies in the 1980s and 1990s tended to support this view, suggesting that consumers have made significant gains from lower prices. One survey estimated that without Airbus commercial aircraft prices would have been 3.5 per cent higher than they currently are, and without both Airbus *and* McDonnell Douglas they would have been 15 per cent higher.

■ Economic spillovers from the Airbus Consortium, such as skills and technology developments, might be expected to benefit other industries. Findings are inconclusive on this point. It is clear, however, that although aggregate R&D in the whole aircraft industry has risen, so has the level of R&D duplication.

Despite Airbus's successes, by 2006 troubles were beginning to emerge. Although it delivered more planes than Boeing, for the first time since 2000 it fell behind in terms of orders – 824, compared with 1050 for Boeing. Also considerable delays (up to two years) and cost-overruns were being experienced with the A380. With falling profitability and falling orders, in February 2007 Airbus announced plans to cut 10 000 jobs from its 57 000 workforce.

Nevertheless, on balance it appears that Airbus has had many positive effects and that the strategic trade theory, which was used to justify state aid, has been largely vindicated. Boeing has a genuine competitor in Airbus and passengers worldwide have benefited from this competition.

? Questions

1. In what other industries could the setting up of a consortium, backed by government aid, be justified as a means of exploiting a potential comparative advantage?

2. Is it only in industries that could be characterised as world oligopolies that strategic trade theory is relevant?

minerals for export may adversely affect the health of miners; the production of chemicals for export may involve pollution; the importation of juggernaut lorries may lead to structural damage to houses; shipping involves large amounts of CO_2 emissions (some 4–5 per cent of total world emissions).

The arguments considered so far are of general validity: restricting trade for such reasons could be of net benefit to the world. There are two other arguments, however, that are used by individual governments for restricting trade, where their country will gain, but at the *expense* of other countries, such that there will be a net loss to the world.

The first argument concerns taking advantage of market power in world trade. If a country, or a group of countries, has monopsony power in the purchase of imports (i.e. they are individually or collectively a very large economy, such as the USA or the EU), then they could gain by restricting imports so as to drive down their price. Similarly, if countries have monopoly power in the sale of some export (e.g. OPEC countries with oil), then they could gain by forcing up the price.

The second argument concerns giving protection to declining industries. The human costs of sudden industrial closures can be very high. In such circumstances, temporary protection may be justified to allow the industry to decline more slowly, thus avoiding excessive structural unemployment. Such policies will be at the expense of the consumer, however, who will be denied access to cheaper foreign imports.

Problems with protection

Protection will tend to push up prices and restrict the choice of goods available. But apart from these direct costs to the consumer, there are several other problems. Some are a direct effect of the protection; others follow from the reactions of other nations.

Protection as 'second-best'. Many of the arguments for protection amount merely to arguments for some type of government intervention in the economy. Protection, however, may not be the best way of dealing with the problem, since protection may have undesirable side-effects. There may be a more direct form of intervention that has no side-effects. In such a case, protection will be no more than a *second-best* solution.

For example, using tariffs to protect old inefficient industries from foreign competition may help prevent unemployment in those parts of the economy, but the consumer will suffer from higher prices. A better solution would be to subsidise retraining and investment in those areas of the country in *new efficient* industries – industries with a comparative advantage. In this way, unemployment is avoided, but the consumer does not suffer.

Retaliation. If the USA imposes restrictions on, say, imports from the EU, then the EU may impose restrictions on imports from the USA. Any gain to US firms competing with EU imports is offset by a loss to US exporters. What is more, US consumers suffer, since the benefits from comparative advantage have been lost.

The increased use of tariffs and other restrictions can lead to a trade war, with each country cutting back on imports from other countries. In the end, everyone loses.

Protection may allow firms to remain inefficient. By removing or reducing foreign competition, firms' incentive to reduce costs may be reduced. Thus if protection is being given to an infant industry, the government must ensure that the lack of competition does not prevent it 'growing up'. Protection should not be excessive and should be removed as soon as possible.

Bureaucracy. If a government is to avoid giving excessive protection to firms, it should examine each case carefully. This can lead to large administrative costs. It could also lead to corrupt officials accepting bribes from importers to give them favourable treatment.

Recap

■ Reasons for restricting trade that have some validity in a world context include: the infant industry argument, the problem of dumping and other unfair trade practices, the danger of the establishment of a foreign-based monopoly, the need to spread the risks of fluctuating export prices, and the problems that free trade may adversely affect consumer tastes and may not take account of externalities.

■ Often, however, the arguments for restricting trade are in the context of one country benefiting even though other countries may lose more. Countries may intervene in trade in order to exploit their monopoly/monopsony power or to protect declining industries.

■ Even if government intervention to protect certain parts of the economy is desirable, restricting trade is unlikely to be a first-best solution to the problem, since it involves side-effect costs.

12.3 The world trading system and the WTO

In 1947, 23 countries got together and signed the General Agreement on Tariffs and Trade (GATT). By 2007, there were 150 members of its successor organisation, the World Trade Organisation (WTO), which was formed in 1995. Between them, the members of the WTO account for over 97 per cent of world trade. The aims of GATT, and now the WTO, have been to liberalise trade.

WTO rules

The WTO requires its members to operate according to various rules. These include the following:

■ Non-discrimination. Under the 'most favoured nations clause', any trade concession that a country makes to one member must be granted to *all* signatories.

■ Reciprocity. Any nation benefiting from a tariff reduction made by another country must reciprocate by making similar tariff reductions itself.

■ The general prohibition of quotas.

■ Fair competition. If unfair barriers are erected against a particular country, the WTO can sanction retaliatory action by that country. The country is not allowed, however, to take such action without permission.

■ Binding tariffs. Countries cannot raise existing tariffs without negotiating with their trading partners.

Unlike the GATT, the WTO has the power to impose sanctions on countries breaking trade agreements. If there are disputes between member nations, these will be settled by the WTO, and if an offending country continues to impose trade restrictions, permission will be granted for other countries to retaliate.

For example, in March 2002, the Bush administration imposed tariffs on steel imports into the USA in order to protect the ailing US steel industry (see Web Case D.28). The EU and other countries referred the case to the WTO, which in December 2003 ruled that they were illegal. This ruling made it legitimate for the EU and other countries to impose retaliatory tariffs on US products. President Bush consequently announced that the steel tariffs would be abolished.

The greater power of the WTO has persuaded many countries to bring their disputes to it. In the first 12 years of its existence it had dealt with 356 disputes (compared with 300 by GATT over the whole of its 48 years).

> **Pause for thought**
>
> *Could US action to protect its steel industry from foreign competition be justified in terms of the interests of the USA as a whole (as opposed to the steel industry in particular)?*

Trade rounds

Periodically, member countries have met to negotiate reductions in tariffs and other trade restrictions. There have been eight 'rounds' of such negotiations since the signing of GATT in 1947. The last major round to be completed was the Uruguay round, which began in Uruguay in 1986, continued at meetings around the world and culminated in a deal being signed in April 1994. By that time, the average tariff on manufactured products was 4 per cent and falling. In 1947 the figure was nearly 40 per cent. The Uruguay Round agreement also involved a programme of phasing in substantial reductions in tariffs and other restrictions up to the year 2002 (see Web Case D.22).

Despite the reduction in tariffs, many countries have still tried to restrict trade by various other means, such as quotas and administrative barriers. Also, barriers have been particularly high on certain non-manufactures. Agricultural protection in particular has come in for sustained criticism by developing countries. High fixed prices and subsidies given to farmers in the EU, the USA and other advanced countries mean that the industrialised world continues to export food to many developing countries which have a comparative advantage in food production! Farmers in developing countries often find it impossible to compete with subsidised food imports from the rich countries.

The most recent round of trade negotiations began in Doha, Qatar, in 2001. The negotiations have focused on both trade liberalisation and measures to encourage development of poorer countries. In particular, the Doha Development Agenda, as it is called, is concerned with measures to make trade fairer so that its benefits are spread more evenly around the world. This would involve improved access for developing countries to markets in the rich world. The Agenda is also concerned with the environmental impacts of trade and development.

The talks were originally scheduled for completion by January 2005, but this deadline had to be extended to December 2005 and then to July 2006, merely for an outline agreement on agricultural and industrial products and later still for an agreement on services. But the deadlines passed with not even an agreement on a 'framework' of what such an agreement should look like!

Box 12.2

Beyond bananas

EU/US trade disputes

Trade relations between the EU and US seem to be at an all-time low. The World Trade Organisation (WTO), set up to manage trade and prevent such disputes arising, appears helpless in resolving the issues and restoring order.

The current round of bad blood between the EU and US started over bananas.

Bananas

The EU/US 'banana war', which has now come to a conclusion, began in 1993 when the EU adopted a tariff and quota system that favoured banana producers in African, Caribbean and Pacific (ACP) countries, mostly ex-European colonies. Predictably, Latin American banana producers, owned by large American multinationals like Chiquita and Dole, took exception to this move. Latin American producers, with huge economies of scale, were able to produce bananas at considerably lower cost than producers in the ACP countries. But, faced with significant tariffs on entry into the EU market, their bananas became more expensive. Championed by the USA, the Latin American producers won the case at the WTO for removing the agreement.

The EU, however, failed to comply, arguing that the preferential access to EU markets for ACP producers was part of a general development strategy, known as the 'Lomé Convention', to support developing economies. Without preferential access, it was argued, ACP banana producers simply could not compete on world markets. As a European Commission document highlighted, 'The destruction of the Caribbean banana industry would provoke severe economic hardship and political instability in a region already struggling against deprivation.'

As the EU refused to comply with the WTO ruling, the USA imposed $191 million worth of tariffs on EU exports in March 1999. After a series of battles over the issue at the WTO, the EU finally agreed to reform its banana protocol and remove all preferential quotas to ACP banana producers by 2006.

Hormone-treated beef

If the banana dispute could be resolved, many equally contentious issues could be found to take its place. The dispute between the EU and USA over hormone-treated beef has been going on for a staggering 20 years. In 1998, the WTO panel ruled against a ban by the EU on imports of hormone-treated beef from the USA and Canada. The ruling permitted the two countries to impose retaliatory sanctions on EU imports. After a process of arbitration, the values were set at $116.8 million for the USA and CDN$11.1 million for Canada.

Despite this, the EU continued to refuse to import any animal products, live or processed, that had received growth hormones. The ban was made on grounds of public health, and this remains the crux of the dispute. The EU argues that it has not been proven that hormone-treated beef is safe. In reply, the Americans argue that the EU has not provided evidence that it is otherwise.

Following an independent assessment of the risks to consumers of hormone-treated meat, which resulted in the EU

The EU and USA blamed larger developing countries, such as Brazil and India, for being unwilling to make reductions in tariffs on manufactured imports. The developing countries, in turn, blamed the unwillingness of the developed countries, and especially the EU and the USA, to make sufficient cuts in agricultural protection. The EU blamed the USA for subsidising its farmers; the USA blamed the EU for high tariffs on imported food.

The talks were restarted in 2007, but were unlikely to be completed before mid 2008 – if at all.

Pause for thought

How can game theory (see section 5.4) help us to understand the difficulty of getting countries to reach and then abide by trade agreements?

banning certain hormones by its farmers, the EU argued that the sanctions should be lifted as it was no longer in breach of the WTO rules. In November 2004, the EU asked the WTO to rule that continued US and Canadian sanctions related to the beef hormone ruling were illegal. In February 2005, a WTO panel was set up to consider the case. The EU, Canada and the USA would all make representations. In addition Australia, Mexico, China and Taiwan were permitted to make 'third-party' representations.

Genetically modified (GM) foods

A more recent trade dispute, again in the field of public health, concerns the development of GM food. GM strains of maize and soya have been available in the USA for many years, but the EU bans imports of such products, whether as seed or food. The US position is that EU consumers should be free to choose whether they have GM food or not. This, not surprisingly, is rejected by the EU on the basis that GM foods might contaminate the entire food supply once introduced. In July 2000, the EU decided to continue with its GM food ban indefinitely.

In response to a complaint to the WTO by the USA, Canada and Argentina, a panel was set up in March 2004 to consider the case. In addition to representations by the four main parties, third-party rights were granted to Australia, Brazil, Chile, China, Colombia, El Salvador, Honduras, Mexico, New Zealand, Norway, Paraguay, Peru, Taiwan, Thailand and Uruguay.

In September 2006, the panel reported that the EU had acted illegally in banning GM imports from 1999 to 2003. Since then, the EU had acted legally in considering 10 specific cases of GM products, but there were undue delays in reviewing 24 out of 27 other products. In December 2006, the EU announced that it accepted the WTO ruling, but would need reasonable time to implement it, given the complexity of the cases.

Airbus

A more recent branch of the current EU/US trade disputes concerns the Airbus Consortium and EU industrial policy (an area which has been a bone of contention for the USA for many years). The current issue concerns the new superjumbo, the A380. The Americans are very unhappy with the loans and subsidies that have been provided by EU members to companies within the Airbus Consortium to develop the aircraft. The American complaint is that such subsidies have broken the WTO subsidy code and, as such, are unfair. Estimated at $4 billion, the subsidies will cover a third of the aircraft's development costs.

In October 2004, the USA requested the establishment of a WTO panel to consider the case. This provoked a counter-request by Airbus, claiming unfair support for Boeing by the USA. In July 2005, two panels were set up to deal with the two sets of allegations.

 Question

Why does the WTO appear to be so ineffective in resolving the disputes between the EU and USA?

Recap

- Most countries of the world are members of the WTO and in theory are in favour of moves towards freer trade.

- The WTO can impose sanctions on countries not abiding by WTO rules.

- There have been various 'rounds' of trade talks, originally under the auspices of GATT and more recently under the WTO. The Uruguay round led to substantial reductions in tariffs and other trade restrictions. The latest 'Doha round', however, has been stalled.

Box 12.3

Preferential trading

The case of NAFTA

The world economy seems to have been increasingly forming into a series of trade blocs, based upon regional groupings of countries: a European region centred on the European Union, an Asian region on Japan, a North American region on the USA and a Latin American region. Such trade blocs are examples of **preferential trading arrangements**. These arrangements involve trade restrictions with the rest of the world, and lower or zero restrictions between the members.

> **Definition**
>
> **Preferential trading arrangements**
> A trading arrangement whereby trade between the signatories is freer than trade with the rest of the world.

Although trade blocs clearly encourage trade between their members, many countries outside these blocs complain that they benefit the members at the expense of the rest of the world. For many developing economies, in need of access to the most prosperous nations in the world, this represents a significant check on their ability to grow and develop.

Types of preferential trading arrangement

There are three possible forms of such trading arrangements

Free trade area. This is where member countries remove tariffs and quotas between themselves, but retain whatever restrictions *each member chooses* with non-member countries. Some provision will have to be made to prevent imports from outside coming into the area via the country with the lowest external tariff.

Customs union. This is like a free trade area, but in addition members must adopt *common* external tariffs and quotas with non-member countries.

Common market. This is where member countries operate as a *single* market. Like a customs union there are no tariffs and quotas between member countries and there are common external tariffs and quotas. But a common market goes further than this. A full common market includes the following features: a common system of taxation; a common system of laws and regulations governing production, employment and trade (e.g. competition law and trade union legislation); and the free movement of labour, capital and materials, and of goods and services (e.g. the freedom of workers from one member country to work in any other).

The effects of preferential trading

By joining a customs union (or free trade area), a country will find that its trade patterns change. Most of these changes are likely to be beneficial.

Countries will probably benefit from 'trade creation'. The removal of trade barriers allows greater specialisation according to comparative advantage. Instead of consumers having to pay high prices for domestically produced goods in which the country has a comparative disadvantage, the goods can now be obtained more cheaply from other members of the customs union. In return, the country can export to them goods in which it has a comparative advantage.

Other advantages from preferential trading include: competition from companies in other member states; economies of scale for firms which now have access to a bigger market; a more rapid spread of technology within the area; the bargaining power of the whole customs union with the rest of the world allowing member countries to gain better terms of trade; increased trade encouraging improvements in the infrastructure

12.4 The European Union and the Single Market

In recognition of the benefits of free trade within the EU, the member countries signed the Single European Act of 1986. This sought to dismantle all barriers to internal trade within the EU by 1993, and create a genuine 'single market'. Although tariffs between member states had long been abolished, there were all sorts of non-tariff barriers, such as high taxes on wine by non-wine-producing of the members of the union (better roads, railways, financial services, etc.).

There are some dangers, however, of customs unions. The first is that 'trade diversion' could take place. This is where countries that were previously importing from a low cost country (which does not join the union), now buy from a higher cost country within the customs union, simply because there are no tariffs on this country's products and hence they can be purchased at a lower price, despite their higher cost of production.

Another danger is that resources may flow from the country to more efficient members of the customs union, or to the geographical centre of the union (so as to minimise transport costs). This can be a major problem for a *common market* (where there is free movement of labour and capital). The country could become a depressed 'region' of the community.

North American Free Trade Agreement (NAFTA)

Along with the EU, NAFTA is one of the two most powerful trading blocs in the world. It came into force in 1994 and consists of the USA, Canada and Mexico. These three countries have agreed to abolish tariffs between themselves in the hope that increased trade and co-operation will follow. Tariffs between the USA and Canada were phased out by 1999 and tariffs between Mexico and the other two countries will be by 2009. New non-tariff restrictions will not be permitted either, but many existing ones can remain in force, thus preventing the development of true free trade between the members. Indeed, some industries, such as textiles and agriculture, will continue to have major non-tariff restrictions.

Concerns were expressed in the USA that jobs would be lost to Mexico as firms took advantage of lower wages there. These fears do not seem to have materialised, however. US manufacturing output has risen rapidly and unemployment has fallen. In Mexico, fears of job losses in agriculture do seem to have been borne out as subsidised US corn and other crops have undercut Mexican prices. In general, however, there have been relatively few trade disputes between the three countries.

NAFTA members hope that, with a market similar in size to the EU, they will be able to rival the EU's economic power in world trade. NAFTA is, however, at most only a free trade area and not a common market. Unlike the EU, it does not seek to harmonise laws and regulations, except in very specific areas such as environmental management and labour standards. Member countries are permitted total legal independence, subject to the one proviso that they must treat firms of other member countries equally with their own firms – the principle of 'fair competition'. Nevertheless, NAFTA has encouraged a growth in trade between its members, most of which is trade creation rather than trade diversion.

Other countries may join in the future, so NAFTA may eventually develop into a western hemisphere free trade association. Leaders of 34 American countries have attempted to create a Free Trade Area of the Americas (FTAA), though no firm timetable has been established. Talks have stalled on a number of occasions and no detailed negotations have taken place.

Questions

1. What factors will determine whether a country's joining a customs union will lead to trade creation or trade diversion?
2. Using the Internet, identify some other preferential trading arrangements around the world and their various features.

countries, special regulations designed to favour domestic producers, governments giving contracts to domestic producers (e.g. for defence equipment), and so on.

Most of the barriers were indeed removed by 1993, and by the mid-1990s it was becoming clear from the evidence that the single market was bringing substantial benefits.

Trade creation. The expansion of trade within the EU has allowed member countries to specialise further in those goods and services that they can produce at a comparatively low opportunity cost. As a result, costs and prices have fallen.

Reduction in the direct costs of barriers. This category includes administrative costs, border delays and technical regulations. Their abolition or harmonisation has led to substantial cost savings, shorter delivery times and a larger choice of suppliers.

Economies of scale. With industries based on a Europe-wide scale, many firms can now be large enough, and their plants large enough, to gain the full potential economies of scale (see Box 4.4 on page 108). Yet the whole European market is large enough for there still to be adequate competition. Such gains have varied from industry to industry, depending on the minimum efficient scale of a plant or firm. Economies of scale have also been gained from mergers and other forms of industrial restructuring

Pause for thought

In what ways would competition be 'unfair' if VAT rates differed widely between member states?

Greater competition. Increased competition between firms has led to lower costs, lower prices and a wider range of products available to consumers. This has been particularly so in newly liberalised service sectors such as transport, financial services, telecommunications and broadcasting. In the long run, greater competition can stimulate greater innovation, the greater flow of technical information and the rationalisation of production.

The economic evidence was backed up by the perceptions of business. Firms from across the range of industries felt that the single market project had removed a series of obstacles to trade within the EU and had increased market opportunities.

Despite these gains, the single market has not received a universal welcome within the EU. Its critics argue that, in a Europe of oligopolies, unequal ownership of resources, rapidly changing technologies and industrial practices, and factor immobility, the removal of internal barriers to trade has merely exaggerated the problems of inequality and economic power. More specifically, the following criticisms are made.

Radical economic change is costly. Substantial economic change is necessary to achieve the full economies of scale and efficiency gains from a single European market. These changes necessarily involve redundancies – from bankruptcies, takeovers, rationalisation and the introduction of new technology. The severity of this 'structural' and 'technological' unemployment (see section 10.5) depends on (a) the pace of economic change and (b) the mobility of labour – both occupational and geographical. Clearly, the more integrated markets become across the EU, the less the costs of future change.

Adverse regional effects. Firms are likely to locate as near as possible to the 'centre of gravity' of their markets and sources of supply. If, before barriers are removed, a firm's prime market was the UK, it might well have located in the Midlands or the north of England. If, however, with barriers now removed, its market has become Europe as a whole, it may choose to locate in the south of England or in France, Germany or the Benelux countries instead. The creation of a single European market thus tends to attract capital and jobs away from the edges of the Union and towards its geographical centre.

In an ideal market situation, areas like Cornwall, the south of Italy or Portugal should attract resources from other parts of the Union. Being relatively depressed areas, wage rates and land prices are lower. The resulting lower industrial costs should encourage firms to move into the areas. In practice, however, as capital and labour (and especially young and skilled workers) leave the extremities of the

Union, so these regions are likely to become more depressed. If, as a result, their infrastructure is neglected, they then become even less attractive to new investment.

The development of monopoly/oligopoly power. The free movement of capital can encourage the development of giant 'Euro-firms' with substantial economic power. Indeed, recent years have seen some very large European mergers. This can lead to higher, not lower prices, and less choice for the consumer. It all depends on just how effective competition is, and how effective EU competition policy is in preventing monopolistic and collusive practices.

Completing the internal market

Despite the reduction in barriers, the internal market is still not 'complete'. In other words, various barriers to trade between member states still remained. Thus, in June 1997, an Action Plan was adopted by the European Council. Its aim was to ensure that all barriers were dismantled by the launch of the euro in January 1999.

To monitor progress an 'Internal Market Scoreboard' was established. This is published every six months and shows progress towards the total abandonment of any forms of internal trade restrictions (Web Case D.29). It shows the percentage of EU Single Market Directives still to be transposed into national law. In addition to giving each country's 'transposition deficit', the Scoreboard identifies the number of infringements of the internal market that have taken place. The hope is that the 'naming and shaming' of countries will encourage them to make more rapid progress towards totally free trade within the EU.

The Action Plan was largely, but not totally, successful. In 1997, the average transposition deficit of member countries was 35 per cent. By 1999, this had fallen to 3.5 per cent and by 2002, to just 1.8 per cent.

In January 2004, the *Implementation Report on the Internal Market Strategy* claimed that, 'Since the abolition of EU internal frontiers ten years ago, the Internal Market has boosted EU economic growth by at least 1.8%, adding nearly 900 billion euro to the EU's collective prosperity and helping create 2.5 million extra jobs.'

Despite this success, national governments have continued to introduce *new* technical standards, several of which have had the effect of erecting new barriers to trade. Also, infringements of single market rules by governments have not always been dealt with. The net result is that, although trade is much freer today than in the early 1990s, especially given the transparency of pricing with the euro, there still do exist various barriers, especially to the free movement of goods.

To counteract new barriers, the EU periodically issues new Directives. If this process is more rapid than that of the transposition of existing Directives into national law, the transposition deficit increases. Thus by December 2004, the average deficit for the original 15 EU members had risen to 2.9 per cent. By December 2006, however, it had fallen to 1.2 per cent (for all 25 members).

> **Pause for thought**
>
> *If there have been clear benefits from the single market programme, why do individual member governments still try to erect barriers, such as new technical standards?*

The effect of the new member states

Given the very different nature of the economies of many of the 12 new entrants to the EU (10 in 2004 and 2 more in 2007), and their lower levels of GDP per head, the potential for gain from membership has been substantial. The gains come through additional trade, increased competition, technological transfer and inward investment, both from other EU countries and from outside the EU.

A study in 2004[2] concluded that Poland's GDP would rise by 3.4 per cent and Hungary's by almost 7 per cent. Real wages would rise, with those of unskilled workers rising faster than those of skilled workers, in accordance with these countries' comparative advantage. There would also be benefits for the existing 15 EU countries from increased trade and investment, but these would be relatively minor in comparison to the gains to the new members.

> **Pause for thought**
>
> *Why may the new members of the EU have the most to gain from the single market, but also the most to lose?*

Recap

- The Single European Act of 1986 sought to sweep away various administrative restrictions to free trade in the EU and to establish a genuine free market by 1993.

- Benefits from completing the internal market have included trade creation, cost savings from no longer having to administer barriers, economies of scale for firms now able to operate on a Europe-wide scale, and greater competition leading to reduced costs and prices, greater flows of technical information and more innovation.

- Critics of the single market point to the costs of radical changes in industrial structure, the attraction of capital away from the periphery of the EU to its geographical centre, possible problems of market power with the development of giant 'Euro-firms'.

- New members have gained substantially from free trade within the EU. There have also been gains to existing member states.

QUESTIONS

1. Imagine that two countries, Richland and Poorland, can produce just two goods, computers and coal. Assume that for a given amount of land and capital, the output of these two products requires the following constant amounts of labour:

	Richland	Poorland
1 computer	2	4
100 tonnes of coal	4	5

[2] M. Maliszewska, *Benefits of the Single Market Expansion for Current and New Member States* (Centrum Analiz Społeczno-Ekonomicznych)

Assume that each country has 20 million workers.

(a) If there is no trade, and in each country 12 million workers produce computers and 8 million workers produce coal, how many computers and tonnes of coal will each country produce? What will be the total production of each product?

(b) What is the opportunity cost of a computer in (i) Richland; (ii) Poorland?

(c) What is the opportunity cost of 100 tonnes of coal in (i) Richland; (ii) Poorland?

(d) Which country has a comparative advantage in which product?

(e) Assuming that price equals marginal cost, which of the following would represent possible exchange ratios?

(i) 1 computer for 40 tonnes of coal; (ii) 2 computers for 140 tonnes of coal; (iii) 1 computer for 100 tonnes of coal; (iv) 1 computer for 60 tonnes of coal; (v) 4 computers for 360 tonnes of coal.

(f) Assume that trade now takes place and that 1 computer exchanges for 65 tonnes of coal. Both countries specialise completely in the product in which they have a comparative advantage. How much does each country produce of its respective product?

(g) The country producing computers sells 6 million domestically. How many does it export to the other country?

(h) How much coal does the other country consume?

2. Why doesn't the USA specialise as much as General Motors or Texaco? Why doesn't the UK specialise as much as Unilever? Is the answer to these questions similar to the answer to the questions, 'Why doesn't the USA specialise as much as Luxembourg?' and 'Why doesn't Unilever specialise as much as the local florist?'

3. To what extent are the arguments for countries specialising and then trading with each other the same as those for individuals specialising in doing the jobs to which they are relatively well suited?

4. The following are four items that are traded internationally: wheat; computers; textiles; insurance. In which one of the four is each of the following most likely to have a comparative advantage: India; the UK; Canada; Japan? Give reasons for your answer.

5. It is often argued that if the market fails to develop infant industries, then this is an argument for government intervention, but not necessarily in the form of restricting imports. What *other* ways could infant industries be given government support?

6. Does the consumer in the importing country gain or lose from dumping? (Consider both the short run and the long run.)

7. What is fallacious about the following two arguments? Is there any truth in either?

(a) 'Imports should be reduced because money is going abroad which would be better spent at home.'

(b) 'We should protect our industries from being undercut by imports produced using cheap labour.'

8. Go through each of the arguments for restricting trade and provide a counter-argument for not restricting trade.

9. If countries are so keen to reduce the barriers to trade, why do many countries frequently attempt to erect barriers?

10. If rich countries stand to gain substantially from freer trade, why have they been so reluctant to reduce the levels of protection of agriculture?

11. Why is it difficult to estimate the magnitude of the benefits of completing the internal market of the EU?

12. Look through the costs and benefits that we identified from the single European market. Do the same costs and benefits arise from a substantially enlarged EU?

Business issues covered in this chapter

- What is meant by 'the balance of payments' and how do trade and financial movements affect it?
- How are exchange rates determined and what are the implications for business of changes in the exchange rate?
- How do governments and/or central banks seek to influence the exchange rate and what are the implications for other macroeconomic policies and for business?
- How do the vast flows of finance around the world affect business and the countries in which they are located?
- What are the advantages and disadvantages of the euro for members of the eurozone and for businesses inside and outside the eurozone?
- How do the major economies of the world seek to coordinate their policies and what difficulties arise in the process?
- What are the causes and effects on business of currency speculation?
- To what extent does the world gain or lose from the process of the globalisation of business?

Chapter map

CHAPTER 13

The global financial environment

When countries sell exports, there is an inflow of money into the economy. When they buy imports, there is an outflow. In this chapter we examine these international financial flows and their implications for business.

But such flows are not just from trade. Inward investment leads to an inflow of money, as do deposits of money in this country made by people abroad. Outward investment and deposits of money abroad from people in this country result in an outflow of money.

All these inflows and outflows of money to and from a country are recorded in the 'balance of payments'. We examine this process in section 13.1.

Trade and investment are also influenced by the rates of exchange between currencies. Rates of exchange, in turn, are influenced by the demand and supply of currencies resulting from trade and investment. We will see what causes exchange rate fluctuations – a major cause of concern for many businesses – and how central banks can attempt to reduce these fluctuations. Section 13.2 looks at exchange rates.

The remaining sections look at various aspects of global finance: how global financial flows affect the world economy; whether the global financial environment can be managed; and how the EU has sought to achieve greater financial stability through the adoption of the euro by many of its members. Finally, by way of a postscript, we ask whether this whole process of economic globalisation with greater and greater economic and financial interdependence has been a 'good thing'.

13.1 The balance of payments

A country's balance of payments account records all the flows of money between residents of that country and the rest of the world. *Receipts* of money from abroad are regarded as *credits* and are entered in the accounts with a positive sign. *Outflows* of money from the country are regarded as *debits* and are entered with a negative sign.

The balance of payments account

There are three main parts of the balance of payments account: the *current account*, the *capital account* and the *financial account*. We shall look at each part in turn, and take the UK as an example. Table 13.1 gives a summary of the UK balance of payments for 2006.

Table 13.1 UK balance of payments, 2006 (£m)

Current account	
Balance on trade in goods and services (exports minus imports)	−54 086
Net income flows (wages and investment income)	+22 801
Net current transfers (government and private)	−12 104
Balance on current account	**−43 389**
Capital account (net capital transfers, etc.)	**+713**
Financial account	
Direct investment	+32 656
Portfolio investment	−20 483
Other investment (mainly short-term flows)	+21 127
Reserves	+426
Balance on financial account	**+33 726**
(Net errors and omissions)	**+8 950**
Total	**0**

Source: *Financial Statistics* (Office for National Statistics). Reproduced under terms of the click-use licence

The current account

The **current account** records (a) payments for exports (+) and imports (−) of goods and services, plus (b) incomes flowing into (+) and out of (−) the country (wages, profits, dividends on shares), plus (c) net transfers of money into (+) and out of (−) the country (e.g. money sent from Greece to a Greek student studying in the UK would be a credit item).

The **current account balance** is the overall balance of all these. A *current account surplus* is where credits exceed debits. A *current account deficit* is where debits exceed credits.

If you want to look purely at the balance of imports and exports (i.e. just item (a) above), this is given as the balance of trade. If exports exceed imports, there is a balance of trade surplus; if imports exceed exports, there is a balance of trade deficit.

The capital account

The **capital account** records the flows of funds, into the country (+) and out of the country (−), associated with the acquisition or disposal of fixed assets (e.g. land), the transfer of funds by migrants, and the payment of grants by the government for overseas projects and the receipt of EU money for capital projects.

The financial account

The **financial account** of the balance of payments records cross-border changes in the holding of shares, property, bank deposits and loans, government securities, etc. In other words, unlike the current account, which is concerned with money incomes, the financial account is concerned with the flows of money for the purchase and sale of assets.

Definitions

Current account of the balance of payments
The record of a country's imports and exports of goods and services, plus incomes and transfers of money to and from abroad.

Balance of payments on current account
The balance on trade in goods and services plus net incomes and current transfers: i.e. the sum of the credits on the current account minus the sum of the debits.

Balance of trade
Exports of goods and services minus imports of goods and services.

Capital account of the balance of payments
The record of transfers of capital to and from abroad.

Financial account of the balance of payments
The record of the flows of money into and out of the country for the purpose of investment or as deposits in bank and other financial institutions.

Some of these flows are for long-term investment. This can involve the acquisition of buildings and equipment (direct investment) or paper assets such as shares (portfolio investment). Some of the flows involve the short-term deposit of money in bank accounts.

Anything that involves an acquisition of assets in *this* country by overseas residents (e.g. foreign companies investing in the UK) represents an inflow of money and is thus a credit (+) item. Any acquisition of assets abroad by UK residents (e.g. UK companies investing abroad) represents a debit (−) item.

> **Pause for thought**
>
> *Where would interest payments on short-term foreign deposits in UK banks be entered on the balance of payments account?*

Flows to and from the reserves. The UK, like all other countries, holds reserves of gold and foreign currencies. From time to time the Bank of England (acting as the government's agent) might release some of these reserves to purchase sterling on the foreign exchange market. It would do so as a means of supporting the rate of exchange (as we shall see in the next section). Drawing on reserves represents a *credit* item in the balance of payments account: money drawn from the reserves represents an *inflow* to the balance of payments (albeit an outflow from the reserves account). The reserves can thus be used to support a deficit elsewhere in the balance of payments.

Conversely, if there is a surplus elsewhere in the balance of payments, the Bank of England could use it to build up the reserves. Building up the reserves counts as a debit item in the balance of payments, since it represents an outflow from it (to the reserves).

Does the balance of payments balance?

When all the components of the balance of payments account are taken together, the balance of payments should exactly balance: credits should equal debits. As we shall see in section 13.2, if they were not equal, the rate of exchange would have to adjust until they were, or the government would have to intervene to make them equal.

When the statistics are compiled, however, a number of errors are likely to occur. As a result there will not be a balance. To 'correct' for this, a **net errors and omissions** item is included in the accounts. This ensures that there will be an exact balance. The main reason for the errors is that the statistics are obtained from a number of sources, and there are often delays before items are recorded and sometimes omissions too.

> **Definition**
>
> **Net errors and omissions**
> A statistical adjustment to ensure that the two sides of the balance of payments account balance. It is necessary because of errors in compiling the statistics.

Does a deficit matter?

If the balance of payments must always balance, then in what sense does the balance of payments matter? The answer is that the individual accounts will *not* necessarily balance. The UK has traditionally imported more than it has exported. The resulting deficit on the current account has thus had to be financed by an equal and opposite surplus on the capital-plus-financial accounts. In other words, the UK has had to borrow from abroad or sell assets abroad to finance the excess of imports over exports. This has meant that it has had to have higher interest rates in order to attract deposits from overseas and have an increased ownership of domestic assets by residents abroad.

Higher interest rates can have a long-term dampening effect on the economy. Inward direct investment, on the other hand, although resulting in increased

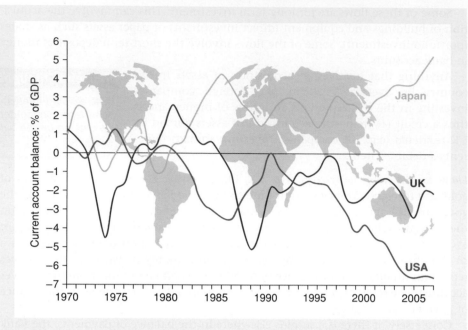

Figure 13.1 Current account balance as % of GDP: 1970–2008

Source: Based on data from *OECD Economic Outlook* (Organisation for Economic Co-operation and Development, 2006). Copyright © 2006 OECD. Reproduce with permission

overseas ownership of assets in the UK, will have the effect of stimulating output and employment.

Figure 13.1 shows the current account balances of the UK, the USA and Japan as a proportion of their GDP. Although the UK has in most years had a current account deficit, this deficit has fluctuated with the business cycle. In times of rapid economic growth relative to other countries, expenditure on imports rises rapidly relative to exports and the current account goes deeper into deficit. You can see this in the late 1980s and late 1990s. In times of recession the current account improves, as it did in the early 1980s and early 1990s. You can also see the effect of oil on the current account. In the late 1970s as North Sea oil was coming on stream, so the current account went into surplus. As oil exports have declined in the early 2000s, so this contributed to a deepening of the deficit.

Figures 13.1 also shows the current accounts of the USA and Japan. They are an approximate mirror image of each other as many of Japan's exports are imported by the USA. Much of Japan's current account surplus is then invested in the USA as direct investment, the acquisition of paper assets, such as shares (portfolio investment), or simply as deposits in US financial institutions. One reflection of this imbalance has been generally much higher interest rates in the USA than in Japan.

Another consequence of the high US current account deficit is that most of it is paid in US dollars. This increases the supply of dollars in the world banking system, much of it on short-term deposit. These deposits can be rapidly transferred from one country to another, wherever interest rates are higher or where speculators anticipate a rise in the exchange rate (see next section). As we shall see, this movement of 'hot money' tends to lead to considerable instability in exchange rates.

Recap

■ The balance of payments account records all payments to and receipts from other countries. The current account records payments for imports and exports, plus incomes and transfers of money to and from abroad. The capital account records all transfers of capital to and from abroad. The financial account records inflows and outflows of money for investment and as deposits in banks and other financial institutions. It also includes dealings in the country's foreign exchange reserves.

■ The whole account must balance, but surpluses or deficits can be recorded on any specific part of the account. Thus the current account could be in deficit but it would have to be matched by an equal and opposite capital plus financial account surplus.

■ The UK has traditionally had a current account deficit, but this has fluctuated with the business cycle.

■ The US and Japanese current accounts are somewhat of a mirror image of each other. One result of large and persistent US deficits has been an increase in 'hot money', which has aggravated exchange rate instability.

The exchange rate   13.2

An exchange rate is the rate at which one currency trades for another on the foreign exchange market.

If you want to go abroad, you will need to exchange your pounds for euros, dollars, Swiss francs or whatever. To do this you will go to a bank. The bank will quote you that day's exchange rates: e.g. €1.45 to the pound, or $1.90 to the pound. It is similar for firms. If an importer wants to buy, say, some machinery from Japan, it will require yen to pay the Japanese supplier. It will thus ask the foreign exchange section of a bank to quote it a rate of exchange of the pound into yen. Similarly, if you want to buy some foreign stocks and shares, or if companies based in the UK want to invest abroad, sterling will have to be exchanged for the appropriate foreign currency.

Likewise, if Americans want to come on holiday to the UK or to buy UK assets, or American firms want to import UK goods or to invest in the UK, they will require sterling. They will be quoted an exchange rate for the pound in the USA: say, £1 = $1.95. This means that they will have to pay $1.95 to obtain £1 worth of UK goods or assets.

Exchange rates are quoted between each of the major currencies of the world. These exchange rates are constantly changing. Minute by minute, dealers in the foreign exchange dealing rooms of the banks are adjusting the rates of exchange.

One of the problems, however, in assessing what is happening to a particular currency is that its rate of exchange may rise against some currencies (weak currencies) and fall against others (strong currencies). In order to gain an overall picture of its fluctuations, it is best to look at a weighted average exchange rate against all other currencies. This is known as the **exchange rate index**. The weight given to each currency in the index depends on the proportion of transactions done with that country.

Definition

Exchange rate index
A weighted average exchange rate expressed as an index, where the value of the index is 100 in a given base year. The weights of the different currencies in the index add up to 1.

Pause for thought

How did the pound 'fare' compared with the dollar, the (former) lira and the yen from 1960 to 2001? What conclusions can be drawn about the relative movements of these three currencies?

Table 13.2 Sterling exchange rates: 1960–2007

	US dollar	Japanese yen	French franc	German mark	Italian lira	Euro[a]	Sterling exchange rate index (1/1/05 = 100)
1960	2.80	1008	13.82	11.76	1747	–	–
1970	2.40	858	13.33	8.78	1500	–	–
1975	2.22	658	9.50	5.45	1447	(1.70)	119.9
1980	2.33	526	9.83	4.23	1992	(1.62)	115.1
1985	1.30	307	11.55	3.78	2463	(1.71)	99.8
1990	1.79	257	9.69	2.88	2133	(1.37)	96.2
1992	1.77	224	9.32	2.75	2163	(1.33)	93.8
1994	1.53	156	8.49	2.48	2467	(1.27)	85.9
1996	1.56	170	7.99	2.35	2408	(1.21)	83.6
1998	1.66	217	9.77	2.91	2876	(1.49)	99.7
1999	1.62	184	(9.96)	(2.97)	(2941)	1.52	99.1
2000	1.52	163	(10.77)	(3.21)	(3180)	1.64	100.9
2001	1.44	175	(10.55)	(3.15)	(3115)	1.61	99.2
2002	1.50	188	–	–	–	1.59	100.4
2003	1.63	189	–	–	–	1.45	96.9
2004	1.83	198	–	–	–	1.47	101.6
2005	1.82	200	–	–	–	1.46	100.5
2006	1.84	214	–	–	–	1.47	101.0
2007 (Q1,2)	1.97	237	–	–	–	1.48	104.4

[a] The euro was introduced in 1999, with notes and coins circulating from 2001. The 'dummy' euro exchange rate figures prior to 1999 are projections backwards in time based on the weighted average exchange rates of the currencies that made up the euro

Source: *Monetary and Financial Statistics Interactive Database* (Bank of England). Reproduced with permission

Table 13.2 shows exchange rates between the pound and various currencies and the sterling exchange rate index from 1960 to 2007.

The determination of the rate of exchange in a free market

In a free foreign exchange market, the rate of exchange is determined by demand and supply. Thus the sterling exchange rate is determined by the demand and supply of pounds. This is illustrated in Figure 13.2.

For simplicity, assume that there are just two countries: the UK and the USA. When UK importers wish to buy goods from the USA, or when UK residents wish to invest in the USA, they will *supply* pounds on the foreign exchange market in order to obtain dollars. In other words, they will go to banks or other foreign exchange dealers to buy dollars in exchange for pounds. The higher the exchange rate, the more dollars they will obtain for their pounds. This will effectively make American goods cheaper to buy, and investment more profitable. Thus the *higher*

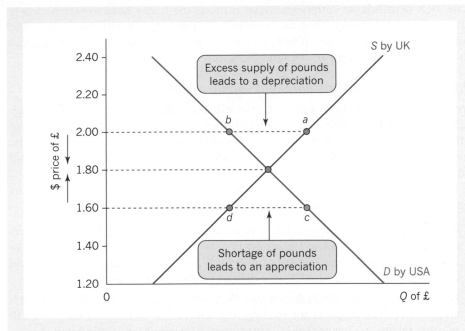

Figure 13.2 Determination of the rate of exchange

the exchange rate, the *more* pounds will be supplied. The supply curve of pounds therefore typically slopes upwards.

When US residents wish to purchase UK goods or to invest in the UK, they will require pounds. They *demand* pounds by selling dollars on the foreign exchange market. In other words, they will go to banks or other foreign exchange dealers to buy pounds in exchange for dollars. The lower the dollar price of the pound (the exchange rate), the cheaper it will be for them to obtain UK goods and assets, and hence the more pounds they are likely to demand. The demand curve for pounds, therefore, typically slopes downwards.

The equilibrium exchange rate is where the demand for pounds equals the supply. In Figure 13.2 this is at an exchange rate of £1 = $1.80. But what is the mechanism that equates demand and supply?

If the current exchange rate were above the equilibrium, the supply of pounds being offered to the banks would exceed the demand. For example, in Figure 13.2, if the exchange rate were $2.00, there would be an excess supply of pounds of *a – b*. Banks would not have enough dollars to exchange for all these pounds. But the banks make money by *exchanging* currency, not by holding on to it. They would thus lower the exchange rate in order to encourage a greater demand for pounds and reduce the excessive supply. They would continue lowering the rate until demand equalled supply.

Similarly, if the rate were below the equilibrium, say at $1.60, there would be a shortage of pounds of *c – d*. The banks would find themselves with too few pounds to meet all the demand. At the same time, they would have an excess supply of dollars. The banks would thus raise the exchange rate until demand equalled supply.

In practice, the process of reaching equilibrium is extremely rapid. The foreign exchange dealers in the banks are continually adjusting the rate as new customers make new demands for currencies. What is more, the banks have to watch closely what each other is doing. They are constantly in competition with each other and thus have to keep their rates in line. The dealers receive minute-by-minute updates on their computer screens of the rates being offered around the world.

Shifts in the currency demand and supply curves

Any shift in the demand or supply curves will cause the exchange rate to change. This is illustrated in Figure 13.3, which this time shows the euro/sterling exchange rate. If the demand and supply curves shift from D_1 and S_1 to D_2 and S_2 respectively, the exchange rate will fall from €1.60 to €1.40. A fall in the exchange rate is called a **depreciation**. A rise in the exchange rate is called an **appreciation**.

But why should the demand and supply curves shift? The following are the major possible causes of a depreciation:

■ *A fall in domestic interest rates*. UK rates would now be less competitive for savers and other depositors. More UK residents would be likely to deposit their money abroad (the supply of sterling would rise), and fewer people abroad would deposit their money in the UK (the demand for sterling would fall).

■ *Higher inflation in the domestic economy than abroad*. UK exports will become less competitive. The demand for sterling will fall. At the same time, imports will become relatively cheaper for UK consumers. The supply of sterling will rise.

■ *A rise in domestic incomes relative to incomes abroad*. If UK incomes rise, the demand for imports, and hence the supply of sterling, will rise. If incomes in other countries fall, the demand for UK exports, and hence the demand for sterling will fall.

■ *Relative investment prospects improving abroad*. If investment prospects become brighter abroad than in the UK, perhaps because of better incentives abroad, or

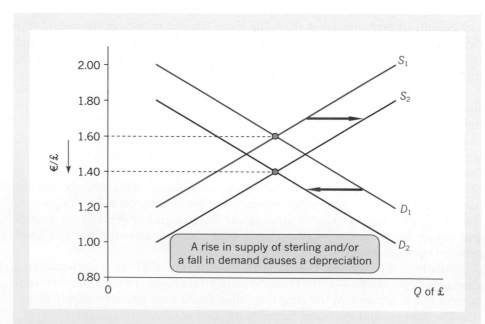

Figure 13.3   Floating exchange rates: movement to a new equilibrium

because of worries about an impending recession in the UK, again the demand for sterling will fall and the supply of sterling will rise.

■ *Speculation that the exchange rate will fall.* If businesses involved in importing and exporting, and also banks and other foreign exchange dealers, think that the exchange rate is about to fall, they will sell pounds *now* before the rate does fall. The supply of sterling will thus rise. People planning to buy sterling will wait until the rate does fall. In the meantime, the demand for sterling will fall.

> **Pause for thought**
>
> Go through each of the listed causes for shifts in the demand for and supply of sterling and consider what would cause an appreciation of the pound.

Exchange rates and the balance of payments

In a free foreign exchange market, the balance of payments will *automatically* balance. But why?

The credit side of the balance of payments constitutes the demand for sterling. For example, when people abroad buy UK exports or assets they will demand sterling in order to pay for them. The debit side constitutes the supply of sterling. For example, when UK residents buy foreign goods or assets, the importers of them will require foreign currency to pay for them. They will thus supply pounds. A **floating exchange rate** will ensure that the demand for pounds is equal to the supply. It will thus also ensure that the credits on the balance of payments are equal to the debits: that the balance of payments balances.

This does not mean that each part of the balance of payments account will separately balance, but simply that any current account deficit must be matched by a capital-plus-financial account surplus and *vice versa*.

> **Definition**
>
> **Floating exchange rate**
> When the government does not intervene in the foreign exchange markets, but simply allows the exchange rate to be freely determined by demand and supply.

Box 13.1

The importance of international financial movements

How a current account deficit can coincide with an appreciating exchange rate

Since the early 1970s, most of the major economies of the world have operated with floating exchange rates. The opportunities that this gives for speculative gain have led to a huge increase in short-term international financial movements. Vast amounts of moneys transfer from country to country in search of higher interest rates or a currency that is likely to appreciate. This can have a bizarre effect on exchange rates.

If a country pursues an expansionary fiscal policy (i.e. cutting taxes and/or raising government expenditure), the current account will tend to go into deficit as extra imports are 'sucked in'. What effect will this have on exchange rates? You might think that the answer is obvious: the higher demand for imports will create an extra supply of domestic currency on the foreign exchange market and hence drive down the exchange rate.

In fact the opposite is likely. The higher interest rates resulting from the higher domestic demand can lead to a massive inflow of short-term finance. The financial account can thus move sharply into surplus. This is likely to outweigh the current account deficit and cause an *appreciation* of the exchange rate.

Exchange rate movements, especially in the short term, are largely brought about by changes on the financial rather than the current account.

 Question

Why do high international financial mobility and an absence of exchange controls severely limit a country's ability to choose its interest rate?

For example, suppose initially that each part of the balance of payments did separately balance. Then let us assume that interest rates rise. This will encourage larger short-term financial inflows as people abroad are attracted to deposit money in the UK: the demand for sterling would shift to the right (e.g. from D_2 to D_1 in Figure 13.3). It will also cause smaller short-term financial outflows as UK residents keep more of their money in the country: the supply of sterling shifts to the left (e.g. from S_2 to S_1 in Figure 13.3). The financial account will go into surplus. The exchange rate will appreciate.

As the exchange rate rises, this causes imports to be cheaper and exports to be more expensive. The current account will move into deficit. There is a movement up along the new demand and supply curves until a new equilibrium is reached. At this point, any financial account surplus is matched by an equal current (plus capital) account deficit.

Managing the exchange rate

The government or central bank (the Bank of England in the UK) may be unwilling to let the country's currency float freely. Frequent shifts in the demand and supply curves would cause frequent changes in the exchange rate. This, in turn, might cause uncertainty for businesses, which might curtail their trade and investment.

Assume, for example, that the Bank of England believes that an exchange rate of €1.60 to the pound is approximately the long-term equilibrium rate. Short-term leftward shifts in the demand for sterling and rightward shifts in the supply, however, are causing the exchange rate to fall below this level (see Figure 13.3). What can be done to keep the rate at €1.60?

Using reserves. The Bank of England can sell gold and foreign currencies from the reserves to buy pounds. This will shift the demand for sterling back to the right. The problem here is that countries' reserves are limited. If people are convinced that the sterling exchange rate will fall, there will be massive selling of pounds. It is unlikely that using the reserves to buy pounds will be adequate to stem the fall.

Borrowing from abroad. The government can negotiate a foreign currency loan from other countries or from an international agency such as the International Monetary Fund. The Bank of England can then use these monies to buy pounds on the foreign exchange market, thus again shifting the demand for sterling back to the right.

Raising interest rates. If the Bank of England raises interest rates, it will encourage people to deposit money in the UK and encourage UK residents to keep their money in the country. The demand for sterling will increase and the supply of sterling will decrease.

This is likely to be more effective than the other two measures, but using interest rates to control the exchange rate may conflict with using interest rates to target inflation. You cannot use one instrument (the rate of interest) to control two separate targets (the exchange rate and the rate of inflation) if the two objectives require a different rate of interest.

Advantages of managed exchange rates

Surveys reveal that most businesspeople prefer relatively stable exchange rates: if not totally fixed, then with minimum fluctuations. The following arguments are used to justify this preference.

Certainty. With stable exchange rates, international trade and investment become much less risky, since profits are not affected by violent movements in the exchange rate.

Assume a firm correctly forecasts that its product will sell in the USA for $1.50. It costs 80p to produce. If the rate of exchange is stable at £1 = $1.50, each unit will earn £1 and hence make a 20p profit. If, however, the rate of exchange fluctuated these profits could be wiped out. If, say, the rate appreciated to £1 = $2, and if units continued to sell for $1.50, they would now earn only 75p each, and hence make a 5p loss.

Little or no speculation. If people believe that the exchange rate will remain constant – there is nothing to be gained from speculating. For example, between 1999 and 2001, when the old currencies of the eurozone countries were still used, but were totally fixed to the euro, there was no speculation that the German mark, say, would change in value against the French franc or the Dutch guilder.

With a totally free floating exchange rate, by contrast, given that large amounts of short-term deposits are internationally 'footloose', speculation can be highly destabilising in the short run. If people think that the exchange rate will fall, then they will sell the currency, and this will cause the exchange rate to fall even further.

Disadvantages of managed exchange rates

Exchange rate policy may conflict with the interests of domestic business and the economy as a whole. Managing the exchange rate will almost inevitably involve using interest rates for that purpose. But this may conflict with other macroeconomic objectives. For example, a depreciating exchange rate may force the central bank to raise interest rates to arrest the fall. But this may discourage business investment. This in turn will lower firms' profits in the long term and reduce the country's long-term rate of economic growth.

Also, if the economy is already in a recession, the higher interest rates could deepen the recession by making borrowing more expensive and thus reducing aggregate demand.

In other words, the rate of interest that is suitable for the exchange rate may be unsuitable for the rest of the economy.

Under a free-floating rate, by contrast, the central bank can choose whatever rate of interest is necessary to meet domestic objectives, such as achieving a target rate of inflation. The exchange rate will simply adjust to the new rate of interest – a rise in interest rates causing an appreciation, a fall causing a depreciation.

Inability to adjust to shocks. Sometimes, it will prove impossible to maintain the exchange rate at the desired level. For example, a sudden increase in oil prices can have a large effect on the balance of payments. Oil-importing countries may find that the downward pressure on their exchange rate is too strong to contain.

Speculation. If speculators believe that the central bank cannot prevent the exchange rate falling (or rising), speculation is likely to be massive. The speculation will bring about the very fall (or rise) in the exchange rate that the speculators anticipated and may well cause the exchange rate to overshoot its longer-run equilibrium rate. At times of international currency turmoil (see Box 13.3), such speculation can be enormous. Worldwide, over two trillion dollars on average passes daily across the foreign exchanges: greatly in excess of countries' foreign exchange reserves!

> **Pause for thought**
>
> *If speculators on average gain from their speculation, who loses?*

Box 13.2

Exchange rate fluctuations and the plight of SMEs

Small businesses and the perils of international trade

As if trading internationally wasn't hard enough for small businesses! It's bad enough trying to compete with large multinational corporations with all their international connections, trying to find a niche market or to offer some specialist service, perhaps, indeed, to multinationals themselves. What makes things doubly difficult for small business are the fluctuations in exchange rates.

In 2002, when asked to identify the main financial factor causing problems for SMEs, easily topping the list was the high exchange rate of sterling against the euro.

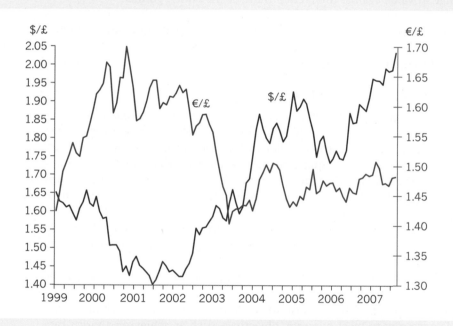

Fluctuations in the euro/pound and dollar/pound exchange rates

Exchange rates in practice

Definition

Adjustable peg
A system whereby exchange rates are fixed for a period of time, but may be devalued (or revalued) if a deficit (or surplus) becomes substantial.

Most countries today have a relatively free exchange rate. Nevertheless, the problems of instability that this can bring are well recognised, and thus many countries seek to regulate or manage their exchange rate.

There have been many attempts to regulate exchange rates since 1945. By far the most successful was the Bretton Woods system, which was adopted worldwide from the end of World War II until 1971. This was a form of **adjustable peg** exchange rate, where countries pegged (i.e. fixed) their exchange rate to the US dollar, but could re-peg it at a lower or higher level (a **devaluation** or **revaluation** of their exchange rate) if there was a persistent and substantial balance of payments deficit or surplus.

Nearly half of the firms in the sample, 47 per cent, say this is very problematic for their business. In addition, more than a quarter responded to the survey by saying it is quite problematic.

The survey figure shows that sterling's strength against Europe's single currency is a problem for more than seven in ten SMEs. For those who sometimes argue that the SME community is less concerned about sterling's strength than its bigger brothers, this survey shows that is far from being the case. SMEs suffer from the strength of the pound.

'It is certainly the case that this is a problem for us, not just sterling against the euro but also against the dollar,' said Bruno Kilshaw, managing director of London-based Sortex. 'We export 95 per cent of our production and would like to operate on the basis of euro and dollar price lists but often that is impossible because it would squeeze our margins too much.'

'We would love to quote in customers' own currency but often we have to quote in sterling and convert at the time of the contract. It is both the high level of sterling and the instability that give us problems. If there was at least stability, we would be happier.'

Sortex manufactures colour-sorting equipment for the agriculture and food-processing industries, mainly coffee, grain and rice producers. The equipment separates good products from waste.[1]

In October 2000, the exchange rate was £1 = €1.71 (see the chart). In other words, UK exporters had to sell €1.71 worth of exports to the eurozone in order to earn £1. From 2002, sterling began to depreciate significantly against the euro. By mid-2003, the rate was around £1 = €1.43. While this was good news for exporters, it was bad news for importers, who were having to pay more in sterling to purchase things priced in euros. Many SMEs rely on key imported components. A rise in their price may force them to pass this on to their customers – making them less competitive with firms that are less reliant on imported components.

But just as sterling was depreciating against the euro, it was appreciating against the dollar (see the chart). In June 2001, the exchange rate was £1 = $1.41. By February 2004, it was £1 = $1.86. Then despite dipping as low as $1.73 in November 2005, in July 2007 it reached $2.05.

The exchange rate against the euro, meanwhile had stabilised considerably. From 2004 to 2007 it remained within the relatively narrow band of £1 = €1.43 to €1.50. Thus while those exporting to the USA were finding it increasingly difficult to make a profit, those trading with the eurozone were under less pressure.

? *Question*
Are SMEs likely to find it easier or harder than large multi-national companies to switch the source of their supplies from countries where the pound has depreciated to ones where it has appreciated?

---

[1] http://www.themanufacturer.com/content_detail.html?contents_id=2653&t=manufacturer&header=reports#

Definitions

Devaluation
Where the government or central bank re-pegs the exchange rate at a lower level.

Revaluation
Where the government or central bank re-pegs the exchange rate at a higher level.

With growing world inflation and instability from the mid-1960s, it became more and more difficult to maintain fixed exchange rates, and the growing likelihood of devaluations and revaluations fuelled speculation. The system was abandoned in

Box 13.3

The euro/dollar seesaw

What is the impact on business?

For periods of time, world currency markets can be quite peaceful, with only modest changes in exchange rates. But with the ability to move vast sums of money very rapidly from one part of the world to another and from one currency to another, speculators can suddenly turn this relatively peaceful world into one of extreme turmoil – a turmoil that can be very damaging for business.

In this box we examine the huge swings of the euro against the dollar since the euro's launch in 1999.

First the down ...

On 1 January 1999, the euro was launched and exchanged for $1.16. By October 2000 the euro had fallen to $0.85. What was the cause of this 27 per cent depreciation? The main cause was the growing fear that inflationary pressures were increasing in the USA and that, therefore, the Federal Reserve Bank would have to raise interest rates. At the same time, the eurozone economy was growing only slowly and inflation was well below the 2 per cent ceiling set by the ECB. There was thus pressure on the ECB to cut interest rates.

The speculators were not wrong. As the diagram shows, US interest rates rose, and ECB interest rates initially fell, and when eventually they did rise (in October 1999), the gap between US and ECB interest rates soon widened again.

In addition to the differences in interest rates, a lack of confidence in the recovery of the eurozone economy and a continuing confidence in the US economy encouraged investment to flow to the USA. This inflow of finance (and lack of inflow to the eurozone) further pushed up the dollar relative to the euro.

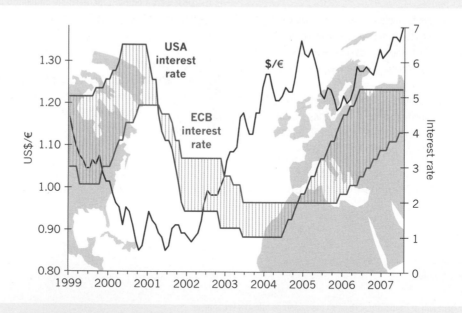

Fluctuations between the euro and the dollar

The low value of the euro meant a high value of the pound relative to the euro. This made it very difficult for UK companies exporting to eurozone countries and also for those competing with imports from the eurozone (which had been made cheaper by the fall in the euro).

In October 2000, with the euro trading at around 85¢, the ECB plus the US Federal Reserve Bank (America's central bank), the Bank of England and the Japanese central bank all intervened on the foreign exchange market to buy euros. This arrested the fall, and helped to restore confidence in the currency. People were more willing to hold euros, knowing that central banks would support it.

... Then the up

The position completely changed in 2001. With the US economy slowing rapidly and fears of an impending recession, the Federal Reserve Bank reduced interest rates 11 times during the year: from 6 per cent at the beginning of the year to 1.25 per cent at the end (see the chart). Although the ECB also cut interest rates, the cuts were relatively modest: from 4.75 at the beginning of the year to 3.25 at the end. With eurozone interest rates now considerably above US rates, the euro began to rise.

In addition, massive debts on the US current account, and a budget deficit nearing 4 per cent of GDP, made foreign investors reluctant to invest in the American economy. In fact, investors were pulling out of the USA. One estimate suggests that European investors alone sold $70 billion of US assets during 2002. The result of all this was a massive depreciation of the dollar and appreciation of the euro, so that by March 2005 the exchange rate had risen to $1.35: a 60 per cent appreciation since June 2001! By 2004, the US budget deficit had risen to 4.5 per cent of GDP – well above the budget deficits in France and Germany (see Box 11.2).

The effects on business in the eurozone

So is a strong euro bad for European business? With over 20 per cent of the eurozone's GDP determined by export sales, and a large part of those exports going to America, the dollar/euro exchange rate will invariably be significant. The question is how significant? The concern was that, with slow growth in the eurozone, the rise in the euro and the resulting fall in exports would slow growth rates even further. With the German economy on the brink of recession, the euro's rise might be simply too much for the German economy to bear. The investment bank Morgan Stanley estimated that for every 10 per cent rise in the value of the euro against the dollar, European corporate profits fall by 3 per cent.

However, the impact of the euro's rise on eurozone business was tempered by a number of other factors:

■ Companies are increasingly using sophisticated management and operational systems, in which value creation is spread throughout a global value chain. Often procurement systems are priced in dollars.

■ Firms hedge their currency risks. BMW, for example, uses forward exchange markets to agree to buy or sell currencies in the future at a price quoted *today* (this, of course, costs it a premium).

■ Many European companies (again BMW is an example) have located some of their production facilities in the USA and use them to help meet demand in the American market. This helps to insulate them from the effects of the rise in the value of the euro.

■ Businesses in the eurozone seem initially to have accommodated the euro's rapid rise.

? Question

Find out what has happened to the euro/dollar exchange rate over the past 12 months. (You can find the data from the Bank of England's Statistical Interactive Database at www.bankofengland.co.uk/statistics) Explain why the exchange rate has moved the way it has.

Definition

Sovereign risk (for business)
The risk that a foreign country's government or central bank will make its policies less favourable. Such policies could involve changes in interest rates or tax regimes, the imposition of foreign exchange controls, or even defaulting on loans or the appropriation of a business's assets.

the early 1970s. What followed was a period of managed exchange rates. Under this system, exchange rates are not pegged but allowed to float. However, central banks intervene from time to time to prevent excessive exchange rate fluctuations. This system largely continues to this day.

The problem of sovereign risk

Uncertainty over exchange rates creates problems for businesses that trade or invest internationally. This is part of the broader problem of **sovereign risk**. These are the risks associated with locating in or dealing with a particular country. For example, there is the risk that a country may raise business taxes or that its central bank may raise interest rates. Its government might impose new stricter regulatory controls that favour domestic firms, or impose stricter competition or environmental policies. There is a risk that the exchange rate may move adversely or that exchange controls may be imposed. In extreme cases, governments may appropriate a firm's assets or prevent it trading.

The greater the perceived level of sovereign risk of a particular country, the less willing will firms be to trade with it or locate there. Countries are thus under pressure to create a more favourable environment for business and reduce sovereign risk.

Pause for thought

Will the pressure on governments to reduce sovereign risk always lead to better outcomes for the citizens of that country?

Recap

■ The rate of exchange is the rate at which one currency exchanges for another. Rates of exchange are determined by demand and supply in the foreign exchange market. Demand for the domestic currency consists of all the credit items in the balance of payments account. Supply consists of all the debit items.

■ The exchange rate will depreciate (fall) if the demand for the domestic currency falls or the supply increases. These shifts can be caused by a fall in domestic interest rates, higher inflation in the domestic economy than abroad, a rise in domestic incomes relative to incomes abroad, relative investment prospects improving abroad, or the belief by speculators that the exchange rate will fall. The opposite in each case would cause an appreciation (rise).

■ The government can attempt to prevent the rate of exchange from falling by central bank purchases of the domestic currency in the foreign exchange market, either by selling foreign currency reserves or by using foreign loans. Alternatively, the central bank can raise interest rates. The reverse actions can be taken to prevent the rate from rising.

■ Managed exchange rates bring the advantage of greater certainty for the business community, which encourages trade and foreign investment. Also, if successful, they reduce speculation.

■ They bring the disadvantages, however, of not being able to use interest rate changes to meet other than exchange rate objectives, the difficulty in responding to shocks and the danger that speculation will be encouraged if speculators believe that the current exchange rate cannot be maintained.

■ There have been various attempts to manage exchange rates, without them being totally fixed. One example was the Bretton Woods system: a system of pegged exchange rates, but where devaluations or revaluations were allowed from time to time. Another was the ERM, which was the forerunner to the euro. Member countries' currencies were allowed to fluctuate against each other within a band.

■ Businesses face sovereign risk when investing in or trading with other countries. These risks relate to unforeseen exchange rate or interest rate movements, or adverse government policies.

The growth of global financial flows   13.3

Financial interdependence

International trade has grown rapidly for many years (see Figure 12.1 on page 340), but international financial flows have grown much more rapidly. On average, over $2 trillion of assets are traded each day across the foreign exchanges. Many of the transactions are short-term financial flows, moving to where interest rates are most favourable or to currencies where the exchange rate is likely to appreciate. Countries have thus become increasingly financially dependent on each other.

Assume that the Federal Reserve Bank (or 'Fed') (America's central bank), worried about rising inflation, decides to raise interest rates. What will be the effect on business in America's trading partners? There are three major effects.

■ If aggregate demand in America falls, so will its expenditure on imports from firms abroad, thus directly affecting businesses exporting to the USA. With a decline in their exports, aggregate demand in these other countries falls.

■ The higher interest rate in the USA will tend to drive up interest rates in other countries. This will depress investment. Again, aggregate demand will tend to fall in these countries.

■ The higher interest rate will attract an inflow of funds from other countries. This will cause the dollar to appreciate relative to other currencies. This will make these other countries' exports to the USA more competitive and imports from the USA relatively more expensive. This will result in an improvement in the current account of the USA's trading partners: their exports rise and imports fall. This represents a *rise* in aggregate demand in these countries – the opposite from the first two effects

There is a simple conclusion from the above analysis. The larger the financial flows, the more will interest rate changes in one country affect the economies of other countries: the greater will be the financial interdependence.

> **Pause for thought**
>
> *What will be the effect on the UK economy if the European Central Bank cuts interest rates?*

The impact of capital flows

Large movements of capital into and out of countries can have serious consequences for business. Some of these capital flows are for direct investment; some are for buying shares and other financial assets; some are simply short-term speculative deposits. The global supply of dollars available for such purposes has grown by some 18 per cent per year since the early 2000s. One of the main reasons for this has been the huge current account deficits of the USA. This has led to vast outflows of dollars from the USA into the world economy as Americans have effectively paid for their deficit by creating more dollars.

Capital inflows. Capital flows will be attracted to countries where investment prospects are good or for speculative purposes. When they are, the financial account of the balance of payments will improve, causing the exchange rate to appreciate. This appreciation, if set to continue, will attract further capital inflows in anticipation of a speculative gain from a rising exchange rate. This will push the exchange rate even higher. Domestic currency will be worth more in dollars and other currencies. In other words, a dollar will buy less of the country's currency.

This will make it harder for firms to export: if exports are priced in foreign currency (e.g. dollars) firms must accept less domestic currency; if exports are priced in the domestic currency, the dollar price must rise. At the same time, imports will be cheaper. This makes it harder for domestic business to compete with imports.

For example, in 2006, capital inflows into the Thai economy pushed up the value of the Thai baht by 16 per cent. As Thai businesses struggled to compete, the Bank of Thailand imposed taxes on inward portfolio investment. But this was not the solution. Share prices fell dramatically, and the tax was hastily withdrawn.

So is the answer to cut interest rates? This would reduce capital inflows and help curb the appreciation of the currency. But it would create another problem. The lower interest rates would encourage more borrowing and hence higher credit growth and higher inflation.

Thus large capital inflows leave countries with an uncomfortable choice: either allow the exchange rate to appreciate, thereby damaging business competitiveness, or cut interest rates, thereby causing higher inflation, which could also damage business competitiveness.

Capital outflows. Just as vast amounts of capital can flow into countries, so they can flow out too. The problem especially concerns money on short-term deposit. If a country's exchange rate is likely to fall, speculators will sell the currency before it does fall. This will then bring about the very depreciation that was anticipated. Such depreciation is likely if the currency had initially appreciated above its long-term equilibrium rate.

Capital controls

Excessive capital flows, whether inward or outward, can be highly destabilising for exchange rates. This makes it very difficult for business to plan and can rapidly turn a profitable business into a loss-making one. The result is to undermine confidence in *long-term* investment. And the problem is getting worse as the supply of dollars and other international currencies continues to grow faster than international trade.

So what can be done? Many commentators have called for capital controls. The aim of such controls is not to *prevent* capital flows. After all, capital flows are an important source of financing investment. The aim is to prevent short-term *speculative* flows, based on rumour or herd instinct rather than on economic fundamentals.

Types of control
In what ways, then, can movements of short-term capital be controlled?

Quantitative controls. Here the authorities would restrict the amount of foreign exchange dealing that could take place. Perhaps financial institutions would be allowed to exchange only a certain percentage of their assets. Developed countries and most developing countries have rejected this approach, however, since it is seen to be far too anti-market.

Alternatively, certain types of inflow could be restricted. China, for example, restricts portfolio capital inflows. This has held down its exchange rate, thereby increasing its competitiveness. But this, in turn, has reduced the competitiveness of other countries in Asia and around the world.

A Tobin tax. This is named after James Tobin, who in 1978 advocated the imposition of a small tax of 0.1 to 0.5 per cent on all foreign exchange transactions, or on just capital account transactions.[1] This would discourage destabilising speculation (by making it more expensive) and would thus impose some 'friction' in the foreign exchange markets, making them less volatile.

Non-interest-bearing deposits. Here a certain percentage of inflows of finance would have to be deposited with the central bank in a non-interest-bearing account for a set period of time. Chile in the late 1990s used such a system. It required that 30 per cent of all inflows be deposited with Chile's central bank for a year. This clearly amounted to a considerable tax (i.e. in terms of interest sacrificed) and had the effect of discouraging short-term speculative flows. The problem was that it meant that interest rates in Chile had to be higher in order to attract finance.

South Korea operates a similar system and in December 2006 it raised the amount that banks must deposit with the central bank in an attempt to stem speculative capital inflows.

Capital controls are a way around what economists call the 'impossible trinity': an economy cannot simultaneously control domestic liquidity [the amount of money], manage its exchange rate and have an open financial account. Only two of the three are possible. Controls on short-term capital inflows, if (a big if) they are implemented in a well-thought-out and transparent way, can offer a viable compromise, curbing capital inflows and excessive money growth, while taking the pressure off the currency.[2]

Recap

- Countries are increasingly financially interdependent. Changes in interest rates in one country will affect capital flows to and from other countries, and hence their exchange rates, interest rates and GDP.

- Capital flows have grown substantially in recent years and can be highly destabilising to an economy. Capital inflows can cause an appreciation, reducing a country's competitiveness.

- If capital flows could be constrained, however, exchange rates could be stabilised somewhat. Forms of control include: quantitative controls, a tax on exchange transactions (a Tobin tax) and non-interest-bearing deposits with the central bank of a certain percentage of capital inflows.

[1] J. Tobin, 'A proposal for international monetary reform', *The Eastern Economic Journal*, 4, no. 3–4, 1978, pp. 153–9
[2] 'The global gusher', *The Economist*, 4 January 2007

13.4 Economic and monetary union in the EU

Although countries around the world generally operate a system of floating exchange rates, small countries sometimes peg their exchange rates to the dollar or other major currencies. Also, on a regional basis, there have been attempts to create greater exchange rate stability by countries pegging their exchange rates to each other.

Such a system was introduced in Europe in 1979 as the forerunner of the adoption of the euro. The name given to the EU system was the **exchange rate mechanism (ERM)**. The majority of the EU countries at the time were members. The UK initially chose not to join the ERM, but eventually did so in 1990.

> ### Definition
>
> **ERM (the exchange rate mechanism)**
> A semi-fixed system whereby participating EU countries allowed fluctuations against each other's currencies only within agreed bands. Collectively they floated freely against all other currencies.

The ERM

Under the ERM, each currency was given a central exchange rate with each of the other member currencies in a grid. However, fluctuations were allowed from the central rate within specified bands. For most countries these bands were set at ±2¼ per cent. The central rates could be adjusted from time to time by agreement, thus making the ERM an adjustable peg system (see page 374). All the currencies floated jointly with currencies outside the ERM.

In a system of pegged exchange rates, such as the ERM, countries should harmonise their policies to avoid excessive currency misalignments and hence the need for large devaluations or revaluations. There should be a convergence of their economies: they should be at a similar point on the business cycle and have similar inflation rates and interest rates.

Shortly after the UK joined the ERM, strains began to show. The reunification of Germany involved considerable reconstruction in the eastern part of the country. Financing this reconstruction was causing a growing budget deficit. The Bundesbank (the German central bank) thus felt obliged to maintain high interest rates in order to keep inflation in check. At the same time, the UK was experiencing a massive current account deficit (partly the result of entering the ERM at what many commentators argued was too high an exchange rate). It was thus obliged to raise interest rates in order to protect the pound, despite the fact that the economy was sliding rapidly into recession. The French franc and Italian lira were also perceived to be overvalued, and there were the first signs of worries as to whether their exchange rates within the ERM could be retained.

In September 1992, things reached crisis point. On 'Black Wednesday' (16 September), the UK and Italy were forced to suspend their membership of the ERM: the pound and the lira were floated and depreciated substantially. The following year, in an attempt to rescue the ERM for the remaining countries, EU finance ministers agreed to adopt very wide ±15 per cent bands.

> ### Pause for thought
>
> *Under what circumstances may a currency bloc like the ERM (a) help to prevent speculation; (b) aggravate the problem of speculation?*

The old ERM appeared to be at an end. The new ±15 per cent bands hardly seemed like a 'pegged' system at all. However, the ERM did not die. Within months, the members were again managing to keep fluctuations within a very narrow range (for most of the time, within ±2¼ per cent). The scene was being set for the abandonment of separate currencies and the adoption of a single currency: the euro.

With a single currency there can be no exchange rate fluctuations between the member states, any more than there can be fluctuations between the Californian and New York dollar, or between the English, Scottish and Welsh pound.

Birth of the euro

In March 1998, the European Commission ruled that 11 of the 15 member states were eligible to proceed to EMU in January 1999. Their economies were deemed to be sufficiently converged in terms of interest rates, inflation rates and government deficits and debt. The UK and Denmark were to exercise their 'opt out', negotiated at Maastricht back in 1992, and Sweden and Greece failed to meet one or more of the convergence criteria.

The single currency, the euro, finally came into being in January 1999 (although notes and coins did not circulate until January 2002). Greece joined the euro in 2001, Slovenia in 2007 and Cyprus and Malta in 2008, making a total of 15 countries using the euro.

With a single currency, countries must have a single central bank (the European Central Bank for the eurozone) and a common monetary policy, involving common interest rates for all member countries. Such a system is known as **economic and monetary union (EMU)**.

Business and the euro

The adoption of the euro has had a profound effect on business, both within the eurozone and outside it. There are significant advantages in terms of greater certainty and greater inward investment, but also various costs in terms of reduced flexibility for governments in managing their economies.

Advantages of a single currency

Elimination of the costs of converting currencies. With separate currencies in each of the EU countries, costs were incurred each time one currency was exchanged into another. The elimination of these costs was, however, probably the least important benefit from the single currency. The European Commission estimated that the effect was to increase the GDP of the countries concerned by an average of only 0.4 per cent. The gains to countries like the UK, which have well-developed financial markets, would be even smaller.

Increased competition and efficiency. Not only has the single currency eliminated the need to convert one currency into another (a barrier to competition), but it has brought more transparency in pricing, and has put greater downward pressure on prices in high-cost firms and countries. This, of course, does not necessarily favour business, which might find its profits squeezed, but it generally benefits consumers.

Elimination of exchange-rate uncertainty (between the members). The removal of exchange rate uncertainty has helped to encourage trade between the eurozone countries. Perhaps more importantly, it has encouraged investment by firms that trade between these countries, given the greater certainty in calculating costs and revenues from such trade.

Definition

Economic and monetary union (EMU)
Where countries adopt a single currency and a single monetary policy. It might also involve other common policies, such as fiscal and supply-side policies.

Increased inward investment. Investment from the rest of the world is attracted to a eurozone of over 300 million inhabitants, where there is no fear of internal currency movements. By contrast, the UK, by not joining, has found that inward investment has been diverted away to countries within the eurozone. From 1990 to 1999, the UK's share of inward investment to the EU was nearly 40 per cent. From 1999 to 2004, it was 16 per cent. By 2006, however, it had risen to 21 per cent.

Lower inflation and interest rates. A single monetary policy forces convergence in inflation rates (just as inflation rates are very similar between the different regions *within* a country). With the ECB being independent from short-term political manipulation, this has resulted in a lower average inflation rate in the eurozone countries. This, in turn, has helped to convince markets that the euro will be strong relative to other currencies. The result is lower long-term rates of interest. This, in turn, further encourages investment in the eurozone countries, both by member states and by the rest of the world.

Opposition to EMU

Monetary union has been bitterly opposed, however, by certain groups. Many 'Eurosceptics' see within it a surrender of national political and economic sovereignty. The lack of an independent monetary and exchange rate policy is a serious problem, they argue, if an economy is at all out of harmony with the rest of the Union. For example, if countries such as Italy and Spain have higher endemic rates of inflation (due, say, to greater cost-push pressures), then how are they to make their goods competitive with the rest of the Union? With separate currencies these countries could allow their currencies to depreciate. With a single currency, however, they could become depressed 'regions' of Europe, with rising unemployment and all the other regional problems of depressed regions *within* a country.

> **Pause for thought**
>
> *How might multiplier effects (see page 283) lead to prosperous regions becoming more prosperous and less prosperous regions falling even further behind?*

The answer given by proponents of EMU is that it is better to tackle the problem of high inflation in such countries by the disciplines of competition from other EU countries than merely to feed that inflation by keeping separate currencies and allowing continued depreciation, with all the uncertainty that that brings. The critics of EMU, however, argue that cost differences, and hence unemployment, could persist.

Perhaps the most serious criticism is that the same rate of interest must apply to all eurozone countries: the 'one size fits all' criticism. The trouble is that while one country might require a lower rate of interest in order to ward off recession (such as Germany in 2003), another might require a higher one to prevent inflation. As convergence between the member economies increases, however, this problem is likely to lessen.

> **Definition**
>
> **Asymmetric shocks**
> Shocks (such as an oil price increase or a recession in another part of the world) that have different-sized effects on different industries, regions or countries.

Another problem for members of a single currency occurs in adjusting to a shock when that shock affects members to different degrees. These are known as **asymmetric shocks**. For example, a sudden change in the price of oil would affect an oil-exporting country like the UK differently from oil-importing countries. This problem is more serious, the less the price flexibility within member countries.

This problem, however, should not be overstated. Divergences between economies are often the result of a lack of harmony between countries in their demand-management policies: something that is impossible in the eurozone in the case of monetary policy, and more difficult in the case of fiscal policy. Also, many of the shocks that face economies today are global and have similar (albeit not identical) effects on all countries. Adjustment to such shocks would often be better with a single coordinated policy, something that would be much easier with a single currency and a single central bank.

Even when shocks are uniformly felt in the member states, however, there is still the problem that policies adopted centrally will have different impacts on each country. For example, in the UK, a large proportion of borrowing is at variable interest rates. In Germany, by contrast, much is at fixed rates. Thus if the UK adopted the euro and the ECB were to raise interest rates, the contractionary effects would be felt disproportionately in the UK. Of course, were this balance to change – and there is some evidence that types of borrowing are becoming more uniform across the EU – this problem would diminish.

The problem for economists is that the issue of monetary union is a very emotive one. 'Europhiles' often see monetary union as a vital element in their vision of a united Europe. Many Eurosceptics, however, see EMU as a surrender of sovereignty and a threat to nationhood. In such an environment, a calm assessment of the arguments and evidence is very difficult.

The UK Labour government specified five convergence criteria that must be met before it would put the question of UK adoption of the euro to the electorate in a referendum. These are examined in Web Case D.38.

Recap

- One means of achieving greater currency stability is for a group of countries to peg their internal exchange rates and yet float jointly with the rest of the world. The exchange rate mechanism of the EU (ERM) was an example. This was seen as an important first stage on the road to complete economic and monetary union (EMU) in the EU.

- The euro was born on 1 January 1999 with euro notes and coins introduced in 2002. There are now 15 countries using the euro.

- The advantages claimed for EMU are that it eliminates the costs of converting currencies and the uncertainties associated with possible changes in former inter-EU exchange rates. This encourages more investment, both inward and by domestic firms, and greater trade between EU countries.

- Critics, however, claim that the loss of independence in policy-making might make adjustment to domestic economic problems more difficult, especially when these problems diverge from those of other members. A single monetary policy is claimed to be inappropriate for dealing with asymmetric shocks.

International economic policy: managing the global economy   13.5

Attempts to coordinate global business activity

There is an old saying: 'If America sneezes, the rest of the world catches a cold.' Viruses of a similar nature regularly infect the world economy. A dramatic example was the 'Asian contagion' of 1997–98. Economic crises spread rapidly around south-east and east Asia and then to Russia and on to Brazil. World leaders were seriously worried that the whole world would plunge into recession. What was needed was a coordinated policy response.

For many years now the leaders of the seven major industrialised countries – the USA, Japan, Germany, France, the UK, Italy and Canada – have met once a year (and more frequently if felt necessary) at an economic summit conference. More recently they have been joined by Russia. Top of the agenda in most of these G8 meetings has been how to generate world economic growth without major currency fluctuations. But to achieve this it is important that there is a **harmonisation** of economic policies between nations. In other words, it is important that all the major countries are pursuing consistent policies aiming at common international goals.

But how can policy harmonisation be achieved? As long as there are significant domestic differences between the major economies, there is likely to be conflict, not harmony. For example, if one country, say the USA, is worried about the size of its budget deficit, it may be unwilling to respond to world demands for a stimulus to aggregate demand to pull the world economy out of recession. What is more, speculators, seeing differences between countries, are likely to exaggerate them by their actions, causing large changes in exchange rates. The G8 countries have therefore sought to achieve greater **convergence** of their economies. However, although convergence may be a goal of policy, in practice it has proved elusive.

Because of a lack of convergence, there are serious difficulties in achieving international policy harmonisation:

■ Countries' budget deficits and accumulated government debt differ substantially as a proportion of their GDP. This puts very different pressures on the interest rates necessary to service these debts.

■ Harmonising rates of monetary growth or inflation targets would involve letting interest rates fluctuate with the demand for money. Without convergence in the demand for money, interest rate fluctuations could be severe.

■ Harmonising interest rates would involve abandoning money, inflation or exchange rate targets (unless interest rate 'harmonisation' meant adjusting interest rates so as to maintain money or inflation targets or a given exchange rate).

■ Countries have different internal structural relationships. A lack of convergence here means that countries with higher endemic *cost* inflation would require higher interest rates and higher unemployment if international inflation rates were to be harmonised, or higher inflation if interest rates were to be harmonised.

■ Countries have different rates of productivity increase, product development, investment and market penetration. A lack of convergence here means that the growth in exports (relative to imports) will differ for any given level of inflation or growth.

■ Countries may be very unwilling to change their domestic policies to fall into line with other countries. They may prefer the other countries to fall into line with them!

If any one of the four – interest rates, growth rates, inflation rates or current account balance of payments – could be harmonised across countries, it is likely that the other three would then not be harmonised.

Definitions

International harmonisation of economic policies
Where countries attempt to coordinate their macroeconomic policies so as to achieve common goals.

Convergence of economies
When countries achieve similar levels of growth, inflation, budget deficits as a percentage of GDP, balance of payments. etc.

Total convergence and thus total harmonisation may not be possible. Nevertheless most governments favour some movement in that direction: some is better than none.

Pause for thought

If total convergence were achieved, would harmonisation of policies follow automatically?

The problem of speculation

One important lesson of recent years is that concerted speculation has become virtually unstoppable. This was made clear by the expulsion of the UK and Italy from the ERM in 1992, a dramatic fall of the Mexican peso and a rise of the yen in 1995, the collapse of various south-east Asian currencies (see Web Case D.26) and the Russian rouble in 1997–98 and the collapse of the Argentinean peso in 2002 (see Web Case D.37). In comparison with the vast amounts of short-term finance flowing across the foreign exchanges each day, the reserves of central banks seem trivial.

If there is a consensus in the markets that a currency will depreciate, there is little that central banks can do. For example, if there were a 50 per cent chance of a 10 per cent depreciation in the next week, then selling that currency now would yield an 'expected' return of just over 5 per cent for the week (i.e. 50% of 10%): equivalent to more than 5000 per cent at an annual rate!

For this reason, many commentators have argued that there are only two types of exchange rate system that can work over the long term. The first is a completely free-floating exchange rate, with no attempt by the central bank to support the exchange rate. With no intervention, there is no problem of a shortage of reserves!

The second is to share a common currency with other countries: to join a common-currency area, such as the eurozone, and let the common currency float freely. The country would give up independence in its monetary policy, but at least there would be no problem of exchange rate instability within the currency area. A similar alternative is to adopt a major currency of another country, such as the US dollar or the euro. Many smaller states have done this. For example, Kosovo has adopted the euro and Ecuador has adopted the US dollar.

Recap

- Currency fluctuations can be lessened if countries harmonise their economic policies. Ideally this would involve achieving common growth rates, inflation rates, balance of payments (as a percentage of GDP) and interest rates. The attempt to harmonise one of these goals, however, may bring conflicts with one of the other goals.

- Leaders of the G8 countries meet regularly to discuss ways of harmonising their policies. Usually, however, domestic issues are more important to the leaders than international ones, and frequently they pursue policies that are not in the interests of the other countries.

- Many economists argue that, with the huge flows of short-term finance across the foreign exchanges, governments are forced to adopt one of two extreme forms of exchange rate regime: free floating or being a member of a currency union.

Postscript: is globalisation a 'good thing'?

We have come across many aspects of globalisation throughout this book, from the operation of international commodity markets (Chapter 2), to global fashions (Chapter 3), to the growth of multinational companies (Chapter 7), to the growth of international trade and financial flows (Chapter 12 and this chapter). Here we reflect on this process and ask whether the world benefits from this growing interdependence.

The supporters

Supporters of globalisation argue that it has massive potential to benefit the entire global economy. With freer trade, greater FDI and greater competition, countries and businesses within them are encouraged to think, plan and act globally. Technology spreads faster; countries specialise in particular products and processes and thereby exploit their core competitive advantages.

Both rich and poor, it is argued, benefit from such a process. Politically, globalisation brings us closer together. Political ties help stabilise relationships and offer the opportunity for countries to discuss their differences. However imperfect the current global political system might be, the alternative of independent nations is seen as potentially far worse. The globalisation of culture is also seen as beneficial, as a world of experience is opened, whether in respect to our holiday destinations, or the food we eat, or the music we listen to or the TV programmes we watch.

Supporters of globalisation recognise that not all countries benefit equally from globalisation: those that have wealth will, as always, possess more opportunity to benefit from the globalisation process, whether from lower prices, global political agreements or cultural experience. However, long term, supporters of globalisation see it as ultimately being for the benefit of all – rich and poor alike.

The critics

Critics of globalisation argue that it contributes to growing inequality and further impoverishes poor nations. As an economic philosophy, globalisation allows multinational corporations, based largely in the USA, Europe and Japan, to exploit their dominant position in foreign markets. Without effective competition in these markets such companies are able to pursue profit with few constraints.

By 'exploiting' low-wage labour, companies are able to compete more effectively on world markets. As competitive pressures intensify and companies seek to cut costs further, this can put downward pressure on such wages – something that workers will find difficulty in resisting, given the monopsony power of multinational employers.

In political terms, critics of globalisation see the world being dominated by big business. As we saw in Table 7.1 on page 194, many multinational companies have a turnover larger than the GDP of whole countries. This gives them huger power in their dealings with such countries and in imposing conditions on them, whether in terms of generous tax regimes, privileged access to markets or limited rights for workers. Multinationals also put pressure on their home governments in America, Europe or Japan to promote their interests in their dealings with other countries, thereby heightening the domination of rich countries over the poor.

Critics are no less damning of the cultural aspects of globalisation. They see the world dominated by multinational brands, western fashion, music and TV. Rather than globalisation fostering a mix of cultural expression, critics suggest that cultural differences are being replaced by the dominant (American) culture of the day.

The above views represent the extremes, and to a greater or lesser degree both have elements of truth within them. The impact of globalisation on different groups is not even, and never will be. However, to suggest that big business rules is also an exaggeration. Clearly big business is influential, but it is a question of degree. Influence will invariably fluctuate over time, between events, and between and within countries.

At present the momentum within the global economy is for barriers to come down. In many global markets, competition rather than monopoly power is becoming the dominant force. This is having profound effects on both multinational business and the peoples of the world.

Recap

- Supporters of globalisation point to its potential to lead to faster growth and greater efficiency through trade, competition and investment. It also has the potential to draw the world closer together politically.

- Critics of globalisation argue that it contributes to growing inequality and further impoverishes poor nations. It also erodes national cultures and can have adverse environmental consequences.

QUESTIONS

1. The following are the items in the UK's 2004 balance of payments:

	£ billions
Exports of goods	190.7
Imports of goods	248.6
Exports of services	95.9
Imports of services	76.8
Net income flows	+24.0
Net current transfers	−10.9
Net capital transfers	+2.1
Net investment in UK from abroad (direct and portfolio)	126.6
Net UK investment abroad (direct and portfolio)	183.1
Other financial inflows	407.5
Other financial outflows	323.8
Reserves	−0.2

Calculate the following: (a) the balance on trade in goods; (b) the balance on trade in goods and services; (c) the balance of payments on current account; (d) the financial account balance; (e) the total current plus capital plus financial account balance; (f) net errors and omissions.

2. Assume that there is a free-floating exchange rate. Will the following cause the exchange rate to appreciate or depreciate? In each case you should consider whether there is a shift in the demand or supply curves of sterling (or both) and which way the curve(s) shift(s).

    (a) More video recorders are imported from Japan.
        Demand curve *shifts left/shifts right/does not shift*
        Supply curve *shifts left/shifts right/does not shift*
        Exchange rate *appreciates/depreciates*

    (b) UK interest rates rise relative to those abroad.
        Demand curve *shifts left/shifts right/does not shift*
        Supply curve *shifts left/shifts right/does not shift*
        Exchange rate *appreciates/depreciates*

    (c) The UK experiences a higher rate of inflation than other countries.
        Demand curve *shifts left/shifts right/does not shift*
        Supply curve *shifts left/shifts right/does not shift*
        Exchange rate *appreciates/depreciates*

    (d) Speculators believe that the rate of exchange will appreciate.
        Demand curve *shifts left/shifts right/does not shift*
        Supply curve *shifts left/shifts right/does not shift*
        Exchange rate *appreciates/depreciates*

3. What is the relationship between the balance of payments and the rate of exchange?

4. Consider the argument that in the modern world of large-scale short-term international financial movements, the ability of individual countries to affect their exchange rate is very limited.

5. Why may capital inflows damage the international competitiveness of a country's businesses?

6. What adverse effects on the domestic economy may follow from (a) a depreciation of the exchange rate and (b) an appreciation of the exchange rate?

7. What are the causes of exchange-rate volatility? Have these problems become greater or lesser in the past ten years? Explain why.

8. Did the exchange rate difficulties experienced by countries under the ERM strengthen or weaken the arguments for progressing to a single European currency?

9. By what means would a depressed country in an economic union with a single currency be able to recover? Would the market provide a satisfactory solution or would (union) government intervention be necessary and, if so, what form would the intervention take?

10. Assume that just some of the members of a common market like the EU adopt full economic and monetary union, including a common currency. What are the

advantages and disadvantages to those members joining the full EMU and to those not joining?

11. What are the economic (as opposed to political) difficulties in achieving an international harmonisation of economic policies so as to avoid damaging currency fluctuations?

12. To what extent can international negotiations over economic policy be seen as a game of strategy? Are there any parallels between the behaviour of countries and the behaviour of oligopolies?

Additional Part D case studies on the *Economics and the Business Environment* website (www.pearsoned.co.uk/sloman)

D.1   **Output gaps.** A way of measuring how far actual output falls short of long-term trend output.

D.2   **The costs of economic growth.** Why economic growth may not be an unmixed blessing.

D.3   **Comparing national income statistics.** The importance of taking the purchasing power of local currencies into account.

D.4   **John Maynard Keynes (1883–1946).** A profile of the great economist.

D.5   **The attributes of money.** What makes something, such as metal, paper or electronic records, suitable as money?

D.6   **UK monetary aggregates.** This examines the various measures of money supply in the UK using both UK and eurozone monetary aggregates.

D.7   **Changes in the banking industry.** This case study looks at mergers and diversification in the banking industry.

D.8   **Technology and unemployment.** Does technological progress destroy jobs?

D.9   **The national debt.** This explores the question of whether it matters if a country has a high national debt.

D.10   **Trends in public expenditure.** This case examines attempts to control public expenditure in the UK and relates them to the crowding-out debate.

D.11   **The crowding-out effect.** The circumstances in which an increase in public expenditure can replace private expenditure.

D.12   **Managing the US economy.** The use of active fiscal and monetary policy in 2001 and 2002 to stimulate the US economy.

D.13 **Discretionary fiscal policy in Japan.** How the Japanese government used fiscal policy on various occasions throughout the 1990s and early 2000s in an attempt to bring the economy out of recession.

D.14 **The daily operation of monetary policy.** What practical steps does the Bank of England take to ensure that the market rate of interest is its own chosen rate?

D.15 **Monetary policy in the eurozone.** This looks at how interest rates are set in the eurozone and what rules govern the behaviour of the European Central Bank.

D.16 **Central banking and monetary policy in the USA.** This case examines how the Fed conducts monetary policy.

D.17 **A new approach to industrial policy.** This looks at changes in the approach to industrial policy around the world.

D.18 **Assessing PFI.** Has this been the perfect solution to funding investment for the public sector without raising taxes?

D.19 **Welfare to work.** An examination of the policy of the UK Labour government whereby welfare payments are designed to encourage people into employment.

D.20 **Fallacious arguments for restricting trade.** Some of the more common mistaken arguments for protection.

D.21 **Free trade and the environment.** Do whales, the rainforests and the atmosphere gain from free trade?

D.22 **The Uruguay Round.** An examination of the negotiations that led to substantial cuts in trade barriers.

D.23 **The Doha Development Agenda.** This looks at the latest WTO trade round.

D.24 **The Battle of Seattle.** This looks at the protests against the WTO at Seattle in November 1999 and considers the arguments for and against the free trade policies of the WTO.

D.25 **The World Trade Organisation.** This looks at the various opportunities and threats posed by this major international organisation.

D.26 **Crisis in south-east Asia.** Causes of the severe recession in many south-east Asian countries in 1997/98.

D.27 **A miracle gone wrong?** Lessons from east Asia crisis of 1997/98.

D.28 **Steel barriers.** The use by the USA of tariff protection for its steel industry and the effects of threats of retaliation by the EU.

D.29 **The Internal Market Scoreboard.** Keeping a tally on progress to a true single market in the EU.

D.30 **The UK's balance of payments deficit.** An examination of the UK's persistent trade and current account deficits.

D.31 **A high exchange rate.** This case looks at whether a high exchange rate is necessarily bad news for exporters.

D.32 **Dealing in foreign exchange.** The operation of international currency markets.

D.33 **Using interest rates** to control both aggregate demand and the exchange rate. A problem of one instrument and two targets.

D.34 **The Tobin tax.** A possible means of reducing exchange rate fluctuations.

D.35 **Currency turmoil in the 1990s.** Two examples of speculative attacks on currencies: first on the Mexican peso in 1995; then on the Thai baht in 1997.

D.36 **Argentina in crisis.** An examination of the collapse of the Argentinean economy in 2001/02.

D.37 **The UK Labour government's convergence criteria for euro membership.** An examination of the five tests set by the UK government that would have to be passed before the question of euro membership would be put to the electorate in a referendum.

D.38 **Attempts at harmonisation.** A look at the meetings of the G7 economies where they attempt to come to agreement on means of achieving stable and sustained worldwide economic growth.

D.39 **High oil prices.** What is their effect on the world economy?

D.40 **Optimal currency areas.** What's the best size for a single currency area such as the eurozone?

Websites relevant to Part D

Numbers and sections refer to websites listed in the Web Appendix and hotlinked from this book's website at www.pearsoned.co.uk/sloman/

■ For news articles relevant to Part D, see the *Economics News Articles* link from the book's website.

■ For general news on macroeconomic issues, both national and international, see websites in section A, and particularly A1–5, 7–9. For general news on money, banking and interest rates, see again A1–5, 7–9 and also 20–22, 25, 26, 35, 36, 37. For all of Part D, see also links to macroeconomic and financial news in A41. See also links to newspapers worldwide in A38, 43 and 44.

■ For macroeconomic data, see links in B1; also see B35. For UK data, see B3 and 34. For EU data, see G1 > *The Statistical Annex*. For US data, see B25 and the *Data* section of B17. For international data, see B15, 21, 24, 31, 33, 35. For links to data sets, see B28, 33.

■ For national income statistics for the UK (Appendix), see B1, *1. National Statistics* > the fourth link > *Economy* > *United Kingdom Economic Accounts* and *United Kingdom National Accounts – The Blue Book*.

(C) Sites for students and teachers of economics

The following websites offer useful ideas and resources to those who are studying or teaching economics. It is worth browsing through some just to see what is on offer. Try out the first four sites, for starters. The Internet Economist is a very helpful tutorial for economics students on using the Internet.

1. Economics Network of the UK Higher Education Academy
2. Biz/ed
3. Ecedweb
4. Econ Links: student resources
5. Economics and Business Education Association
6. Tutor2U
7. Economics America
8. The Internet Economist (tutorial on using the Web)
9. Oxford School of Learning
10. Teaching resources for economists
11. Resources for University Teachers of Economics (University of Melbourne)
12. Federal Reserve Bank of San Francisco: Economics Education
13. Federal Reserve Bank of Minneapolis Economic Education
14. WebEc resources
15. BibEc papers
16. Online Opinion (Economics)
17. The Idea Channel
18. History of Economic Thought
19. Resources For Economists on the Internet (RFE)
20. Classroom Expernomics
21. VCE Economics (Economics teaching resources – Australian)
22. Why Study Economics?
23. JokEc: economics jokes!
24. Veconlab: Charles Holt's classroom experiments

(D) Economic models, simulations and experiments

Economic modelling is an important aspect of economic analysis. There are a number of sites that offer access to a model for you to use, e.g. Virtual economy (where you can play being Chancellor of the Exchequer). Using such models can be a useful way of finding out how economic theory works within an environment that claims to reflect reality.

1. Virtual economy
2. Virtual factory
3. Virtual Learning Arcade
4. About.com Economics
5. Classroom experiments, Internet experiments and Internet simulations
6. *Economics Network Handbook*, chapter on simulations, games and role-play
7. Estima (statistical analysis)
8. SPSS (statistical analysis)
9. National Institute of Economic and Social Research
10. Software available on the Economics Network site
11. RFE Software
12. Virtual Chancellor
13. Veconlab: Charles Holt's classroom experiments
14. EconPort
15. Denise Hazlett's Classroom Experiments in Macroeconomics
16. Games Economists Play
17. Finance and Economics Experimental Laboratory at Exeter (FEELE)
18. Classroom Expernomics
19. *The Economics Network's Guide to Classroom Experiments and Games*

UK government and UK organisations' sites   (E)

If you want to see what a government department is up to, then look no further than the list below. Government departments' websites are an excellent source of information and data. They are particularly good at offering information on current legislation and policy initiatives.

1. Gateway site (DirectGov)
2. Communities and Local Government
3. Central Office of Information
4. Competition Commission
5. Department for Education and Skills
6. Department for International Development
7. Department for Transport
8. Department of Health
9. Department for Work and Pensions
10. Department of Trade and Industry (DTI)
11. Environment Agency
12. UK euro information site
13. Low Pay Commission
14. Department for Environment, Food and Rural Affairs (DEFRA)
15. Office of Communications (Ofcom)
16. Office of Gas and Electricity Markets (Ofgem)
17. Official Documents OnLine
18. Office of Fair Trading (OFT)
19. Office of the Rail Regulator (ORR)
20. The Takeover Panel
21. Sustainable Development Commission
22. OFWAT
23. National Statistics (NS)
24. National Statistics Time Series Data
25. HM Revenue and Customs
26. UK Intellectual Property Office
27. Parliament website
28. Scottish Executive
29. Scottish Environment Protection Agency
30. Treasury
31. Equal Opportunities Commission
32. Trades Union Congress (TUC)
33. Confederation of British Industry
34. Adam Smith Institute
35. Chatham House
36. Institute of Fiscal Studies
37. Advertising Standards Authority
38. Small Business Service
39. Transport 2000

Sources of monetary and financial data   (F)

As the title suggests, here are listed useful websites for finding information on financial matters. You will see that the list comprises mainly central banks, both within Europe and further afield.

1. Bank of England
2. Bank of England Monetary and Financial Statistics
3. Banque de France (in English)
4. Bundesbank (German central bank)
5. Central Bank of Ireland
6. European Central Bank
7. Eurostat
8. US Federal Reserve Bank
9. Netherlands Central Bank (in English)
10. Bank of Japan (in English)
11. Reserve Bank of Australia
12. Bank Negara Malaysia (in English)
13. Monetary Authority of Singapore
14. Bank of Canada
15. National Bank of Denmark (in English)
16. Reserve Bank of India
17. Links to central bank websites from the Bank for International Settlements
18. The London Stock Exchange

(G)   European Union and related sources

For information on European issues, the following is a wide range of useful sites. The sites maintained by the European Union are an excellent source of information and are provided free of charge.

1. Economic and Financial Affairs: (EC DG)
2. European Central Bank
3. EU official Web site
4. Eurostat
5. Employment and Social Affairs: (EC DG)
6. Booklets on the EU
7. Enterprise: (EC DG)
8. Competition: (EC DG)
9. Agriculture and Rural Development: (EC DC)
10. Energy and Transport: (EC DG)
11. Environment: (EC DG)
12. Regional Policy: (EC DG)
13. Taxation and Customs Union: (EC DG)
14. Education and training: (EC DG)
15. European Patent Office
16. European Commission
17. European Parliament
18. European Council

(H)   International organisations

This section casts its net beyond Europe and lists the Web addresses of the main international organisations in the global economy. You will notice that some sites are run by pressure groups, such as Jubilee Research, while others represent organisations set up to manage international affairs, such as the International Monetary Fund and the United Nations.

1. Food and Agriculture Organisation
2. International Air Transport Association (IATA)
3. International Labour Organisation (ILO)
4. International Monetary Fund (IMF)
5. Organisation for Economic Co-operation and Development (OECD)
6. OPEC
7. World Bank
8. World Health Organisation
9. United Nations
10. United Nations Industrial Development Organisation
11. Friends of the Earth
12. Jubilee Research
13. Oxfam
14. Christian Aid (reports on development issues)
15. European Bank for Reconstruction and Development (EBRD)
16. World Trade Organisation (WTO)
17. United Nations Development Programme
18. UNICEF
19. EURODAD – European Network on Debt and Development
20. NAFTA
21. South American free trade areas
22. ASEAN
23. APEC
24. United Nations Conference on Trade and Development (UNCTAD)

Economics search and link sites   (I)

If you are having difficulty finding what you want from the list of sites above, the following sites offer links to other sites and are a very useful resource when you are looking for something a little bit more specialist. Once again, it is worth having a look at what these sites have to offer in order to judge their usefulness.

1. Gateway for UK official sites
2. Alta Plana
3. Data Archive Search
4. Inomics (search engine for economics information)
5. RePEc bibliographic database
6. Links to economics resources sites
7. Intute: Social Sciences (Economics)
8. WebEc
9. One World (link to economic development sites)
10. Economic development sites (list)
11. Biz/ed Internet catalogue
12. Web links for economists from the Economics Network
13. Yahoo's links to economic data
14. OFFSTATS links to data sets
15. Excite Economics links
16. Internet Resources for Economists
17. Google Web Directory: Economics
18. Resources for Economists on the Internet
19. UK university economics departments
20. Economics education links

Internet search engines   (J)

The following search engines have been found to be useful.

1. Google
2. Altavista
3. Whoosh UK
4. Excite
5. Infoseek
6. Search.com
7. MSN
8. UK Plus
9. Yahoo
10. Ask
11. Kartoo
12. Blinkx (for videos and audio podcasts)

Key ideas

1 **The principal–agent problem.** Where people (principals), as a result of a lack of knowledge (asymmetric information), cannot ensure that their best interests are served by their agents. Agents may take advantage of this situation to the disadvantage of the principals. (See page 10.)

2 **The behaviour and performance of firms is affected by the business environment.** The business environment includes social/cultural (S), technological (T), economic (E), ethical (E), political (P), legal (L) and environmental (E) factors. The mnemonic STEEPLE can be used to remember these. (See page 13.)

3 The **opportunity cost** of something is what you give up to get it/do it. In other words, it is cost measured in terms of the best alternative forgone. (See page 25.)

4 **Rational decision making involves weighing up the marginal benefit and marginal cost of any activity.** If the marginal benefit exceeds the marginal cost, it is rational to do the activity (or to do more of it). If the marginal cost exceeds the marginal benefit, it is rational not to do it (or to do less of it). (See page 26.)

5 **People respond to incentives, such as changes in prices or wages.** It is important, therefore, that incentives are appropriate and have the desired effect. (See page 34.)

6 **Changes in demand or supply cause markets to adjust.** Whenever such changes occur, the resulting 'disequilibrium' will bring an automatic change in prices, thereby restoring equilibrium (i.e. a balance of demand and supply). (See page 34.)

7 **People's actions are influenced by their expectations.** People respond not just to what is happening now (such as a change in price), but to what they anticipate will happen in the future. (See page 38.)

8 **Partial analysis: other things remaining equal (ceteris paribus).** In economics it is common to look at just one determinant of a variable such as demand or supply and see what happens when the determinant changes. For example, if price is taken as the determinant of demand, we can see what happens to quantity demanded as price changes. In the meantime we have

to assume that other determinants remain unchanged. This is known as the 'other things being equal' assumption (or, using the Latin, the 'ceteris paribus' assumption). Once we have seen how our chosen determinant affects our variable, we can then see what happens when another determinant changes, and then another, and so on. (See page 38.)

9 **Equilibrium is the point where conflicting interests are balanced.** Only at this point is the amount that demanders are willing to purchase the same as the amount that suppliers are willing to supply. It is a point which will be automatically reached in a free market through the operation of the price mechanism. (See page 44.)

10 **Elasticity.** The responsiveness of one variable (e.g. demand) to a change in another (e.g. price). This concept is fundamental to understanding how markets work. The more elastic variables are, the more responsive is the market to changing circumstances. (See page 51.)

11 **The principle of diminishing marginal utility.** As you consume more of a product, and thus become more satisfied, so your desire for additional units of it will decline. (See page 66.)

12 **Adverse selection.** Where information is imperfect, high-risk/poor-quality groups will be attracted to profitable market opportunities to the disadvantage of the average buyer (or seller). (See page 71.)

13 **Moral hazard.** Following a deal, if there are information asymmetries (see page 10), it is likely that one party will engage in problematic (immoral and/ or hazardous) behaviour to the detriment of the other. In other words, lack of information by one party to the deal may result in the deal not being honoured by the other party. (See page 71.)

14 **The law of diminishing marginal returns.** When increasing amounts of a variable input are used with a given amount of a fixed input, there will come a point when each extra unit of the variable input will produce less extra output than the previous unit. (See page 92.)

15 **Sunk costs and the 'bygones' principle** states that sunk (fixed) costs should be ignored when deciding whether to produce or sell more or less of a product. Only variable costs should be taken into account. (See page 94.)

16 **Transactions costs.** The costs associated with exchanging products. For buyers it is the costs over and above the price of the product. For sellers it is the costs over and above the costs of production. Transactions costs include search costs, contract costs, monitoring and enforcement costs, and transport and handling costs. (See page 106.)

17 **Market power benefits the powerful at the expense of others.** When firms have market power over prices, they can use this to raise prices and profits above the perfectly competitive level. Other things being equal, the firm will gain at the expense of the consumer. Similarly, if consumers or workers have market power they can use this to their own benefit. (See page 124.)

18   **People often think and behave strategically.**   How you think others will respond to your actions is likely to influence your own behaviour. Firms, for example, when considering a price or product change will often take into account the likely reactions of their rivals. (See page 135.)

19   **Nash equilibrium.**   The position resulting from everyone making their optimal decision based on their assumptions about their rivals' decisions. Such an outcome, however, is unlikely to maximise the collective benefit. Nevertheless, without collusion in this 'game', whether open or tacit, there is no incentive to move from this position. (See page 142.)

20   **Competitive advantage.**   The various factors that enable a firm to compete more effectively with its rivals. These can be supply-side factors, such as superior technology, better organisation, or greater power or efficiency in sourcing its supplies – resulting in lower costs; or they could be demand-side ones, such as producing a superior or better-value product in the eyes of consumers, or being more conveniently located – resulting in higher and/or less elastic demand. (See page 162.)

21   **Core competences.**   The areas of specialised expertise within a business that underpin its competitive advantage over its rivals. These competences could be in production technologies or organisation, in relationships with suppliers, in the nature and specifications of the product, or in the firm's ability to innovate and develop its products and brand image. (See page 170.)

22   **Efficient capital markets.**   Capital markets are efficient when the prices of shares accurately reflect information about companies' current and expected future performance. (See page 184.)

23   **Social efficiency.**   This is achieved where no further net social gain can be made by producing more or less of a good. This will occur where marginal social benefit equals marginal social cost. (See page 244.)

24   **Externalities are spillover costs or benefits.**   Where these exist, even an otherwise perfect market will fail to achieve social efficiency. (See page 244.)

25   **The free-rider problem.**   People are often unwilling to pay for things if they can make use of things other people have bought. This problem can lead to people not purchasing things which would be to their benefit and that of other members of society to have. (See page 246.)

26   **Economies suffer from inherent instability.**   As a result, economic growth and other macroeconomic indicators tend to fluctuate. (See page 286.)

27   **The distinction between real and nominal values.**   Nominal figures are those using current prices, interest rates, etc. Real figures are figures corrected for inflation. (See page 304.)

28   **The law of comparative advantage.**   Provided opportunity costs of various goods differ in two countries, both of them can gain from mutual trade if they specialise in producing (and exporting) those goods that have relatively low opportunity costs compared with the other country. (See page 342.)

29 **The competitive advantage of nations.**   The ability of countries to compete in the market for exports and with potential importers to their country. The competitiveness of any one industry depends on the availability and quality of resources, demand conditions at home in that industry, the strategies and rivalry of firms within the industry and the quality of supporting industries and infrastructure. It also depends on government policies, and there is also an element of chance. (See page 345.)

Glossary

Absolute advantage A country has an absolute advantage over another in the production of a good if it can produce it with fewer resources than the other country.

Accelerator The *level* of investment depends on the *rate of increase* in consumer demand, and as a result is subject to substantial fluctuations. Increases in investment via the accelerator can compound the multiplier effect.

Adjustable peg A system whereby exchange rates are fixed for a period of time, but may be devalued (or revalued) if a deficit (or surplus) becomes substantial.

Adverse selection Where information is imperfect, high-risk/poor-quality groups will be attracted to profitable market opportunities to the disadvantage of the average buyer (or seller).

Aggregate demand for labour curve A curve showing the total demand for labour in the economy at different average real wage rates.

Aggregate supply of labour curve A curve showing the total number of people willing and able to work at different average real wage rates.

Appreciation A rise in the free-market exchange rate of the domestic currency with foreign currencies.

Asymmetric information A situation in which one party in an economic relationship knows more than another.

Asymmetric shocks Shocks (such as an oil price increase or a recession in another part of the world) that have different-sized effects on different industries, regions or countries.

Average (total) cost (*AC*) Total cost (fixed plus variable) per unit of output: $AC = TC/Q = AFC + AVC$.

Average cost or **Mark-up pricing** Where firms set the price by adding a profit mark-up to average costs.

Average fixed cost (*AFC*) Total fixed cost per unit of output: $AFC = TFC/Q$.

Average revenue Total revenue per unit of output. When all output is sold at the same price, average revenue will be the same as price: $AR = TR/Q = P$.

Average variable cost (*AVC*) Total variable cost per unit of output: $AVC = TVC/Q$.

Backward integration Where a firm expands backwards down the supply chain to earlier stages of production.

Balance of payments on current account The balance on trade in goods and services plus net incomes and current transfers: i.e. the sum of the credits on the current account minus the sum of the debits.

Balance of trade Exports of goods and services minus imports of goods and services.

Bank (or deposits) multiplier   The number of times greater the expansion of bank deposits is than the additional liquidity in banks that caused it: $1/L$ (the inverse of the liquidity ratio).

Barometric forecasting   A technique used to predict future economic trends based upon analysing patterns of time-series data.

Budget deficit   The excess of central government's spending over its tax receipts.

Budget surplus   The excess of central government's tax receipts over its spending.

Business cycle or **trade cycle**   The periodic fluctuations of national output round its long-term trend.

Business ethics   The values and principles that shape business behaviour.

Capital account of the balance of payments   The record of transfers of capital to and from abroad.

Cartel   A formal collusive agreement.

Cash in circulation   The measure of narrow money in the UK. This is all cash outside the Bank of England: in banks, in people's purses and wallets, in businesses' safes and tills, in government departments, etc.

Change in demand   The term used for a shift in the demand curve. It occurs when a determinant of demand *other* than price changes.

Change in supply   The term used for a shift in the supply curve. It occurs when a determinant other than price changes.

Change in the quantity demanded   The term used for a movement along the demand curve to a new point. It occurs when there is a change in price.

Change in the quantity supplied   The term used for a movement along the supply curve to a new point. It occurs when there is a change in price.

Claimant unemployment   Those in receipt of unemployment-related benefits.

Collusive oligopoly   When oligopolists agree (formally or informally) to limit competition between themselves. They may set output quotas, fix prices, limit product promotion or development, or agree not to 'poach' each other's markets.

Collusive tendering   Where two or more firms secretly agree on the prices they will tender for a contract. These prices will be above those which would be put in under a genuinely competitive tendering process.

Command-and-control (CAC) systems   The use of laws or regulations backed up by inspections and penalties (such as fines) for non-compliance.

Comparative advantage   A country has a comparative advantage over another in the production of a good if it can produce it at a lower opportunity cost: i.e. if it has to forgo less of other goods in order to produce it.

Competition for corporate control   The competition for the control of companies through takeovers.

Competitive advantage   The various factors, such as lower costs or a better product, that give a firm an advantage over its rivals.

Competitive advantage of nations   The various factors that enable the industries in a particular country to compete more effectively with those in other countries.

Complementary goods   A pair of goods consumed together. As the price of one goes up, the demand for both goods will fall.

Complementors   Firms producing complementary goods.

Conglomerate merger   Where two firms in different industries merge.

Conglomerate multinational   A multinational that produces different products in different countries.

Consortium   Where two or more firms work together on a specific project and create a separate company to run the project.

Consumer durable A consumer good that lasts a period of time, during which the consumer can continue gaining utility from it.

Consumption The act of using goods and services to satisfy wants. This will normally involve purchasing the goods and services.

Consumption of domestically produced goods and services (C_d) The direct flow of money payments from households to firms.

Convergence of economies When countries achieve similar levels of growth, inflation, budget deficits as a percentage of GDP, balance of payments, etc.

Core competences The key skills of a business that underpin its competitive advantage.

Corporate social responsibility Where a business takes into account the interests and concerns of a community rather than just its shareholders.

Cost-push inflation Inflation caused by persistent rises in costs of production (independently of demand).

Credible threat (or promise) One that is believable to rivals because it is in the threatener's interests to carry it out.

Cross-price elasticity of demand The responsiveness of demand for one good to a change in the price of another: the proportionate change in demand for one good divided by the proportionate change in price of the other.

Crowding out Where increased public expenditure diverts money or resources away from the private sector.

Current account of the balance of payments The record of a country's imports and exports of goods and services, plus incomes and transfers of money to and from abroad.

Decision tree (or game tree) A diagram showing the sequence of possible decisions by competitor firms and the outcome of each combination of decisions.

Deindustrialisation The decline in the contribution to production of the manufacturing sector of the economy.

Demand curve A graph showing the relationship between the price of a good and the quantity of the good demanded over a given time period. Price is measured on the vertical axis; quantity demanded is measured on the horizontal axis. A demand curve can be for an individual consumer or a group of consumers, or more usually for the whole market.

Demand-deficient or cyclical unemployment Disequilibrium unemployment caused by a fall in aggregate demand with no corresponding fall in the real wage rate.

Demand-pull inflation Inflation caused by persistent rises in aggregate demand.

Demand schedule for an individual A table showing the different quantities of a good that a person is willing and able to buy at various prices over a given period of time.

Demand-side (or demand management) policy Policy to affect aggregate demand (i.e. fiscal or monetary policy).

Depreciation A fall in the free-market exchange rate of the domestic currency with foreign currencies.

Derived demand The demand for a factor of production depends on the demand for the good that uses it.

Devaluation Where the government or central bank re-pegs the exchange rate at a lower level.

Discretionary fiscal policy Deliberate changes in tax rates or the level of government expenditure in order to influence the level of aggregate demand.

Diseconomies of scale   Where costs per unit of output increase as the scale of production increases.

Disequilibrium unemployment   Unemployment resulting from real wages in the economy being above the equilibrium level.

Diversification   A business growth strategy in which a business expands into new markets outside of its current interests.

Dominant strategy game   Where the firm will choose the same strategy, no matter what assumption it makes about its rivals' behaviour.

Downsizing   Where a business reorganises and reduces its size, especially in respect to levels of employment, in order to cut costs.

Dumping   Where exports are sold at prices below marginal cost – often as a result of government subsidy.

Economic and monetary union (EMU)   Where countries adopt a single currency and a single monetary policy. It might also involve other common policies, such as fiscal and supply-side policies.

Economic growth   The rise in GDP. The rate of economic growth is the percentage increase in GDP over a 12-month period.

Economies of scale   When increasing the scale of production leads to a lower cost per unit of output.

Economies of scope   When increasing the range of products produced by a firm reduces the cost of producing each one.

Efficiency wage hypothesis   A hypothesis that states that a worker's productivity is linked to the wage he or she receives.

Efficiency wage rate   The profit-maximising wage rate for the firm after taking into account the effects of wage rates on worker motivation, turnover and recruitment.

Efficient (capital) market hypothesis   The hypothesis that new information about a company's current or future performance will be quickly and accurately reflected in its share price.

Elastic demand   If demand is (price) elastic, then any change in price will cause the quantity demanded to change proportionately more. (Ignoring the negative sign) it will have a value greater than 1.

EMU   (see **Economic and monetary union**).

Environmental scanning   Where a business surveys social and political trends in order to take account of changes in its decision-making process.

Equilibrium   A position of balance. A position from which there is no inherent tendency to move away.

Equilibrium GDP   The level of GDP where injections equal withdrawals and where, therefore, there is no tendency for GDP to rise or fall.

Equilibrium price   The price where the quantity demanded equals the quantity supplied: the price where there is no shortage or surplus.

Equilibrium ('natural') unemployment   The difference between those who would like employment at the current wage rate and those willing and able to take a job.

ERM (the exchange rate mechanism)   A semi-fixed system whereby participating EU countries allowed fluctuations against each other's currencies only within agreed bands. Collectively they floated freely against all other currencies.

Exchange rate index   A weighted average exchange rate expressed as an index, where the value of the index is 100 in a given base year. The weights of the different currencies in the index add up to 1.

Explicit costs   The payments to outside suppliers of inputs.

External benefits   Benefits from production (or consumption) experienced by people *other* than the producer (or consumer).

External costs   Costs of production (or consumption) borne by people *other* than the producer (or consumer).

External diseconomies of scale   Where a firm's costs per unit of output increase as the size of the whole industry increases.

External economies of scale   Where a firm's costs per unit of output decrease as the size of the whole *industry* grows.

External expansion   Where business growth is achieved by merging with or taking over businesses within a market or industry.

Externalities   Costs or benefits of production or consumption experienced by society but not by the producers or consumers themselves. Sometimes referred to as 'spillover' or 'third-party' costs or benefits.

Financial account of the balance of payments   The record of the flows of money into and out of the country for the purpose of investment or as deposits in bank and other financial institutions.

Financial flexibility   Where employers can vary their wage costs by changing the composition of their workforce or the terms on which workers are employed.

Fine-tuning   The use of demand management policy (fiscal or monetary) to smooth out cyclical fluctuations in the economy.

First-mover advantage   When a firm gains from being the first to take action.

Fiscal policy   Policy to affect aggregate demand by altering government expenditure and/or taxation.

Fiscal stance   How expansionary or contractionary the Budget is.

Fixed costs   Total costs that do not vary with the amount of output produced.

Fixed input   An input that cannot be increased in supply within a given time period.

Flat organisation   One in which technology enables senior managers to communicate directly with those lower in the organisational structure. Middle managers are bypassed.

Flexible firm   A firm that has the flexibility to respond to changing market conditions by changing the composition of its workforce.

Floating exchange rate   When the government does not intervene in the foreign exchange markets, but simply allows the exchange rate to be freely determined by demand and supply.

Forward integration   Where a firm expands forward up the supply chain towards the sale of the finished product.

Franchise   A formal agreement whereby a company uses another company to produce or sell some or all of its product.

Free market   One in which there is an absence of government intervention. Individual producers and consumers are free to make their own economic decisions.

Free-rider problem   When it is not possible to exclude other people from consuming a good that someone has bought.

Frictional (search) unemployment   Unemployment that occurs as a result of imperfect information in the labour market. It often takes time for workers to find jobs (even though there are vacancies) and in the meantime they are unemployed.

Functional flexibility   Where employers can switch workers from job to job as requirements change.

Game theory (or the theory of games)   The study of alternative strategies that oligopolists may choose to adopt, depending on their assumptions about their rivals' behaviour.

General government debt The accumulated central and local government deficits (less surpluses) over the years: i.e. the total amount owed by central and local government, both to domestic and overseas creditors.

Globalisation The process whereby the economies of the world are becoming increasingly integrated.

Goodhart's Law Controlling a symptom or indicator of a problem is unlikely to cure the problem; it will simply mean that what is being controlled now becomes a poor indicator of the problem.

Goods in joint supply These are two goods where the production of more of one leads to the production of more of the other.

Gross Domestic Product (GDP) The value of output produced within the country over a 12-month period.

Growth maximisation An alternative theory which assumes that managers seek to maximise the growth in sales revenue (or the capital value of the firm) over time.

Growth vector matrix A means by which a business might assess its product/market strategy.

Harmonisation (international) of economic policies Where countries attempt to coordinate their macroeconomic policies so as to achieve common goals.

Historic costs The original amount the firm paid for inputs it now owns.

Holding company A business organisation in which the present company holds interests in a number of other companies or subsidiaries.

Horizontally integrated multinational A multinational that produces the same product in many different countries.

Horizontal merger Where two firms in the same industry at the same stage of the production process merge.

Imperfect competition The collective name for monopolistic competition and oligopoly.

Implicit costs Costs which do not involve a direct payment of money to a third party, but which nevertheless involve a sacrifice of some alternative.

Import substitution The replacement of imports by domestically produced goods or services.

Income effect The effect of a change in price on quantity demanded arising from the consumer becoming better or worse off as a result of the price change.

Income elasticity of demand The responsiveness of demand to a change in consumer incomes: the proportionate change in demand divided by the proportionate change in income.

Independent risks Where two risky events are unconnected. The occurrence of one will not affect the likelihood of the occurrence of the other.

Indivisibilities The impossibility of dividing an input into smaller units.

Industrial sector A grouping of industries producing similar products or services.

Industry A group of firms producing a particular product or service.

Inelastic demand If demand is (price) inelastic, then any change will cause the quantity demanded to change by a proportionately smaller amount. (Ignoring the negative sign) it will have a value less than 1.

Infant industry An industry which has a potential comparative advantage, but which is as yet too underdeveloped to be able to realise this potential.

Inferior goods Goods whose demand falls as people's incomes rise. Such goods have a negative income elasticity of demand.

Information asymmetry A situation in which one party in an economic relationship knows more than another.

Infrastructure (industry's)   The network of supply agents, communications, skills, training facilities, distribution channels, specialised financial services, etc. that support a particular industry.

Injections (J)   Expenditure on the production of domestic firms coming from outside the inner flow of the circular flow of income. Injections equal investment (I) plus government expenditure (G) plus expenditure on exports (X).

Interdependence (under oligopoly)   One of the two key features of oligopoly. Each firm will be affected by its rivals' decisions. Likewise its decisions will affect its rivals. Firms recognise this interdependence. This recognition will affect their decisions.

Internal expansion   Where a business adds to its productive capacity by adding to existing, or by building, new plant.

International harmonisation of economic policies   Where countries attempt to coordinate their macroeconomic policies so as to achieve common goals.

Joint-stock company   A company where ownership is distributed between shareholders.

Joint venture   Where two or more firms set up and jointly own a new independent firm.

Just-in-time methods   Where a firm purchases supplies and produces both components and finished products as they are required. This minimises stock holding and its associated costs.

Kinked demand theory   The theory that oligopolists face a demand curve that is kinked at the current price: demand being significantly more elastic above the current price than below. The effect of this is to create a situation of price stability.

Labour force   The number employed plus the number unemployed.

Law of comparative advantage   Trade can benefit all countries if they specialise in the goods in which they have a comparative advantage.

Law of demand   The quantity of a good demanded per period of time will fall as the price rises and rise as the price falls, other things being equal (*ceteris paribus*).

Law of diminishing (marginal) returns   When one or more inputs are held fixed, there will come a point beyond which the extra output from additional units of the variable input will diminish.

Law of large numbers   The larger the number of events of a particular type, the more predictable will be their average outcome.

Leading indicators   Indicators that help predict future trends in the economy.

Lender of last resort   The role of the Bank of England as the guarantor of sufficient liquidity in the monetary system.

Licensing   Where the owner of a patented product allows another firm to produce it for a fee.

Limited liability   Where the liability of the owners for the debts of a company is limited to the amount they have invested in it.

Liquidity ratio   The ratio of liquid assets (cash and assets that can be readily converted to cash) to total deposits.

Liquidity trap   When interest rates are at their floor and thus any further increases in money supply will not be spent but merely be held in bank accounts as people wait for the economy to recover and/or interest rates to rise.

Lock-outs   Union members are temporarily laid off until they are prepared to agree to the firm's conditions.

Logistics   The business of managing and handling inputs to and outputs from a firm.

Long run   The period of time long enough for *all* inputs to be varied.

Long run under perfect competition   The period of time which is long enough for new firms to enter the industry.

Long-run average cost curve   A curve that shows how average cost varies with output on the assumption that *all* factors are variable.

M0   Cash plus banks' balances with the Bank of England. Note that this definition of narrow money is no longer used (see **cash in circulation** for the current measure of narrow money).

M4   Cash outside the banks plus all bank and building society deposits (including cash).

M-form business organisation   One in which the business is organised into separate departments, such that responsibility for the day-to-day management enterprise is separated from the formulation of the business's strategic plan.

Marginal benefits   The additional benefits of doing a little bit more (or *1 unit* more if a unit can be measured) of an activity.

Marginal cost (*MC*)   The cost of producing one more unit of output: $MC = \Delta TC/\Delta Q$.

Marginal costs   The additional cost of doing a little bit more (or *1 unit* more if a unit can be measured) of an activity.

Marginal revenue   The extra revenue gained by selling one or more unit per time period: $MR = \Delta TR/\Delta Q$.

Marginal revenue product of labour   The extra revenue a firm earns from employing one more unit of labour.

Marginal social benefit (*MSB*)   The additional benefit gained by society of producing or consuming one more unit of a good.

Marginal social cost (*MSC*)   The additional cost incurred by society of producing or consuming one more unit of a good.

Marginal utility (*MU*)   The extra satisfaction gained from consuming one extra unit of a good within a given time period.

Market   The interaction between buyers and sellers.

Market clearing   A market clears when supply matches demand, leaving no shortage or surplus.

Market demand schedule   A table showing the different total quantities of a good that consumers are willing and able to buy at various prices over a given period of time.

Market experiments   Information gathered about consumers under artificial or simulated conditions. A method used widely in assessing the effects of advertising on consumers.

Market niche   A part of a market (or new market) that has not been filled by an existing brand or business.

Market surveys   Information gathered about consumers, usually via a questionnaire, that attempts to enhance the business's understanding of consumer behaviour.

Marketing mix   The mix of product, price, place (distribution) and promotion that will determine a business's marketing strategy.

Merger   The outcome of a mutual agreement made by two firms to combine their business activities.

Merit goods   Goods which the government feels that people will underconsume and which therefore ought to be subsidised or provided free.

Mobility of labour   The ease with which labour can either shift between jobs (occupational mobility) or move to other parts of the country in search of work (geographical mobility).

Monetary policy   Policy to affect aggregate demand by central bank action to alter interest rates or money supply.

Monopolistic competition   A market structure where, like perfect competition, there are many firms and freedom of entry into the industry, but where each firm produces a differentiated product and thus has some control over its price.

Monopoly   A market structure where there is only one firm in the industry.

Monopsony   A market with a single buyer or employer.

Moral hazard   Following a deal, if there are information asymmetries, it is likely that one party will engage in problematic (immoral and/or hazardous) behaviour to the detriment of the other. In other words, lack of information by one party to the deal may result in the deal not being honoured by the other party.

Multinational corporations   Businesses that either own or control foreign subsidiaries in more than one country.

Multiplier   The number of times a rise in GDP (ΔGDP) is bigger than the initial rise in aggregate expenditure (ΔE) that caused it. Using the letter k to stand for the multiplier, the multiplier is defined as $k = \Delta GDP/\Delta E$.

Multiplier effect   An initial increase in aggregate demand of £xm leads to an eventual rise in GDP that is greater than £xm.

Multiplier formula   The formula for the multiplier is $k = 1/(1 - mpc_d)$.

Nash equilibrium   The position resulting from everyone making their optimal decision based on their assumptions about their rivals' decisions. Without collusion, there is no incentive to move from this position.

Nationalised industries   State-owned industries that produce goods or services that are sold in the market.

Natural monopoly   A situation where long-run average costs would be lower if an industry were under monopoly than if it were shared between two or more competitors.

Net errors and omissions   A statistical adjustment to ensure that the two sides of the balance of payments account balance. It is necessary because of errors in compiling the statistics.

Network   An informal arrangement between businesses to work together towards some common goal.

Non-collusive oligopoly   When oligopolists have no agreement between themselves – formal, informal or tacit.

Non-excludability   Where it is not possible to provide a good or service to one person without it thereby being available for others to enjoy.

Non-price competition   Competition in terms of product promotion (advertising, packaging, etc.) or product development.

Non-rivalry   Where the consumption of a good or service by one person will not prevent others from enjoying it.

Normal goods   Goods whose demand increases as consumer incomes increase. They have a positive income elasticity of demand. Luxury goods will have a higher income elasticity of demand than more basic goods.

Normal profit   The opportunity cost of being in business. It consists of the interest that could be earned on a riskless asset, plus a return for risk taking in this particular industry. It is counted as a cost of production.

Numerical flexibility   Where employers can change the size of their workforce as their labour requirements change.

Observations of market behaviour   Information gathered about consumers from the day-to-day activities of the business within the market.

Oligopoly A market structure where there are few enough firms to enable barriers to be erected against the entry of new firms.

Oligopsony A market with just a few buyers or employers.

Open-market operations The sale (or purchase) by the authorities of government securities in the open market in order to reduce (or increase) money supply.

Opportunity cost The cost of any activity measured in terms of the best alternative forgone.

Organisational slack When managers allow spare capacity to exist, thereby enabling them to respond more easily to changed circumstances.

Overheads Costs arising from the general running of an organisation, and only indirectly related to the level of output.

Perfectly competitive market (preliminary definition) A market in which all producers and consumers of the product are price takers.

PEST (or STEEPLE) analysis Where the political, economic, social and technological factors shaping a business environment are assessed by a business so as to devise future business strategy. STEEPLE analysis would also take into account ethical, legal and environmental factors.

Picketing Where people on strike gather at the entrance to the firm and attempt to dissuade workers or delivery vehicles from entering.

Plant economies of scale Economies of scale that arise because of the large size of the factory.

Preferential trading arrangements A trading arrangement whereby trade between the signatories is freer than trade with the rest of the world.

Price-cap regulation Where the regulator puts a ceiling on the amount by which a firm can raise its price.

Price discrimination Where a firm sells the same product at different prices in different markets for reasons unrelated to costs.

Price elasticity of demand A measure of the responsiveness of quantity demanded to a change in price.

Price elasticity of supply The responsiveness of quantity supplied to a change in price: the proportionate change in quantity supplied divided by the proportionate change in price.

Price leadership When firms (the followers) choose the same price as that set by one of the firms in the industry (the leader). The leader will normally be the largest firm.

Price mechanism The system in a market economy whereby changes in price in response to changes in demand and supply have the effect of making demand equal to supply.

Price taker A person or firm with no power to be able to influence the market price.

Primary labour market The market for permanent full-time core workers.

Primary market in capital Where shares are sold by the issuer of the shares (i.e. the firm) and where, therefore, finance is channelled directly from the purchasers (i.e. the shareholders) to the firm.

Primary production The production and extraction of natural resources, plus agriculture.

Principal–agent problem One where people (principals), as a result of lack of knowledge, cannot ensure that their best interests are served by their agents.

Prisoners' dilemma Where two or more firms (or people), by attempting independently to choose the best strategy for whatever the other(s) are likely to do, end up in a worse position than if they had cooperated in the first place.

Privatisation   Selling nationalised industries to the private sector. This may be through the public issue of shares, by a management buyout or by selling it to a private company.

Product differentiation   Where a firm's product is in some way distinct from its rivals' products. In the context of growth strategies, this is where a business upgrades existing products or services so as to make them different from those of rival firms.

Production   The transformation of inputs into outputs by firms in order to earn profit (or meet some other objective).

Productivity deal   Where, in return for a wage increase, a union agrees to changes in working practices that will increase output per worker.

Profit-maximising rule   Profit is maximised where marginal revenue equals marginal cost.

Profit satisficing   Where decision makers in a firm aim for a target level of profit rather than the absolute maximum level.

Public good   A good or service which has the features of non-rivalry and non-excludability and as a result would not be provided by the free market.

Public-sector net cash requirement (PSNCR)   The (annual) deficit of the public sector (central government, local government and public corporations), and thus the amount that the public sector must borrow.

Pure fiscal policy   Fiscal policy which does not involve any change in money supply.

Quantity demanded   The amount of a good that a consumer is willing and able to buy at a given price over a given period of time.

Quota (set by a cartel)   The output that a given member of a cartel is allowed to produce (production quota) or sell (sales quota).

Random walk   Where fluctuations in the value of a share away from its 'correct' value are random. When charted over time, these share price movements would appear like a 'random walk' – like the path of someone staggering along drunk.

Rate of inflation   The percentage increase in prices over a 12-month period.

Rational choices   Choices that involve weighing up the benefit of any activity against its opportunity cost.

Rationalisation   The reorganising of production (often after a merger) so as to cut out waste and duplication and generally to reduce costs.

Real growth values   Values of the rate of growth in GDP or any other variable after taking inflation into account. The real value of the growth in a variable equals its growth in money (or 'nominal') value minus the rate of inflation.

Real-wage unemployment   Disequilibrium unemployment caused by real wages being driven up above the market-clearing level.

Recession   A period of falling GDP: i.e. of negative economic growth. Officially, a recession is where this occurs for two quarters or more.

Regional unemployment   Structural unemployment occurring in specific regions of the country.

Repeated or **extensive-form games**   Where firms decide in turn in the light of what their rivals do. Such games thus involve two or more moves.

Replacement costs   What the firm would have to pay to replace inputs it currently owns.

Resale price maintenance   Where the manufacturer of a product (legally) insists that the product should be sold at a specified retail price.

Revaluation   Where the government or central bank re-pegs the exchange rate at a higher level.

Risk This is when an outcome may or may not occur, but where the probability of its occurring is known.

Sale and repurchase agreement (repo) An agreement between two financial institutions whereby one in effect borrows from another by selling some of its assets, agreeing to buy them back (repurchase them) at a fixed price and on a fixed date.

Sales revenue maximisation An alternative theory of the firm which assumes that managers aim to maximise the firm's short-run total revenue.

Scarcity The excess of human wants over what can actually be produced to fulfil these wants.

Seasonal unemployment Unemployment associated with industries or regions where the demand for labour is lower at certain times of the year.

Secondary labour market The market for peripheral workers, usually employed on a temporary or part-time basis, or a less secure 'permanent' basis.

Secondary market in capital Where shareholders sell shares to others. This is thus a market in 'second-hand' shares.

Secondary production The production from manufacturing and construction sectors of the economy.

Self-fulfilling speculation The actions of speculators tend to cause the very effect that they had anticipated.

Share (or stock) options The right to buy shares in the future at a fixed price set today. When granted to senior executives as a reward they do not involve any outlay by the company. They act as an incentive, however, since the better the company performs, the more the market value of its shares is likely to rise above the option price and the more the executive stands to gain by exercising the option to buy shares at the fixed price and then selling them at the market price.

Short run The period of time over which at least one input is fixed.

Short run under perfect competition The period during which there is too little time for new firms to enter the industry.

Short-run shut-down point Where the *AR* curve is tangential to the *AVC* curve. The firm can only just cover its variable costs. Any fall in revenue below this level will cause a profit-maximising firm to shut down immediately.

Short-termism Where firms and investors take decisions based on the likely short-term performance of a company, rather than on its long-term prospects. Firms may thus sacrifice long-term profits and growth for the sake of quick return.

Single-move or **single-period** or **normal-form game** Where each firm makes just one decision without at the time knowing the decision of the other.

Social benefit Private benefit plus externalities in consumption.

Social cost Private cost plus externalities in production.

Social efficiency Production and consumption at the point where *MSB* = *MSC*.

Sovereign risk (for business) The risk that a foreign country's government or central bank will make its policies less favourable. Such policies could involve changes in interest rates or tax regimes, the imposition of foreign exchange controls, or even defaulting on loans or the appropriation of a business's assets.

Specialisation and division of labour Where production is broken down into a number of simpler, more specialised tasks, thus allowing workers to acquire a high degree of efficiency.

Speculation This is where people make buying or selling decisions based on their anticipations of future prices.

Spreading risks (for an insurance company)   The more policies an insurance company issues and the more independent the risks of claims from these policies are, the more predictable will be the number of claims.

Stakeholder   An individual affected by the operations of a business.

Stakeholders (in a company)   People who are affected by a company's activities and/or performance (customers, employees, owners, creditors, people living in the neighbourhood, etc.). They may or may not be in a position to take decisions, or influence decision taking, in the firm.

Standard Industrial Classification (SIC)   The name given to the formal classification of firms into industries used by the government in order to collect data on business and industry trends.

Standardised unemployment rate   The measure of the unemployment rate used by the ILO and OECD. The unemployed are defined as people of working age who are without work, available for work and actively seeking employment.

STEEPLE analysis   Where the social, technological, economic, ethical, political, legal and environmental factors shaping a business environment are assessed by a business so as to devise future business strategy. (See also **PEST analysis**.)

Stock options   (see **share options**)

Strategic alliance   Where two firms work together, formally or informally, to achieve a mutually desirable goal.

Strategic management   The management of the strategic long-term decisions and activities of the business.

Strategic trade theory   The theory that protecting/supporting certain industries can enable them to compete more effectively with large monopolistic rivals abroad. The effect of the protection is to increase long-run competition and may enable the protected firms to exploit a comparative advantage that they could not have done otherwise.

Structural unemployment   Unemployment that arises from changes in the pattern of demand or supply in the economy. People made redundant in one part of the economy cannot immediately take up jobs in other parts (even though there are vacancies).

Subcontracting   Where a firm employs another firm to produce part of its output or some of its input(s).

Substitute goods   A pair of goods which are considered by consumers to be alternatives to each other. As the price of one goes up, the demand for the other rises.

Substitutes in supply   These are two goods where an increased production of one means diverting resources away from producing the other.

Substitution effect   The effect of a change in price on quantity demanded arising from the consumer switching to or from alternative (substitute) products.

Supernormal profit   The excess of total profit above normal profit.

Supply chain   The flow of inputs into a finished product from the raw materials stage, through manufacturing and distribution right through to the sale to the final consumer.

Supply curve   A graph showing the relationship between the price of a good and the quantity of the good supplied over a given period of time.

Supply schedule   A table showing the different quantities of a good that producers are willing and able to supply at various prices over a given time period. A supply schedule can be for an individual producer or group of producers, or for all producers (the market supply schedule).

Supply-side policy   Policy to affect aggregate supply directly.

Tacit collusion   When oligopolists take care not to engage in price cutting, excessive advertising or other forms of competition. There may be unwritten 'rules' of collusive behaviour such as price leadership.

Takeover   Where one business acquires another. A takeover may not necessarily involve mutual agreement between the two parties. In such cases, the takeover might be viewed as 'hostile'.

Takeover constraint   The effect that the fear of being taken over has on a firm's willingness to undertake projects that reduce distributed profits.

Tapered vertical integration   Where a firm is partially integrated with an earlier stage of production: where it produces *some* of an input itself and buys some from another firm.

Tariffs   Taxes (customs duties) on imports. These could be a percentage of the value of the good (an 'ad valorem' tariff), or a fixed amount per unit (a 'specific' tariff).

Taylor rule   A rule adopted by a central bank for setting the rate of interest. It will raise the interest rate if (a) inflation is above target or (b) economic growth is above the sustainable level (or unemployment below the equilibrium rate). The rule states how much interest rates will be changed in each case. In other words a relative weighting is attached to each of these two objectives.

Technological unemployment   Structural unemployment that occurs as a result of the introduction of labour-saving technology.

Technology transfer   Where a host state benefits from the new technology that an MNC brings with its investment.

Terms of trade   The price index of exports divided by the price index of imports and then expressed as a percentage. This means that the terms of trade will be 100 in the base year.

Tertiary production   The production from the service sector of the economy.

Tit-for-tat game   Where you will copy whatever your rival does. Thus if your rival cuts price, you will too. If your rival does not, neither will you.

Total consumer expenditure (*TE*) (per period)   The price of the product multiplied by the quantity purchased. $TE = P \times Q$.

Total cost (*TC*) (per period)   The sum of total fixed costs (*TFC*) and total variable costs (*TVC*): $TC = TFC + TVC$.

Total revenue (*TR*) (per period)   The total amount received by firms from the sale of a product, before the deduction of taxes or any other costs. The price multiplied by the quantity sold. $TR = P \times Q$.

Tradable permits   Each firm is given a permit to produce a given level of pollution. If less than the permitted amount is produced, the firm is given a credit. This can then be sold to another firm, allowing it to exceed its original limit.

Transactions costs   The costs associated with exchanging products. For buyers it is the costs over and above the price of the product. For sellers it is the costs over and above the costs of production.

Transfer payments   Moneys transferred from one person or group to another (e.g. from the government to individuals) without production taking place.

Transfer pricing   The pricing system used within a business to transfer intermediate products between its various divisions, often in different countries.

U-form business organisation   One in which the central organisation of the firm (the chief executive or a managerial team) is responsible both for the firm's day-to-day administration and for formulating its business strategy.

Uncertainty   This is when an outcome may or may not occur and where its probability of occurring is not known.

Unemployment rate The number unemployed expressed as a percentage of the labour force.

Unit elasticity When the price elasticity of demand is unity, this is where quantity demanded changes by the same proportion as the price. Price elasticity is equal to -1.

Value chain The stages or activities that help to create product value.

Variable costs Total costs that do vary with the amount of output produced.

Variable input An input that *can* be increased in supply within a given time period.

Vertical integration A business growth strategy that involves expanding within an existing market, but at a different stage of production. Vertical integration can be 'forward', such as moving into distribution or retail, or 'backward', such as expanding into extracting raw materials or producing components.

Vertical merger Where two firms in the same industry at different stages in the production process merge.

Vertically integrated firm A firm that produces at more than one stage in the production and distribution of a product.

Vertically integrated multinational A multinational that undertakes the various stages of production for a given product in different countries.

Wage taker The wage rate is determined by market forces.

Withdrawals (*W*) (or leakages) Incomes of households or firms that are not passed on round the inner flow. Withdrawals equal net saving (S) plus net taxes (T) plus import expenditure (M): $W = S + T + M$.

Working to rule Workers do no more than they are supposed to, as set out in their job descriptions.

Index

Also written by John Sloman and published by Pearson Education

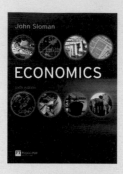

Economics
(with MyEconlab)

A well-known and loved, comprehensive and up-to-date introduction to economics, carefully designed to enhance learning. Suitable for use on principles of economics courses as part of a single or joint-honours economics degree programme.

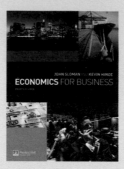

Economics for Business
John Sloman and Kevin Hinde
(with Grade Tracker)

Provides appropriate coverage of microeconomic, macroeconomic and international economic issues for business students. Its focus throughout is firmly on applying economic principles to the world of business.

Essentials of Economics
(with MyEconLab)

The market-leading concise text in introductory economics is an abridged version of *Economics*, making it the ideal companion for shorter courses or courses for non-specialist students of economics.

MyEconLab

An interactive website that enables students to assess their learning and test their understanding of economics. It provides a personalised study plan with a variety of tools including: a range of exercises and problems with graphs that students can manipulate, guided solutions, animated key models with audio narration, monthly updated links to news articles and an online workbook.

Grade Tracker

A full Companion Website with a range of online tools including case studies, topical economic issues and hotlinks, answers to in text questions, an online glossary, an online workbook and multiple choice questions automatically graded and entered in the student's personal gradebook.

For more information on these titles please visit **www.pearsoned.co.uk/sloman** or contact your local Academic Sales Representative at **www.pearsoned.co.uk/replocator** to request a sample teaching copy and brochure with a CD-ROM enabling you to view samples of all online resources.